ANOTHER LIFE:
LAWRENCE AFTER ARABIA

ANOTHER LIFE: LAWRENCE AFTER ARABIA

ANDREW R. B. SIMPSON

SPELLMOUNT

In memory of my father
Wing Commander L.J. Simpson, R.A.A.F., R.Aux. A.F., D.F.C. (1918-2007)
Loved and remembered by many

One day I said to Lawrence:
'. . . The greatest employments are open to you if you are to pursue your new career in the Colonial Service.'
He smiled his bland, beaming, cryptic smile and said: 'In a very few months my work here will be finished. The job is done, and it will last.'
'But what about you?'
'All you will see of me is a small cloud of dust on the horizon.'

Winston Churchill to T.E. Lawrence on leaving the Colonial Office, January 1922. (From *Great Contemporaries*, W.S. Churchill, Thornton Butterworth, 1938)

First published 2008

Spellmount Publishers
The History Press Ltd.
Cirencester Road, Chalford,
Stroud, Gloucestershire, GL6 8PE
www.thehistorypress.co.uk

Spellmount Publishers are an imprint of The History Press Ltd.

British Library Cataloguing in Publication Data.
A catalogue record for this book is available from the British Library.

ISBN 978 1 86227 464 8

Typesetting and origination by The History Press Ltd.
Printed in Great Britain by Ashford Colour Press Ltd, Gosport, Hampshire.

Contents

List of Maps and Diagrams

Abbreviations used in the Text

AEC	Associated Engineering Company
AID	Air Inspection Department
Air Min	Air Ministry
ATB	Armoured Target Boat
AV-M	Air Vice-Marshal
AW or AWL	Arnold Walther Lawrence
B-G	W.E.G. Beauforte-Greenwood
BPBCo	British Power Boat Company
CAS	Chief of the Air Staff
CB	Confined to Barracks or ' Jankers'
CO	Commanding Officer
CSM	Company Sergeant Major
DH	de Havilland Aircraft Company
DOSD	Directorate of Service Duties
DPP	Director of Public prosecutions
E.6	Air Ministry's Marine Craft Service or Boat Section
Flg Off	Flying Officer
Flt Lt	Flight Lieutenant
GBS	George Bernard Shaw
GW2275	Lawrence's Brough Superior 'George VII'
HSF	RAF's Schneider Trophy High Speed Flight
JIC	Joint Intelligence Committee
MAEE	Marine Aircraft Experimental Establishment (Originally the Marine and Armaments Experimental Establishment)
MBC	Motor Boat Crew
MCS	Marine Craft Service
MCU	Marine Craft Unit
MI5	Military Intelligence Department 5 (Internal)
MIS	Military Intelligence Department 6 (Foreign/External)

MTB	Motor Torpedo Boat
QMSI	Quarter Master Sergeant Instructor
RAC	Royal Aeronautical Club, also Royal Automobile Club
RAF	Royal Air Force
RAMC	Royal Army Medical Corps
RAOC	Royal Army Ordnance Corps
RASC	Royal Army Service Corps
RFC	Royal Flying Corps
RSM	Regimental Sergeant Major
RTC	Royal Tank Corps
SBAC	Society of British Aircraft Constructors
S-P	Hubert Scott-Paine
TE	T.E. Lawrence
TEL	T.E. Lawrence
TES	T.E. Shaw
Tes	Sydney Smiths' nickname for Lawrence
US	Unserviceable
W	H.B. Walters, who vetted Lawrence's translation of the *Odyssey*
WIG	Wing in Ground Effect
Wing Cdr	Wing Commander
W/T	Wireless Telegraphy

Acknowledgements

Thanks to the late Arthur Russell, Colin Bradley of the *Western Morning News*, the late Frank Gordon, R. James Hargreave (for information on his grandfather Alec Dixon), Vera M. Hewitt, Ingrid Keith, Mrs. Betty Kent (for the reminiscences of Leslie Edward Gates), Philip Knightley (for permission to quote from the Knightley and Simpson files in the IWM), Terence Phillips (owner of 2, Polstead Road), Godfrey Runyard; Jeremy Whitehorn, Heartland Old Books, Tiverton (for proof reading); Phyliss Whowell (for permission to use the material from *T.E. Lives* magazine); all those who replied to my advertisements., the staff of the Modern Papers Room, the Bodleian Library, Oxford; the staff of the Imperial War Museum Reading Room; Mike O'Hara (curator of Wareham Museum, Dorset), the Trustees of the *Seven Pillars of Wisdom* Trust (for copyright permission to quote from the letters of A.W. and T.E. Lawrence in the *Bogus Biographers* and *An Impersonation* sections); the staff of Wareham Reference Library, Dorset; the staff of Dorset County Museum, Dorchester; the staff of the Dorset Record Office, Dorchester and Exeter University Oriental Studies Library, and the staff of the RAC Tank Museum Archives Library, Bovington, Dorset.

Thanks also to the British Library Newspaper Archive, Colindale; Gerald Wasley (for proof reading and help on Mount Batten); Pieter Shipster (for proof reading and help on the Schneider Cup); the technical staff of the Solent Sky Museum, Southampton; Exeter University Library; the Roger Friedman Rare Book Studio, US (for the original Bruce Rogers' roundel from the *Odyssey*); the staff of the Imperial War Museum Reading Room; Stuart Haddaway and the staff of the RAF Museum Reading Room; the Fleet Air Arm Museum, Yoevilton; the late Dennis McDonnell; Brian Riddle, the Royal Aeronautical Society; the National Maritime Museum; Alistair Arnott, Southampton Maritime Museum Special Collections; the Military Power Boat Association, Hythe; the National Archives, Kew; the staff of Plymouth City Reference Library; the staff of 3, Elliot Terrace, Plymouth; Colin Harris and the staff of the Bodleian Library Modern Papers Room, Oxford; Alan Thomas, the Air Historical Branch (RAF) Ministry of Defence; Susan Walker, Antiquities Curator, the Ashmolean Museum, Oxford; Jeremy Whitehorn.

Special thanks to Richard M. Bennett, Nick Birnie, Colin Bradley, Mike Chapman, Tony Cripps, Joe Fletcher, Ray Gurven (for proof reading), Ian Handoll, Philip Knightley, Rodney Legg, Alex May, Nigel Neville-Jones, Mike O'Hara, Andrew Perrin (for information on GW2275), Godfrey Runyard, Colin Simpson, Geoff

Titman (for photographs of the 1962 film's Chobham crash site), the Trustees of the *Seven Pillars of Wisdom* Trust (for permission to quote the two letters of Captain Lettman-Johnson), Jeremy Whitehorn, Anne Williamson (for information on her father-in-law Henry Williamson), Colin Wilson, Jeremy Wilson and the T.E. Lawrence Society, and *Saga* magazine.

Many thanks to the following, who replied to my letter in *Saga* magazine in March 2005: Mrs. Julia Anderson, Mr. Philip Bailey, Mrs. Anne I. Baker, Mr. Cyril Blackshaw, Mr. Colin Bristow, Mr. Gordon Brooks, Mr. Barry Burgess, Dr. Julia Burton-Brown, Mrs. E. Bush, Mr. Norman Dawkins, Mr. Nicholas Dewey, Mrs. Margaret Emerton, Mr. Vernon Fewtrell, Mrs. Rosemary Gaston-Grubb, Mr. Peter F. Goodwin, Mr. Roger Hallett, Mrs. Vera M. Hewitt, Mrs. Diane M. Horner, Mr. Ralph Hyde, Mrs. Pat Jilkes, Mrs. Betty Kent, Mrs. M.A. King, Mrs. Y.J.T. Kingdom, Mr. Dave Linguard, Professor James S. Malpas, Mr. Dave Micholly, Mrs. Tessa Morrish, Mr. D.W. Noakes, Mrs. Greta Parker, Mr. R.E. Poole, Mr. John Powell, Mr. Ian Ralph, Mr. E. Reynolds, Rev. L.S. Rivett, Mrs. W.M. Robertson, Mrs. E. Rowbottom, Mr. Godfrey Runyard, Mrs. Jillian A. Shepherd, Mrs. J. Simpkins, Mrs. Margaret Simpson, Mrs. Valery Thompson, Mrs. D.H. Thompson, Mrs. D.H. Thorne, Mrs. Nora Thornton, Mr. H.B. Webster, Mrs. Nora Wise. Of the original interviewees, Arthur Russell, Frank Gordon, Roland Hammersley, Margaret Montague, Joyce Knowles, Joan Hughes, and Bob Hunt have now sadly passed away.

Although a number of members of the T.E. Lawrence Society kindly assisted in the research for this book the Society does not officially support it. I would particularly like to thank Society Committee member Pieter Shipster, Gerald Wasley, and Jeremy Whitehorn, whose large collection of books was a great help.

Photographs
The Bodleian Library, Oxford for permission to use the photograph of T.E. Lawrence on 'George V', RK4907, at Cranwell, and the full length photograph of T.E. Lawrence in a Bombardier Corporal's blouse.
The Archive Library, R.A.C. Museum, Bovington for the photograph of E.S. 'Posh' Palmer and other general photographs of Bovington Camp.
The National Archives Photographic Department for the photographs of RAF 200 on trial at Mount Batten.
The Special Collections Department, Southampton Maritime Museum for a selection of photographs from the Scott-Paine Archive.

As far as possible T.E. Lawrence has been referred to by only two names throughout: 'Lawrence' and the more informal 'T.E.', although Lawrence changed his name by deed poll to Thomas Edward Shaw in the 1920s.

Preface: The Patroclus of the Piece

This book originated with an interview I conducted with Arthur Russell at his home in Coventry in 1985. Russell had served as a private in the Tank Corps with Lawrence from 1923 to 1924 and had been, in his own words, his 'constant companion'. One day, when they were in the cottage at Clouds Hill, the poet Siegfried Sassoon came to visit. In the course of the conversation, as they were sitting in the music room, Sassoon suddenly exclaimed 'Little Russell, the Patroclus of the Piece.' (Patroclus was of course the constant companion of Achilles.) 'So that's how he dubbed me,' said Russell, 'as his constant companion.' One would have thought that spending time with someone who had known T.E. that well would have brought one closer to the man, but I did not feel that. After an hour or

Arthur Russell at his home in Coventry, December 1985. Brought up in the city Russell ended up in the same barrack block as Lawrence in March 1923 and became his constant companion during his initial period at Bovington. Mr Russell died in 1991 aged 87. (Author)

so of conversation, in which Mr Russell kindly answered many of my questions, T.E. Lawrence remained an enigma.

Russell had married in 1939, settled in Coventry and had a daughter and two grandsons. In April 1995 he was confined to the Aavon Grange Old People's Home. Although many people went to see him subsequently, gradually, as the years passed, the intensity of his recollections faded. He had taken the well known photograph of Lawrence reading *The Times* outside the Quartermaster's Stores at Bovington in 1923, and also donated a bench, carved with his name, to the cemetery at Moreton. Lawrence had changed his life and been an inspiration, as he had for many people. Transferred to Warwick Hospital, Arthur Russell died there on 7th November 1997, a very charming old man, who outlived the friend he was devoted to by 62 years.

I had been given Russell's details by Ingrid Keith. Ingrid was a teacher in Wareham at the time and all her life she had a fascination for Lawrence, such that in 1985 she decided to form her own T.E. Lawrence Society. It had humble beginnings, starting off with a small meeting in Wareham Museum where the founder members included Ronald Knight, Roland Hammersley and John Weekly. This tiny seed grew to proportions that many would have never believed possible. There are now thousands of members worldwide, with splinter groups in the US and even one in Japan. This book, therefore, was born out of the enthusiasm of others and a frustrations of an inconclusive interview. I hope the reader senses the former and not the latter within these pages.

Andrew R.B. Simpson

Introduction

Thomas Edward Lawrence was born in 1888 at Tremadoc, North Wales, the second son of an Irish landowner who fled Ireland after a bigamous relationship with his housekeeper, who bore him five sons. From Wales they travelled to Scotland, France, Guernsey, the New Forest, eventually settling in Oxford. All five boys were educated at Oxford High School, eventually matriculating to the university. Although not the oldest, T.E. was the natural leader of the group, being a stronger character than the others. T.E.'s elder brother submitted to the dominant character of his mother Sarah Junner, whose, according to some judges, hypocritical religious beliefs filtered into his character. He became bound to her and served as her companion and fellow missionary for the rest of his life. The other Lawrences were strong enough to assert themselves against Sarah, and to escape on different paths.

Educated at Jesus College, Oxford, Lawrence made a walking survey of all the important Crusader castles in Syria for his degree thesis, which was awarded a First. In 1910 he was invited by D.G. Hogarth of the Ashmolean Museum, Oxford, to assist at a Hittite excavation at Carchemish in Syria and gradually his knowledge of the Arab peoples began to accumulate and was applied when he went to work for British Intelligence in Cairo in 1914. The tribes in Arabia were preparing a revolt and needed a charismatic leader and Lawrence was sent to find one, in the hope it would revitalize the Allies' failing fortunes in that theatre. Not only did he do this but, by a series of brilliant moves, long distant rides, tactical attacks and strategic campaigns, manage to harass the Turks from Medina to Damascus, delaying them from transferring their troops northward and preparing the ground for the final Allied offensive in 1918.

Lawrence's leadership ability, charisma, and genius for guerrilla warfare meant that by 1918 he was leading a united Arab irregular force. The responsibility and the stresses he experienced deeply affected him so that the end of the campaign he was physically and emotionally exhausted. Those experiences would never leave him. He was not yet thirty.

After the War he was employed as an adviser to the Arab forces at the Paris Peace Conference. He failed to get the concessions he had promised to his Arab friends. This was partially, but only temporarily, righted by Churchill's mandates defined at the Cairo Conference in 1921, held to settle the Middle East question.

The rivalries amongst Britain, the Arabs, and France, particularly over the question of Syria and Trans-Jordan, had to be settled. But Lawrence felt betrayed, he had failed his Arab followers. By this time he had become a celebrated international figure, owing to the films made of him in Arabia by the American Lowell Thomas, which were shown in cinemas worldwide. These made him one of the most glamorous figures of the First World War, in a war with little glamour. Lawrence had craved celebrity all is life but when he got it, he despised it.

In Arabia he had realised air warfare would be the overriding factor in any future conflict and, in 1922 joined the RAF under a pseudonym, deciding, much to the consternation of his sophisticated friends, to disappear into the obscurity of the ranks.

This book is about Lawrence's life after Arabia, his service in the RAF and the Tank Corps and details, hopefully as no other book before has done, how he became an expert in the technology of the new RAF. It examines the work he did for the 1929 Schneider Trophy Race, the development of the new RAF 200 seaplane tender, and the development of its armour-plated offspring, the Armoured Target Boat. During this period he was involved in a number of literary projects. As well as *Seven Pillars of Wisdom* he created an important study of the early days of the RAF, *The Mint*. This was ground breaking in its realism, so much so that its ' home truths' were hidden from public view until 1950. His other important literary work, a prose translation of Homer's *Odyssey,* took four years to finish and proved almost as arduous a task as *Seven Pillars.*

What is remarkable about these projects is that, for most of the time they were being written, he was working as an ordinary serviceman where, particularly at Bovington, he lived amongst company that was anything but intellectual. He spent his days doing hard physical work that might have left him little energy for more cerebral pursuits; the fact that he was able to produce such remarkable work in such circumstances, and, in his latter period in the Air Force was able to undertake other important and useful practical work is a testimony to his character. Although the likes of Robert Graves commented on his working man's accent, gold teeth, roughness of hands and fading literary output, Lawrence took great pride in the fact that he could strip an engine down and rebuild it to running condition. This seemed to be a part of his struggle to escape the 'Lawrence of Arabia' image. Where other men from such a position would have risen effortlessly in the diplomatic world, he chose to redirect his abilities to smaller, more mundane matters that, in the long term, were of almost equal importance. It was this progression ' from ink to oil' that was the key to Lawrence's life in the 1920s and '30s. It was not something forced upon him, but work that came about through a series of tragic circumstances, creating a product that gave him great joy.

T.E. Lawrence was one of the most mystifying and charismatic figures of the twentieth century. The dashing desert warrior clad in flowing Arab clothes and headdress bears little resemblance to the truth. This was partly set right in 1962 – though there was still plenty of dash – in David Lean's film, *Lawrence of Arabia,* which gave a more accurate insight into his psychological conflicts as they were understood at the time; but this still was not the Lawrence known by those close to him. His achievements in World War One were remarkable, and understood by fellow officers who encountered him, and it was this that gave birth to the legend, more so than the books that were written about him, for a legend cannot persist for 70 years without some truth behind it.

Ever since Thomas's biography appeared in 1925 there has been a regular series of biographies that vary from the excellent, such as J.M. Wilson's, to those that are so full of exaggerations and downright lies that it is difficult to believe they were published at all. But what they all illustrate is that that there has been an increasing fascination with him, or with the myth that he left behind, ever since his death, the circumstances of which only served to reinforce that myth; some say, because that is the way his admirers want it to be. He is especially attractive to a particular type of person. They tend to be loners or in some way social misfits. A.W. Lawrence, his brother, concluded it was a form of religion to them, such that, after T.E.'s death, many tried to make him a St. Paul. However, A.W. declined to lead the new sect.

Liddell Hart, when writing his biography in the 1930s intended to create a record of the Arab Revolt. However, as he researched the subject more deeply he realised that the contribution Lawrence made was much greater and had more effect than he had originally thought. Eventually he concluded that because Lawrence played such an important part, it was incumbent upon him to write a biography of the man himself and not of the movement. A series of personal interviews with him in the late 1920s and '30s led him to conclude that, despite his quiet subtlety, Lawrence was a man with a greater force of personality than any he had ever known.

PART ONE

A Voyage all out of Reckoning

CHAPTER ONE

Motivation: Colonial Office to AC2

Why did Lawrence return to the ranks? In Chapter 1 of Lawrence's *Seven Pillars of Wisdom*, his account of the part he played in the Arab Revolt of 1917, is a famous passage that begins 'All men dream: but not equally. Those who dream by night in the dusty recesses of their mind wake in the day to find that it was vanity.' What follows is an explanation of the dream he had to create a new nation and restore a 'lost influence, to give twenty millions of Semites' the foundation of their national 'dream palace'. With typical self-deprecation Lawrence minimized his contribution to the aim, declaring that his was only a 'mock primacy'. He realised from early on that the British Cabinet had engineered a conspiracy, conspiring to persuade the Arabs to fight on 'definite promises of self-government'. Only Lawrence's word would assure them of the truth of this, as they had no use for written promises. This deception continued for two years, during which Lawrence was always aware of the dishonesty of his task: 'Instead of being proud of what we did together', he later wrote 'I was continually and bitterly ashamed'. His planned solution was to make the Arabs politically strong enough to convince the Allies to grant their wishes at the Peace Conference.

Lawrence explains that there were two deceptions he perpetrated in the war. Firstly 'a pugnacious wish to win the war' controlled him, but this was impossible without Arab help, so it was better for them to win on a dishonest premise than to lose. Secondly, since he was fighting under a false flag, a deception even his immediate superior was unaware of, he refused to accept any conventional rewards or recognition for his success: to prevent any 'unpleasantness arising' he began to falsify his reports, 'to conceal the true stories of things',[1] the second deception.

In Arabia Lawrence of course encountered a completely different concept of life with entirely different values to those with which he had been brought up. He explained much of his thoughts on Semitic beliefs in the introduction he wrote to C.M. Doughty's *Travels in Arabia Deserta* in 1921:

> The desert is a place of passing sensation, of cash-payment of opinion. Men do not hold their minds in suspense for days, to arrive at a just and balanced average of thought. They say good at once when it is good, and bad at once when it is bad.

The different perspective led Lawrence to re-evaluate his own values. After the War he abandoned the concept of the progress of mankind. His belief in God, certainly the Christian God, disappeared in Arabia and he gave up the idea of a conventional career. He tried in his life for an absolute value, a standard, but, in his own eyes, fell far short of it: Basil Liddell Hart concluded 'His peak was so high that few other men could even see it through the mist of life.'[2] Churchill once said that Lawrence moved at a different speed and on a different level to the ordinary man. During the war other men began to move at his pace, but after it was over, he was left alone on his own plane once more.

In 1919 the Peace Conference in Paris ended in political decisions that gave the Arabs almost nothing, causing T.E. extreme depression and bitterness. All the promises he had made to his friends had not been met. He had entered the conference with a cry for Arab unity fresh on his lips but soon found that he was surrounded by parties witrh no interest in the Arab Question. The Conference, he found to his disgust, was more concerned with the settlement of the European War than with petty squabblings in Arabia.

Still, he had other dreams, an important one being the conquest of the air. He also had to write the story of the Arab Revolt, a task for which only he was qualified. He signed a contract with the new publisher Jonathan Cape, one condition of which was the writing of a second book of his choice.

Although profoundly changed by the War, that Lawrence's psychological problems afterwards were caused by his experiences in the War itself is a misconception. He was actually fairly well balanced at the Armistice. The economist J.M. Keynes, who met him in Paris, found a natural aloofness in him, but reckoned him a fit man and later concluded 'It was the subsequent events that twisted him.'[3] Professor John Mack, a biographer of Lawrence, commented that he had turned inward, his mother describing how in the winter of 1919–1920 'He would sit for hours in a state of marked despondency without moving or changing his facial expression.'[4] John Buchan met him at this time and observed that he was in a trough of depression caused by 'the failure of his work for the Arabs, which involved for him a breach of honour.'[5] It was during this period that he at last learned the truth of his deceased father's adulterous background, his own illegitimacy (which he had suspected as a youth), and the fact that an inheritance of large estates in Ireland, which otherwise would have been his, had been forfeited. Simultaneously, Lowell Thomas was eulogizing him before thousands, and in a few years his picture shows would be seen by millions worldwide. The high profile was initially encouraged by T.E. in the hope that it would help the Arab cause; but after the Conference it was clear that it would have no effect. So against his will, he became transformed into a national hero, a society demagogue, and a matinee idol.

His psychological problems actually began to beset him whilst writing his account of the Revolt in an attic room of a terraced house at 14 Barton Street,[6] London, in the winter of 1921–22. Here he worked day and night on the book, going without food and sleep for long periods in order to focus. His changing mental state is reflected in his letters. In December 1917 his correspondence is, if anything, jaunty, but in those written later in the 1920s there is a pronounced tone of self deprecation, a kind of masochistic desire for punishment. The consequence of his sense of failure with the Arabian affair was a desire not to have any form of responsibility over men or to make any decisions of consequence again. A step towards this, he felt, was to accept the lowest status possible, which in the ranks of the RAF was Aircraftman 2nd Class. Arthur Russell explained:

> Because he'd been let down with the Arabs: he had to go down and promise them things. He knew most of it would never come off but he had to carry on and pretend, but he thought most of them wouldn't. It was due to the French government and the Indian government. And he told me then that – I don't know why the Indian government got involved – they didn't want the Indian government to have these concessions. He told me his life was forfeit if he went back to England.[7]

There were other, more straightforward reasons for enlisting. He had to find something that would put food on the table: by 1922 he was so poor he had to wait outside his friends' clubs and ask them to buy him lunch. He had been awarded a research fellowship by All Souls College, Oxford, but this was not worth a great deal[8] and also he had his Foreign and Colonial Office salary[9] that ended in July 1922. So the ranks offered him some kind of living, if only a meagre one. He had enjoyed the fellowship he had shared with ordinary soldiers with the Handley Page and Armoured car crews in Arabia, and imagined the peacetime ranks would recreate this. Joining the RAF, he hoped, would provide him with material for a second book, which he had been contracted by Cape to produce; and the 'monastic' environment of the ranks also offered a chance to escape from the attention the Lowell Thomas lectures created.

The memories of the war his writing brought back to him upset him greatly, so much so that when he joined up in August 1922 he was on the verge of a nervous breakdown. He told Robert Graves he hoped that being 'ordinary in a mob of likes'[1] would cure his mental exhaustion. The day before he joined he wrote to George Bernard Shaw:

> You see the war was, for us who were in it, an overwrought time, in which we lost our normal footing. I wrote this thing in the war atmosphere, and believe that it is stinking with it. Also there is a good deal of cruelty and some excitement. All these things, in a beginner's hands, tend to force him over the edge.[11]

The conclusion must be that his motivations for joining the ranks were disillusionment with the deceitfulness of the Arabian campaign and subsequent shunning of any form of responsibility; his desire for a life of discipline – a military straitjacket, perhaps – that would kerb the wanderings of his will until his body and mind returned to a more normal state; plus the more prosaic need for a regular income and the chance to write a 'Day Book' of the RAF.

Notes

1 *Seven Pillars of Wisdom*.
2 *T.E. Lawrence in Arabia and After*. 2nd Edition. B. Liddell Hart. 1934.
3 Friends: Keynes contribution.
4 Mack.
5 Buchan.
6 The building still stands to this day.
7 Arthur Russell. Interview with author, Coventry, December 1985.
8 £300 p.a.
9 £1200 p.a.
10 B:RG.
11 Letter to G.B. Shaw, 27th August 1922. MB.

CHAPTER TWO

The First RAF Period: The Mint

I am convinced that some quality departed from Lawrence before he became the RAF
recruit. Lawrence of Arabia had died.

(Charles Findlay, Adjutant, RAF Farnborough, 1922)

Lawrence joined the Air Force as John Hume Ross on Monday 28 August 1922.
There had been rain generally the night before. Around Westminster and the RAF's
Henrietta Street Recruiting Office that morning it was suitably cloudy. His entry to
the RAF was not as straightforward as he assumed it would be, his first application
being refused because he had no documentation. When he returned with the forms
they were judged to be forgeries. By this time the recruiting officer – W.E. Johns,
the creator of 'Biggles'– had contacted Somerset House and discovered that no
John Hume Ross had ever been born on the date specified. Lawrence returned to
the Air Ministry to retrieve a minute, probably from Trenchard, the Chief of the Air
Staff, to Air Vice-Marshal Swann (of the Air Council), that ordered his enlistment.
Despite this he still had to get through the medical examination: his physical
condition was so poor through malnutrition and stress that he was failed the first
time, and the second. The whip lash scars on his body aroused suspicion and even
after his identity had been revealed the doctors still refused to admit him. Only
after an outside doctor was called in were the admittance forms signed.

Lawrence came from the educated middle classes, a more privileged background,
of course, than his colleagues. It was unheard of for high ranking officers to enter
the ranks. But the Air Force was a new body utilising new technology, and this
affected the relationship between the officers and the men. Now the fitter could
know a great deal more about his specialization than his officer. Consequently the
social hierarchy in the RAF in the 1920s was something different and the technician
had a much higher standing than his earlier military or naval counterparts; there
was far more team work.

Lawrence started making notes for *The Mint* in August 1922, shortly after
his arrival at Uxbridge. He was given the service number 352087 and was an
Aircraftman 2nd Class. The book would not be released to the public until 1955,
fulfilling a promise Lawrence had made to Trenchard, and ensuring that any of
the staff mentioned in the text would be dead or retired when it came out. He did

however lend segments of the notes to friends. This caused serious trouble in 1931when portions of it appeared in a service journal. Fortunately, the section came from a later part of the work, which was not as critical as the earlier text. There was an official publication in 1935 in the United States however, precipitated by a fear of a pirated edition. To ensure the American copyright, a limited edition had to be published. Lawrence had encountered a similar problem in 1920 when his introduction to an edition of Doughty's *Arabia Deserta* was pirated by an American firm.

The Mint was constructed in three parts, the first dealing with the basic training of the 'raw material' at Uxbridge in 1922. The second part, 'In the Mill', covered N.C.O.'s, school instruction, stock-taking and guard room duties etc. Part Three was different and much mellower in tone than the earlier chapters. The Uxbridge chapters depicted the harsh discipline and brutality of barrack-room life. At the Depot he had been miserable and the toughness of the basic training shocked him. When other recruits had no option but to stick it out, he could have left of his own accord and it required great will power on his part not to do so. The comradeship he had enjoyed during the war with the crews of Armoured Cars and Handley Page aircraft did not exist at Uxbridge and he rapidly became disillusioned:

> Out hut is a fair microcosm of unemployed England: not of unemployable England, for the strict R.A.F. standards refuse the last levels of the social structure. Yet a man's enlisting is his acknowledgement of a defeat by life. Amongst a hundred serving men you will not find one whole or happy. Each has a lesion, a hurt open or concealed, in his late history.[1]

This was the first time he had bunked with enlisted men and, although the conditions were extreme, they paled in comparison to what he was later to suffer at Bovington. One veteran who was in the same hut at Uxbridge was Aircraftman A.G. Turner. Turner was also quiet and short – 5' 6" (about the same height as T.E.). He swore less than the other men. He and T.E. were placed together on parades. Turner recalled that Lawrence was 'a very quiet sort, did not smoke, drink, swear or express much about things going on in camp. He was a loner, did not make friends easily, always went out of camp after duty hours by himself, mostly to London.'[2]

Turner was 70 years old when he recalled these memories in 1973. He conducted a lengthy correspondence, from August 1973 until March 1974, with Group Captain P.E. Raymond of Uxbridge and the Ministry of Defence, representing the Air Historical Branch. Turner wrote a series of letters elaborating on his experience of 'Ross'. He found the person he knew in 1922 did not match the man who wrote *The Mint*. 'Ross' was very thin, often fumbling with his weapon on parades. The Drill Sergeant would take it from him telling him 'he was like an old woman who'd never had it and shewed him how to handle the rifle'.[3]

Lawrence was then in an extremely weak and neurotic condition, still suffering from the malnutrition and exhaustion that had nearly overwhelmed him at Barton Street. Nobody at the Depot believed such a small, emaciated figure could be the man who led the desert Arabs. This was not an uncommon assessment at the time. The American author Robert McAlmon met him in Paris in 1919, whilst McAlmon was being sculpted by a man named Dobson. Lawrence sat in and discussed excavation work he had done in the Middle East and brought a small statuette, which he gave to Mrs Dobson. Only after he left did McAlmon realise that it was the famous Colonel Lawrence of Arabia. McAlmon found great difficulty in conceiving of him as the 'bold leader of the desert Bedouins'. The impression he left was not a deep one.[4]

After the six weeks initial drill at the Uxbridge Depot he became fitter and more settled. Turner found him reluctant to talk about himself. So did other soldiers upon first meeting him. In the Tank Corps his immediate superior in the Quartermaster's Stores at Bovington found he did not seem to care for anyone at first and was disliked for it initially. He told Turner after some time he had signed on for 7 and 5,[5] stating when asked that he was a writer. He then changed the subject immediately to discuss the poor food at the Depot, where the menu was monotonous and unappetizing. But the recruits were so hungry they always ate it. The service pay was three shillings a day, and by Thursday most of the squad were out of money. Lawrence, despite representing himself otherwise, had more cash reserves than the average airman: 'The fact was, he was about the only airman not short of money on a Wednesday or Thursday; Friday was pay day.'[6] It was simply Lawrence's character that made him adopt a spartan lifestyle.

Turner said of the other men at Uxbridge: 'We had some pretty tough characters in the squad, costermongers, Merchant Navy men, taxi drivers, farm workers and army officer types. Consequently the language at times was a bit strong, which Ross did not like.'[7] A photograph was taken of his squad outside Hut IV, in 1922, by an Army photographer. Lawrence was reluctant to divulge his identity. He can be seen tucked away on the extreme left of the photo, hiding behind the window mullions. Turner could never understand how such a weak man as 'Ross' could be passed fit by the stiff RAF medicals. 'Did someone in the Air Ministry know that he was going to join and so stretch the regulations [?] Every time I see a picture of a thin man it reminds me of Ross at Uxbridge. Life there must have been hell for him.'[8] Occasionally Lawrence invited Turner to the Y.M.C.A. for tea and cake: 'He used at first to go by himself in the evenings but he got pestered so much he started asking me to go with him, seeming to use me as a buffer against other men questioning him. I did not mind, he always paid.'[9]

Turner found Lawrence never seemed to smile, always appearing to be worried about something and noticed he had a peculiar, strained look about his eyes. Only later, when serving in the Middle East, did Turner realize this was caused by the glare of the sun on the desert sand. Lawrence often stayed in the barracks in the evenings. He would sit on his bed writing, his knees drawn up with his back resting against the palliasse and blankets and would do this for about two hours

Lawrence's squad at the Uxbridge Depot in 1922. Foreground is R.S.M. 'Taff' Davis. Second soldier from the right is AC2 E.G. Turner. (via Hyde)

at a time. Turner, only discovered after he had left the Depot that it was material for *The Mint.*

Many of Lawrence's notes for this were written up much later, but some remain from this period. These are a few pages of the rough notes he made about his experience at Uxbridge. They have been written specifically for an unidentified person, possibly Trenchard or Jonathan Cape.[10] Lawrence explained in his introduction his reason for writing them:

> I tried to write the monograph on the school as an independent force: but failed, since the whole current of my endeavour at Uxbridge is to see it in general. Consequently all my notes have been of the school in relation to the Depot.
>
> I tried the second time to write up these notes into a coherent form: but my sense of authorship impeded me. It is too soon. So I have chosen some of these in initial m/s & edited them severely. To me now they seem mild: but if they are improper, & if no use for your purpose, I hope that you will destroy them promptly. It is my wish to remain peacefully in the shadow here.[11]

The spindly handwriting contrasts with a handwritten report Lawrence made at the end of his service in 1935. Both texts are obviously written by the same person, but the later one is significantly more precise and confident. The 1923 unpublished notes appear to be a rough draft of what was later worked up, probably in stages, to be the final draft of *The Mint*. They are now part of an Air Ministry archive file.[12] A number of passages were meticulously rewritten for the final draft.

> Hut IV besides being a pack of as-yet unlevelled personalities has (without me) a common character and [illegible] a group opinion, which is usually arrived at by contrarying the too quick judgement of the reactive talkers. We are also developing a group instinct (Lamarck would have loved the order of our growth) and this is gradually enabling us to act together, tautly, as the majority desire.[13]

In Part Two, Chapter 21 of *The Mint* we find the final form of this:

> Our hut used to arrive at an opinion by discussion, by contradicting the early word that the first fool rushed out. Later this turned into instinct. We have come, unknowing to a corporate life. Today we think, decide, act on parade without a word said. Men are becoming troops when they act like one body. . . [14]

The following passage from the original notes also became part of Chapter 21:

> It is inevitable that each such place should have a master spirit; and as it has been the lot of Uxbridge to find it in one who does not pretend to be an officer, and who holds perhaps a latent grudge against the professional class of officer. At least he is not reluctant to make clear to them and to us their awkwardness on parade.[15]

This became:

> Every camp needs its dominant: and ours has drawn the lot of Stiffy, who is very masterful. He does not pretend to be an officer: perhaps he harbours a latent grudge against the officer class: he so likes to take them down before us. 'Mr. Squire, your damned cap isn't fit for parade'. Indeed he wants to be the sole ruler here and humiliates the Sergeant Major, the sergeants, even the corporals, by public curses.[16]

According to A.G. Turner, 'Stiffy' was ex-Guardsman Flt/Lt Wombwell, so nicknamed because he was a very erect, big, broad man, over six feet tall, who was the officer in charge of drill parades and had a voice like a fog horn. It was said in the camp that his voice was so loud it caused the windows to break in 'M' section.[17] Michael Yardley and other biographers however identify 'Stiffy' as G.F. 'Stiffy' Breeze, the Squadron Commander at Uxbridge.[18] Turner agreed with Lawrence in identifying the C.O. as Group Captain 'Pegleg' Bonham-Carter.[19] Lawrence's original notes stated:

But that is the spirit of technical incompetence in those officers we meet. They are not carefully enough chosen, or careful enough to know their subjects, & that is dangerous with our mixed classes.[20] In that 4 are experts on thirty matters, more skilled men than could be plucked from an entire army division. It is good form to conceal this knowledge: but instructors should guard against it. We have been set to learn the handling of aircraft. One expert talked wrongly of the purpose and effect of the dihedral. Another tapped the epicyclic casing and said 'That's the Constantinesco gearing by which the propellor is worked up to twice the engine speed.' One of us was foreman in the C.C. workshop. Two are ex-aerial gunners. One has his certificate. [21]

This was rewritten in Chapter 15 as:

Wasted, too, I fancy are the hours devoted to teaching the manhandling of aircraft. Probation-officers take us for that: and they do not put enough effort into it to meet our demand. We have almost a habit of trying hard, now. Some of us have read a little aerodynamics; so we expect the officers to know a great deal. Troops ask everything of their officers. Yet at the first lecture in the gloomy shed through which the wind blew damply upon the carcass of the imprisoned Bristol Fighter, Flying Officer Bayes confused incidence with dihedral . . .

...It was worse later, on October the twenty sixth, when another young officer deputized for Bayes. He tapped the epicyclic gear case with his cane and airily told us, 'This is the Constantinesco gear. I won't muddle your heads explaining how it works: but take it from me that it revs up the prop to twice the engine speed.' Our Allen, a country-bred, has been an air gunner. I saw his legs wilt and his ears redden with the news. [22]

The published passages are much more lucid and comprehensive (and more amusing) than the original notes. This contrasts with his rewriting of *Seven Pillars* to create the 1926 abridged edition, which produced a thinned down, etiolated version of the original Oxford text.

In November 1922 he was transferred to Farnborough. He arrived there one day late for a nine-month photography course and was refused entry. He was told he would have to wait until the first week in January for the next intake. This arranged, he was appointed to the Adjutant's office as an orderly and his duties were to sweep the office, light the fire and run errands during the day. Charles Findlay the Adjutant saw him as an average recruit, performing his duties efficiently. Although he was heartened by the transfer away from the depot, he was anxious to employ his well honed photographic talents, skills he had been instructed on by his father. He had undertaken work before the war photographing pottery at Carchemish.

Neither Findlay, nor the Station Commander, Guilfoyle, suspected his true identity and it was only after Oliver Swann telephoned to ask why Aircraftman Ross hadn't started his course that they realised something was afoot; it was most unusual for a high ranking Air Ministry official to telephone a Station. Findlay later commented that 'Nothing about him ever suggested that here was the most amazing aircraftman ever to join the RAF.'[23] Lawrence was called into the Station-Commander's office, and Guilfoyle noticed something familiar about him as he had once seen him in Cairo in 1914. He informed Findlay that he thought it was Lawrence of Arabia and instructed him to contact the Chief Instructor.

Lawrence enjoyed the course and later found the enlarging and mosaic work, learned in two of the later months, extremely useful. In August 1929 the Committee of the Schneider Trophy would require an aerial mosaic to be made of the course. Farnborough assigned a Flight Sergeant to the task who conducted an aerial photo survey, but the work was considered inadequate and Lawrence was asked to produce a replacement.

In the barrack hut at Farnborough Lawrence met A.E. 'Jock' Chambers, the hut orderly, a rugged Scotsman who was later to prove a life-long friend. Chambers didn't think much of the new arrival at the outset because of his short stature and general air of loneliness. Unaware of who he was, Chambers tried to belittle Lawrence in front of the men and told him to scrub his bed, 'no tide marks', addressing him as 'shortarse'. After half an hour, despite being an officer type, he was accepted by the other men in the hut and he and Chambers soon became close friends. He borrowed two of Lawrence's books, *Also Sprach Zarathustra* and *The Brothers Karamazov*. Although he was not educated Chambers was intelligent and found the books interesting. On one occasion Chambers gave Lawrence a bear hug from behind, pinning his arms behind his back, but sensed immediately that he did not like this and quickly withdrew. Chambers recalls an occasion when the Press was looking for Aircraftman Ross at Farnborough and Lawrence was standing guard duty by the camp gate. 'Here, you aren't him are you?' one of them asked him. The little man replied 'Now, do I look like a soldier?'[24] Some of Chambers' later comments about the closeness of their friendship were moving, startling even in their depth of feeling: 'He was my only real friend, the only one I've ever had. He was one of the finest men who ever trod the globe, better than Christ or any of them.'[25]

Lawrence continued making his notes for *The Mint* at Farnborough. An article by Findlay in *The Listener* of June 1958 gives an insight into Lawrence at this time: He was keenly interested in photography and felt that, when engaged in any other task, he was misemployed. He told Findlay that service as an officer would have 'spoiled' the experience for him. He wanted to see the RAF from the ranks' point of view and could only do this by sharing life in the barracks. Findlay found he was but a shadow of the man who had led the Arab Revolt. He noted: 'I am convinced that some quality departed from Lawrence before he became the R.A.F. recruit. Lawrence of Arabia had died.'[26]

Lawrence also befriended another airman at Farnborough named Robert 'Bob' Guy. R.A.M. Guy, young, short and fair haired, was particularly handsome – 'like a Greek God' Chambers thought – and Lawrence said he represented the best of the Air Force ranks as he pictured them. He was probably attracted to Guy by

'Looking like a retired pirate' was how Malcolm Brown described A.E. 'Jock' Chambers when he appeared for the BBC film of Lawrence's life in 1962. Chambers first met Lawrence at the Cadet College, Cranwell in August 1925. (Tunbridge)

his good looks, the image somewhat marred by a broad Birmingham accent. Guy transferred stations but still kept in touch and sometimes visited Clouds Hill. He tended to sponge off T.E.

It was not generally known that Lawrence was in the RAF. After the *Daily Express* revealed his presence at Farnborough in December 1922, Trenchard told him the only way he could continue in the service was to accept a commission, but he refused. The Air Minister Samuel Hoare was horrified when he heard.[27] Lawrence's enlistment, when concealed, was 'delicate' but it became untenable when revealed and he was discharged from the RAF by Air Ministry Order in February 1923.[28] From that point until August 1925 his research for *The Mint* stopped abruptly.

Lawrence did not finish *The Mint* until 15th March, 1928, at Karachi. Between then and 1935 he sent manuscripts[29] to his friends G.B. Shaw, E.M. Forster, Siegfried Sassoon, both the Garnetts, and John Buchan, who all praised it for its honesty. 'It is a document . . . made at a cost of experience and with a literary power that makes it rare and valuable as a record' said Shaw. Buchan was also full of praise: 'The kind of document which has never been produced before about any service.' Buchan, with typical astuteness, also wrote that it was a 'picture of the impact of this kind of life upon a man of your calibre, who is capable of setting down exactly his impressions and reactions . . . your visualizing and observing powers are perfectly uncanny.'[30]

E.M. Forster did not think it to be as great a work as the *Seven Pillars* in 'colour or form' but he found it more 'startling and heartening' than anything else he had read. The first two parts he found 'superbly written', but the third part 'a little odd'. Edward Garnett described it as 'first rate stuff'. The style was 'elastic, sinewy, terse'. The 'feeling of Hut and Fatigue life', he thought, 'swept out of existence all former states of consciousness and riveted one horribly.'[31] His son David Garnett's first impression was that Lawrence was 'a queerer man' than he revealed in the *Seven Pillars*. The Lawrence of *The Mint* was not 'intellectual at all'. He found a tendency for Lawrence to 'regard all sorts of incidents as illuminating and valuable', when they were neither.[32] Siegfried Sassoon saw it as 'a bit of a shock to the squeamish mind . . . a drama of mind versus body . . . can one achieve mental "perfect fitness", or whatever it is – in defiance of physical comfort?'[33] The book's descriptions of barrack room life reminded him starkly of 'the gross brutality of "unprotected" human existence'.[34]

The Publication of *The Mint* in the US

Shortly after Lawrence's death in May 1935 Trenchard, then Commissioner of the Metropolitan Police, contacted the Air Ministry to enquire what the position was with regards to the publication of *The Mint* in the United States. On 15th July the Secretary of the Air Ministry, Sir Christopher Bullock [35] wrote to him:

> My dear Trenchard,
> In pursuance of our telephone conversation of the other morning, I have been following up the question of 'The Mint'.
> I have spoken both to Jack Salmond and Ellington,[36] who saw the book in typescript, and also got young Lawrence[37] to come round to see me.
> There does appear to be a real danger of a printed version appearing in America, and the only way to bar this seems to be on the lines suggested by Lawrence, viz. that a strictly limited edition should be 'published' in the States in order to ensure the copyright position. This entails *inter alia* the deposit of one or two copies in the Library of Congress and also in our own libraries entitled to copies of all books published, e.g. the University libraries of Oxford and Cambridge.[38]

Bullock had earlier contacted Sir Stephen Casalec, the Foreign Office Librarian and an expert in such matters, for his opinion. He advised that the Library of Congress was usually very amenable in this type of case, recommending an arrangement be made through diplomatic channels.

Over a year later, in November 1936, the Air Ministry wrote to Sir Stephen reminding him of 'the question of the protection of Lawrence's *The Mint* from general publication in America'.[39] A.W. Lawrence, a partner in the firm of Lawrence's literary agent Raymond Savage Ltd., had contacted the Air Ministry, advising them it would be necessary to take early action to prevent the appearance of a pirated edition. He had realised that, in view of its stark descriptions of RAF life and certain personalities, the book was potentially explosive. Trenchard and Sir John Salmond, each having read a typescript copy, agreed with this emphatically.

The problem arose from an aspect of American copyright law. Bullock: 'Savage's secretary added, what is a little obscure to me, that a ruling has recently been given in the States to the effect that when copyright is taken out for any book it is not legally proper to withhold access to it from American citizens generally.'[40] An unsigned, undated note remains from this period, officially for the attention of 'Raymond Savage – publishers' and 'A.W. Lawrence' that resides in the National Archives:

> *Ruling now given in the States –*
> *copyright cannot prevent publt[ion]*
> *for American Citizens.*
> *Diplom. refuses [us] to prevent general distrib[tion].*
>
> *British*
> ---------------------
> *Stephen Gaselec.*
> ---------------------
>
> *Action by F.O.*
> *(1) Stay publ[tion]. in U.S.A. – pirated.*
> *(2) Tell Embassy we are taking out copyright – here & in U.S.A.*
> *(3) In spite of the recent ruling*
>   *can they arrange for the book*
>   *to be kept confidential in two or three libraries?*[41]

Gaselec, in an earlier telephone call with an Air Ministry official, agreed that the British Embassy in Washington should contact the American authorities for help. Consequently the Secretary of State for Air requested that he should ask the Americans, firstly that they take any steps required to stay publication of a pirated edition, and secondly that they uphold any confidentiality safeguards in copyright law over copies deposited in the Library of Congress.

Somehow, however, the Air Ministry's plans failed. When *The Mint* was published in the US in 1935 the publishers Doubleday, Doran, Incorporated, in order to protect their copyright, offered 10 copies for sale at $500,000. Naturally there were no purchasers.[42] But under law two copies had to be sent to the Library of Congress. The editors of America's *Saturday Review of Literature* realised that this was a golden opportunity for them to examine it, and sent a man to Washington to watch for the copyright confirmation. He waited a year before it was granted, then, on 13th November 1936, after ensuring legality, the *Review* editors sent the paper's critic, Henry Siedel Canby, to review it. Savage's secretary had been right: under U.S. copyright law anyone could see the books after they were lodged at the Congressional Library.

On November 21st an article by Canby appeared in the *Saturday Evening Review,* New York:

> *The Mint*, the name a symbol of a man's desperate mood, may be the last book of Arabian Lawrence, later known as 352087 A/c Ross of the R.A.F. Visitors of the Book Fair have seen one of the twelve printed copies under burglar proof glass with a price of $500,000 on its head . . .
>
> Night by night he wrote these notes in bed, intending to select from them afterward, and presumably to prune the rank abundance of homely Saxon words, which he faithfully copied from his companions indescribably profane and obscene conversation, though he could not use them himself. In this James Farrell, James Joyce, and Ernest Hemingway might well envy his dialogue.[43]

Canby later wrote a similar, but reworded, review, for a New York paper in December 1936. Examining the Library of Congress books, valued at £200,000, Canby wondered 'whether one of them was worth half of it'. He realized that it was an incomplete book, since Lawrence was expelled from the Air Force before it was finished. The second part, written after Lawrence's return of 1925, Canby saw as only a series of notes: 'It is not a book; it is the foundation porch to a great edifice that was never built; a torso with a sketch of the whole added.' But Canby concluded it *was* written with 'deep psychological insight' and 'being a replica of reality it puts art to shame'. It was probably the unexpurgated version, for he refused to describe the language Lawrence's companions, 'ordinary, coarse, unheroic men' used, language he again called 'indescribably profane and obscene'.

On December 14th 1936 a memorandum was produced by the Air Ministry explaining the Library of Congress's custody of the book.[44] J.M.K. Vyvyan, a British official in Washington, was one of five people, aside from Congressional Library officials, allowed to see the book, after Canby and a *Washington Post* reporter had examined it. Security was absurdly high. In a steel lined strong room, surrounded by incunabula (books printed before 1500) and overseen by the Superintendent of the 'Rare Book Section' where it resided, Vyvyan spent half an hour examining the uncut pages. Readers were not allowed to copy or quote from the work. Who was allowed to examine it was apparently at the discretion of the Library authorities, but legally anyone could. An Air Ministry memorandum of December 1936 stated:

> Rights in the 'Mint' were sold to Doubleday-Doran subject to a delay of *de facto* publication until 1950. The firm could have safeguarded this by locking up the typescript in a strong room or by securing a copyright. They chose the latter.[45]

For some reason news of the 'sensational' American review, a two and a bit page scoop, did not appear in the British Press until December 17th, 1936. Headlines were printed in various newspapers such as the *Daily Telegraph* and *Morning Post* of 18th December. The *Evening Standard* got to the nub of it:

£100,000 Book by T.E. Lawrence Traced:
Not to be published until 1950:
Bitter Attacks on Officers at the R.A.F. Training School[46]

Raymond Savage, the owner of the English copyright, told the press that there would be no publication in England for 25 years. Out of deference to Trenchard, Lawrence had stipulated in his will that the book was not to be published until 1950. At the end of December 1936, Gaselec sent a copy of the article to the Air Ministry. Although the action they requested appeared to have been taken, reports appearing in the British Press suggested that something had gone wrong. The Air Ministry's comment was that 'So far we do not see that anything more has now to be done about it. We hope that the sensation will soon blow itself out – till 1950.'[47] There is no record that any pirated editions of *The Mint* ever appeared before 1950.

Lawrence's introduction to life in the ranks had come as a shock to him. He had taken for granted the fact that his entry to the RAF would be relatively easy, which it was not. When he was admitted, he found it a much tougher life than he had anticipated and that the wartime style comradeship he had anticipated no longer existed. However, he was able to pursue his writing project. The first two parts of *The Mint* made the experience worthwhile. Few books had been written that gave such a 'warts and all' view of barrack room life. Whether, as Aircraftman Turner questioned, this was an actual picture of life as it was, or simply Lawrence's interpretation of it for the sake of vivid literary effect is another matter. When it was published in the US the book caused a sensation because of its visceral imagery and strong language, and its closeting for a further 20 years only served to increase its notoriety. T.E.'s lack of diligence in concealing his identity and his naivety concerning the seriousness of the consequences of his writings eventually led to him being banished from the RAF for two-and-a-half years.

Notes

1 Letter to G.B. Shaw, 27th August 1922. MB.
2 National Archives AIR 1/2697 A.G. Turner to Group Captain P.E. Raymond, Eastbourne, Sussex. 20/8/1973.
3 Ibid.
4 Source: *Being Geniuses Together*, Robert McAlmon and Kay Boyle, Paris, 1938.
5 Seven years in the colours, five in the reserve.

6 National Archives AIR 1/2697 A.G. Turner to Group Captain P.E. Raymond, Eastbourne, Sussex. 20/8/1973.

7 A.G. Turner to Group Captain P.E. Raymond, Eastbourne, 22/3/1974.

8 Ibid.

9 Ibid.

10 Cape requested, as part of the contract for the *Seven Pillars*, that Lawrence supply them with a second book, which *The Mint* eventually became.

11 National Archives: AIR 1/2697 *Notes Made of Uxbridge Service*. J.H. Ross, c. 1923.

12 Ibid.

13 Ibid.

14 *Mint:* unexpurgated.

15 National Archives: AIR 1/2697 *Notes Made of Uxbridge Service*. J.H. Ross, c. 1923.

16 *Mint:* unexpurgated.

17 A.G. Turner to Group Captain P.E. Raymond, Eastbourne, 20/08/1973. National Archives: AIR 1/2697.

18 A.B. Tinsley in his 1984 book *One Rissole on My Plate*, which gave a nostalgic account of RAF life between the wars, also identified 'Stiffy' as Flight Lieutenant Wombwell, an ex-Guardsman appointed as Uxbridge's Drill Adjutant after receiving an RAF commission.

19 Yardley's source is listed as a postscript to Aldington's *Lawrence of Arabia – a Biographical Enquiry.*

20 Working and middle classes, or less likely, mixed ability. T.E. decried the lack of technical competence of the officers at Uxbridge but not at Bridlington in 1935.

21 National Archives: AIR 1/2697 *Notes Made of Uxbridge Service*. J.H. Ross, c. 1923.

22 *Mint:* unexpurgated.

23 *The Amazing AC2*, C. Findlay, *The Listener*, 5/06/1958.

24 A.E. Chambers in the 1962 BBC film *T.E. Lawrence 1888–1935.*

25 Mack.

26 *The Amazing AC2*, C. Findlay, *The Listener*, 5/06/1958.

27 Sir Samuel J.G Hoare, 1st Viscount Templewood, was Conservative MP for Chelsea who served in the Conservative and National Governments in the 1920s and 1930s. He was appointed Secretary of State for Air from 1922 to 1924 and from 1924 to 1929. During the National Government of 1931 he became Secretary of State for India until 1931, negotiating the India Act 1935, and in 1935 became Foreign Secretary, negotiating the Hoare-Laval Agreement with the French for Italian territorial concessions in Ethiopia. Following that he was successively appointed First Lord of the Admiralty (1936–37), Home Secretary (1937–1939), Lord Privy Seal (1939–40), Secretary of State for Air (1940), and was sent as Ambassador to Spain when Churchill became Prime Minister (1940–1944).

28 B: RG.

29 It was probably the same manuscript that went to all of them.

30 John Buchan to T.E. Lawrence, 12/3/1935. LTEL.

31 Edward Garnett to T.E. Lawrence, 22/4/28. LTEL.

32 David Garnett to T.E. Lawrence St. Ives, Huntingdonshire, 20/05/1928.

33 Siegfried Sassoon to T.E. Lawrence, London, 13/11/1930. LTEL

34 Quotes 30 to 33 above all from LTEL.

35 Sir C.D. Bullock, then at the height of his career, was Personal Secretary to the Secretary of State for the Air.

36 Air Chief Marshal Sir Edward Ellington, Chief of the Air Staff. He replaced Air Marshal Sir John Salmond, 'Jack', on 22nd May 1933.

37 A.W. Lawrence.

38 National Archives: AIR 1/2701 Air Ministry to Lord Trenchard, London. 15/7/1935

39 National Archives: AIR 1/2701 Air Ministry official to Sir Stephen Casalec, London, 18/11/1935.

40 National Archives: AIR 1/2701 Air Ministry to Lord Trenchard, London. 15/7/1935. The Subscribers' Edition of the *Seven Pillars* had also caused him concern in 1924 because of the copyright loophole.

41 National Archives: AIR 1/2701 Unsigned Air Ministry note, London, c. November 1936.

42 George Doran, publishers of New York, had used exactly the same method with the *Seven Pillars* in 1925.

43 National Archives: AIR 1/ 2697 *Lawrence after Arabia*, from *The Saturday Evening Review, New York.* 21/11/1936.

44 National Archives: AIR 1/2697 *The Custody of the 'Mint' by the Library of Congress.* Air Ministry Memorandum, London, 14/12/1936.

45 Ibid.

46 *Evening Standard*, 17/12/1936.

47 National Archives: AIR 1/2697 *The Custody of the 'Mint' by the Library of Congress.* Air Ministry Memorandum, London, 14/12/1936.

CHAPTER THREE

Bovington

Here every man has joined because he was down and out: and no one talks of the Army or of promotion, or of trades and accomplishments . . . there cannot be classes in England much more raw, more free of all that the upbringing of a lifetime has plastered over you and me.

T.E. Shaw to Lionel Curtis,
Bovington Camp, 27th March, 1923

. . . of course they were a pretty low lot. The language and the talk was pretty awful . . . I always said there it was the finest institution in the world for demoralizing the human emotions.

A. Russell to author,
December 1985

Lawrence's enlistment in the Tank Corps was a direct result of his dismissal from the RAF, it being a crude irony that the only publicity the Air Force received during this period was caused by his expulsion. He gave the impression that his money had run out shortly after he moved into a small hotel at Frensham near Farnborough. He returned temporarily to the old rooms in Westminster of 1922, above Herbert Baker's office at 14 Barton Street and tried to persuade Trenchard to post him to a remote station, but this fell on deaf ears. The sudden end of the RAF life had left him with a blank and he implored Trenchard for a second chance. The Chief of the Air Staff was tired with the triviality of it all and recommended he accept a short service commission as an Armoured Car officer. His Adjutant at Farnborough, Charles Findlay, concluded that Lawrence 'was searching for something new in life – but had not found it.' Findlay thought his participation in the Air Force was only a partial solution to his problem, he still seemed to be trying to shake something off. In that sense any structured way of life may have appealed to Lawrence, and he toyed with various alternatives, contacting Leo Amery, then First Lord of the Admiralty, for help.[1] He mooted a storekeeper's position in Bermuda and there was also an offer from the Irish Free State Army that he did not take up. Amery suggested being a lighthouse keeper or a Coastguard, but the Navy wasn't interested, so Sir Phillip Chetwode at the War Office, an old friend from Arabian days, informed him it was possible he could enlist in the Tank

Corps as a private soldier. (Perhaps we should pause here a moment to remind ourselves what an extraordinary story this is: Lawrence of Arabia as a storekeeper? A lighthouse keeper?)

He had hit rock bottom and had few other means of supporting himself, no trade or profession, little money and was in a state of depression. Only a job could save him, he thought. The most attractive thing about the Tanks, apart from it being a technical branch, was that there had been cases of its troops transferring to the RAF. So began one of the most miserable and unfulfilling years of Lawrence's short life, where he was thrown into a rawness of existence he had never encountered before; the only compensations the friends he made and his love of literature and music.

On Monday 12th March 1923 Lawrence arrived at Bovington Camp, Dorset for eighteen weeks basic training, enlisting as Trooper Shaw, T.E., No. 7875698. He spent most of the first few months living with 'the lowest of the low', as a friend later described them, and regarded this period as a waste of time, for himself and for the army.

Dorset in the mid 1920s was an extremely remote and rural county and Bovington Camp was a much more basic affair than it is today. It was founded in 1899 after the Army purchased 1000 acres of privately owned land for a rifle range and tented camp, consisting of a collection of corrugated tin huts and row upon row of wooden buildings. The Tank Training Centre moved there in 1916, as the terrain resembled the Western Front. One soldier visiting in the 1920s reported it to be a unique establishment, a friendly, peaceful place, where the recruits appeared unharrassed, the most pleasant camp he had ever experienced. The surrounding heathland and pine forest leant it a bucolic calm. When he was posted there later, however, he changed his mind and looked back on the experience with disdain.

By 1920 the Tank Corps had been reduced from its wartime status to a depot with four battalions. In 1923 it was granted the prefix 'Royal' by King George V, its Colonel-in-Chief since 1918. Two men who served there remembered well Lawrence's first arrival at Bovington. To Captain G.E. Kirby, a former infantryman who joined the Tanks in 1917 and Sergeant W.E. Jeffrey who enlisted in the Corps in 1922, it was quite obvious that Lawrence was no ordinary recruit. Both his age and height made him ineligible. Kirby was the same age as Lawrence but his superior officer, and Jeffrey was only 20. Years later Kirby commented on Lawrence's arrival at Bovington in the Dorset *Daily Echo:*

> It was just as an ordinary recruit that Shaw came to the depot, signed the necessary Army forms, as all other recruits must, and was drilled with other newcomers for two months.[2]

Rumours circulated that 'he had been attested for service under special authority given by the War Office'[3] which proved to be true. One of the first exercises he had to do was write a short essay on 'Your First Impression of Bovington Camp'. It was late in the evening when he arrived. The result of his efforts was a single sentence: 'I arrived in darkness, and have not yet had time to look around.'[4]

He was assigned to hut F12 in Macelhayes Road. The first person he met was a short, stocky 18-year-old named Arthur Russell:

> It was early in March 1923; I joined in Coventry, via Budbrooke[5]... Well, it's strange, but we were all in civilian clothes. His bed was just the opposite side of the bed to mine and we sort of took to each other right away. Why I don't know, probably the conversations or some like ... of course they were a pretty low lot. The language and the talk pretty awful.[6]

Russell came from Coventry and had joined the Army on a whim, arriving at Bovington two days before Lawrence. He later recalled that the first thing T.E. had said to him was 'I am illegitimate.'[7] Russell was short with a bullet-shaped head and nicknamed 'Cov' or 'Bullet'. He was practical and could drive a car and a motorbike, unusual for those times, and later went with Lawrence to visit Thomas Hardy or G.B. Shaw, or up to London to see a show or for tea. In December 1923 Lawrence told an RAF friend that Russell was 'the best fellow I can find in the camp, and he's decent in suffering my fancies patiently'. Although Lawrence at 35 was 17 years older, Russell was unaware of any age difference:

> [I] didn't notice ... there was no hero worship. I didn't know who Lawrence of Arabia was in those days. Then he told me he'd been in the Army. Now, next bed to him was Taffy Watkins, he was ex-service. The one by the side of me, Shadbob, he was ex-service. I was the odd one out in these four.

Life in the Tank Corps in those times could be hard. The duties included cleaning out the bathhouse.

> Now things were pretty disgusting up there. His first job was looking after a Bath House. We were allowed one change of clothes a week. You slept in your shirt. You were allowed one bath a week. If you missed it on that night when you were supposed to have your bath you had to go the next week. That was the army in those days. Dirty.

Charles R. Bourne, from Parkstone, Dorset was at Bovington in the 1920s. In 1923 he had 18 months service behind him and was an 'old soldier' in charge of recruits. He recalls that the Corporal in charge of education, Higgins, told Lawrence that he would have to undergo the preliminary examination in education. Lawrence contested this, saying he would sit for the final examination. The Corporal explained that he had to take the preliminary first, to see if he was qualified to take the first, second and third tests in that order. The Corporal wrote the questions on a blackboard, and then covered them with a sheet until the exam began. After the sheet was removed the candidates were allowed two hours to finish the exam. Within 15 minutes Lawrence put his pen down and sat back. 'Are you stuck, lad?' The Corporal asked him. Lawrence replied he was not and had finished. When his paper was handed in it was found he had answered each question in a different language. He was put on orders for insolence.[8] Arthur Russell recalled the same educational tests:

> Now we were in the same hut and the same squad together on the square. We both wanted to go in for our Third Class Certificate of Education, but they said no, we've got to hold back with the rest. We couldn't go in for it. And we had to wait for the rest of the squad. We would have passed. But no.

Russell also recalled that it was so disgusting in the mess hall they decided not to go again and went into the camp whilst the money lasted and fed there. However, after three months they were broke.

> When we got broke I said to him: 'I'm going to do Mess Orderly tomorrow' and I wangled myself onto it.[9] 'Course the Mess Orderly, although the table was for twelve there were only six on it. They used to throw the tray of food into the middle of the table and they grabbed it with their hands. That's why we didn't go. Anyway as Mess Orderly I put it on the table and they were gonna grab and I said 'I'll dish it out'. And before I got it dished out the table was full and it started it. People started dishing it out then, so we fed up there. And the food was not bad.

There were a number of cafes in the camp they could go to: 'There was one just by the huts, "The Elite", which everyone called "The Eeelite" so you can guess how ignorant they were. "Smiths" was a big one and "Miss Fawkes". That was a nice little cafe and she used to look after us, and it was cheap.'

Trooper John Smith was also at Bovington when Lawrence was there. He joined the Tank Corps in 1924, aged 17. To get away with it he added to his age by a number of years and in 1991, aged 84, he still did not know how he managed it. He well remembered the 'Elite' café:

> It was early midnight when I arrived at Wool Station, rain pouring. I had no mackintosh, my shoes leaked and still two miles to walk to Bovington Camp. I reported to the guardroom and was directed to the stores. There, to my surprise, was Lawrence. I was so wet he gave me a complete change of clothing, army of course, a cup of coffee and helped me to take my bedding over to the recruits hut. Just a few days later I met Shaw, or Lawrence, in the Elite café. It was a very small place where you could get 2d square, something like bread pudding, and a 1d cup of tea. We came to become very friendly and met very often.

George F. Preedy (left) and friend on Wareham station c. 1923. He joined the Tank Corps in 1921 and worked in the cookhouse at Bovington. In March 1923 Private T.E. Shaw joined his hut. (Emerton)

There were a number of reports of Lawrence being put on 'Jankers' (Confined to Barracks) shortly after his arrival at Bovington. Mr. H. Searle of Bournemouth recalled that Lawrence was put on a charge for not reporting on Pay Parade and told his CO he had no desire to pick up his pay as it could be given to the other men. He was told he had to parade and was given seven days CB. While serving out his punishment a signal came for him to go immediately to London and he replied: '"Regret unable attend: serving seven days CB". Needless to say he was instantly released.'[10] In 1935 Captain Kirby and Sergeant Jeffrey recounted another version of the incident. Some time after his arrival, for some slight contravention of regulations, Lawrence was ordered to be confined to barracks. To his great pleasure he then received a communication requesting him to report to the Air Ministry and, without hesitation telegraphed the reply; 'Unable to reply to request, as am a defaulter'. 'The military authorities were instructed to arrange for him to be sent on leave without delay.'[11] Arthur Russell had yet another version of the story. 'Once the War Office sent for him, and he sent a telegram back: "Can't come. On Jankers." They didn't even know what Jankers meant. "Confined to barracks! Punishment!" So they sent for him and he had one of 'em drive him down there. And when they got there, they [the staff] looked at him and they said: "Well, this is how you call in today".'[12]

After completing recruit training Lawrence was employed in the Quartermaster's Stores where he was mainly marking and fitting clothing. Basil Liddell Hart pointed out: 'It was, on the whole, a "cushy job" and had the advantage of giving him the privacy of an office in which he could work at night on the final revisions of the *Seven Pillars*.'[13] He was employed there for the remainder of his period at Bovington, until August 18th, 1925. Even here Lawrence's leadership qualities came to the fore. He became the driving force behind the work of reorganising the stores. He was 'highly delighted to have been chosen to carry out duties which entailed so little responsibility.'[14] Captain G.E. Kirby who was, at one point, the Captain in charge of the Stores, recalled that despite having been a Colonel, which was never discussed or used in his favour, Lawrence was much more amenable to discipline than the average squaddie. His reasons for joining were never revealed. Although he hardly ever mixed with the other men, he was soon accepted as an equal. His normal duties were from 8.30 to 4.30 p.m., with Wednesday and Saturday afternoons off, and like any other soldier he had to obtain a pass for special leave. Lawrence found the senior officers and N.C.O.s had little mechanical knowledge, button cleaning being their forte.

The 1923–25 Army Form B 2066 Employment Sheet entry for T.E. Shaw for November 30th 1923 stated: 'Duty now employed in Q Master's Stores. Very clean, hardworking and conscientious. A very reliable man.' The 1924 entry stated: 'Q.M. Stores. A highly intelligent man. Very reliable and works well.'

Lawrence was precise in his tasks and displayed some humour: 'When, for example, he had occasion to issue a beret . . . to a rather starchy warrant officer, whose size happened to be $7^3/_8$ he sent up a 7¼ – the largest size in the store at the time. This was returned with the message that it was too small, and a $7^3/_8$ was required. So slight an obstacle was overcome by altering the marking to $7^3/_8$ and stretching the cap band. Later he was informed that the second cap was a perfect fit.'[15]

To say Lawrence 'stood out' was an understatement. He later described life in the ranks as like being 'a unicorn in a racing stable'. Arthur Russell commented:

He was different to the rest, vastly different. We went everywhere together. We used to go up to the Proms together, to see the plays in London. We seemed to like the same things. I wasn't well educated. He was, of course, but we took to each other. We could

John Bruce. An 18-year-old Scot, Bruce shared Lawrence's hut in Macelhayes Road, Bovington in 1923. In 1968 he revealed to the *Sunday Times* his flagellation of Lawrence in the 1920s and '30s. (John Bruce estate)

talk, converse easily. I don't think I was quite as low as the others. Even Bruce said he was pleased that I was his friend, but he preferred Palmer, because Palmer I think had read a little bit more than I had.[16]

At the end of November 1923, eight months after joining, Lawrence and Russell went on Lawrence's Brough to see Hardy's *The Famous Tragedy of the Queen of Cornwall* at the Dorchester Corn Exchange. He mentioned Private Russell a number of times in letters to friends. On 2nd December he wrote to Florence Hardy at Max Gate, saying he was glad he had enlisted. The troubles of the day sharpened his pleasure in leisure hours: 'One of the best hours I've had in my life was that one in the Corn Exchange.' That evening the audience was raucous and Russell had difficulty hearing:

He said again that the audience was unworthy: that they interrupted his notice of the play. He much liked the chorus: its slow speech, and the continuity it gave the action and the brevity. The two songs were 'luvely': the words spoken in the balcony were superfluous. A look and a gesture would have been enough.[17]

They were late back to camp and the Orderly Sergeant reported them. They were not allowed out late again. Some time after that Florence invited him over for Christmas dinner but Lawrence had to decline: a 'villain' had borrowed his motorbike and crashed it into a ditch. On Christmas Day he wrote to Russell's mother. Lawrence and Russell spent all Christmas day at Clouds Hill, sitting and talking, the celebrations in the camp being too wild for them:

> Does it feel queer to be Arthur's mother sometimes I expect? He is rather an uncommon person. I don't know of course what stories he has told you about me. The truth is that he gives up a good deal of his spare time to showing me about: and in return for his kindness I try to be as tiresome to him as I can. The debt is all mine, to him.[18]

Lawrence now realized what he had involved himself in. He had not taken in that the Tank Corps had the same basic training as the infantry. For each initial period at Uxbridge and Bovington he had to undergo six weeks of basic drill. The average office worker can have little understanding of the physical hardships this entails. Drill in the army is the same now as it was at the beginning of the 20th century. One has to learn to present and order arms, march in time in formation, stand in line at attention, about wheel in time with other men. This is about team work: the ranks do not suffer loners, which is what T.E. was. There was also of course a dress code that with his earlier slovenly ways he would have found anathema. He was not designed for this type of life: a sophisticated, highly educated, extremely gifted but physical inferior man, he was in a totally alien environment. Back then of course a working class man was just that, he could perform hard physical, repetitive tasks regularly day after day for months on end with very little complaint, which the average white collar worker would find difficult. Some of the men in the ranks would have been unable to read or write. There would have been no relief from the mindless mockery, the worst of which was reserved for the more educated or smaller men, from the N.C.O.s. Lawrence was a romantic, an adventurer. He would have found this barren, heartless existence the antithesis of anything adventurous, save in his own mental excursions. The period marks the beginning of his deliberate rejection of his privileged background.

Alec L. Dixon was at Bovington in 1923. A banker before joining up and therefore atypical, he described their fellow soldiers as being the most mean, bestial men he had ever met, as being of the worst type. Any virtues they may have possessed were concealed by a degree of avarice and a tendency to lie that led them to deceive and swindle their fellow squaddies as much as they would a complete stranger. They were a parcel of rogues.

Lawrence himself said the men were 'social bed-rock', 'unfit for life by competition', each placing 'no more value on his fellows than his own cheapness'. From 19th March to 27th June 1923 he wrote a series of five letters to his old friend Lionel Curtis[19] in which he poured out his sufferings with sometimes harrowing descriptions of the viciousness of barrack room life. On one occasion drunken troopers broke his arm as he lay sleeping in his bunk.

> There cannot be classes in England much more raw, more free of all that the upbringing of a lifetime has plastered over you and me ... here these masses are as animal, as carnal as their ancestors were before Plato and Christ and Shelley and Dostoevsky taught and thought.[20]

What he found difficult to accept was the inability to escape from a 'black core of things', and the consequent obligation to take the carnality of spirit on trust. Every word and action and thought of the men in his hut was clouded by this, informed by it. It may be that the average man would not have been as affected by these impressions, and would rapidly have hardened himself to them. But Lawrence the Sunday school teacher could not. Even in Arabia he had been able to distance himself in leadership from the Bedouins' similar appetites. Here he possessed no barrier, apart from what men sensed in him, there being no refuge from these streetwise, desensitised creatures.

In view of the painfulness of his circumstances and the fact that he found the experience a waste of time and intelligence one has to ask why he stayed there. He could have left voluntarily whenever he wanted. Churchill had told him in January 1922 that the greatest employments were open to him in the Colonial Service. But Lawrence turned his back on this. He had his mind set on the Air Force. But after his exposure at Farnborough, there was only a remote possibility he would be allowed back into the RAF. Although his belief that good conduct reports could see him to where he wanted to go, as others had done before, and that to facilitate a return to RAF ranks he had to remain in the Army must have been a motivation, it would seem that the self-punishing, masochistic tendency that was part of his character must also have had a part to play.

Not many of his elevated friends agreed with Lawrence's retreat into the ranks; in fact most of them were alarmed, George Bernard Shaw referring to it as 'shocking tomfoolery'. Lawrence visited Curtis at the Colonial Office some time in 1923 and Curtis was appalled by his appearance:

> He turned up in the uniform of a private soldier covered in dirt like some amphibious creature rising to the surface for a momentary breath of the atmosphere to which he naturally belongs ... He seems to have imbibed a strain of eastern asceticism and the only explanation he vouchsafes of his conduct is a desire to kill his marvellous mind by burying it amongst people as different as possible from himself ... It is a tragedy.[21]

The Civil List Pension

Bernard Shaw was regularly petitioning the Government in 1923 and 1924 for Lawrence to be awarded a Civil List pension. He approached two successive Prime

Ministers at different extremes of the political spectrum. The first was Stanley Baldwin who, in 1923, was at the head of a weak Conservative government. The second was Shaw's fellow-member of the Fabian Society and Labour party leader Ramsay MacDonald.

Baldwin was at the head of the 'Second Eleven' – a Conservative administration containing all that remained after Chamberlain and his fellow high flyers abandoned the Tory front bench. The sickly Bonar Law was left to choose from what remained. GBS was granted an audience with Baldwin in May 1923, shortly after writing to him of Lawrence's situation, requesting that he be granted the pension of £500 for a commanding officer. Although Baldwin appeared to agree to this arrangement it was never followed through. Shaw later commented 'That was Baldwin's way and the secret of his promotion. He could always be depended on to smoke amiably and do nothing.' But behind Baldwin's outward pose of being the amiable gentleman farmer, the 'man of the people', there was a subtler character. He may have resisted GBS's petition for a number of reasons. One: the recent dismissal of Lawrence from the Air Force, with its consequent publicity, would have made any further press attention an award would have attracted extremely difficult, in view of the government's unstable political position. Two: after the First World War Baldwin had felt it his duty to try and supply the 'missing generation' (those killed in the war), who would otherwise have guided Britain's future. He wrote to *The Times* saying he was giving 20% of his estate to the nation's Treasury to help pay the war debt. Few men followed his example. The idea of financing a 35-year-old (relatively) fit and glorious survivor of the conflict would probably not have sat well with him. This was the man who later persuaded Edward VIII to abdicate, saving the government's face and indirectly taking all real power away from the monarchy forever.

The second time Shaw approached him in June 1924, Baldwin was in the last two months of office. Within two weeks he had vacated Chequers. He set aside the idea of a Civil List pension. The alternative, he said – that the House of Commons could decide to make a special award – was unworkable since it was too busy trying to get rid of Baldwin to become embroiled in another controversy.

When Baldwin's Tory administration was brought down with a vote of no-confidence at the end of 1923, GBS's ability to help Lawrence became even weaker. The new Labour P.M. Ramsay MacDonald was not the man many of his supporters imagined. He was as dormant as Baldwin on the home front and did little to enact strong Socialist measures, even supporting employers against workers. Shaw, who had worked hard for a first Labour government, concluded MacDonald had 'abandoned the faith' and, although he reportedly approached MacDonald regarding Lawrence, he can only have done this halfheartedly.

In March 1924 Lawrence had written to the Air Ministry requesting to be returned to the Air Force. Although this was supported by one senior officer, Air Vice-Marshal Game, who suggested that he be stationed abroad with his C.O. informed of his identity beforehand, this was vetoed.

On October 25th 1924, four days before the General Election, the *Daily Mail* published the notorious letter from Grigori Zinoviev, the head of the Comintern or internal Communist organisation. While there was a movement to normalize relations between the USSR and Great Britain (which the Conservatives opposed), the letter recommended that this was an opportune moment to encourage 'agitation propaganda' in the armed forces and increase 'sympathetic forces' within the British Labour movement. The *Mail* headlines reported a 'Civil War Plot by Socialists' Masters: Moscow Orders to Our Reds'. MacDonald later told the Cabinet he felt 'like a man sewn in a sack and thrown into the sea'. The letter had been widely circulated, including to senior army officers, and, presumably, the RAF, to inflict maximum damage on the Labour government. In the ensuing election, Labour, although it had increased its support by over two million before office, was forced into a general election which it lost by a landslide. The Zinoviev letter, we now know of course, was fraudulent. A Foreign Office historian concluded (as late as 1996) that it had been concocted by officers of the Secret Intelligence Service (MI6) based in Latvia, supported by White Russians opposed to any Anglo-Soviet Treaty, to assist a Conservative victory.[22] After MacDonald's fall Bernard Shaw did not petition the government directly on Lawrence's behalf again.

Serving at Bovington in the Quartermaster's Stores in 1923 was a Corporal named Leslie Edward Gates. Gates had transferred from 2nd Battalion the Suffolk Regiment to 'A Company', the Tank Corps Depot in 1923. He was promoted to Corporal and put in charge of Lawrence from August 1923 until February 1925:

Well, my Q.M. left me to it and I began to see this chap Shaw did not care for anyone and he was never willing to take an order or even help with the work. He was not liked much by any of the other chaps. I found him to be a very hard and off hand sort of chap. I made a report to my Q.M. After one week he said 'We'll put him on a charge' but nothing came of it. So, after a few weeks of this sort of thing, I was sent for, to report to my C.O. I did so and it was then I was told who Private Shaw really was and also told that no charge was to be made against him.[23]

After a time Gates got to know Lawrence better but found he would never open up about himself or talk about other people. Gates had worked in the rubber plantations of Brazil before the army, leading gangs of native rubber tappers. Lawrence was very interested to listen to his experiences but still kept to himself. Then one day he began to talk, instructing Gates to call him 'Neddy'. Gates gradually began to realise that the trooper he knew as 'Shaw' had somehow become a friend. When they went wandering over the moors together Lawrence would tell him more about himself and of all the great cities he had been to. They would walk across Egdon Heath together:

So, we would often walk and talk, in Neddy I found a good pal and I spent all my spare time with him, forever talking. It was after I had been down to Lulworth Cove for my Gunnery course with Neddy, as we were both good shots; I was I feel, a far better shot than him with a rifle, as I had had a lot of practice while in the Suffolks and at sea.

Also in the Quartermaster's Stores was a soldier named E.S. Palmer, whom everyone called 'Posh'. Palmer was Lawrence's main companion after Russell was posted to Perham Down, Tidworth, Wiltshire, in 1924. He was one of the more articulate soldiers and had 'read a bit'. In September 1925 Lawrence wrote to him from Cranwell telling him he missed 'the quietude of the office' they had shared in the Quartermaster's Stores. He and Palmer had shared a close relationship: he said there was no one at Cranwell as 'tuned to his pitch' as Palmer.

Postcard sketch of Private Edward S. 'Posh' Palmer by Gilbert Spencer, 1925. It was given to Palmer by Private W.C. Jeffrey on 7th September 1925. Inscribed '7/9/25. To: "Posh" from "JEFF".' (R.A.C. Tank Museum)

E.S. 'Posh' Palmer was one of Lawrence's closest companions at Bovington, serving in the Quartermaster's Stores with him 1923–25. He was a friend of E.M. Forster and more tuned to Lawrence's 'pitch' than most of the other soldiers. (R.A.C. Tank Museum, Bovington)

Despite Lawrence being a more or less exemplary recruit Liddell Hart mentions two occasions when he overstepped the mark. On one he left his overalls on his bed and was confined to barracks[24] for three days. Whilst Robert Graves was researching his biography of Lawrence in 1927, Palmer recalled in detail Lawrence's other misdemeanour: 'the Corporal incident':

> The Corporal was a Scotsman of the old school, an ex-officer, overbearing, with a wonderful idea of his own importance. T.E. used to rag him unmercifully. The corporal had a habit of laying the dust in the hut with a bowl of water sprinkled on the floor. This performance annoyed T.E. and everybody else, so one day T.E. got up early and swamped the hut with I forget now how many bowls of water. We all paddled. Later a man in the hut received a few days 'Confined to Barracks' unfairly, through the corporal. T.E. simply slung the corporal's suitcase into the sanitary bin.

R.S.M. Harry Banbury joined the Army in 1905 having spent five years in a Military School. In 1905 he enlisted in the Dorset regiment and joined the Tank Corps in 1917, in which he was awarded both the Meritorious and Long Service Medals. He first met T.E. in 1924 at Bovington and was referred to in some of Lawrence's letters as 'H.H.B'. Private Ingham introduced him to Lawrence:

> The impression persisted in every meeting and, having then been among soldiers for twenty years, it was not a feeling to be imagined. There was no propulsion in this

feeling, but rather the feeling that he was deliberately playing down to me to lead me; yet in doing so he slowed my brain and tied my tongue: always there was an intense self-consciousness, a littleness of mind in the presence of a great brain force. I felt a mental pygmy in his company, even to our last meeting shortly before his end. Others of the circle have told me that they felt the same, and my wife, after her only meeting with him, spoke of the magnetic attraction of his eyes.[25]

Another Tank Corps soldier later commented on this friendship: 'He made great friends with his Company Sergeant Major, a man named Harry Banbury, a first class chap; in itself this was unusual, private soldiers didn't make friends with CSMs but he did all right.'[26] This particular soldier, who had encountered Lawrence in the Middle East, commented that he got 'all sorts of minor privileges' as a result of the friendship. This seems to confirm that many of Lawrence's supposed privations were exaggerated. When he was at Uxbridge he wanted his own room and later at Mount Batten had his own table in the canteen and own office. He was able to mix and talk freely with celebrities and members of the aristocracy until an incident in 1929 during the Schneider Trophy competition. The fact that he was able to run a motorbike with a 0.998 litre engine (which would have burnt more fuel than present day ones) all over southern England suggests he had money. L.E. Gates recalled that, during his time at Bovington, Lawrence never went on Pay Parade. He said his money was always paid into the bank.

On 1st March 1926 Banbury wrote a heartfelt letter to 'Posh' Palmer from the Sergeants Mess, 1st Depot Battalion R.T.C., Bovington, about his affection for Clouds Hill:

Dear Posh,
A line to bid you 'goodbye'. Since you left I have been recalled and sent to Catterick on a wild goose chase and returned here on Saturday, spending the weekend at Clouds Hill with Arthur Knowle[s] … Arthur Knowles gave me a lovely weekend to salve my sorrows and I leave him perfectly content. I wish I had seen T.E. before I left for that would have been the culmination of happiness. I would [have] greatly liked to thank him for his many kindnesses to me since I have been here. If there has been one thing, Posh, that has helped me over the last two years, it has been the happiness of my hours at C.H. [Clouds Hill]. I shall ever look back to the times when Ingham introduced me there when E.M.F. was visiting and made up for it ever since. I would write to T.E. but for the fact he might think it pre-emption on my part, and again, the linnet does not address the eagle. Would you thank him for me?[27]

Banbury was clearly overawed by Lawrence, irrespective of his lower rank, even more so than the other soldiers who visited Clouds Hill. Harry Banbury found Lawrence stronger than himself in every area, from wrestling, to pistol shooting, to mental gymnastics. He derived great pleasure from his advice on books and literature and Lawrence later set him parcels of books 'to bestow on whomsoever he please'.

Banbury found it difficult to get Lawrence to refer to his past: he still suffered mental anguish when referring to the Arab Revolt and the R.S.M. tactfully avoided the subject. Lawrence was only focussed on the present and future, to avoid the personal agony of reminiscence. Banbury last saw Lawrence in 1935, shortly after he left the RAF, and found him noticeably aged and disappointed. He said Lawrence treated him as an equal without affectation.

T.E.'s other main companion at Bovington was Alec Dixon, an engineering draughtsman. He did not encounter Lawrence until 1924, and gradually developed a friendship with him. Dixon was an educated former bank clerk, enthusiastic writer and watercolourist, his paintings being remarked upon by many of the soldiers. He used to take commissions for scenes from the War. He had three books published with Lawrence's assistance: *Tinned Soldier*, on life in the Army; *Singapore Patrol*, about the Straits Settlements police, and a novel, *Extreme Occasion*. A solemn and melancholic air, Dixon said, distinguished Lawrence's behaviour during his early months at Bovington. He told John Mack that Lawrence's views of the differences between the RAF and the Tank Corps were greatly exaggerated and thought Lawrence was popular with the other men in the Tanks because (like Nancy Astor!) he had a sympathy for the underdog. It was some time before Dixon discovered who Trooper 'Shaw' really was. He was invited to ride on Lawrence's Brough to Salisbury one Sunday afternoon in 1924 and it was in the 'Golden Rule' tearooms near the Cathedral that Lawrence informed him. They remained firm friends until Lawrence left the Corps in August 1925. Dixon witnessed T.E. carving 'the jape on the architrave'[28] at Clouds Hill on the stone lintel above the front door the week before he left.

Drawing Office at Bovington c. 1923 where Alec Dixon would have worked. (R.A.C. Tank Museum)

Alec L. Dixon, whose book *Tinned Soldier* contained a lengthy section on his relationship with Lawrence, was one of his closest friends at Bovington and often visited Clouds Hill with Russell and Palmer. The photograph was taken in 1968 when he was awarded the Imperial Service Medal after retiring, aged 67, as a draughtsman from R.E.M.E. workshops, Aldershot. He died in 1970 after a long illness. (Hargreave)

A number of other soldiers remember Lawrence at Bovington. Ronald Shewry of Weymouth was a private in the Tanks. Although not a close friend he would often study him in the camp. Whilst walking back along the road past Clouds Hill, during his courting days, he sometimes saw Private Shaw standing outside his cottage, staring at the stars. Walter Charles Alcock also served at Bovington in the 1920s, and had joined the Army in 1914 aged 14 after running away from home. From 1922 to 1925 he was serving as a Major at Bovington and his daughter remembered he put Lawrence on a charge for going A.W.O.L. The son of an N.C.O. in the Tank Corps, W.M. Robertson of Pontefract, West Yorkshire, recalled his family lived in the married quarters in the 1920s, one of the perks of which was the weekly delivery of free rations. A 'very gentle, polite and well-spoken private' quite often made the delivery and made a big impression on Mrs Robertson. When she enquired who he was she discovered it was Private T.E. Shaw of Clouds Hill. 'N.W.D.' was stationed at Bovington in 1922 doing his recruit officer courses for acceptance as a Regular Officer in the Tank Corps. He was attached to the Depot and someone came to tell him that Lawrence of Arabia had joined up.

I didn't believe the story at first but it was him all right. I didn't pry and never referred to the fact that we had met earlier ['N.W.D.' had served in the Palestine campaign] but I talked to him on occasions, principally about motorcycles. He used to ride Brough Superiors.[29]

'N.W.D' was recently identified as Colonel Nigel Duncan (1900–1987), seconded from the Black Watch to the Tank Corps in 1922. He said Lawrence did his recruit training in exemplary fashion but hated it and the soldiers as well. He concluded Lawrence thought the training a waste of time, the instructors mindless, and the squaddies' existence earthbound.

On conclusion of his recruit training he was posted to the administrative company – don't ask me how it was done, for it was theoretically illegal, but posted he was and became a storeman in the Quartermaster's Stores, a busy job with the depot running up to 2,000 strong and all having to be kitted out in the stores. The Q.M., a great character, was delighted; nothing will go wrong with that chap here, he used to assert, and sure enough, nothing did.[30]

Lawrence presented the Depot with some unusual problems. On one occasion

He went out at lunchtime and was late back. Challenged about this he explained that he had been detained by his host at a lunch party which he had gone to. This was received with evident disbelief and he was asked who was there: he replied that in

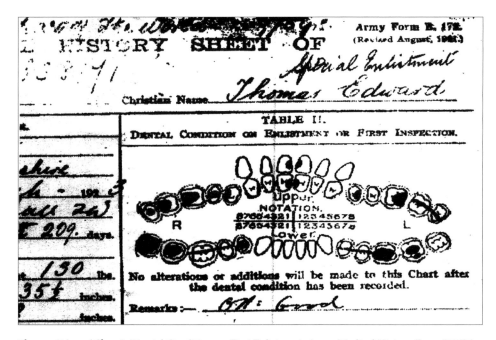

Thomas Edward Shaw's 'Dental Condition on First Enlistment. Army Medical History Form B.178.' Marked 'Special Enlistment' this inspection was made at Bovington on 28th March 1923 by a Captain Wilkinson, 16 days after T.E. arrived. He had 14 fillings with six teeth removed. (National Archives)

addition to his host there was the Archbishop of Canterbury, Mr. Winston Churchill and Lady Violet Bonham Carter. The disbelief changed into incredulity [sic] and he was placed on a charge for being absent, and all the rest of the might of disciplinary procedure, which suffered a severe jolt when, just to check, his host was rung up and confirmed that in fact Lawrence had been there, and that he had correctly stated his fellow guests. He was hastily released from all threatened penalties.[31]

Soon the press tried to sniff Lawrence out. The Quarter Master was an enormous man named Barnham who came from the Border Regiment. He put a lot of value on Lawrence's work: 'I remember coming down to the QM stores to find Bill Barnham dancing with rage and telling a reporter from whichever paper it was that was involved that he . . . blank . . . blank . . . couldn't see anyone on his staff and that he had never heard of Lawrence or Shaw . . . and that if the reporter didn't take himself off, he Bill, would break the aforesaid reporter's neck.'[32]

As a child, Mrs. Y.J.T. Kingdon, of Eastleigh, Hampshire met Lawrence. Her father, Company Sergeant Major David Black had served with the Royal Tank Corps in Bovington. Some time after her father's death Mrs. Kingdon's family was visiting her mother's friend Joyce Knowles, Lawrence's neighbour at Clouds Hill, when he arrived on his Brough:

We heard a motorbike approaching and were told it was 'Shaw'. He came straight to Mrs. Knowles house, he was introduced as her neighbour, she kept an eye on his house. After a few pleasantries 'Shaw' took us across the road and gave us a personally conducted tour of his cottage. He told us he planned to use paper plates, to avoid washing up, I had never heard of such things then! He also told us he planned to plant a variety of rhododendrons to supplement the wild variety that already exists on the surrounding sloping countryside. Many, many years later I saw that this had been achieved, the land was just a mass of rhododendrons. He also objected to overhead electricity wires, saying they should all be underground. I can remember this quite plainly; I was twelve years old at the time. It was several years later that I realized the significance of this meeting and the importance of the man.[33]

The fun Lawrence had on his motorbike was recalled by many old soldiers. A resident of Bovington recalled in the 1960s the story of a tall major who was an Orderly Officer in 1923/24. He housed a lightweight two-stroke motorbike in the lock up at the garrison's Red Garage on King George V Road. One day he pushed the bike out of its garage in full dress uniform, complete with sword and scabbard, in order to inspect the sentries on duty. The major push-started the bike and advanced up the hill to the camp, his sword scuffing the dirt road surface. Lawrence had witnessed this stately progress a number of times and this time he followed on his Brough. The camp was criss-crossed by numerous dirt roads and, as the Major advanced, Lawrence deliberately cut across the front on his bike with a roar of acceleration. The Orderly Officer's bike swayed about uncontrollably.

Duncan recalled that Lawrence used to go off every weekend on his motorbike but would never put in for a leave pass. After a time he was reprimanded for this. He eventually submitted one and for his destination wrote 'any part of England'. When questioned about such vagueness he explained that the previous Saturday he had intended to visit his mother in Brighton but when he got to the Wareham turning he was travelling so fast he went straight across, being unable to turn, and went to see his brother in Cornwall. 'So you see, sir, it is difficult for me to tell were I am going,' he told his company commander. The man was not amused, but Lawrence continued to go his own way, submitting fictitious destinations to soothe the military administrative conscience.

Almost all witnesses remark upon how reckless Lawrence was on his Broughs. Lesley Gates recalled: 'You could see this very small, thin, brown man coming up from Wool on his great machine, a Brough Superior, doing anywhere over 80 miles per hour. It was a masterpiece how he could control this monster of a bike.'[34] One day Lawrence took Gates on the Brough to Wool, about three miles from Clouds Hill, and Gates never forgot the experience. Although there was no mishap, he declined to go again.

C.W. Jukes of Bournemouth was a Royal Army Service Corps clerk at Bovington from 1924 to 1927. He remembered Lawrence calling daily at his office to deliver and collect correspondence, riding his Brough like 'a jockey on a racehorse'.[35] A First World War veteran of the Suffolks and the Somme, W.C. Packham M.S.M., T.D, served at Bovington. His daughter recalled him saying Lawrence was 'a most interesting man, and he couldn't understand when he came to Bovington why he had such a low rank'. Packham used to go up to Clouds Hill on Lawrence's bike. He said he rode 'like a bat out of hell' and he was 'not surprised when he eventually got killed'. Lesley Gates:

> We all knew what he was like for speed. Many times he would put in for a weekend pass, go off on a Friday night, where to no one knew. On Monday morning you would hear the roar of his bike coming up the hill that led to the camp and in no time he would be alongside you with a great big grin on his face. I would say, 'Well you have made it, Neddy', meaning he beat his pass time by about two minutes.[36]

When he first rode into Bovington he had an S.S. 80, on which he had travelled down from the north of England. Arthur Russell recalled 'He changed the bike to an SS 80 Solent. I think just before he relinquished that and had the SS100, he had a little Francis Barnett with a geodesic frame – you could pick it up with one hand, the actual opposite!' Lawrence used the lightweight Francis Barnett on short journeys of a few 100 yards to 'the lines' of huts. In less than two months a soldier had borrowed it without permission and driven straight into a nearby gravel quarry, bending it irreparably. Lawrence sold it back to the Red Garage for a nominal sum.

The Red Garage in Bovington village was so named because of its red corrugated metal roof, and the proprietor was A.H.'Roy' Reiffer. Reiffer had been brought up in London and before the War worked for the Port of London Authority. He had served in the First World War and was with the Tank Corps from the beginning. He took part in the attack on Delville Wood and the Battle of Flers Courcellette on the Somme in 1916. He was also twice in action at Arras and was awarded the MM. The Red Garage was located in a small tin shed next to the Bovington cinema. In 1923 he met Lawrence, who wanted to rent a lockup for his Brough. They remained firm friends until Lawrence's death.

Reiffer's mechanics were Godfrey and Frank Runyard, local boys, who had been brought up in Wool village. They were employed by Reiffer from 1923 and were responsible for servicing all Lawrence's Broughs. It was the Runyards who picked up the bike from Clouds Hill after the accident. Godfrey was a trials rider for Douglas and Rudge Ulster and he and Lawrence often discussed motorcycles. Godfrey Runyard worked at the Red Garage from the age of 16 in 1924. From 14 he also worked as a part-time projectionist at the camp cinema and Lawrence would often pop in see him in the evening and have a chat. He remembered T.E. as 'a very quiet and reserved man' with a passion for motorcycles. 'When talking with Lawrence it was always motorcycles. He did take a ride on my Rex Acme with a 250 cc Blackburn engine. He commented that the petrol tank was large like his bike. He was a very interesting man to talk with and very polite.'[37]

Some time in 1923 or 1924 Lawrence visited the Archbishop of Canterbury. As an unbeliever he had, for a long time, felt dissatisfaction with the compulsory requirement for all rankers to attend church parade. Arthur Russell:

> We used to go to church, only Church Parade. As far as the Army was concerned church was an excuse to have a parade and a band out. It didn't matter what you were, you went on this parade. If you were not Church of England you stayed outside the church 'til you marched back. A lot of people say, 'Did we go to church in Moreton?' We never did. I don't think either of us were real churchgoers then. We just had to go. Duty!

Lawrence made the long journey to Canterbury dressed in the uniform of a private. When he arrived in a bedraggled state, he was received by the archbishop's butler who was shocked at the sight of a lowly, dirty private from the Tank Corps on the doorstep. He asked who he was. Lawrence replied 'Lawrence of Arabia' and was invited in. Unsurprisingly, the Archbishop would not agree to Lawrence's request, as he knew attendances would fall off if church parades were made voluntary. Lawrence subsequently developed a very irreverent opinion of the most senior Anglican in England.

Clouds Hill

In 1924 Lawrence rented a small cottage at Clouds Hill from his relative, Henry Featherstonehaugh-Frampton, buying it in 1929. Arthur Russell described his first encounter with the cottage:

He'd been to see Thomas Hardy and on the way back we used to cut through the back roads and we used to pass by Clouds Hill, down that road where the cottage is. And we stopped there one day and he said, 'Want to have a look at something?' So we walked down and saw this cottage, practically no roof on it. It was derelict. He said: 'A relative of mine, as far as I know, owns this. I'll go and see her about it, see if I can have it.' He didn't mind walking back to camp. 'I'll go and see her now; she only lives down the road.' I walked back to camp. I hadn't been there long when he said, 'We've got it.' Not 'I've got it' but 'We've got it.' I was always included in with him everywhere.

Clouds Hill is the name of the hillside on which both the Knowles' bungalow and Lawrence's cottage stood. When Sergeant Knowles was digging out the foundations for their cottage in the early 1920s he found the remains of some small, blue, glass beads, enough to make a necklace. The museum in Dorchester identified them as Phoenician.[38] Lesley Gates recalled Lawrence talking of his desire for a home:

> I remember one afternoon when we were way out over the moors, he said 'Tankey, what I should like is to find a place, a little house, where I could go and play my records and carry on writing my book.' We were walking across the moor up near the village of Moreton and near to the foot of Clouds Hill and we saw a small woodsman's cottage. We did after some hard work get the door open. As we went in he said,

Clouds Hill cottage today. Rear of the building showing Sgt. Knowles' dormer window for the Music Room on the right, with Lawrence and Russell's work in the centre. There are more drainpipes than in 1935. (Author)

Looking across Egdon Heath from the hill of rhododendrons to the cottage's east, where Lawrence and Pat Knowles discussed their plan for a printing press in May 1935. (Author)

Interior of the upstairs Music Room, where T.E. entertained his Tank Corps and literary guests such as George Bernard Shaw and E.M. Forster. It was in this room that Lawrence punched an intrusive reporter in the eye in 1935 and where John Bruce administered at least one beating. The large gramophone speaker is not the original.

'This is my place, Tankey'. Well, after many days and lots of letters he went off for a weekend to London. On the Monday morning he said, 'I've got the house.' Well, why he should want a place like that, no windows, one door, no toilet, and trees growing out of the places where the windows should have been, beat me.[39]

A while before this Pat Knowles and his father, Pioneer Sergeant Arthur Knowles, had been painting the outside woodwork of the cottage. Lawrence appeared with two other soldiers who stood at a respectful distance. Lawrence asked Sergeant Knowles if there was any possibility of renting it. Sergeant Knowles had intended building a wing on it for his four sons (he had built his own cottage over the road the year before). Knowles agreed to talk it over with his family. Lawrence said he would return the following week. Lawrence appeared again when Sergeant Knowles was cutting glass and commented favourably on Knowles' skill. A temporary lease was arranged after Lawrence offered to help in financing the new building work. Pat was slightly afraid when he first encountered Private Shaw. He seemed entirely out of place in uniform, having a strained air about him.

Lawrence rented the cottage from Henry Rupert Fetherstonehaugh-Frampton in 1923, buying it in 1929 for £450. Henry Frampton was the High Sheriff of Dorset that year and donated the plot in which Lawrence was buried six years later, as the graveyard at Moreton Church was full. They came from different sides of the Fetherstonehaugh-Frampton family. Lawrence's great-great-grandfather, James Fetherstonehaugh of County Westmouth, Ireland, was Henry Fetherstonehaugh-Chapman's great grandfather. Henry was 19 years older than Lawrence.

Whilst he used the cottage as a personal retreat Lawrence also used to invite friends from all strata of society to visit. He invited his literary friends as well as men from the camp. The National Trust has owned the cottage since 1937 when Arnold Lawrence donated it. Arthur Russell remembered the work that was done on the cottage in the 1920s:

> Sergeant Knowles was the Pioneer Sergeant for Bovington Camp. So he approached him and asked him, would he see to the roof? To preserve the cobwebs – they were big ones. He said yes. He did a lot of work on it himself, and I believe he got someone from Moreton village down to do the tiling and that. And he did the woodwork. Now while it was in progress Shaw and I did one of the dormer windows. There were three little dormers. Sergeant Knowles was doing one of the others and we were just copying him. On the inside the wall is only about three and a half feet high round and then going up to the roof. We covered it with hessian, stuck it on. It was nice. It's now panelled, and the cobwebs were preserved.

After Lawrence moved into the cottage he had Sergeant Knowles knock down a partition in the upper room and put a skylight in the roof. A leather settee arrived and it was necessary to remove a window to get it in; then a table, a green carpet and two leather upholstered chairs. These were probably the ones Lawrence received as a gift from an American oil financier whilst he was at All Souls College, Oxford. One friend in the ranks remembered Lawrence telling him that he sold his gold Arabian dagger to pay for the restoration. After the structure was made watertight, furniture, books, pictures and a Columbia gramophone with many records were brought in.

Lesley Gates also remembered working on the cottage:

> I built a new fireplace and put down many new bricks on the floor. One day he came up the hill with a lump of wood under his arm, which when trimmed down made the mantle shelf. Neddy never sat down to eat and drink, so the mantle shelf he had put at just the height he could stand and rest his arm on. He ate and drank very little.[40]

Almost all those who remembered life at Clouds Hill had very fond recollections. In a 1938 radio broadcast E.M. Forster, (whose *A Passage to India* was influenced by Forster's early access to *Seven Pillars*), recalled:

> In those days the two bottom rooms were full of firewood and lumber. We lived upstairs, and the sitting room there looks now much as it did then, though the gramophone and books have gone, and the fender with its bent ironwork has been remodelled. It was, and it is, a brownish room – wooden beams and ceiling, leather covered settee.[41]

Lesley Edward Gates, 1976. Ex-Corporal Gates, a former rubber plantation supervisor in Brazil and infantryman in the Suffolk Regiment, served in the Quarter Master's Stores at Bovington with Lawrence, 1923–25. (Kent)

Forster stayed at least once in the small bunkroom with the porthole window on the first floor. At other times, when the cottage was full, he would rent a room at the Black Bear Hotel in Wareham. Arthur Russell remembered the work they did on the interior:

> We got some dye from Bournemouth, Johnson's spirit dye, and dyed the bedroom floor black. He had the fireplace there; a sort of fender was in the front. He had that made by a blacksmith who lived in one of the houses just beyond the camp. Feeding up there, I think all we ever did was toast. We had the fire – we used to collect the old wood from around the woods.

By September 1924 Clouds Hill had developed a neglected air. Lawrence had to spend all his time, nights included, in re-sorting the store books of 'A' company, a process that would take at least a month. He wasn't able to get to Clouds Hill and it was abandoned. Palmer and Russell seldom went there since they found the atmosphere 'flat' without Lawrence. Russell recalled:

> I did make a radio set. I put a pole on top of Clouds Hill and ran the aerial down to the cottage and in. This set I made in a type of suitcase, a wooden one. But that was stolen within a month. I think I know who had it. He used to make radio sets in those days and sell them. Just like my own. But we didn't say anything. We'd sit up at the cottage probably over an hour, and never even need to speak to each other. He used to do food up there, but that was always toast. There were no cooking facilities and no water laid on. No toilet. We'd do a huge plate of toast, I would toast it; he would butter it and stack it up on a plate. Stand it on the mantlepiece. We could make tea, used to boil the kettle there on the fire - we never used to let the fire go out.
>
> We used to live mainly on toast and fruit and cream. Up at the cottage, if you look in the room downstairs you'll see some 'black lustre' crockery or 'lack lustre' crockery with a dull finish. He bought that specially, had it made for him for one specific reason – it was black.

A gramophone and books completed the furnishing of the upstairs room.

> He was fond of music. Now if you remember, Gustav Holtz, when he did 'The Planets', I think he sent them to him. But we did have all 'The Planets' – he used to love those. Another record I remember was Elmer Gluck and Caruso singing. That was lovely. The only time they ever sang together. He used to love listening to music. All sorts of music there. I don't know what records are there now, but they were all 78s of course.

In the late 1920s and early 1930s Lawrence and Charlotte Shaw, the wife of GBS, a much older woman who, with her partner's mutual agreement, lived in an unconsummated marriage, conducted a lengthy and extremely intimate correspondence only revealed after her death. The letters he wrote to her from the ranks touched upon such intimate subjects as the details of his flagellation at Deraa. This was not a one-sided correspondence, they had a natural mental rapport and after Lawrence's death Charlotte described the relationship as 'the strangest contact' of her life. Both Russell and Corporal Gates remembered meeting her:

> I recall one lady he thought a great deal of that was Mrs Shaw. He looked upon her as a second mother and as I saw it they were very good friends. When we got the little house at Clouds Hill round a bit, [Charlotte Shaw] came down and brought bedclothes, knives and forks, teacups, plates, teapot. Oh, and a lot of other things. I gave her a hand to put down the great old carpet that had been sent up from Poole and I found both G.B. and Mrs Shaw, very nice people. On many occasions I found myself in their company, while I was with T.E.[42]

When asked whether George Bernard Shaw had much to do with the writing of *Seven Pillars* Russell recalled that the playwright refused to edit chapters of the book until Charlotte made him do it: 'He wasn't interested. He didn't think he [Lawrence] ought to be in the Army.'

> I'll set this record straight. They always wanted to know what I thought or said. I liked the Hardys; they were a lovely couple, and the Shaws. Not so much GBS, but Charlotte Shaw she was nice, a lovely person.

Russell remembered meeting E.M. Forster, Siegfried Sassoon, R.A.M. Guy, the Astors and the Hardys. Forster also remembered the visit of the Hardys one afternoon:

> I don't know whether I'm at all conveying . . . the atmosphere of the place – the happy casualness of it, and the feeling that no one particularly owned it. T.E. had the power of distributing the sense of possession among all the friends who came there. When Thomas Hardy turned up, for instance, as he did one sunny afternoon, he seemed to come on a visit to us all, and not especially to see the host. Thomas Hardy and Mrs Hardy came up the narrow stairway into the little brown room and there they were – the guests of us all. To think of Clouds Hill as T.E.'s home is to get the wrong idea of it. It wasn't his home, it was rather his pied-a-terre, the place where his feet touched the earth for a moment, and found rest.[43]

Russell said the visitors would talk about anything. When G.B. Shaw and Charlotte made what was probably their first visit Russell was amongst the group. He heard a phrase used that later became the title of a book.[44] George Bernard Shaw was berating Lawrence for joining the Tank Corps:

> And he said 'Behold Public Shaw and Private Shaw'. Now there was controversy about why he used the name Shaw. He told me. When he was first in the Air Force he

was Ross. But when he was changed to the Tank Corps they said, 'What name do you want?' So he opened a telephone directory, put his finger on it, said 'That one, what is it? Shaw.' It just happened to be Shaw.[45]

Alec Dixon used to visit the cottage two or three evenings a week. He would spend his spare time there reading, writing, and talking with soldier friends. Lawrence encouraged these gatherings. When asked if Lawrence liked to surround himself with mystery Russell replied:

> No. The media tried to make a mystery of him. He was very self-effacing. He didn't want publicity. He was trying to escape from it. He wanted to lead a quiet life. No decision-making. He'd been let down that badly over the Arabian do. He just wanted to sink away from things. He threw his medals in the Thames – didn't want them.

T.E. enthusiastically oversaw the group, holding picnics and music sessions during all daylight hours. He would respnd to any queries and mediate any contentions with patience, all being washed down by mugs of China Tea. Whilst some sat on chairs and some on the floor, Lawrence would stand with his elbow resting on the mantleshelf, stoking the fire as he ate. As Lawrence was such a short man, he built the mantleshelf himself at just less than four feet above the floor level, where he could rest his shoulder on it. It is still there. The upper room, the music room, where these meetings were held, was remarkably small for such gatherings. It measured only 10 feet by 12. The men's ranks were unimportant, there was no social distinction. Lawrence had successfully integrated himself into a completely different society from that he had known in 1922, indeed at Clouds Hill he had built his own society. He was humbler, more disciplined and mentally fitter.

There was one crowded Christmas in 1924 that Leslie Gates later remembered: 'There were about 15 in the cottage for five days, friends of Neddy's and boys from the camp. They had stacks of wood all down one side of the living room. Neddy didn't bother with coal because there was such a good supply of wood available.'[46]

A.W. Lawrence came two or three times; Captain Basil Liddell Hart occasionally; and there was one who was a great friend, Eric Kennington. Lawrence would sleep in the cottage at weekends and often take breakfast at the Knowles', there being no washing or cooking facilities at Clouds Hill in the early days. A form of mutual healing occurred between Lawrence and Arthur Knowles. Pat said he once saw them talking to each other in the garden: 'They must have been enjoying something funny because first one would talk animatedly and then the other, with broad grins and laughter between.'[47] After Lawrence's identity was revealed Knowles refused to betray his privacy and told the press 'to clear off in no uncertain terms.' Knowles' died in 1931 aged forty-nine from the effects of a wartime gas attack.

Shortly after arriving at Cranwell in August 1925, Lawrence described his Tank Corps experiences as 'a voyage all out of reckoning'. At Bovington, particularly in the earlier period, he experienced one of the unhappiest periods of his life. Apart from his work on the *Seven Pillars*, he achieved hardly anything creative. If any good did emerge from this self-imposed hardship it was the inspiration and encouragement he gave to the men around him. He became for them the most unlikely of friends. Few men can be said to have the ability to really change and enrich the lives of those around them but Lawrence most certainly did; the effect he had on some of his companions was so profound that they remained influenced by it for the rest of their days.

Notes

1 Leopold Charles M.S. Amery (1873–1955) a Conservative MP originally for Birmingham (South), was educated at Harrow with Winston Churchill and at Balliol College, Oxford. Like Lawrence he became a fellow of All Souls College. He was noted for his interest in India, the British Empire and military preparedness. Despite being competent, hardworking and equally as intelligent as Churchill, Amery lacked Churchill's glamour and his brilliance at writing and oratory.
2 Dorset *Daily Echo*, 20/05/1935.
3 Friends, Captain G.E. Kirby and Sergeant W.E. Jeffrey
4 Ibid.
5 Budbrook Barracks, near Warwick.
6 All the Arthur Russell quotations are from an interview with him about his experience in the Tank Corps, Bovington, 1923–24, recorded by the author at Mr Russell's home in Coventry, December 1985.
7 *T.E. Lives* magazine.
8 *Dorset Echo*, February 3rd, 1972
9 'Mess' was normally a British Army term for a group of 16 men. Two mess tables would accommodate 16 men.
10 *Bournemouth Evening Echo*, 05/1964.
10 Friends.
12 Arthur Russell. Interview with author. December 1985
13 *T.E. Lawrence – in Arabia and After*, Captain Sir Basil Liddell Hart, Jonathan Cape, 1934.
14 One story has it that after a few weeks Shaw wanted a day off and asked the Quartermaster's permission. The Q.M. took him to see the C.O. who refused him point blank. The next day the camp received a telegram from Winston Churchill ordering Private Shaw's immediate furlough.
15 *T.E. Lawrence by his Friends*, Captain G.E. Kirby and Sergeant W.E. Jeffrey Jonathan Cape, 1937.
16 Knightley and Simpson quote John Bruce: 'There was only about a handful of them fit to be in his [Lawrence's] company, and we arrived at a short list of two: Privates Russell and Palmer. Russell was a nice fellow, thick set and strong, and looked as if he could use

himself if need be. He was my choice for that reason. Palmer was Lawrence's choice. He was a gentler kind of chap, without brawn, and seemed to have read a little.'

17 T.E. Lawrence to Florence Hardy, 2/12/1923. DG.

18 T.E. Lawrence to Mrs Russell, 25/12/1923. MB.

19 Curtis was an imperialist and one of 'Milner's Kindergarten' in South Africa. A member of the Round Table group, he shared an All Souls Fellowship with Lawrence and was one of the founders of Chatham House in London.

20 T.E. Lawrence to Lionel Curtis.

22 *The Guardian*, 04/02/1999; *Desmond Morton: Churchill's Man of Mystery and the World of Intelligence*, G. Bennett. 2006; *Private Shaw & Public Shaw*, Stanley Weintraub, 1963.

23 This report was concealed amongst family possessions for many years until remembered by Gates' daughter in 2005 responding to enquiries by the author. As it is the only unpublished reminiscence available on Lawrence's service in the Quarter Master's Stores it is included here. Certain passages later in the record about Lawrence's character have been omitted because they were obviously inspired by observations in Liddell Hart's biography.

25 Friends, R.S.M. H.H. Banbury.

26 Recollections of 'N.W.D' Bovington Camp Archive Library, deposited in 1982.

27 Letter from H.H. Banbury to E.S. Palmer, 1st March 1926.

28 This was an inscription in Ancient Greek with no literal translation, but roughly meaning 'Why Worry?' or 'Why care?'. It implied T.E.'s guests were to adopt such an attitude whilst they stayed there.

39 Recollections of 'N.W.D.'

30 Ibid.

31 Ibid.

32 Ibid.

33 Mrs Y.J.T. Kingdom, letter to author, 2005.

34 Recollections of Lesley Edward Gates.

35 Quote from the *Bournemouth Evening Echo*, 13th May 1964.

36 Recollections of Lesley Edward Gates.

37 Godfrey Runyard, *T.E. Lawrence Society Newsletter* no. 68.

38 *An Handful With Quietness*, P. Knowles/ E.V.G. Hunt.

39 Recollections of Lesley Edward Gates.

40 Ibid.

41 Forster stayed at least once in the small bunk room with the porthole window on the first floor at Clouds Hill.

42 Recollections of L.E. Gates.

43 E.M. Forster. *The Listener*. September 1st, 1938.

44 *Public Shaw and Private Shaw*, Stanley Weintraub, Cape, 1963.

45 Lawrence changed his name to Shaw by deed poll in 1924. The generally accepted account (Wilson p. 710) is that he selected the first monosyllabic name he found in the Army List.

46 Recollections of L.E. Gates.

47 From Pat Knowles account in *An Handful with Quietness*. ed. E.V.G. Hunt, 1990s.

CHAPTER FOUR

The Abridgements of Seven Pillars of Wisdom

This book is by no means a literary study, but Lawrence's writing is of course central to his life after Arabia, so it cannot be ignored. It is generally recognised that Lawrence's supreme literary achievement was *Seven Pillars of Wisdom*. He half killed himself in writing it, much as he had virtually destroyed himself creating the events it described. That, Siegfried Sassoon concluded, was one of his greatest talents: he had the ability 'make things happen', to be an originator of great events. The book's style was in parts archaic, and despite being written largely from memory it lacked continuity, changing as it was affected by contemporary writers. *Seven Pillars* was a book about war. The title misleads one to think it was a was a philosophical study, but this is a misconception owing to the use of the title of an earlier book that Lawrence had been planning before the War on seven cities in the Middle East. *Seven Pillars* is in fact a day-to-day account of one Englishman's part in the Arab Revolt. This was not a Jihad, or holy war, but an attempt by the people of Arabia to win back their territory from the Turkish Empire after centuries of Ottoman rule. It is grand and sweeping in its concept and full of remarkable, memorable stories, but the accuracy of some of its accounts, and the claims Lawrence made, have been questioned by scholars. Although modern research has supported some of these claims and even judged them to be understated on occasion, Lawrence later confessed that he had 'bent the truth' in some passages for the sake of literature.

The book was written between 1919 and 1926 and its gestation and creation were, to say the least, unusual. By November 1919 he was living at All Souls College, Oxford where he had been granted a Research Fellowship, mainly at the instigation of another Fellow, the *Times* editor Geoffrey Dawson, for the purpose of 'prosecuting his researches' into the antiquities, ethnology, and history of the Near East. This included rooms in the college and an annual research grant of £200. However, Lawrence found the atmosphere at All Souls inconducive to writing and from December 2nd 1919 he was allowed the use of the attic floor in a three-storey terraced house in Barton Street near the palace of Westminster. He hoped that he would be able to recreate the excitement and passion of the war on paper; he wrote Book XXXIII within 24 hours,[1] later claiming that 95% of the second draft was finished in three months.

From January to December he went to work for Churchill in the Colonial Office for the Cairo Conference. Churchill told his wife Clementine that he had 'got Lawrence to put on a bridle and collar.'[2] Here T.E. continued the work begun in Paris and renewed his acquaintanceship with Richard Meinertzhagen, an Intelligence officer he had met in the desert. And it was of course the desert that first inspired Lawrence. As early as 1910, before leaving on a walking tour of Syria, he had read C.M. Doughty's *Travels in Arabia Deserta*, a meticulous study of an Englishman's two-year walking tour of northern Arabia, from Damascus to Jedda. The book was so accurate it was used by British Intelligence in Cairo during the War and inevitably the style of *Seven Pillars* was compared with Doughty. Although admitting he was influenced by it, Lawrence drew mainly from his own resources for *Seven Pillars*. Another influence, it was suggested, was the meticulously detailed style of the 19th-century writer George Borrow, who, like T.E., 'described every blade of grass and foot of gravel he walked over'.[3] If this was so, Lawrence did this unconsciously, later writing to Edward Garnett for advice on how to interpret the comparison. Three drafts of the book had been produced. The first he lost on Reading Station in 1919; all but three of its eleven books. The second had been worked on, mainly from memory and using the remaining notes he had, from December 1919 until May 1920, after the Peace Conference. This was a far more difficult task than the first as all the field notes he had used as a source had been destroyed as he wrote. For the second draft he had to rely almost entirely on his memory and persevered only because of the encouragement he received from D.G. Hogarth, who had read the original draft. Through Charlotte Shaw he obtained a number of copies of the *Arab Bulletin*, the journal of the Arab Bureau,[4] and used this as a source also.

He took draft two as the basis for a third draft, from December 1921 to February 1922, after he had returned from Transjordan, which became the 'Oxford Text', eight copies of which were printed by the *Oxford Times*. These were produced to ensure the manuscript did not disappear as the first had done. It was during this period in London that he drove himself into a state of complete nervous exhaustion through long periods of deliberately going without food and sleep. In spite of his success in the campaign, as already outlined, he had known since 1917 that he was fighting the War on a lie. He explained much of his concern about this in the first chapter of *Seven Pillars*, which reads like a personal admission of guilt. Chapter 1 has an immediacy and displays a penetrating insight into his feelings as it was written directly after his return from Transjordan in December 1921, and allowed him to state the truth of what happened. His friends, however, pressed him for a more commercial work.

The *War in the Desert* Abridgement
In the winter of 1924–25 Lawrence was worrying about his bank overdraft and the following spring offered Jonathan Cape an abridgement of 125,000 words (less than half of *Seven Pillars*), promising to remove every sixth word (which, while a

good trick to pull off, wouldn't have been enough).[5] He was toying with the idea of using a previous abridgement Edward Garnett had worked on in 1922, known as *The War in the Desert*.[6] The chronology of Garnett's abridgement was a saga in itself, one of eventual failure caused by Lawrence and the machinations of George Bernard Shaw, who had his own ambitions for the publication of *Seven Pillars*. The jealousy and possessiveness of G.B. and Charlotte Shaw eventually sank Garnett's abridgement and forced Lawrence to remain in the ranks for a further 12 years.

Edward Garnett was a reader for Jonathan Cape who had championed Joseph Conrad in the 1890s and encouraged D.H. Lawrence early in the 20th century. T.E. was encouraged by any approval Garnett gave him, which he indefatiguably provided. In August 1922 Garnett mooted an abridgement, and suggested himself for the editing. Garnett had produced a popular abridgement earlier of Doughty's *Arabia Deserta*. Lawrence was unhappy with *Seven Pillars* but realised an efficient abridgement would pay, and in September he sent Garnett an unbound copy. Garnett commenced work, aiming to reduce it to 150,000 words. On 9th October 1922 Lawrence wrote to him from Uxbridge: 'I wonder how the reduction seems to you now? If you get it to 150,000 and satisfy, and then I take it to 20,000 or so, that should do the trick.'[7]

By October 15th Garnett had completed the first draft. In November, whilst still at Uxbridge, Lawrence returned this edited proof, and three days later Garnett wrote and told him the abridgement was finished. It was indeed 150,000 words long. Lawrence realised that the work, unofficially titled *War in the Desert*, could make him a rich man. By 6th November Lawrence had transferred to Farnborough and had more leisure time than at Uxbridge. He told Garnett on the 12th that the 'cutting up process' gave him a 'horrible satisfaction'[8] On 1st December George Bernard Shaw told him that he recommended an abridgement.[9]

But the self-lacerating tendency in Lawrence again came to the fore: he told Garnett on 7th December that he intended to remain in the Air Force, fearing that that any living 'of a workless character' (from royalties, for example) would entice him back to 'the fleshpots' of London. Consequently he resisted any loan to finance the project from Cape as his 'puritan self' hoped failure would compel him to 'dwell longer in the barracks.'[10] He wrote again to Cape on the 14th asking for a minimal advance of £200 to £300, suggesting he was 'completely broke' and that any money he received from the project would enable him to set up a private printing-press, which had been a life-time dream.[11]

Bernard Shaw was pushing for his own publishers, Constable. He told Lawrence on the 17th that he could not do better, unless he 'would prefer a brace of thoroughgoing ruffians' (Cape) 'who would begin with exploiting the serial rights in English and American papers.'[12] Shaw had blundered into this situation. He had only met Lawrence once and regarded his enlistment as a 'maddening masquerade'.[13]

Lawrence did not receive Shaw's letter until Christmas day. By the 21st he had already told Cape that his literary agent Raymond Savage had made him hope that they would publish the book.[14] On 27th December he wrote again to GBS. Constable had told Shaw that they 'would be very pleased and honoured to be entrusted with the publication'. Lawrence naturally found it difficult to accept Shaw's description of the *Seven Pillars* as 'the greatest book in the world', with the grand old man on the verge of winning the Nobel Prize for Literature. No doubt Lawrence was touched by his comment but told him 'I care very much for this, as it's been my ambition all my life to write something intrinsically good. I can't believe that I've done it, for it's the hardest thing in the world.'[15]

He still felt he had not expressed all he wanted to say. Only if he wrung his mind out could he take the work to a higher plane. But fear that the intense effort would rekindle his earlier neurosis prevented this.[16] By that time Charlotte Shaw had read all of the *Seven Pillars,* but GBS had not. In a letter Lawrence rejected Shaw's publishing advice unequivocally: 'I believe Cape, a new publisher of the respectable sort (he runs that divine book of extracts from yourself) is first in the running for the thing.'[17] The 'divine book of extracts' was a collection of Shaw's writings, *Selections,* which Charlotte had compiled.

At this moment the *Express* revealed that Lawrence was serving in the RAF at Farnborough. When GBS wrote to him the same day, he apparently still had not received T.E.'s letter describing Cape as a 'respectable' publisher. But he had read a report in the *Daily News* to the effect that Cape had pre-empted Constable. Shaw was extremely upset by this.

> The cat being now let out of the bag, presumably by Jonathan Cape with your approval, I cannot wait to finish the book before giving you my opinion, and giving it strongly. IT MUST BE PUBLISHED IN ITS ENTIRETY, UNABRIDGED. Later on an abridgement can be considered, though it may take the shape of a new book . . . You must not for a moment entertain the notion of publishing an abridgement first, as no publisher would touch the whole work afterwards; and I repeat THE WHOLE WORK MUST BE PUBLISHED. If Cape is not prepared to undertake that he is not your man.[18]

Only four weeks before, Shaw had urged Lawrence to publish an abridgment and give a history of the Arabian campaign 'for working purposes'. Apart from Shaw's approach to Constable, what had changed? On 31st December Charlotte Shaw wrote to Lawrence, describing Seven *Pillars* as 'one of the most amazing individual documents that has ever been written'. She added:

> About these *** publishers . . . I am told I must be 'very careful': that anything I say is sure to be libellous. I only want to say one thing, I am greatly honoured by your phrase 'divine book of' *selections,* please, not 'extracts', since it is I who selected them, but the fact that Cape has that book is an accident. He did not publish it but took it over from a little friend of mine (A.C. Fifield) who, to my regret, gave up business. I had practically no say in the matter.[19]

Arthur Fifield was a close friend of the Shaws who had earlier published a number of Shaw's shorter works. Cape bought the firm out. Recently published letters suggest that when Cape took the Fifield deal over, publishing *Selections*, the Shaws felt railroaded, if not betrayed. So perhaps they fostered a grudge against Cape and persuaded Lawrence not to publish with them. But there were other reasons for urging Lawrence not to publish the abridgment with Cape. Shaw was a professional author and aware of how unscrupulous publishers could be. He feared that if an abridgement appeared the complete version would never be printed. Also, he felt a loyalty to Constable, a more established and, he thought, prosperous, publisher.

Lawrence had the opportunity to leave the Air Force right in front of him, as the publication of an abridgement would have provided with him with an assured income for many years. J.M. Wilson's view is that Shaw's meddling ruined this chance and changed the course of T.E.'s life,[20] ensuring he remained on service pay until the mid 1930s. Lawrence had no contact with the Shaws for nearly a year, which suggests he was hurt by the affair. But of course it was his decision, and once again we can only speculate as to motivation: perhaps Lawrence was to some extent in thrall to the brutality and harsh discipline of the ranks and the publication of the abridgement threatened to take this away from him.

The Garnett abridgement never happened. On January 7th 1923, Lawrence wrote to Cape saying he was pulling out of the project, after Trenchard told him how unstable his position in the RAF was. In January however, his lack of caution regarding concealing his identity resulted in nationwide publicity that ensured his position was untenable. On 23rd January, 1923 Trenchard dismissed him from the RAF. There had been a general unease amongst the officers at Farnborough with his presence; they feared he was spying on them, or would 'show them up' and it was one of them who gave him away.[21]

Lawrence was a little coy about the cancellation, trying to cover it up. J.L. Garvin, the editor of the *Observer*, had planned to serialise but Lawrence told him that he had changed his mind after sleeping on it.[22] In August 1927 he told Robert Graves he did not want the story of the death of his servant Farraj covered in any detail. Farraj was the Arab boy he had a great affection for, whom he had been compelled to shoot dead after he was wounded by the Turks. He told Graves: 'Garnett included it in his abridgement, which is a main reason why his abridgement was superseded by my own.'[23] This seems pretty thin.

The *Subscribers' Edition* Abridgement

Relief from the emotional turmoil the *Oxford Text* had caused was one of the reasons Lawrence joined the RAF in 1922. However, during the following 18 months, rather than his mental state improving, it became more agitated. This was the period, from 19th March until 27th July 1923, when a series of highly emotive letters to his friend Lionel Curtis were written. His mental condition had reached such a point of deterioration by December 1923 that concerned friends encouraged him as a form of cure to produce a private subscription edition.

Many of the soldiers at Bovington remembered Lawrence working on *Seven Pillars of Wisdom*.The Bovington text was not a new version of the book. By that time it was nearly five years after the War and Lawrence had lost the freshness of immediate recollection. Because of this, and because his writing style had changed under the influence of post-war authors, he realised his only option was to produce an abridgement of the material he already had. This was done entirely without reference to Edward Garnett's work. He had done some work on this at Uxbridge but at Bovington he continued the work in earnest. In a circular sent to would-be subscribers he explained:

> For copyright reasons, and because the book is somewhat outspoken regarding myself, I am not publishing it, but am trying to raise enough money to raise enough private subscribers to cover the cost of production. Estimates (necessarily provisional) for block making and printing total about £3000. Consequently I've suggested 100 subscribers at 30 guineas. If the bills come to more I'd print 105 or 110 copies (suppose extra subscribers are to be found). If it costs less I'll dock its tail off the list. Circumstances make me unable to profit by it. Type, paper, and illustrations will be decent of their kinds (I hope!) and the complete work, as sent to subscribers, will not be reissued in my lifetime.

One great benefit the Quartermaster's Stores gave him was a time and place to work on the book. At times the recollections upset him greatly. Lesley Gates recalled

> ...It was, I feel sure, his knowledge [of the Arabs] and his great success [in Arabia] that gave him the power to write his book . . . He applied for a sleeping out pass and got it, so he set to work, writing and writing, and when he wasn't doing that he had his gramophone playing all the classical records he could buy. To him, a day in camp in the Q.M. stores was a long day. When he had been writing the manuscript of his book, which he often passed to me to read, he would come on duty very agitated and it would be hours before he was himself again. He would sit in his corner of the stores, speaking to no one and continue to write. It would take a long time to clear up his mess when he had gone. I had been with him on Parade and at no time could he stand still, all the time he was very agitated: it put everyone who was near him into a flat spin, but . . . he never got put on a charge.[24]

In 1923 George Bernard Shaw agreed to edit portions of the book and Lawrence welcomed the offer. With his wife Charlotte, Shaw meticulously examined and altered the early proofs. Chapter 1 did not have the 'furious rush of words' he found in Chapter 2 and was initially abandoned as too introspective and for casting doubt on the British government's motivations in Arabia. Perhaps this excision was for other, pressingly personal reasons. At the time *Seven Pillars* was being re-edited Lawrence was pushing to be restored from the Army to the RAF:

opening his great work with an expression of disillusionment with unscrupulous British diplomacy would hardly put him in a strong position with Trenchard. Some of the chapter's statements also appeared to contradict each other, further reducing its credibility.

Lawrence did widespread cutting for the *Subscribers' Edition* and 84,000 words disappeared. This would account for any discrepancies that that those who retraced his operations (such as Michael Asher and the 1985 Royal Greenjackets expedition) found. Rewriting the abridgement was a solitary experience for him but sometimes, at Clouds Hill, he asked Russell or Palmer what they thought of it. Russell recalled:

> He was telling me a lot of his adventures out there and then he started to write the book, rewrite the book. And as he finished a chapter he would give it to me to read and say, 'Find fault with that.' and I would have to read it through and make suggestions. Some he followed, some he didn't. But I made suggestions.

Of the printing timetable for the abridgement Lawrence observed: 'The printers estimate that they will take ten months block making (fifty illustrations); and I don't propose to put the work in hand except as subscriptions to cover each section of it are assured. You will be lucky to get the finished work in 1924 . . . it may drag till the summer of '25. I promise no date.'

The printer he chose was Manning Pike of Westbourne Terrace, London W2. On one occasion, a Sunday morning, when Lawrence and Russell visited, Pike was setting out the typeface:

> All hand set that book, no linotype, all hand set individual type. And he was tearing off a chapter, just tearing off like that. And he said to me, 'You think you could do that?' I said 'Yes, why?' He said, 'have a go then'. So I set it up, tailoring his type, whilst he was talking business with Lawrence. When he came back he said, 'There's nothing wrong with that' He said, 'You can keep that as it is', and that went in the book. I don't know the chapter though. I wish I knew.[25]

During the course of rewriting, Lawrence, continued to undervalue his talents. He regarded himself as an imitator, working without justification, producing a static work.[26] He felt profoundly dejected by the experience and continued to underestimate its worth, describing it as inferior to nearly every book of the many he had read. Books were his passion and pleasure. They had trapped him into the 'hopelessness of trying to create'.[27]

He told Forster the book 'stank' of himself. To Doughty he apologised for the nature and tone of it, and said that he did not regard it as fit for general reading, owing to the horrible nature of his Arabian experiences. He sent Robert Graves a copy for criticism, saying it was sincere but admitting to having distorted the truth. He also sent a copy to Lady Sandwich in August 1924, warning her: 'Bits of it are decently written, but the whole lacks design and unity.'

Nevertheless, in the same month he told Robin Buxton that the subscription was slowly gaining momentum, and he was intending to print 200. In September he was having problems with the proofs but by 6th October the proofing had reached page 55 and it looked to be an 'exceptionally fine edition'. On the 15th Manning Pike told him that they were still in profit. George Bernard Shaw continued to consider every paragraph.

In June 1925 Lawrence sent a section of the revised *Seven Pillars* to Garnett. Although he still regarded it as a deplorable work it was less cut about than any previous attempts and had lost only 15% of its length. His self-deprecation was still extreme: 'There isn't a scribbler in Fleet Street who wouldn't have got more fire and colour into every paragraph.'[28] This increasing sense of worthlessness was prompted in part by the feeling that his re-entry into the RAF was not going to happen: '. . . that, and the closer acquaintance with the *Seven Pillars* . . . have convinced me that I'm no bloody good on earth. So I'm going to quit: but in my usual comic fashion I'm going to finish the reprint and square it up with Cape before I hop it!'[29]

It was this intimation of suicide that finally persuaded Trenchard to let him back into the RAF. He was allowed back on 16th July and in a letter to Garnett from Clouds Hill on the 27[th,] displayed much more self-confidence and energy: 'Here is the contracted book IX for which you asked. They take long to do; and besides them I've to read and correct proofs of three or four earlier books. We have in hand, at the moment, the whole text from page 80 upwards to this point. Alas it is too long!'[30]

The Revolt in the Desert Abridgement

By the spring of 1926 the rewriting of the *Subscribers' Edition* was complete. To cover the fees of the book's artists he used the royalties from his own abridged version, now entitled *Revolt in the Desert*, published by Cape. After all the hesitations and false starts, he finally produced this by simply hacking his way through a complete set of *Seven Pillars* sheets with a pair of scissors and some Indian ink. The result was an uncontroversial book of 335 pages and 35 chapters, as opposed to the 122 chapters of the original.[31] The first seven chapters were simply dropped altogether, along with another eight. The Deraa incident was also excised. 'My sense of proportion made me sacrifice purple bit after purple bit.' Almost all the self analysis went. An American edition was produced, with hand cut pages, by George H. Doran and Company of New York in 1927.[32] In the foreword to this edition he wrote:

> If I am asked why I have abridged an unsatisfactory book, instead of casting it as history, I must plead that to do so nice a job in the barracks which have been my home since 1922 would need a degree of concentration amounting in an airman to moroseness: an interest in the subject which was exhausted long ago in the actual experience of it.[33]

Revolt in the Desert was hugely successful. The English print run alone sold 90,000 copies. In 1935, after his death, Cape intended to issue a reprint but was prevented by A.W. Lawrence. T.E. had not wished for a further appearance of an abridgement of *The Seven Pillars*. Six weeks after Lawrence's death, Cape, with A.W.'s permission, rushed out a trade edition of the 1926 *Subscribers' Edition* abridgement.

The Anonymous Education Fund

One of the stipulations T.E. made for the 1926 *Subscribers' Edition*, was that he would not make any personal profit from it. But if he profited from the publication of *Revolt in the Desert*, which inevitably undermined the value of the Subscribers' Edition, it would appear he had cheated on his subscribers' investment. Consequently he made the copyright of *Revolt* over to the charitable trust he had set up with £20,000 of the proceeds from its sales, the 'Anonymous Education Fund' for the education of children of disabled or deceased RAF officers.

In 1931 the Inland Revenue made a claim for income tax on the fund. Edward Eliot, Lawrence's solicitor, questioned this and in November 1931 pointed out that it was Lawrence's intention that all the net profits from *Revolt*, after his overdraft to the bank and advance royalties from the publisher had been paid off, would go to the charity. The net money had been assigned to charity from the outset, without restriction on the amount. This was intended to be in the form of annual payments. Eliot felt this should be enough to circumvent legally the income tax demand.

In 1926 Lawrence printed the *Subscribers' Edition* of the *Seven Pillars*. This cost £10,126. Sales amounted to £4,324. Martin's Bank financed him and an overdraft of £7,030 resulted. *Revolt in the Desert* was published by Jonathan Cape in January 1927. Over the three April-to-April tax years 1927–1929, the ostensibly taxable royalties for *Revolt* amounted to £16,637 (income tax was four shillings in the pound, i.e. £3,327). The royalties for the first year, April 1927 to April 1928 amounted to £14,032.

Lawrence arranged for the royalties to be disposable under three deeds:

1) The first deed, in November 1926, assigned the rights of his book to his Trustees.[34] They were to clear his overdraft on the *Seven Pillars* of £7,030 and to cover the advance paid to him of £3,000. The balance was to be paid to the RAF Memorial Fund (the Anonymous Education Fund was part of this). This was to be irrevocable.

2) The second deed was assigned in October 1928. This was a declaration of trust between Lawrence's trustees, the managing trustees for the Memorial Fund, and Martins Bank as custodian trustees for the money. This defined in detail the Trust's conditions. By November 1931 £10,000 had accumulated and was available to the charity. The Committee of the RAF Memorial Fund was made the Executive Committee for the management of the subsequent income.

3) The third deed was assigned in April 1929. This was a supplemental declaration of trust. Herein a further sum of £5,000 that had accrued from *Revolt's* net profit was added.

The Inland Revenue's claims for income tax were aimed at the two last lump sums. A year after Eliot's notes for the Inland Revenue, the Fund's case was still being contested.

In June 1938 a 'Secret' *Summary of Personal File of 338171 A/C2 Shaw, T.E.*, consisting of three red folders and two yellow ones, was examined by David Garnett at the Air Ministry. In one of the red folders he found 'an enormous correspondence' of 'perhaps 200,000 words' that concerned the income tax charges on the Anonymous Education Fund.[35] This dealt with a series of missives that passed from March 1931 until March 1934 between the Air Ministry, Inland Revenue, the RAF Memorial Fund and Lawrence's solicitors, Tamplin, Joseph, Posonby, Ryde and Flux.

Involved in this were Lawrence's solicitor Edward Eliot (Messrs. Tamplin and Co.), whom Lawrence had granted Power of Attorney over his estate in 1926; Air Marshal Sir Edward Ellington (Air Officer Commander in Chief, Air Defence of Great Britain); Sir Cecil Owen (Solicitor to the Treasury); S.E. Minnis (Assistant Secretary to the Secretary's Office, Inland Revenue); Sir Charles McLoud (RAF Memorial Fund); W.E.S. Burch (RAF Memorial Fund); Group Captain Carmichael (Secretary, RAF Memorial Fund); J. Stirling Ross C.B., C.B.E. (Messrs. Tamplin and Co.) and 'Mr. X' (Aircraftman Shaw). At first the contention was whether or not Lawrence was liable to taxation on the royalties he had received from *Revolt in the Desert*. Ross, at Lawrence's solicitors, stated:

> It seems clear that the Inland Revenue claim is based on the contention that the first receipt of the profits is part of the ordinary income of the author. The claim, if good, would lie against him.[36]

He concluded that the legality of the I.R. claims rested on whether Lawrence had formerly received the royalties and paid them into his bank, or whether a deed had assigned his interest in the work to the Trustees for a charitable purpose. In the first case any receipts would have been part of his income. In the second case the receipts 'wouldn't have been his money'. On 13th April 1931 Ross told Owen that Ellington had questioned whether the Trustees should make it easy for the I.R. to get the money: 'Mr. X is only an aircraft-hand getting 3/- a day and the Trustees cannot themselves pay, in ordinary cause, without breach of trust.'[37]

On 11th February 1932 a test transaction was suggested of £10 to make a case for an appeal, thus bringing it within the scope of the Appeal Commissioners. It was intended to mimic the earlier payments of £5,000 and £10,000 'so as to be on all fours with them [the I.R.]'.[38] Ross and the Trustees wanted to know that the case would go to the Commissioners without the Trustees 'going through the elaborate formality of a deed.'[39] Minnis presumed that, after the test payment, the Trustees would formally reclaim the deducted tax 'and then put the matter in hand.'[40] On 8th March 1932 Ross wrote to Eliot 'I think we can assume that the Inland Revenue agree that we can proceed without a formal deed.[41] But it was, Minnis told Ross, taking a while to get the case 'in trim'.[42] Ross thought the Memorial

Fund authorities were making a draft appeal. On 13th October Minnis told Ross the appeal case was due to be heard on November 11th at 2 pm. Ross told Sir Charles McLoud a week later:

> I am given to understand that the Trustees could pay over the money if they got a rectification of the Deed of Trust by the appropriate court, or if the Attorney General . . . is willing to acquiesce.[43]

He wrote to Ellington on the 26th to say the Air Ministry was still undecided. By the 3rd November Mr Bowe at the Air Ministry Council was 'still getting a good knowledge' of the case.[44] The following day a submission to the Appeal Court was made. Ross seemed to think there was a 'difference of opinion' at that stage, it being 'inadvisable to butt in.'[45] On the 5th of the following month Burch received an Income Tax Repayment Claim Form from the Chief Inspector of Taxes (Claims). Ross said the decision now rested with the courts who would be 'content to hear the appeals of both parties'.[46] Earlier some party, probably Eliot, had prepared a report on the case: *Draft Notes for the Secretary of State*. These isolated two main questions: was the claim good and if it was good, how was the amount due to the Inland Revenue to be found? On point 1 the conclusion was that the income tax claim was legally correct. Lawrence had not assigned the profits, or the balance of the profits, to any trust body without receiving them first. If he had done this it is possible the profits would not have been regarded as personal income, and, as charitable income, have been free from tax. Although Lawrence may have intended this, he did not do it.

On point 2, Owen, the Treasury Solicitor, who had shown an interest in the case, concluded that the tax could not be paid out of the capital or income of managing trustees without a breach of trust:

> . . .The claim lies primarily against Mr. X (or his trustees). If he refuses to pay (and he must refuse, if, as we believe, he has no means) and the Inland Revenue press their claim against him, then a refusal by the Trustees to take any legal means to make possible the payment by them would force Mr. X into a position which would be unfair to him without his own consent.[47]

The supposition that Lawrence had 'no means' seems to be a common, but wrong, assumption. In 1931 his solicitors produced a Statement of Account for the Trustees of Colonel Lawrence. This gave a detailed breakdown of the receipts and payments of the estate between the years 1926 to 1931. It showed:

Dec 30 1926 – Dec 9, 1927

Total receipts: £20,872 4s 4p. (This included over £4,173 in 1926 for *Seven Pillars* subscriptions, £1,800 royalties for sales of *Revolt in the Desert*, and £107 2s on sales of the German, Swedish, Dutch and French rights to *Revolt*).

Total payments: £10,759 9s 4 p (including over £4,069 personal loans and £1,215 to Manning Pike).

Jan 1 – Nov 6 1928

Total receipts: £25,783 5s (including £2,453 3s 1p for the English, Canadian and Australian sales of *Revolt*, and £900, the first instalment on sales of the film rights for *Revolt*).

Total payments: £20,091 18s 1p (including £10,000 transferred to a Deposit Account on April 16 and £10,000 transferred to the Trustees Department, Martins Bank).

Jan 3– Oct 31 1929

Total receipts: £6,449 9s 2p (including £448 3s 7p American royalties, less tax and commission, and £172 for Canadian and German rights for *Revolt*).

Jan 1 – Nov 4 1930

Total receipts: £1,880 10s 11p (including total American, Canadian, Australian, Dutch and French sales for *Revolt* of £422 3s).[48]

Revolt in the Desert was making Lawrence a rich man. By 1931 the book's total sales (including royalties and sale of film and book rights) amounted to over £19,736. His estate's total receipts 1927–1930 were over £57,985. This, with the government pension Bernard Shaw had been pressing for, would have left Lawrence extremely well off.

In November 1932 Lawrence wrote from Mount Batten to Clare Sydney Smith to say that there was an income-tax case in London of the RAF Memorial Fund for hearing that Friday and Saturday, and he was to appear as a witness.[49] On 2nd December the Office of Special Commissioners of Income Tax contacted the RAF Memorial Fund's solicitors, enclosing a copy of the Appeal Commission's decision. They were invited to 'carry the matter further' if they wished.

The Appeal on November 11th failed for one main reason; because Lawrence's trustees were paying the balance of the royalties, after certain costs and liabilities had been met, to the RAF Memorial Fund in lump sums, i.e. £5,000 and £10,000, and not in annual periodical payments, the claim for income tax exemption was declared invalid.

Apart from that the Commissioners had 'considerable doubt' as to whether the balance of Lawrence's Trust Fund, insofar as it arose from royalties, could be regarded as income for the RAF Fund. They also questioned whether his fund should not be regarded as the trustees' own income, in view of the discretion he allowed them. Thus any payments made to the RAF fund could be regarded as discretionary applications by Lawrence's trustees of their own income. The Commissioners did not feel obliged to elaborate on this point in view of their original decision.[50]

Months after the Appeal Court decision was made the RAF Benevolent Fund was finding difficulty in making the payments. In March the Air Member for Personnel at the Air Ministry pointed out that if liability was placed with Lawrence's trustees they would only say that the only way they could pay would be from royalties that had accumulated since 1929, which he thought totalled around £2,000. But there would be a tax on this as well, of about £500, leaving only a residue of £1,500 to pay a total of £4,000. An alternative was to pay the balance from the RAF Memorial Fund's general funds, rather than from the Education Trust.

In October Tamplin and Co. told the RAF Memorial Fund that the chargeable tax that had accumulated from 1926 to 1933 amounted to £3,364 14s, of which Lawrence's trustees had already paid £2,093 for the year 1927–28. The trustees had only just over £64 left, leaving a balance outstanding of £1,271 10s. The I.R. were anxious to know when this balance would be paid.[51]

Ross asked Minnis if it was possible to have dispensation to pay by instalments over a period of two to three years, it being preferable to meet the cost from the Fund's income (which was around £500 per annum) rather than capital, although a partial realisation of capital may be necessary. The RAF main fund was at that time suffering from a 'falling off of income', which increased the difficulty.[52] Minnis agreed to this but the Finance Committee at the RAF Fund found they were unable to meet this unless they entirely closed the Fund for Educational purposes for over two years. As it was at that time supporting eighteen cases, all of them widows entirely dependent on the Fund for the education of their children, this course was not acceptable.

The RAF Fund's only recourse seemed to pay by capital. Since its only income was from fixed rate dividends that were unlikely to increase in value and since royalties would no longer be added to the general capital, the Fund would suffer a permanent reduction in income. The Finance Committee's solution was to make a lump sum payment of £1,000 by the end of 1933. Group Captain Carmichael at the RAF Memorial Fund asked for sympathetic consideration from the Inspector of Taxes, in view of the effect any depletion of capital would have 'on the several cases dependent on [the Anonymous Education Fund] for support'. He also pointed out that advantages would accrue for the Inland Revenue 'through the immediate payment of a lump sum'.[53]

On the same day Carmichael wrote to Ross reiterating the dual advantages of a lump sum payment and enclosed a copy of the letter to the I.R.[54] The Inland Revenue Department appears to have reneged on their original stipulation. Six months later, on 20th March 1934, Carmichael again wrote to them to say that the Trustees of the RAF Benevolent Fund [55] had agreed to payments of £40 a month from the charity's General fund to meet the debt.[56]

We can thus see how successful Lawrence's benevolence had been and would become through its support for the education of ex-servicemen's children. By 1935 the later renamed Lawrence of Arabia Fund was educating 13 children a year and is still operating as part of the RAF Benevolent Fund.

Notes

1 Book XXXIII was one of the key sections in *Seven Pillars*. It describes how Lawrence,
   laid up sick for ten days, rethought the Arab campaign using mathematical techniques,
   realizing that the only effective strategy would be one of detachment, of the
   containment of the enemy by silent threat.
2 W.S. Churchill to C.S. Churchill, War Office, London, 16/2/1921.
3 Sidney Webb to G.B. Shaw, Ayot-St. Lawrence, 1923.
4 The Arab Bureau was set up in the war to monitor the Middle East war and the
   progress of the Arab revolt.
5 This was not the *Subscribers' Edition* abridgement, which amounted to 250,000 words.
6 This would have been a 'popular' abridgement, unlike the *Subscribers Edition*.
7 Letter from 'E.L.' to Edward Garnett. Uxbridge, 9th October, 1922.
8 T.E. Lawrence to Edward Garnett, Farnborough, 12/11/1922. DG.
9 G.B. Shaw to T.E. Lawrence 01/12/1922. LTEL.
10 T.E. Lawrence to Edward Garnett, Farnborough, 7/12/1922.
11 T.E. Lawrence to Edward Garnett, Farnborough, 7/12/1922.
12 G.B. Shaw to T.E. Lawrence, Adelphi Terrace, London, 17/12/1922. LTEL.
13 G.B. Shaw to T.E. Lawrence, Adelphi Terrace, London, 17/12/1922. LTEL.
14 T.E. Lawrence to H.J. Cape, 21/12/1922.
15 T.E. Lawrence to George Bernard Shaw, Farnborough, 27/12/1922.
16 Ibid.
17 Ibid.
18 G.B. Shaw to T.E. Lawrence, Ayot St. Lawrence, 28/12/1922.
19 C.F. Shaw to T.E. Lawrence. 31/12/1922. BL Add 45903.
20 Wilson, p. 699.
21 To a certain extent Lawrence brought this on himself by writing openly to relative
   strangers of his situation.
22 Letter from T.E. Lawrence to J.H. Garvin. 14, Barton St., 30th January 1923.
23 *B: RG*. P. 99.
24 Recollections of Leslie Edward Gates.
25 Arthur Russell. Interview with author. 1985.
26 Letter to E.M. Forster, 20th February, 1924.
27 Ibid.
28 T.E. Lawrence to Edward Garnett, 13/06/1925.
29 Ibid.
30 T.E. Lawrence to Edward Garnett, 27/07/1925.
31 The *Subscribers' Edition* was also a 'hacked about' abridgement of the 1922 edition.
32 Sales of this would have been helped by extracts from *Seven Pillars* being published in
   a number of American magazines including *The World's Work* in 1927. This was at the
   suggestion of Lowell Thomas.
33 *Revolt in the Desert*, T.E. Lawrence, George H. Doran, New York, 1927.
34 The Trustees of the fund were Edward Eliot, Robin Buxton and D.G. Hogarth.
35 MS Eng. d.3343 Bodleian Library Modern Papers Room. This file now resides under a
   high security classification in the National Archives.

36 J.S. Ross to Sir Edward Ellington. 18/03/1931. National Archives AIR 1/2695

37 J.S. Ross to Sir Cecil Owen. 13/4/1931. National Archives AIR 1/2695

38 The amount of income tax payable on £15,000 was around £4,000. So at a tax rate of 5s in the pound, the amount payable on £10 was £2 10s.

39 National Archives AIR 1/2695

40 Ibid.

41 J.S. Ross to E. Eliot. 8/3/1932. National Archives AIR 1/2695

42 S.E. Minnis to J.S. Ross. 21/4/1932. National Archives AIR 1/2695

43 J.S. Ross to Sir C. McLoud. 21/10/1932. National Archives AIR 1/2695

44 Air Ministry to J.S. Ross. 3/11/1931. National Archives AIR 1/2695

45 J.S. Ross to ? National Archives AIR 1/2695.

46 J.S. Ross to ?. 7/11/1932. National Archives AIR 1/2695.

47 *Draft Notes for Secretary of State*. National Archives AIR 1/2695

48 *Trustees of Colonel Lawrence: Statement of Account for Years 1926 to 1931*. Tamplin Joseph Ponsonby Ryde and Flux, 1931. National Archives AIR 1/2695.

49 *Golden Reign*.

50 *Royal Air Force Memorial Fund Decision*. Office of the Special Commissioners of Income Tax. 2/12/1932. National Archives AIR 1/2695.

51 Tamplin Joseph Ponsonby Ryde and Flux to RAF Memorial Fund, 6/10/1933. National Archives AIR 1/2695.

52 Tamplin Joseph Ponsonby Ryde and Flux to S.B. Minnis, 11/10/1933. National Archives AIR 1/2695.

53 Group Captain Carmichael to Inspector of Taxes, London, 27/10/1933. National Archives AIR 1/2695.

54 Group Captain Carmichael to J.S. Ross 27/10/1933. National Archives AIR 1/2695.

55 The name of the Fund appears to have been changed to its present title some time between October 1933 and March 1934.

56 Group Captain Carmichael to Inspector of Taxes, London, 20/3/1934. National Archives AIR 1/2695.

PART TWO

In the Racing Stable

Do explain to your successor what his chief liability is: & that I am less trouble to the C.A.S. when I am inside the service than when outside it: but a trouble anyhow. It is like having a unicorn in a racing stable. Beast doesn't fit.

T.E. Lawrence to Sir Hugh Trenchard, Miranshah, 26th December, 1928

CHAPTER FIVE

The Second RAF Period:
Cranwell, India and Beginning the Odyssey

Despite Lawrence's endless entreaties to Trenchard, in the summer of 1925 he was still at Bovington. Although the Chief of Air Staff had approved a transfer, the new Air Minister, Sir Samuel Hoare, refused to warrant it. This was a source of constant unhappiness to Lawrence, such that, by the time of his 6th June letter to Edward Garnett he viewed his life as worthless. After Garnett received the intimation of suicide he contacted Bernard Shaw and Shaw wrote to Baldwin in his second period of premiership. But Hoare still refused to reinstate him. Baldwin[1] only intervened when John Buchan also protested. So, on a warm day of blue cloudless skies, Thursday 16th July 1925, the Chief of the Air Staff signed the order for Lawrence to return to the Air Force.

This was to lead to some of his happiest days since Carchemish and there is no doubt that Trenchard's action saved Lawrence's life. It was Trenchard who, despite personal misgivings, had helped him enter the service in 1922 and now his old friend did it again. There is also little doubt that it was only Lawrence's personal contacts that made it happen. By August 1925 he had spent two-and-a-half years in the Tank Corps and his emergence from it back into the RAF led to an immediate uplift in spirits: 'The oracle responded nobly . . . The immediate effect of this news was to send me lazily and smoothly asleep: and asleep I have been ever since. It's like a sudden port, after a voyage all out of reckoning.'[2]

After recruit processing at RAF West Drayton and Uxbridge, within weeks he was cleaning aircraft at the Cranwell Cadet College and living in a hut of fourteen men, a corporal and a sergeant. It was tough, but nothing like as barbaric as life in the Tanks.

He still has some fondness for some of his time at Bovington: seven days after rejoining the Air Force, on Tuesday 25th August 1925, he wrote to 'Posh' Palmer from the RAF Cadets College:

When I entered the R.A.F. station at West Drayton (a derelict misery-stricken unfinished factory-place) from its upper windows came 'The Lass of Richmond Hill', violently sung. At once I remembered Clouds Hill and you and H.H.B. and I hung my kit-bag on a willow tree and wept.[3]

Life was less harsh than that at the Uxbridge Depot of 1922. He was exulted by the sound in the early morning of the running up of a 260 h.p. Rolls-Royce engine at nineteen hundred revs.

Two Air Force men who encountered Lawrence during this period, an officer and an aircraft hand, left accounts. He helped Rupert de la Bere edit the Cadet College journal and whilst at Cranwell Lawrence attended a lecture course de la Bere was giving on Imperial geography. In the midst of this he gave his own talk on the Middle East that would never be forgotten by those who heard it.[4]

At Cranwell he served in 'B' Flight, billeted in Hut 106. According to R. Hales, also at Cranwell, his duties would be cleaning and tidying the Flight hangar and living quarters. Hales was a Carpenter/Rigger who had a lot of friends in the same hut as Lawrence. De la Bere remembered he was responsible for tidying the Flight office and lighting the fire. They were tasks he did uncomplainingly and Hales concluded that the *esprit de corps* was so high at the Cadet College that the kindness of his fellow airmen, officers and N.C.O.s completed his rehabilitation

Other personalities at the College at that time were the Duke of York (later king George VI) and Wing Commander 'Razzo' Rees V.C., who radiated coolness and courage in the air and on the ground. 'B' Flight maintained Bristol Fighters, whilst 'C' Flight was more experimental, having training aircraft such as the Avro 504K and Sopwith Snipes and one of the early Gloster Schneider Trophy aircraft.[5]

Both de la Bere and Hales agree that Lawrence wrote part of *Seven Pillars of Wisdom* in his rooms near Lindum Hall, Lincoln, whilst at Cranwell. He also gave a first edition of the book to a fitter in 'B' Flight, Sergeant Pugh. Lawrence contributed a number of articles to the College journal at de la Bere's request.[6] His capacity for compassion and generosity was well known by his colleagues. One example at the Cadet College of such empathy only came to light in 2002, when his records were released to the public. Lawrence was friendly with an airman at Cranwell named Greyham Bryant. Bryant, like Lawrence, loved racing motorcycles around Lincolnshire. In September 1926 T.E. attended an RAF dance at the Cadet College and here he met Bryant's 24-year-old sister Ruby. The girl was not impressed when they met, later describing him as 'quite a pathetic figure with a weak handshake'.[7]

Lawrence learned somehow of her tragic background. Her father had been a private in the Essex Regiment and was shot in the back on the Western Front by a sniper in 1915. His death overwhelmed his widow and she died a short time later. The girl was cruelly treated and took a job as a maid. But her circumstances worsened. By the time Lawrence met her Miss Bryant was noticeably underweight. and he took pity on her. According to an 'Allotment of Pay' order in his RAF pay book, he shortly afterwards set aside two-thirds of his pay, two shillings a day, to her. This continued for 14 months, from September 1925 to November 1926 and it transformed her life, enabling her to leave work and attend secretarial college. It was well known amongst her relations that Miss Bryant knew Lawrence, but they did not know of the help he had given her. Ruby Bryant died in 1980, aged 76.[8]

To India

Lawrence was allowed to transfer abroad and at his own request was posted to India as an ordinary aircraftman at the beginning of December 1926. This was largely to avoid press attention in England following Cape's publication of *Revolt in the Desert*. He sailed on 7th December 1926 on the troopship *Derbyshire*[9] with 1200 other officers and men and spent some time at Drigh Road, Karachi, a camp he later described as 'new stone-built and spacious'. This was an RAF Depot which focussed on highly technical work.[10] The provisioning section, which had to order all the required stores from England, had to allow for a time delay in all its deliveries to be efficient.[11] Lawrence was, at one stage, responsible for organizing the records in the engine repair department. He never ventured into the city but confined himself voluntarily within the camp boundaries, which allowed time to begin a literary project that would engage him for the next four years.

Bruce Rogers from Linwood, Indiana, had earned international acclaim for outstanding typography, and was a highly respected advocate of good book design. In 1928 he received a commission from Random House publications for a book on any subject he liked. He chose a translation of Homer's *Odyssey*. Rogers considered all the existing translations, and was drawn to the 1900 translation of Samuel Butler.[12] He then came across that of George Herbert Palmer, an old acquaintance of his from Boston, an 88-year-old Harvard Philosophy Professor who had written a number of academic books, including a popular school text of the *Odyssey* in the 1900s. However Rogers felt he still had not found what he was looking for. Rogers had read *Seven Pillars of Wisdom* and despite being uninterested in the subject matter, found the text gripped him. If the style could be applied to the *Odyssey* they would have a version that outstripped every existing translation.[13] 'Here at last was a man who could make Homer live again – a man of action who was also a scholar and could write swift and graphic English.'[14]

Rogers did not know how to contact Lawrence. Then he met a 37-year-old American and former British Staff Colonel named Ralph Isham, who had been corresponding with Lawrence at Karachi. The American had suggested that if Lawrence came to the US. he could work on Boswell's papers, a suitable use for his talents. Lawrence declined, on the fairly firm grounds that he knew nothing about Boswell, so Isham suggested he write a novel.[15] Lawrence replied:

> I can't write a novel, and if I did it would not be a good novel, probably. I do not like the idea of struggling for 20 years, with a pen, pot boiling, with the risk always of running dry. I can't, of course, write about Arabia. That is covered by the self-denying ordinance.[16]

Isham had known Lawrence since 1919. He was dining with Rogers on the night he received his letter and showed it to Rogers,[17] who urged Isham to write to T.E. about the *Odyssey*. This he did on December 6th 1927, suggesting a payment of £800. Lawrence predicted it would take two years to complete, immediately realizing the enormity of the task. He confessed that he carried a copy to every camp but only read it for pleasure, often needing a dictionary. However he was reluctant to take the job on: '[I] tried to see myself translating it, freely, into English. Honestly it would be most difficult to do. I have the rhythm of the Greek so in my mind that it would not come readily into straight English.'[18]

He told Rogers he would abandon the project if the publishers expressed any misgivings. He had admired Rogers' work for years, and was wary of not living up to his standard – or Homer's for that matter. In fact, he as much as told Isham he could not do it. He thought none of the 26 existing prose translations were exceptional. He proposed a fee of fifteen to twenty pounds, with the strictest possible terms: he would not sign it, nor have his name on it. He felt the whole of the style of the translation would be determined by the way he treated Book I of the 24 books, and so he must complete that first book within six months, for a fraction of the total fee. (Eventually he would go back on this.)

His fear of the project is constantly to the fore. If previous translators like Morris, Butler and Butcher and Lang couldn't get it right, he thought, how could he?

> My strongest advice is for you to get someone better, to do you a more certain performance. I am nothing like good enough for so great a work of art as the *Odyssey*. Nor, incidentally, to be printed by B.R ... Do realise that I have no confidence in myself, and what I'd like is some little job, unquestionably within my strength and within my leisure hours in the R.A.F.[19]

The following Spring Isham and Rogers were still gently cajoling and in early March Rogers sent him Palmer's American prose version. It arrived in April: 'It is very wholesome and very loving. Do you think I'll do better? I'd suggest you get a lien on Palmer, in case my sample book is less noteworthy of preservation.'[20]

Lawrence felt frightened by the size of the poem. To transform the ancient text into modern, everyday language was a daunting task: 'I do it tacitly every time I read him: but that is for my own belly.'[21]

One bar to getting started was his work on *The Mint*. The effort of finishing this by the 15th of March had exhausted him and his first reaction to the *Odyssey* was a characteristic one: withdrawal. He may have feared the translator's solitary creative process: but he also feared, as he had with the abridgements, any rekindling of the earlier mental breakdown he suffered at Barton Street. At some point, like so many writers before him, he realised the solution lay in making a start, in getting Book I out of the way. On 16th April he wrote to Rogers 'I want to do it and am afraid: but can get over that difficulty by doing the sample book for you.'[22] He was still uncertain of Rogers' view of him and realised that a work without his name on it would be of little financial value, *Revolt in the Desert*'s success in America having left him with the publishing world at his feet.

Reluctantly, through an old friend Lawrence had now been persuaded to get involved in Rogers' project, despite realizing how difficult it would be. The problem he was faced with was how to better all the existing translations, and produce something fresh. How long it would take him and how far he would draw on his previous experiences, both as a writer, soldier and archaeologist, he underestimated.

Notes

1 Baldwin was an astute political animal. In 1937 he persuaded Edward VIII to abdicate in the face of public indignation at the coronation of Wallis Simpson. Edward had been a thorn in the flesh of the government for years, with his potential erratic behaviour. The abdication was an adroit move by Baldwin, whereby he sidestepped the inclinations of Churchill and Beaverbrook and saved the government's face in the eyes of the people, the Conservatives appearing still to be on the side of the Windsors.

2 T.E. Lawrence to John Buchan, 5/7/1925. DG. In a letter to E. Garnett on 17th July he took the analogy further, comparing himself to 'the ship Argos, when Jason last drew her up on the beach'.

3 DG:L

4 *Aircraftman Shaw in Lincolnshire (a Last Conversation)*, Professor R. De La Bere M.A., F.R.Hist.S. *The Lincolnshire Magazine*, Vol.2, No.7, Sept. to Oct. 1935.

5 *Recollections of R. Hales*. Lincoln, February 1971. I.W.M.

6 *Aircraftman Shaw in Lincolnshire (a Last Conversation)*, Professor R. De La Bere M.A., F.R.Hist.S. *The Lincolnshire Magazine*, Vol.2, No.7, Sept. to Oct. 1935.

7 *Daily Telegraph*, June 9th 2006.

8 Ibid.

9 In the 1920s all British troopships were named after British counties. They were supplied by the 'Bibby Shipping Line' and known as the 'Shire Boats'.

10 At that time there were eight RAF Squadrons in India: four Army Co-operation Squadrons and four day bombing Squadrons. Karachi acted as a supply depot to all of them.

11 *The Autobiography of Group Captain R.J. Bone*, I.W.M.

12 Butler had argued that Homer was a 'young, headstrong and unmarried' woman.

13 B. Rogers to T.E. Lawrence. 4/3/1928. Bodleian reserve.

14 From the introduction by Bruce Rogers to *Letters from T.E. Shaw to Bruce Rogers*.

15 See *Typescript Account of the* Odyssey *Project*, Ralph Isham, Bodleian Library.

16 Ibid.

17 Ibid.

18 T.E. Lawrence to R. Isham. 2/1/ 1928. L-BR.

19 T.E. Shaw to Bruce Rogers, 2/1/1928. Letters-Brown.

20 T.E. Lawrence to Bruce Rogers. Karachi. 16/4/1928. L-DG.

21 Ibid.

22 T.E. Lawrence to Bruce Rogers. 16th April 1928.

CHAPTER SIX

The Problems of a Translator; and Mired in the Great Game

It is generally conceded that the *Odyssey* was written in the 8th century B.C. It concerns Odysseus's 20-year journey back from the Trojan Wars, and the adventures and trials that beset him. In his Translators Note, originally intended to be at the end of the book, Lawrence described the *Odyssey* as 'the oldest book worth reading for its story and the second novel of Europe'; (the first was the *Iliad*).

In 1928 Homer was even more of a mystery than today. Scientific archaeology was still in its infancy, but it had confirmed that there was a 'real' Bronze Age which supported the authenticity of Homer's tales. It had also been proved, by anthropologists[1] working in Yugoslavia and Greece, that oral recitation of poetry was quite common. This led to the conclusion that little writing was done in the *Odyssey*'s composition. But this was not made public until 1932, by which time T.E.'s translation was finished. A third discovery also confirmed a link between Homer and the Bronze Age. This was that the Minoan hieroglyphic tablets,[2] found by a British archaeologist in Athens earlier in the century, were in Greek, but again, these were not translated until 1952. Lawrence had very little evidence that there was a real Homer, and no idea how the *Odyssey* was recorded.[3]

How close was Lawrence's translation to the original? Was it a word for word translation or an interpretation? This was an epic poem recited by illiterate singers about the former Heroic times in the Bronze Age, sung in chanting stanzas to the background music of a lyre. Because of this, contemporary verse translations are more in keeping with the original than Lawrence's version.[4] The problem of the modern translator is how to preserve these rhythmic patterns and forms in a sensible, lyrical narrative.

There is no hard evidence as to who Homer really was: whether he was one poet, two, or many, whether he was illiterate, blind or even a woman. In order to record and remember this lengthy work, singers would prepare so-called 'formulae' which were whole sections of verse (resembling the procedures of modern computer programming) that could be called upon at any time to describe a scene. For example three short sections in the last four books of the *Odyssey* are exactly the same. These concerned Penelope, Odysseus's wife, and her tricking of her suitors: her scheme was to weave a shroud for a dead warrior to avoid their attention. Until the weave was finished she could not choose a suitor, but every night she undid the day's weave, thus putting off the moment. In the original, Homer used the exactly same wording for this 'formula' or section in three different places. Lawrence, however, rather than employing the same words each time as Homer did, translated each section differently. Other examples of similar treatment of formulae can be found elsewhere in the poem. His three separate interpretations were:

(i)   One trick her subtlety devised was to install in her apartments a huge loom, and set up on this a fine, wide weave; and ever she would say to us, 'Sweet hearts go slow. Your burning intent to have me married. The death of royal Odysseus lays on me the duty of completing this linen shroud, to save its gossamer threads from being scattered to the winds. It is for the burial of Laertes, the aged hero, and it must be ready against the inevitable day when fate will pull him to the ground and death measure out his length.'

(ii) I was inspired to build me a monster loom upstairs, on which I set up a fine, gold-threaded linen weave, telling them by and by, 'My lords and suitors be patient with me (however much you wish me wedded now great Odysseus is lost) till I complete this shroud against the inevitable day that death shall smite Laertes, the aged hero, low.

(iii) . . . for the moment she imagined another device, by setting up a very broad, fine warp on a great loom in her chamber; and pleading to us regarding it, 'My lords and courtiers, as great Odysseus is dead, can you not bridle thy haste to have me wedded, until I finish this winding sheet against hero Laertes' burial on the fateful day that all-conquering death lays him low?'

One of the aims Lawrence stated in his Translator's Note was generally to 'raise the colour' of the text, his slavish devotion to this creating a great deal of work. He made supreme efforts to translate 'in context' with forceful expressions, often creating compound words (eminently in keeping with the original), much as he had in *Seven Pillars*. 'Suitor-maggots' replaced 'men' when referring to the parasitic nature of the suitors; 'winged scavengers of the wind' replaced 'whirlwind' when referring to Odysseus being blown off course by Harpies. Rogers wanted a gutsy, dramatic presentation and Lawrence worked himself to distraction to achieve this. Whether Lawrence was conscious of it or not, his use of multiple interpretations of formulae, although meant to colour the translation, radically altered the style. He changed Butler's 'the women of the place will talk' to 'I will be the pointing-block of every Achean woman within our neighbourhood': the distance between the two is enormous.

In Butcher and Lang's words, a prose translation[6]

. . . only gathers, as it were, the crumbs which fall from the richer table, only tells the story without the song.

Butcher and Lang felt that neither verse nor prose translations told the whole truth; and that any modern translation would be temporally constricted, reflecting its era and the character of its translator. Because of this there could be no definitive translation of Homer.

Lawrence decided on prose partly because of his limitations in rhyming verse. His poems written at or about Clouds Hill in the 1920s were simple rhyming stanzas. Another reason may have been that he saw the *Odyssey* 'as primarily a story'[7] and prose therefore the best medium to tell it. Prose also allowed him a greater opportunity for orginality.

In his letters Lawrence annotated the problems with the work: one incorrect phrase could ruin a whole passage; everything he did was an 'approximation' of what Homer may have said; if he introduced anything of his own character into the poem it did not work; different styles in the original, perhaps caused by there being more than one Homeric author, further confused matters.

He later considered he had failed in his attempts to take liberties with, or rather liberate, the original Greek. Typically, he modestly stated, he had 'no originalities of his own to express'. In view of his genius this can hardly be true. His 'Englishness' also tended to cloud the translation. And an embarrassment with his own acquisitive motivation[9] contributed to his disillusionment.

Owing to difficulties with his relationship with an incoming officer at Karachi, he asked to be transferred, explaining the reason for this in a letter to Trenchard on 1st May 1928. The C.O. at Karachi had told a friend[10] in a club after dinner that he had Lawrence 'taped',[11] if he got the chance he intended to 'jump on'[12] him. Lawrence told Trenchard he had no means of verifying the story, but he was 'tired of fighting'.

Miranshah

On Saturday 26th May 1928 he was moved to Peshawar on the North-West Frontier, and, after two days, assigned to a tiny outpost in the province of Waziristan, near the Afghan border; a brick and earth fort surrounded by barbed wire, complete with searchlights and machine guns, containing seven hundred Waziristan scouts, 21 RAF men and five officers. The barbed wire was there for a reason, as according to one source the locals 'thought it great fun to murder any white person'.[13]

Miranshah was the smallest RAF detachment in India. With its setting in a sun-scorched, barren plain near the Afghan foothills it possessed an encouragingly Homeric ambience. The detachment rotated once every two months and the remoteness made it a much sought-after post, aircrew going there for a few months to take charge of a flight and liaise with the Waziristan scouts.[14] Wireless operator Jack Easton worked in a small cabin set apart from the rest of the fort. Lawrence described it to Charlotte Shaw:

> ... a 15 foot square whitewashed cube, with cement floor. In the centre is the fan,[15] underneath it the officer's table: against the far wall my table, covered with white

American cloth, and carrying the typewriter, which I've taught to produce pages of Homer, as well as daily Routine Orders![16]

The radio cabin was an ideal place to work on the *Odyssey* for two or three hours a day. Easton later recalled:

> He had steely blue eyes, a very sharp chin and you could tell when he was talking that he was well educated. He always kept to himself. He never talked about any of his exploits. He used to come in the cabin and talk but he didn't make trouble for himself. Everyone seemed to like him.[17]

On 30th June he completed Book I of the *Odyssey*. This was six months after he had accepted the work and did not include the time, up until mid-March, when he was finishing *The Mint*. It had taken six drafts, afterwards he felt 'beaten to his knees'. He found Homer 'baffling'[18] and understood why all the previous translations had been inadequate.

Book II took four months and was even harder than Book I. Despite scouring Palmer's translation for inspiration he still had to refer to Morris's and Butler's books, which he had earlier dismissed as 'too literary'. He wanted to opt out of the project at this point but Isham told him this was impossible; he and Emery Walker, the publishers, would not let it go.[19] He then requested the employment of an expert scholar to check Book 1 for 'howlers'. Rogers agreed and chose H.B. Walters, an antiquities expert at the British Museum, thereafter referred to as 'W' by Lawrence. He told Isham of his financial expectations:

> That cottage in Dorset will be mine, in consequence: and the surplus will get me a motor-bike and make my 1930–1935 years in England very good.[20]

Rogers sent Book I for review by the Cambridge University Press, who were not enthusiastic, criticising the text for containing a mixture of classic and modern narrative styles; and they were unable to support T.E.'s anonymity, since anonymous authorship was not only illegal but also a common publisher's cost-cutting dodge at the time.

In October 1928 the Under Secretary of State for Air, Sir Phillip Sassoon, visited the base. He had just undertaken a massive aerial journey from RAF Cattewater, Plymouth, to India, to test the feasibility of the flying boat for commercial travel. They had come via Paris, Naples, Athens, Baghdad and Basra in a Blackburn Iris II with two other aircraft, in one day seeing three of the seven wonders of the ancient world. Sassoon was a millionaire and member of the Sassoon and Rothschild families,[21] the type who 'went about without a penny in his pocket' according to Group Captain R.J. Bone, who knew both Sassoon and Lawrence in India. Bone described Sassoon as 'an enthusiastic Under Secretary who flew and understood Air Force work'.[22] He introduced his estimates quoting precise sums without looking at a note. 'This performance of memory has never been equalled', Bone recalled, '– indeed it has never been attempted by anyone else.' Sassoon was then one of England's most eligible bachelors. (He used to dress particularly flamboyantly for official events and on one occasion, whilst inspecting a University Air Squadron, arrived with an Air Chief Marshal Sir Dulline Longmore in a white hat, white trousers, white shoes, and a blue blazer. The RAF officer receiving them for parade, astonished, called the squad to attention. Afterwards Sassoon commented, 'Did you notice that moment of horror when I got out of the aeroplane? You know what was the matter with DL, don't you? He thought I'd forgotten my banjo'.)[23]

After returning to England, Sassoon (a cousin of Siegfried), published the only book he ever wrote, *The Third Route*, which described the flying boat journey. Despite his high station, Sassoon had an ability to relate easily with airmen. He had a long talk with Lawrence at Miranshah. He found him 'happy in his self chosen exile'[24] but still suffering from his fear of being dismissed. The chafing was unnecessary, as his service was extended for another five years 'of peaceful and useful obscurity'.[25]

In December a bomb dropped. A confused article was published by the London *Daily News* describing Colonel Lawrence's desire to lead an 'obscure existence' in Waziristan. It added he was learning Pushtu, implying he was intending to move to Afghanistan. It appears an airman on the camp may have seen an original Greek *Odyssey* on Lawrence's desk and erroneously concluded it was in the language. A few weeks later, on December 16th, a sensationalist Manchester newspaper, the *Empire News*, published an entirely false story that an English medical missionary had encountered Lawrence in Afghanistan. There had been a minor rebellion in the country in November and the world's press was encouraged to believe 'Colonel Lawrence' was mixed up in it. The rumours were crudely contrived, but there was very little news at that time of year and Lawrence made good copy.

At the end of December 'Boom' Trenchard resigned as Marshal of the Royal Air Force. Lawrence heard the news on the camp radio. He had a high regard for 'Boom' and regretted his passing. The *Odyssey* continued to challenge his intellect and he sent the corrected proofs of Books I to III, 14,000 words, off to Emery Walker on Christmas Day. It had taken him 500 hours, 'a very skilful literary performance . . . but not epic at all'.[26]

Following the lies about him leading a rebellion, by then spreading across the globe, the Indian Government became seriously concerned. At that time there was a strong movement amongst the British government at home and in India for the sub-continent to become a 'brown dominion'. This became even more strident when Labour won the general election in June 1929. Independence was far in the future, and, although a part of the administration had come into Indian hands, there was still unrest. In a political situation such as this the last thing His Majesty's Government in India wanted was a confrontation on its borders. Increasing speculation in the Indian and Afghanistan press began to appear about Lawrence's activities, fuelled by the Russian and Turkish Ambassadors implying there was British support for the rebellion. Sir Francis Humphreys, the British Minister in Kabul, cabled Delhi and London on 3rd January 1929 requesting that Lawrence be removed from the frontier until the uprising had ended.

The British Government in India contacted Sir Geoffrey Salmond, the Air Officer Commanding India, who sent a cable to Trenchard on January 4th requesting instructions. Trenchard remained Chief of the Air Staff and knew Lawrence could be a peg on which to hang all kinds of propaganda, but was still sympathetic to his ambitions in the RAF. So he told Salmond to withdraw T.E. from the sub-continent, but he would be allowed to go wherever he chose. Salmond was an old friend from Arabian days. His daughter Anne Baker later emphasised: 'My father helped Lawrence to return to England from Miranshah, after the crisis in Afghanistan in which Lawrence was <u>not</u> involved.'[27]

Lawrence's posting overseas was for five years, so he was delighted when he heard he would return home prematurely. On January 8th he was flown from Miranshah to Lahore and Group Captain Bone was given strict instructions to see him safely on board his ship, the SS *Rajputanah*, in Bombay docks. Bone took him down to the ship in his car, on the way asking him why he had enlisted instead of taking some post at the universities. 'He said he would have liked that but to take such a post one had to have a dinner jacket and he did not possess one.'[28]

On January 12th 1929 Lawrence embarked on the *Rajputanah* for England. Arthur Russell was also in Bombay:

> After a while I went to India and he went to India. Different parts. He was probably a couple of thousand miles from me. He was up at Drigh Road, Karachi; I was down at Pernot. Very peculiar because I used to visit Bombay quite a bit on duty. I was always on the move, and was standing down at the docks one day looking at a boat. And it was the only time when I was in India, I said to myself, 'Well, I wish I was on that'. That was the boat he was on, sending him back to England. The only time I wished I was going back was when I was looking at that boat. It was the only time I walked down to the docks as a matter of fact to look at the boats. Strange coincidence?[29]

A few months later Lawrence wrote to Russell from England, explaining what had happened. 'You probably saw the hullabaloo over me in the Press, and that I was shot out of India and home. I'm glad to be in England, but sore at the manner of the return: for I needn't tell you that I was never in Afghanistan – or outside either Karachi or Miranshah whilst stationed in them'[30] Fortunately the SS *Rajputanah* was half empty for the trip and he had a cabin to himself. Within weeks he had completed two whole Books of the *Odyssey*; the same output that had taken him seven months at Miranshah. He disembarked at Plymouth on Saturday 2nd February 1929.

In the middle of March 1929 his anonymity was deceitfully compromised. The magazine *John Bull* publicised 'Lawrence of Arabia's' authorship of the translation. T.E. was overwhelmed by despair and for two-and-a-half months he could not work at all; but at the end of April he despatched the corrected Walter proofs back to Emery Walker and by the beginning of May had finished Books VII to IX.

The work had taken much longer than he predicted: by December 1929 he was up to book XX, but was still revising XVIII and XIX. The more corrections he made, the more former thoughts would reappear, partly owing to the exhaustion brought on by his fitting the translation into his busy RAF schedule. At the end of January 1930 he returned the corrected proofs of XVIII to XX. By the end of January 1931 he and Rogers were discussing Book XXI.

Notes

1 Milman Parry and Albert Lord.

2 These were the *Linear B* tablets discovered by Arthur Evans.

3 Source: Wood. The problem with the 'Bronze Age' was that it had a chronology that varied with geographical location. It started where the copper and tin occurred as natural outcroppings, and when they were first smelted together. The first use of bronze occurred in the Near East around 3500 BC, whereas in Mycenean Greece it did not occur until 1600 BC and ended in 1200 BC. This was a period of extensive trading and great wealth. The so-called Dark Ages that followed it were characterised for the most part by poverty and illiteracy. In much of sub-Saharan Africa, where there were no tin or copper outcrops, there was no Bronze Age at all.

4 Early Greek poetry used two main types of structure: the iambic pentameter and the hexameter. These two forms determined the shape of the work.

5 *Homer's* Odyssey *and Lawrence's*, N. Postlethwaite, The Journal of the T.E. Lawrence Society, Vol.5 No. 1, Autumn 1993. Postlethwaite used the three formulaic translations quoted.

6 Ibid.

7 Source: Mack, p. 519, Fn. 42.

8 Introduction to *On Translating Homer*, Matthew Arnold, London 1905.

9 He described it as a 'pot boiler' (he was able to pay for renovations at Clouds Hill with the royalties).

10 T.E. Lawrence to C.F. Shaw, 11/6/1928. Bodleian Add. MS 45904.

11 T.E. Lawrence to Sir H.M. Trenchard, 1/5/1928.

12 Ibid.

13 *The Autobiography of Group Captain R.J. Bone*, I.W.M. The local tribes were known collectively as the Pathans, it being the RAF's duty to police the 27,000 square miles of unadministered territory that contained them.

14 On these remote posts with their inhospitable surroundings *esprit de corps* was a natural outcome. Lawrence may at last have found something of the comradeship he had been hoping for since first joining the RAF. In the background of a photograph of him reading a book in the barracks at Miranshah is a case of chained rifles. The chain was to prevent theft by the local tribesmen, who cherished the British Lee Enfield but were unable to make the bolts required to fire them. Source: Tinsley.

15 Some form of air conditioning was essential in North West India. Temperatures could soar to 112 degrees during the day and drop to below zero at night.

16 T.E. Lawrence to Charlotte F. Shaw, 25/6/28 BL Add MS 45904.

17 Interview with Ingrid Keith. TEL Soc. Journal, 1988.

18 T.E. Lawrence to Bruce Rogers, 30th May 1928. *Letters from T.E. Shaw to Bruce Rogers.* 1938. Houghton Library.

19 Rogers had known Emery Walker Ltd. since 1917. He chose them because they were not professional publishers and the best chance for anonymous authorship lay with them.

20 *Account of the* Odyssey *Project*, Ralph Isham, Bodleian Library.

21 His father was Sir Edward Sassoon, 2nd baronet, MP, and his mother Aline Caroline de Rothschild. He succeeded Edward as MP for Hythe, Kent as the youngest Member of Parliament in 1912.

22 Sassoon served as Under-Secretary for Air under Sir Samuel Hoare from 1924 to 1929, and again from 1931 to 1937. His other political office was First Commissioner for Works 1937 to 1939. In World War One he had been private Secretary to Field Marshal Haig and in 1920 he served as Parliamentary Private Secretary to Lloyd George.

23 *The Autobiography of Group Captain R.J. Bone*, I.W.M.

24 *The Third Route.* Sir Philip Sassoon.

25 Ibid.

26 T.E. Lawrence to E. Walker, 25/12/1928 from Bodleian reserve.

27 Letter to the author, 2006.

28 *The Autobiography of Group Captain R.J. Bone.* I.W.M.

29 A. Russell: interview with author, 12/1985.

30 T.E. Lawrence to A. Russell, Plymouth, 20/3/1929. Private collection, courtesy *T.E.Lives* magazine.

Lawrence on the Miranshah landing ground, one of the pictures taken by Fl Lt S.J. Smetham. He cradles his wrist in a habitual pose, having broken it in an accident at Cranwell in 1926.

CHAPTER SEVEN

The Book XXI Controversy

This chapter, it must be confessed, is something of an aside, treating as it does with an academic squabble between classical historians; but it does reveal something more about the way Lawrence thought: in the reliance upon his own experiences, the tenacity, in the openness to new ways of thinking, and at the same time, the obduracy.

Early in January 1931 Lawrence began to disagree with Walters over certain archaeological and technical questions in the translation. He refused to accept Walters' authority or that of any other translator, arguing that his knowledge gained whilst digging in Syria and Egypt before the War and his experiences in Arabia and the Mediterranean more than adequately qualified him for the task. His disagreement particularly concerned Book XXI, which many scholars consider the finest book in the tale. Here, and in the next book, the suitors of Penelope were despatched in a final blood letting. For many years Book XXI had been the focus of academic controversy, scholars producing conflicting theories to explain the sense of the text. It concerns a ceremony termed 'The Trial of the Bow' or 'The Trial of the Axes'.

Lawrence's time was limited by a deadline he had promised Rogers: he had to complete the translation by the end of August. In 1931 two disastrous events occurred that had effects on his work. In February a Blackburn Iris III flying boat crashed in Plymouth Sound, killing nine men. He assisted in the rescue and was a witness at the public inquest. One of the factors that may have made the disaster worse than it could have been was the inefficiency of the RAF's seaplane tenders attending the accident. As a result, T.E. spent much of his time in the first seven months of 1931 conducting the trials of a much faster tender design, aimed specifically at the Schneider Trophy race that September. This limited the time he had to spend on the translation. At the beginning of August the results of his labours stood in a boatyard at Hythe, Southampton. A fire on 3rd August burnt out all the tenders bar one. The only positive result was that he had the whole of August free to work on Homer.

Lawrence first contested Walters' conclusions in a letter of 31st January. He had returned books XVIII to XX and included Walters' corrections. With Book XXI however, he had more difficulty. At that time he thought his service in the RAF was almost over.

I return XVIII-XX, with some minor changes and the necessary embodying of the W. corrections. . . . Only I have refused to accept his championing of the ancient theory of hollow-bladed axes. The metaphor from ship-building seems as clear as daylight. I have odd knowledges that qualify me to understand the *Odyssey*, and odd experiences that interpret it to me. Therefore a certain headiness in rejecting help . . . I have no more for you yet. My R.A.F. interruption is almost over, *pro tem*, and I hope to get XXI into shape before another week is passed.[1]

This was the first time he had challenged Walter's authority. In view of the fact that Book XXI took him seven months, his reticence may have been a mistake. Walters was Keeper of Greek and Roman Antiquities at the British Museum and an authoritative Hellenic scholar,[2] but it was his archaeology that Lawrence felt was in error: 'You may have thought me cavalier in preferring my own ways to W's professional suggestions, sometimes: not his verbal suggestions but his archaeology. Yet, actually I'm in as strong a position vis-à-vis Homer as most of his translators.'[3]

The passage that led to this disagreement describes the solution Penelope found to having seven suitors pursuing her. The failure of her husband, Odysseus, to return from the Trojan Wars had meant the suitors were becoming increasingly frustrated. Her earlier deception to offset their attentions was exposed and since Odysseus had not returned, she had to choose one suitor. To solve this problem she employed an ancient court ceremony named the 'Trial of the Bow'. Here is Lawrence's translation:

> Presently will dawn the illfamed day which severs me from the house of Odysseus. To introduce it I am staging a contest with those axes my lord (when at home) used to set up, all twelve standing together, like an alley of oaken bilge-blocks, before standing well back to send an arrow through the lot. Now will I put this same feat to my suitors: and the one who easiest strings the bow with his bare hands and shoots through the twelve axes, after him will I go, forsaking this house of my marriage.[4]

Lawrence's language here is precise, and unadorned; he uses the vulgar colloquialism, 'lot'. Book XXI described the proceedings. Before the contest could begin, Telemachus arranges the axes: 'hollowing one long trench for them all, getting them exactly in line and forming the earth about them with his foot. Every onlooker was amazed at how regularly he set them, despite having never done it before.'[5] So the 12 court axes were set in a line, with a trench dug to hold their bases. As the axes stood upright the suitor sat at one end of the line, 20 feet away, and was supposed to shoot an arrow through the iron of one axe head after another. He also had to restring a recurved bow before he did this. None succeed with the stringing, let alone the axe-heads: 'The young warmed the bow and did their best to string it, but failed. They showed themselves not nearly strong enough.'[6]

Odysseus returns from his travels disguised as a swineherd. He reveals his identity and subsequently undertakes the test:

. . .changing the bow to his right hand he proved the string, which sang to his pluck, sharp like a swallow's cry . . . he snatched up the keen arrow which lay naked there upon his table . . . and set it firmly upon the grip of the bow. He notched it to the string and drew; and from his place upon his settle, just as he sat, sent the arrow with so straight an aim that he did not foul one single axe. The bronze-headed shaft threaded them clean, from the leading helve onward, till it issued from the portal of the last ones.[7]

The problem scholars have wrestled with ever since the poem was written was how Odysseus managed to perform such a feat. What exactly had he *done*? Various theories were put forward:

Theory 1: Butcher and Lang, 1928; the axe-heads had apertures

This was, apparently, supported by H.B. Walters. Lawrence had heard of this theory and referred to it in his letter of 25th February:

…Yes I know the Butcher and Lang view of the axes trial. All other scholars have followed them, more or less.[8]

In Butcher and Lang's 1928 translation was an end-note containing sketches of five different axes: three were with open-work blades. If the holes were enlarged one could shoot through them. Lawrence discounted the theory having found similar copper axe-heads before the war. He told Rogers that it would have been impossible to shoot through one axe-head at twenty yards, let alone twelve.

Lawrence's sketch that accompanied his dismissal of the Butcher and Lang theory of the axe-trial. He had found 'copper axe-heads with openings in them like that' before the war. One 'could not have shot through one of them . . . much less 12'.

Theory 2: A. Goebel, 1876; double-headed

This was also presented by Butcher and Lang. Goebel's idea was that if a row of 12 double-headed axes, in which the two blades almost met, formed a ring at the top of the handle the contestant could shoot through the two 'ears' of the axe head. Examples of these axes were found by Heinrich Schliemann at Mycenae, and Arthur Evans during his excavations at Knossos on Crete. Lawrence drew a sketch of one in his letter showing an arrow passing 'through' it, but he also discounted the theory:

> Whereas your suggestion of shooting through the ears of 12 axes so, it would require a slow motion cinema to prove that his arrow passed so and no higher: and the trajectory and angle of stance would both complicate the point.[9]

Theory 3: Butcher and Lang; hafts removed

This was suggested in antiquity, fell out of favour and was then revived. Here the handle was removed and the axe-head was stuck in the ground by the blade. The archer then shot through the handle hole. The low height of the heads seems to discount this theory, since Odysseus was seated when he performed the shot. But Lawrence found difficulty because the handles did not resemble bilge-blocks. He thought Homer could not have meant 'only axe-heads' for

One of the roundels Rogers designed for the book, based on Greek pottery motifs. (via Roger Friedman Rare Book Studio)

The talented American book designer Bruce Rogers, who designed Lawrence's *Odyssey* translation. (Estate of Bruce Rogers)

The bull's horns religious symbols that Arthur Evans found all over the Palace of Knossos and dubbed 'horns of consecration'.

Lawrence's sketch of the double bladed Mycenean axe with the arrow passing between its 'ears': 'it would require a slow motion cinema to prove his [Odysseus's] arrow passed so and no higher'.

shooting through the handle-holes as then he would not have referred to them as 'bilge-blocks of oak'.[10] bilge-blocks being almost as high as a man and always coming in pairs. He also pointed out that most ancient archers with these short bows shot kneeling.

Theory 4: Denys Page; a line inverted

The Greek word for axe means not only a cutting tool, but also a ceremonial cult object. Antiquarian scholar Denys Page concluded: 'There is one great difference between the household-axe and the cult-axe – a difference which explains why axes should be selected to compose a target for the exhibition shot.[11] Since the timber handle of the household axes perished, none have survived intact, but a few ceremonial axes, having a haft of iron or bronze, have. In the Minoan and Mycenean period these were hung upside down on Palace walls. The bases of these hafts were often pierced with a ring for suspension. The theory, presented by Page long after Lawrence's death, was that the line of 12 double-headed axes was placed upside down and the archer shot through the suspension rings. This would account for the need for a trench. The line of rings might appear too narrow, but Arthur Evans found one axe four feet long with a ring five inches in diameter. Lawrence said that the axe would not be a grown man's height but that 'a four foot axe-handle would be ample' [12] – most battle axes were 4½ to 5 feet long.

Theory 5: Lawrence's solution; rows of six

The axes were not in a perfectly straight line: '. . . the text shows that they were not put up with a plumb line and spirit level, only stamped firmly into a trench scratched by Telemachus into the earth floor of the hall.' Telemachus, he concluded, had not set out axes before so the blades must have 'been in only a rough line.'[13] His explanation was simple, two rows of axes, six a side 'Nothing else fits all the Greek and yet remains a possible feat. I admit that possibility is not what the public prefer . . . only I feel that the *Odyssey* should, as far as possible, make sense.'[14] By shooting between the rows of axes an archer could shoot through all the iron blades. Some discount this theory, arguing it does not correspond to the original Greek. Russo, Fernandez and Hanebeck discounted it. Lawrence, seeing the description as implying only a single row of targets, apparently noticed a discrepancy and alluded to it in his letter of 25th February, 'Nothing else fits *all* the Greek and yet remains a possible feat.' *All* would include Chapter XIX, where Penelope mentioned '*an alley* of oaken bilge bocks.' Lawrence confirmed this in the same letter 'A 5 foot 6 inch man standing 20 yards off could easily shoot through *an alley* of them.' The definition of an *alley* is a narrow passage or lane, a narrow way bounded on two sides. Lawrence's arrangement of two rows of axes fits this more than any other and explains how Odysseus was able to shoot between the irons. However, Lawrence's arrangement, as with all the other theories, bore no resemblance to 'oaken bilge-blocks' in any form. He pointed out to Rogers that bilge-blocks always came in pairs, they supported both the stern and the fore part of the bilges of a ship. He also said in his January letter that there was 'a clear metaphor from ship building'. [15] If six ships were laid in two rows, one behind the other, and the hulls removed to leave only the bilge-blocks, then, viewed on end, an alley two bilge-blocks wide and six rows deep of each would remain.

It is possible Lawrence arrived at this theory through his work at Carchemish before the War. On 1st March 1902 in a ceremonial room in the excavations at the Minoan palace of Knossos, Crete, the archaeologist Arthur Evans discovered two pairs of religious symbols resembling the horns of the bull. At the centre of each of these horns he found a hole. He concluded this was to take the shaft of a double-headed axe.[16] This may have been the origin of Lawrence's answer to the axe shot. On top of the timber base of each bilge-block is a set of horn-like crucks. Replace the blocks with twelve Knossos horns, each carrying a double-headed axe and you have what bears a resemblance to 'an alley of oaken bilge-blocks'. Lawrence may have arrived at this conclusion from his work in Syria. D. G. Hogarth replaced Evans as curator of the Ashmolean Museum in Oxford in 1909, where one of his young charges was Lawrence. In 1911 Hogarth invited him out to excavate at Carchemish, where the foreman was the Greek Cypriot Gregori Antoniou, with whom Hogarth had worked on Crete.[17] It is postulated that Gregori and Hogarth discussed the findings at Knossos with Lawrence, laying the foundations of T.E.'s axe theory.

There are several flaws in this theory:
1) Homer is normally thought to evoke the world of Mycenean Greece, not earlier Minoan Crete.
2) Evans's reconstructions at Knossos were an early 20th-century, hypothetical view of things, not actual archaeological evidence.
3) Evans believed in Minoan superiority, such that Mycenean civilization originated on Crete and the Greek islands, a theory that has later been discounted.
4) He became obsessed with the double-axe motif and attributed an unwarranted religious significance to it that is not supported by archaeologists today.[18]

So the Knossos horns' theory is flawed in that it solves a mystery of the Mycenean period, with Minoan evidence.

In his February 25th letter Lawrence also described the bow used in the contest. This was a Scythian bow, the stringing of which he thought was more difficult than the trial itself. He suspected that they were making 'too much of the shooting test'. As there was no great astonishment at it in Homer's text he concluded that 'stringing the bow' was much more difficult:

> These re-curved bows (I was handling one yesterday) are most cunning things built up of sinew and birch bark and wood and horn. Relaxed they are an oval about 30 inches by 18: strung they are 4½ to 5 feet long.[19]

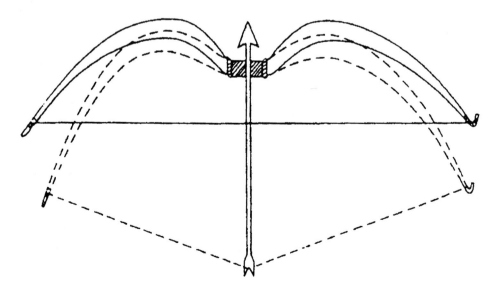

The Scythian bow; a mighty trial of strength to string.

The Mycenean bow was smaller than the medieval longbow and because of its reflexed shape, it required great strength to string it, even if warmed beforehand and, in the *Odyssey*, only Odysseus succeeded. Lawrence's understanding was that they were strung half sitting, 'putting the one end between the thighs and pulling down on the other horn, whilst pressing down the centre grip.'[19] When it was bent right out and over the other side one slipped the string up the blade and notched it. But Russo, Fernandez and Hanebeck's description was different: 'The archer. . . put one end of the bow over one knee, the middle under the opposite thigh, and pulled up the other end.'[20]

Rogers had returned Chapter XXI to Lawrence with his and Walters' changes. At the beginning of August 1931 T.E. took a month's leave and went to his old lair at Barton Street, to try and finish off the chapter by the end of the month. By that time he was 'sicker than ever of the great work'.[21] He worked on the book day and night until the 12th but it remained unfinished. Despite toiling seventeen hours a day, the book was only creeping along and he wondered if it would ever end. During this period he checked Rogers and Walters' addenda and added a few minor alterations of his own.[22]

In August he took a few days off to visit the Smiths at Thurlestone on the South Devon coast, then returned to London. On 15th August his leave was unexpectedly cut short by the Air Ministry. He finished the chapter, then returned it to Roger's secretary. He had struggled with Chapter XXI for seven months and found XXII and XXIII nearly as arduous and slow. Although he had completed the final page of the *Odyssey* by 15th August, he still had to correct the returned proofs for Books XXII to XXIV. Rogers told him Book XXI was 'a disappointment' and Lawrence had to agree, thinking 'it was the worst Homeric writing of all'.[23]

He had become frustrated by flaws he perceived in the original work. Although he thought the Homer of the *Iliad* had an epic quality, the *Odyssey* lacked this, it felt unreal and had little drama, despite being concise and replete with detail, it lacked *integritas*. The poem had no overall structure: the final books did not sit with with the rest of the poem, suggesting they had different authors. In the resolution of the story, he found uncertainty.

It was not until March 1932 that all the ends were tied up. After over four years, the ordeal was ended. He had almost fulfilled Rogers remit, a realistic, up-to-date, vibrant translation, but Lawrence remained dissatisfied. The translation was ground-breaking in its realism, reflecting his own experiences, as he said it would. But this worked best in the militaristic passages, and elsewhere the interpretation could be completely askew. Its initial publication in America was anonymous and received little interest. When his authorship was revealed, the book's sales inevitably increased. Although at the time it was acclaimed for its realism, the translation has since been declared to have numerous errors.

It took Lawrence nearly forty months to complete the translation of Homer's epic. In order to produce the effect Rogers wanted – similar dynamics to the

Seven Pillars – Lawrence adopted techniques that were unnecessarily laborious. Like *Revolt*, his *Odyssey* was a child of the style of *Seven Pillars*. He imagined that his archaeological investigations in Syria, the war in Arabia and his marine craft work in the Air Force would all give him a much better insight into the author's mind than any of the hide-bound scholars who would normally have attempted such work. He finished it after his testing of the RAF 200, demanding work. The interruptions he suffered, such as the Schneider Trophy competition and the various seaplane crashes, meant that maintaining an overview was extremely difficult, but his success despite this shows how committed he was to fulfilling Rogers' ambition.

Notes

1 T.E. Lawrence to Bruce Rogers, 31/1/1931. DG

2 *T.E. Lawrence and the Translating of the* Odyssey, *1928-1931*. J.M. Wilson, The Journal of the T.E. Lawrence Society, Vol. III, No. 2, Spring 1994.

3 T.E. Lawrence to Bruce Rogers, 31/1/1931. DG.

4 *The* Odyssey *of Homer,* Book XIX, translated by T.E. Shaw. Oxford University Press, 1935.

5 *The* Odyssey *of Homer,* Book XXI, translated by T.E. Shaw. Oxford University Press, 1935.

6 Ibid.

7 Ibid.

8 T.E. Lawrence to Bruce Rogers, 25/2/1931. DG.

9 Ibid.

10 Ibid.

11 *Folktales in Homer's* Odyssey, Denys Page.

12 T.E. Lawrence to Bruce Rogers, 25/2/1931. DG.

13 Ibid.

14 Ibid.

15 T.E.'s letter of 31/1/1931 intimates that H.B. Walters attached little importance to the connection with ship-building.

16 *Minotour.*

17 Ibid.

18 Dr Susan Walker, Dept. of Antiquities, Ashmolean Museum, Oxford. Communication with author, 2006. The museum further commented that many of Evans' conjectures are now regarded as fanciful. 'The Aegean Bronze Age remains a highly controversial period.'

19 T.E. Lawrence to Bruce Rogers, 25/2/1931. DG.

20 *A Commentary on Homer's* Odyssey *Vol. 3*, Russo/Fernandez-Latiano/Havebeck. Clarendon Press, Oxford, 1992.

21 T.E. Lawrence to Clare Sydney Smith, 3/8/1931.

22 There is no record of what any of these were.

23 T.E. Lawrence to Bruce Rogers, 30/10/1931. Houghton Library, Harvard.

CHAPTER EIGHT

Mount Batten

When Lawrence returned to England in 1929 he had been out of the country for two years. He returned to a nation in the grip of the Great Depression and must have been happy to be in employment. His news value was even more of a burden to him when he returned home than when abroad, as it would be for the rest of his life. Mount Batten marked the beginning of a new, more successful life for him, during which he did some extremely useful work. With a less understanding C.O. this may never have happened. As it was, Sydney Smith was astute enough to realise he had a unique opportunity with a man of Lawrence's abilities on the station and employed him to the best of his ability. It was Smith's encouragement that led to Lawrence's work later with Scott-Paine. He began the transfer from clerical and literary work to devoting all his energies to boat development. It was certainly Clare Sydney Smith's relationship with him and their trips around the local coastline that contributed to his mental healing. (The darker side to his character, practically unknown to his friends, would manifest itself in a bizarre holiday in 1930.) Mount Batten was the setting for some of the most important work in his life, work that some say had more long-term practical value than any of his successes in Arabia. But the Lawrence of Arabia was a different creature to Aircraftman Shaw of the RAF, and the achievements of each cannot be measured against the other in any meaningful way.

A newsreel film was made of his return from India. This shows, in poor quality monochrome, a solitary aircraftman wrapped in a greatcoat and service cap, descending a rope ladder into a waiting pinnace moored directly below.[1] This is one of the few films of Lawrence that still exist. By 1929 he was known throughout the world; the post-war cinema films of Lowell Thomas had been a distraction from the awful wartime destruction. In London alone a million people watched the show *With Allenby in Palestine and Lawrence in Arabia*. The Prime Minister and Cabinet watched, as did General Allenby, the Emir Feisal, and many who taken part in the desert campaign. There was a Royal Command Performance at Balmoral. For the rest of his life Lawrence's fame pursued him like a dog snapping at his heels. His return to England, in keeping with this, was a media event.

Saturday 2nd February 1929 was a foggy day with very poor visibility in Plymouth Sound. There was drizzle and a strong southerly wind, low stratus covered the sky. The pinnace stopped on the other side of the ship allowing Lieutenant-Commander D'Arcy-Evans and Wing Commander Smith to board the *Rajputanah*. The boat then went around to the other side where Lawrence, informed of the plan to deceive the press by radio, was waiting. On the opposite side the remaining passengers disembarked into a P&O tender as hoards of press boats milled around eager for his appearance. But on Lawrence's side there was a delay when a rope ladder fouled in the doorway and the ruse did not work. As soon as he disembarked he was whisked away.

As the boat drove towards Sutton Harbour he was handed a month's supply of mail and immediately threw all of it into Plymouth Sound. Smith, who commanded the nearby flying boat and seaplane base at RAF Cattewater was piloting. Rather than catching a train at Plymouth to London, where he had to meet Trenchard, Smith drove him to Newton Abbot, where they entrained. It was the P&O boat train from Plymouth containing the press, and, although by this time Lawrence despised their intrusion into his life, the mishap amused him. He was subsequently assigned to RAF Cattewater at Plymouth at his own request, the Air Ministry allowing he could be based anywhere on the condition it was not near London.

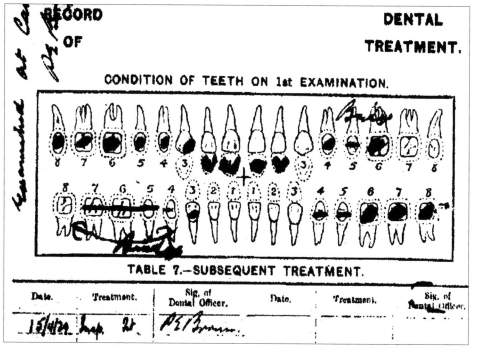

Lawrence's dental chart 1929. By the time of the inspection of 15th April 1929 by Flight Lieutenant P.E. Brown at Cattewater there were marked signs of further deterioration: 16 fillings with six teeth removed. Teeth 7 and 8 of the upper jaw appear to have been replaced. By early 1930, according to Robert Graves, Lawrence had a 'mouthful of gold'. (National Archives)

His new C.O., Sydney William Smith, was 41, the same age, and coincidentally exactly the same height.[2] It could not have hurt their relationship. He and his wife Clare had first met Lawrence in Egypt in 1921 at the Cairo Conference. Five years after T.E.'s death, Clare would publish *The Golden Reign*, one of the most endearing books ever written about Lawrence. In it she recalled that her first meeting, with the quiet, withdrawn, fair-haired Englishman had little effect upon her – so characteristic of Lawrence. The next day though, the impression he made was much stronger. Lawrence arrived at Groppi's Restaurant where they were dining and came straight to their table. His attractive Irish voice and quiet presence now struck her.[4]

Even before he arrived in England, Parliament had discussed his use of a false name. This preceded his posting to Cattewater, when he was staying temporarily back in Herbert Baker's flat in central London. On 30th January[5] Ernest Thurtle, the Labour M.P. for Shoreditch, asked the Secretary of State for Air Sir Samuel Hoare whether it was known that Aircraftman Shaw had enlisted under a pseudonym; a nom de paix to replace one of the most famous noms de guerre in history. Hoare replied that Lawrence's identity was known when he transferred from the Army to the Air Force under the name of Shaw. Since he preferred to be known by that name 'no objection was seen to his being accepted for service under it'.[6]

But Thurtle wasn't satisfied. He did not know Lawrence and was inclined to believe the rumour that the man was an imperialist spy, 'being used for sinister purposes'. Thurtle later realised how foolish his assumptions were, but the secretive nature of the man's homecoming only served to reinforce his suspicions. Thurtle did not understand the trouble the tabloid press had caused the British Government in India. His assumptions were not those of an isolated crank: in January Lawrence had been burned in effigy by anti-imperialist Socialists on Tower Hill.

When he heard of this persecution, Lawrence was disturbed by two possibilities: first that he would again be asked to leave the Air Force, and second – the more dreadful – that his illegitimacy would be revealed, which could have serious consequences for his family. On 5th February he wrote to E.M. Forster from Barton Street. He told Forster that he was 'being hunted . . . When the cry dies down I'll come out of my hole and see people – unless of course the cry doesn't die down, and the catchers get my skin.'[7]

Thurtle continued to pose questions in the Commons. On the 6th he asked Hoare if it was customary for the RAF to accept recruits under a known pseudonym and Hoare replied that it was hardly 'customary' but it was well known that men did enlist under assumed names, for a variety of reasons.[8] The regulations provided that if a man had done so he could have his true name recorded by making a statutory declaration.

Some time after this Lawrence decided to resolve the situation.[9] In the Order Paper of the Commons Thurtle had indicated he would be asking further questions.

Barton Street was little more than five minutes away from the House of Commons and Lawrence went there in an unsuccessful bid to find him. After Thurtle returned from the Commons that evening he was interrupted by an unwelcome telephone call. He did not catch the name the speaker gave, so he asked him to repeat it and Lawrence spelled out the name 'Shaw'. Thurtle furiously complained that he did not know him, but Lawrence's calculated reply was soft enough to assuage the angry MP: 'You don't know me, but you've been asking questions about me in Parliament.'[10]

Thurtle suspected the caller was an imposter. Lawrence remained good humoured and arranged to meet him in the House. The next day, when the diminutive figure appeared, the M.P.'s doubts were cast aside. He described the man with the unimpressive uniform as having 'an almost devastating air of intelligence about him and a great poise of manner.'[11] In the smoking-room downstairs, fellow Socialists James Maxton M.P, and Lieutenant-Colonel Cecil Malone (who had known him in Arabia) joined them. The meeting soon became amicable, but Lawrence's discovery of his illegitimacy had deeply affected his thinking and he explained to them his fears,[12] answering their questions freely. What they could not extract from him was what led him to abandon the glittering prizes before him and join the ranks. Thurtle found 'There was something enigmatic about him that bewildered us all . . . His mind was of a very unusual order indeed, and his sense of values was more unusual still.'[13] He was later severely reprimanded by the Air Ministry for the Commons visit. He lent Thurtle a copy of *Seven Pillars* and an early edition of *The Mint* and advised him later to be 'uncommonly discreet', particularly with *The Mint's* return.[14]

At the War Office there was consternation over his change of name and whether he should be allowed to retain his Lieutenant Colonelcy. On 6th March Mr Widdows in the office of the Under Secretary of State wrote to the Air Ministry asking what their views were on the procedure to be adopted:

> Sir
> I am commanded by the Army Council to state that it is usual to withdraw the rank previously granted in the cases of ex-officers enlisting in the Army, during the period covered by such enlistment, and restore it on completion of service in the ranks, should such service have been of a satisfactory nature.
> No action has so far been taken in the case of Lieutenant-Colonel Lawrence, as the statement made by Sir Samuel Hoare was the first official intimation that Lieutenant-Colonel Lawrence had so enlisted.[15]

On receipt an official at the Air Ministry filed a note on the 8th to the new Chief of the Air Staff (CAS) Sir John Salmond 'He is no longer Lawrence and possibly the question of retention of rank does not arise.'[16] Salmond said he would make enquiries. Ministry official J.A. Webster, was asked to prepare a letter from a minute to be issued on the 12th by Salmond. This he later did with slight emendations. The original stated:

A.M.P.[17]

Will you please have a letter sent to the War Office on the following lines:

In the first case, it is not correct to say that the first official intimation that Lieut. Colonel Lawrence had enlisted was the statement made by Sir Samuel Hoare as No. 7876598 Pte T.E. Shaw was transferred from the Royal Tank Corps to the Royal Air Force and the correspondence that took place between the Adjutant-General and Sir Hugh Trenchard will show that the War Office had full official cognizance of the whole of this case.

Secondly, the War Office might like to know that his name is not Lawrence but is now Shaw and that he never uses the rank of Lieutenant Colonel Lawrence himself: this is done by the press, but that is not his fault, and we should consider it extremely unwise to withdraw his commissioned rank after all these years as it would only make for greater publicity and press comment. We therefore hope that no action will be taken.[18]

After Lawrence and Smith arrived in London they discussed the matter of his next station with Trenchard. Smith recalled the conversation many years later:

Following Shaw's conversation, the C.A.S. told him to go on leave and he would, in the meantime, think over his posting. Lawrence however wrote to Sir Hugh and said he would like to be posted to my station at Mount Batten since he was interested in flying boats and marine craft in general. The C.A.S. eventually agreed to his request and he reported to me there in 1928.[19]

He was allowed to take a month's leave before travelling to Plymouth and appeared at Cattewater on March 10th 1929. Clare Smith remembered 'a shining and powerful Brough motor-cycle roared to a standstill at the gates of Cattewater.'[20] T.E. dismounted in peaked cap, goggles, and gauntlet gloves with a small dispatch-case slung on his back framing a uniform of smart Air Force blue. The bike was a 1000cc Brough SS80 Superior, a gift from the Shaws at the instigation of George Bernard's wife Charlotte. Its value was equivalent to three years pay and Lawrence accepted it reluctantly, fearing that he would feel too indebted to Charlotte, who had showered him with gifts for years. The Shaws were immensely fond of T.E. and Charlotte, unbeknown to her husband, had become a close confidante.

The base was a tiny station on a promontory projecting into Plymouth Sound, with around 100 airmen and six huts; a popular camp, but communication with the mainland was difficult. Water lay 60 yards to the north and the beach at high tide was 30 yards southwards. On the second day he started work. Two RAF

Squadrons were based at Cattewater from 1929 to 1934, 204 and 209. Lawrence and Smith were not attached to a squadron but on the staff of the station itself. Lawrence's duties included cleaning the barracks he shared with twenty other airmen, daily drill, and four hours on and four off duty watch. He also rowed out to check the flying boats' moorings, fixed on riding lights in rough seas and checked for anchor drag.

On 3rd October 1929 R.A.F. Cattewater became R.A.F. Mount Batten at the suggestion of Smith and T.E.[21] The name derived from the pier on the opposite side of the promontory, the name 'Batten' from a Captain Batten who had been in charge of the defences during a siege of the city in 1643. Lawrence also designed the squadron motif, a cormorant with wings outstretched perching on a rock.

On Wednesday 20th March T.E. wrote to Russell saying he was glad to be back in England, but not with the manner of the return, as he was never in Afghanistan. He had visited Clouds Hill on the way down from London and found it 'as lovely as ever'. His service time had just been extended to 1935 and he was pleased with the camp, which felt comfortable, being 'very small and quiet'. He told Russell he had received a 1929 Brough presented to him by friends. 'He did not name them'.[22] After less than a month he wrote to Jack Easton:

> Dear Corporal,
> You'll envy me, here. There is an H.Q. Flight (Office and motorboat and transport personnel, & W/T) and a squadron under W/Cdr. Smith. About 150 in all. They are going to add a second squadron, later. This one has no flying boats yet, but hopes for them, this month. It is a quiet, decent station; not windy, but all new as yet. We'll see in six months how it shapes. I'm typing DRO's for a living. What a change you'll say. That's about all I do, too. But I'm to go to marine section and do something on a motor boat, this month.

For nine days of the first three weeks at Cattewater he had been on station fire piquet duties but more interesting work came along when Smith appointed him to the Marine Craft Section. He was given an office over the workshops with Flt. Lt. Jinman, the station Engineering Officer, and immediately was told to organise a workshop routine. As the workshop was completely empty, he protested he was only an aircraft hand and so not used to such responsibility. He had to deal with a mountain of paperwork. These were simple but irksome clerical tasks, like typing out daily routine orders, and with other tasks like standing station orders it meant a lot of paperwork.

Subsequently, when Clare Smith visited, the workshops were a hive of activity. His office was at the top of a steep stair like a ladder and was 'a long, low room lined with rough shelves around the walls for storing instruments and files.'[23] He received any amount of requests for inspecting, editing or prefacing unknown authors' books after *Seven Pillars* was published, and many of these lay scattered haphazardly about the room. It had a rough wooden floor, two small wooden stools, and the only comfortable piece of furniture was a revolving office chair. His desk, a purloined barrack room table, stood covered with files and other stationery in the centre.

He often had to sweep out the office after morning parade. Sometimes he would deliberately wait until the men were dismissed, then, as they passed underneath, would surprise them with a shower of dirt and dust.[24] On another occasion after parade he is said to have picked up the shaft of a heavy sledge-hammer, head uppermost and threw it into the air. He smacked the handle with a sharp blow in mid flight so that it turned a complete revolution in mid-air. He then neatly caught the shaft and lowered it head-first to the floor. Other airman tried to do this but failed hopelessly. Asked to repeat the performance he said 'I only do that sort of thing once, next time I may not be so lucky'.[25]

Later in March, as he had promised, Lawrence made a point of visiting Jack Easton's wife and her two children one evening on the Plymouth Barbican. She had been ill, and looked 'washed out, but well.' He told Easton:

A quaint district that Barbican. It is full of old streets. Your house must be pretty old itself. I was in a room on the first floor. In a fortnight or so I hope to go across again. This time I'll try and warn Mrs. Easton that I'm coming . . . I'd been to dinner with Lady Astor and we talked a lot about Plymouth. She's going to spend May here fighting the general election. I rather think she's nervous about getting the push. All the beer interests are down on her for being too TT [teetotal]. A fine creature all the same, Nancy is.[26]

Nancy Astor, M.P. for Sutton East in Plymouth, lived within sight of Mount Batten in what is now the Mayor's Parlour on top of Plymouth Hoe.[27] The Astors had bought the grand five-storey Victorian terraced house at 3 Eliot Terrace that faced the Sound in 1919. Some said the south facing stone balcony had the grandest view in Europe. Batten was less than a mile to the south-east of it. That Lawrence and Nancy 'got on' is surprising: but their divergent characters and backgrounds acted to attract each other. She had first corresponded with Lawrence in 1922, requesting a copy of *Seven Pillars*. She was a naturally witty, sociable extrovert, who liked to be the centre of attention, the opposite of the withdrawn, introspective T.E. However, they both shared a disturbed childhood with a dominant parent, a large family and a compassion for the underdog. They also disliked physical contact and practised an outwardly celibate existence in later life. Nancy called him 'Airman' and Lawrence addressed Nancy as 'Peeress', sharing a simple affection for each other. In the third week of April he passed Nancy on his Brough in Plymouth and she screamed 'Aircraftman' at him from her car, later inviting him to her country home at Cliveden on the Thames. But he declined, telling her he was happier staying on the base where he felt he belonged.

Aerial view of RAF Mount Batten seaplane station in 1933/34, facing north. The Napoleonic Martello Tower in the centre of the peninsula, the two seaplane hangers, the slipways on the east side and the pier to the west still exist today. On the opposite side to the Cattewater to the north is Plymouth Hoe. where the Astors lived. The south side of the peninsula now contains a large housing development. The small road to the south was the only land route to the mainland. Lawrence was billeted at one time in a house near there, to the south of the hangars. (RAF Museum)

150 airmen lived at Cattewater and were known as 'Lady Astor's Air Force' as she had arranged for many of them to be posted to the promontory on compassionate grounds, fifty because they were married locally. She often went out on T.E.'s pillion. In 1986 an eyewitnesses recalled

> In 1931 a friend and I were in Crownhill when a Brough motorcycle pulled up at the traffic lights. I looked and saw that the motorcyclist was T.E. Lawrence . . . His passenger on the pillion seat, also wearing leathers and other motorcycle gear was Lady Astor.[28]

Many years later, Nancy told the witness that 'His Lordship [Waldorf] would be very angry if he knew. Only my maid knew that I went out as Lawrence's passenger.'[29] She realized he liked taking her as a passenger because she would balance on the seat without touching him: both disliked physical contact.[30]

Lawrence stayed at Mount Batten for over four years. Three of these, from August 1929 until October 1931, were the period he described as 'The Golden Reign'. According to some biographers, including Clare Smith, his special friendship with the Smiths was accepted without resentment by most of the RAF men at Mount Batten as he never used it to gain any special favours.[31] But it does seem that certain officers intensely disliked his presence in the ranks, some reports stating that the 'pull' he had with authority caused rancour. Gerald Wasley, an historian of Mount Batten, disagreed with Clare Smith in *The Golden Reign*: he thought that Lawrence certainly did receive special favours at Cattewater.

Although he was kind and generous and did not talk down to his fellow aircraftmen, the differences between them were obvious. His unkempt hair irritated many: whilst most airmen had to have it shaven to the skin, Lawrence's stuck up from the roots and was only cut once a month. He shared Hut 7 with 14 deckhands and coxswains who tended the Supermarine Southampton and Scapa flying boats and motor launches in the Sound. He sometimes ate in the NAAFI canteen but was always standing up and preferred using a spoon to a knife and fork.[32] He used his influence to ensure that the airmen's mess had dining tables, stainless steel cutlery, water-jugs and glasses, white table-cloths and flowers on the tables. Although he could rib people mercilessly with a perfectly straight face, he was never seen to laugh, and disdained shaking hands. His locker was full of books and contained one of the few private radio sets on the station. This upset one new Warrant Officer to such an extent that he tried to put Lawrence on a charge, but this was not processed as the man found himself immediately transferred to another station. Other officers were known to step respectfully out of Lawrence's way and even salute him at Mount Batten.

Sydney Smith employed him in the Marine Craft Section at Cattewater after noticing an unusual tenseness and nervousness in him when he first arrived there, which he thought the work would eradicate. The station motor-boats suffered from engine trouble and were out of date and inadequate and Smith thought Lawrence would be more gainfully employed working on these than on normal duties. Lawrence, not content with second-hand knowledge, began stripping down the engines to study every detail. This tendency to learn by doing rather than merely absorbing knowledge, is, some say, the true mark of genius. He soon realised that the craft were of the wrong design altogether for their purpose, being expensive to run, unduly slow, over-crewed, and generally antiquated.

Lawrence told his biographer Liddell Hart that he had only 'done an ordinary Aircraftman's job until the Schneider Cup', so that his transition from 'ink to oil'[33] (his concentration on mechanical work rather than literature) did not take place until around the time of the competition in September 1929. However, it would seem that this statement represented a characteristic downplaying of his work. Clare Smith recalled that he had 'all the technical correspondence turned over to him'[34] early on at Plymouth. This was work that was 'well beyond the level of responsibility normally accorded to an aircraftman'[35] and led to some radical developments well before the Schneider races.

Cattewater was a flying boat station. Although seaplanes and flying boats obviously had advantages in not requiring a hard landing ground, they needed specialized maintenance vessels to service them. As time progressed and aircraft design advanced, so the vessels attending them became more sophisticated, requiring greater speed, power, and storage. Most of the RAF launches were ex-RNAS boats, 35-foot launches, with some 50-foot paraffin driven Kelvins. These were inadequately powered for the work, a fact that became obvious during the 1927 Schneider Cup. Here, for the first time, Britain was represented by a Service team whose sophisticated machines required much faster servicing than the old aircraft. So in 1928 the Admiralty, on the RAF's behalf, began searching for newer marine craft to replace the existing ones.

Lawrence learned a lot from working on the engine of a Biscayne Baby speedboat (the *Biscuit*) that he had been given at the 1929 Schneider competition. The engine was malfunctioning badly when he received it and replacement parts had to be ordered from the US. Only an expert could cope with the intricacies of the machinery, which had a tendency to catch fire. It suffered from oil and water leaks and the hull, being of lightweight construction, often needed repairing. By 16th July he had finished working on the engine, but had to wait for a replacement coupling before installing it.

Lawrence with Clare and friends made the most of the *Biscuit*. Because it was not an ocean-going craft it was not possible to take it out to sea, so all its runs had to be

The central slipway on the east side of Mount Batten, where RAF 200 arrived on 18th June, 1931. On the slipway is a Fairey IIIF floatplane and its trolley. In front of the Martello tower, moored in the Cattewater, are two Blackburn Irises. (RAF Museum)

Facing south-east across the Cattewater from Mount Batten's northernmost slipway, c. 1934. In the background is a Blackburn Iris flying boat. (RAF Museum)

confined to the rivers of the Tamar valley. Gerald Wasley points out that they only went out to the English Channel once and soon turned back: 'Off they would steer a course up the River Lynher in search of a quiet place. These were halcyon days: picnics among the wild foxgloves, Lawrence sitting on the river bank reading the fashion magazine *Vogue*.'[36]

T.E., the Sydney Smiths and a friend once stayed in a bungalow on the South Devon coast at Thurlestone, near Kingsbridge, belonging to Major A.A. Nathan, a pilot friend of Smith, set apart from its neighbours in an idyllic location close to a golf course. Lawrence would get up at dawn and pick mushrooms for breakfast. Whilst Wing Commander Smith played golf, Lawrence and Clare would go out picking blackberries and shrimping in the local rock pools. In a photograph taken by Sydney Smith, which T.E. named 'The Judgement of Paris', Mrs. Smith, her sister Lily and a friend, Mrs Galpin, stand staring at Lawrence's tiny body sitting to their left, his hair askew. Mrs Galpin, nicknamed 'Pippin', had her mind read by Lawrence, as had many others. She noticed his work-soiled hands and thought silently 'He really ought to take more trouble to clean up before he came here'. Lawrence smiled. Holding up his hands and, examining them, he exclaimed: 'Yes, they are shameful – but I had no time.'[37]

Lawrence found himself some biking enthusiasts in the vicinity, William Harris and Harold Short. The two would often go out on their motorbikes, Harris having

Aircraftman Shaw and W Sydney Smith at Thurlestone, c. 1931. Major A.A. Nathan owned a bungalow at Thurlestone that the Smiths often visited. (Bodleian)

a Norton, and one day they met Lawrence on Dartmoor, and would often meet up with him afterwards, going for rides across the open moor.

Clare Smith, her friends and Lawrence often visited Port Eliot in Cornwall where the brother of Lawrence's solicitor Edward Eliot, the Earl of St. Germans, lived. T.E. also went to Cornwall with Basil Liddell Hart and his wife once and stayed at the Headland Hotel, Newquay where he was ignored by the staff when they saw his uniform, taking him for the chauffeur.[38] At weekends he sometimes dined with Admirals and Generals at Government House, Devonport, as Lieutenant-General Sir George Jeffeys' guest,[39] and at Admiralty House, Mount Wise, as the guest of

Sir Rudolf Bentinck. He gave a ride in the *Biscuit* once to Viscountess Cantalupe, General Jeffreys' friend, when Lawrence and Clare Smith went for dinner at the General's house. Thursday evenings however, were reserved for a favourite of the ranks, 'tea and wads' in the NAAFI.[40]

During this period of merry sociability however, the other, darker Lawrence lying deep beneath the surface would emerge. In September 1930, which he described as a 'thin' year for him; he took part in a bizarre 'holiday'. He wrote a letter to the American publisher F.N. Doubleday about it, published in the 1938 edition of *The Letters of T.E. Lawrence* but there is no indication of the darker purpose behind it. He arranged to go on holiday in Scotland with his old acquaintance from Bovington, John Bruce. On the instructions of 'The Old Man'[41] Bruce had to rent a cottage owned by a Mr Ross on the coast 16 miles north of Aberdeen at Collieston. This was for the specific purpose of performing a ritual beating on Lawrence. Bruce told the *Sunday Times* 'Insight' team in 1968 that he had flogged Lawrence 11 times since first meeting him.[42] The reasons for this behaviour were complex and difficult to understand but their origins almost certainly go back to the War.

On November 20th 1917 Lawrence, with an accomplice, made a reconnaissance of the defences of the Turkish held town of Deraa, Syria, a focal point for the

Lady Cantalupe (often confused here with Nancy Astor) and Lawrence in the *Biscuit* motor boat off Devonport, probably in August 1930. The occasion was a lunch party given by Major-General Sir George Jeffreys, which Lawrence attended with Clare Sydney Smith. (Southampton City Council)

Arab offensive in 1917. This followed an unsuccessful attempt to destroy the rail bridge at Tel el Shehab, the aim being to cut rail communication from Damascus to Palestine to facilitate Allenby's advance in Palestine. Returning south to Azrak afterwards they decided to compensate for their failure by blowing up a train. This was also was bungled at first, only being successful after Lawrence had sat 50 yards from the track in full view of the Turks and waved at them to alleviate suspicion. On the third attempt his toe was broken by a piece of flying metal from the explosion.

The Deraa reconnaissance was intended to find a southern entry to the town. What happened that day has been debated ever since. Lawrence later gave three different accounts of the incident, which differed slightly; some scholars have argued that the incident never happened at all. By Lawrence's account, he was arrested by a Turkish guard and escorted to the headquarters of the Bey of Deraa, the Turkish Army governor. What happened next, he suggested, was a form of male rape, or attempted rape. The trauma would be terrible for anyone, but the effect on Lawrence, particularly since his feeling towards sex seemed to be one of repulsion, was devastating.[43] On 28th June 1919 he described the incident to W.F. Stirling: 'I went into Deraa, in disguise, to spy out the defences, was caught, and identified by Hajim Bey, the governor . . . Hajim was an ardent pederast and took a fancy to me. So he kept me under guard until night and then tried to have me.'[44]

It can be argued that the molestation at Deraa became the focus of his life and later sufferings. The event almost certainly happened. Although there is no hard evidence to confirm it, Lawrence's behaviour after the war displayed all the symptoms of a victim of male rape. Eyewitnesses told Liddell Hart whilst he was researching his 1934 biography that when Lawrence returned to Akaba from Deraa he was 'badly shaken, pale and obviously distraught'. Some sources suggest that the Bey was actually an ardent heterosexual and it was members of the guard that performed the act.[45]

At the time the event did not have any immediate effect upon him, however, after the war, when he had time to reflect upon it, it disturbed him greatly. Whilst rewriting *Seven Pillars* in 1922 the recollection of it profoundly upset him and it was the subject of one of the earliest chapters he wrote. Its effect on him has been most graphically illustrated by a letter he wrote to Charlotte Shaw on March 26th 1924: 'For fear of being hurt, or rather to earn five minutes respite from a fear which drove me mad, I gave away the only possession we are born with – our bodily integrity . . . it's an unforgivable matter, an irrevocable position: and it's that which has made me foreswear decent living, and the exercise of my not contemptible wits and talents.'[46]

Although many scholars have claimed that the beating and sexual assault never happened, it is hard to deny that there was some kind of beating at some stage; some soldiers saw the marks on Lawrence's back when he was in the ranks. Arthur Russell recalled that some time in 1923 or 1924 he went swimming with T.E. at tiny Arishmael Cove, between Worbarrow Bay and Lulworth Cove on the Dorset coast. They were both keen swimmers, he said. 'He stripped off and I said 'You've been beaten'. He said 'Oh, my back, yes, I'll tell you about that some time.' After the swim Lawrence explained to him how he was beaten by the Turks. '"He tore a piece of flesh out here or skin out here and stuck a bayonet through it and turned it." He showed me the scars, you know. You could see the double scar.' Mrs Helen Beaumont, wife of one of T.E.'s machine gunners in Arabia, said an airmen at Mount Batten wrote to her: 'he saw T.E. in a shower one day with his back to him and observed the scars – which he thought at first to be burn marks.'[47] Rather than there being a limited number of weals on his torso Arthur Russell had seen what appeared to be dozens of scars all over his upper body.

For Eric Kennington, his friend who helped to illustrate *Seven Pillars,* the Deraa incident was the key to Lawrence's behaviour after the War; he 'made the rest of his life an intermittent struggle to reclaim or re-create his soul, by altruistic labour, self denial and penance.'[48] The disturbing, long-term effect of the incident did not become public until 1968; that over a period of 12 years he had a series of systematic ritual beatings administered upon him by another soldier from the Tank Corps.[49] J.M. Wilson's conclusion was that, since the psychology of a person is peculiar to himself , such abnormal private behaviour could appear as insane to one party, but may be the only certain way for the subject concerned to attain 'psychological equilibrium'. Lawrence's mental imbalance brought on by the writing of *Seven Pillars* at Barton Street appears to have been one of the catalysts that started this behaviour.

There is nothing in the letter to Doubleday about what actually happened at Collieston:

What are we doing here? Nothing, practically. There are three of us –Jimmy who used to work in Canada but came home in 1914 and was a gunner for four years in France: now he jobs horses in Aberdeen – Jock the roughest diamond of our tank corps hut in 1923; and me . . . But what do we do? Why nothing as I said. Jimmy has his horses to groom and feed and exercise. Sometimes we do the last for him. Jock fishes.[50]

There is no indication here of anything untoward and John Buchan later opined that Lawrence never wrote better prose than in this letter. Bruce told the *Sunday Times* that three horses were hired and Jimmy Nicholson was employed to act as a groom. Lawrence undertook a strict programme of self-discipline: He rose at six thirty; swam in the sea for fifteen minutes (the water was very rough and so cold at that time of year that even the locals would not bathe in it), then had breakfast in the local Post Office that doubled as a general store and café. He next rode on the moors for two hours until twelve, had lunch, rode for another two hours until four, swam for half an hour, had another meal and went to bed. By the end of the first day Bruce said Lawrence had a high temperature and had to be dosed up with whisky. This ritual went on for seven days, whereupon Bruce beat him severely with a birch. Nicholson was sick as he witnessed it, whilst Bruce wrote a report. All this was done of Lawrence's own free will and Bruce later said he found it almost impossible to understand him: 'Here is a man subjecting himself almost beyond human endeavour, willingly, and in the midst of it all he writes a four page letter in the gayest possible manner.'[51] The beatings were repeated in Aberdeen in 1931 and in Edinburgh in 1934.

Scott-Paine

On the night of October 5[th,] 1930 the R101 crashed. A log entry was made in the marine workshops at Mount Batten recording that Lawrence was on the duty crew that night. This led to an incorrect assumption that he had attended the crash.[52] What was significant about it for him was that Lord Thompson, the Minister for Air, died in the crash and with him perished the stricture that T.E. was forbidden to fly. Thompson had been appointed Viceroy of India, the reason he had made the trip.

In the following month there was a seaplane crash; one of three serious crashes that occurred at Mount Batten between 1930 and 1932. A float on an aircraft flown by Flying Officer S.K. Wood came off in mid air and when it landed the aircraft cart-wheeled and sank in 30 feet of water.[53] When Lawrence was watching the salvage operation he realized that it was going wrong. He took a motor-boat out to the wreck, stripped off to his singlet, dived in and put a hawser around the tail. He performed in a few minutes a task that the salvage team had spent hours on. This sort of action brought him great respect from his fellow RAF men.

Also in November came the Southampton boat builder Hubert Scott-Paine's invitation to Flight Lieutenant Beauforte-Greenwood and his colleagues in the RAF to examine a new type of tender he had designed for the British services. Hubert Paine was born at Shoreham near Southampton in 1890 to an ironmonger and chandler named Henry Paine and his wife Rosannah (nee Scott). He adopted his mother's maiden name when he became successful. As a youth he had a natural aptitude for mechanics and his strength of mind and force of character enabled him to overcome obstacles in his career that would have overwhelmed most men. He was a very large man, a redhead with his whole upper body a mass of red freckles leading to his nickname, 'The Red Fox of Hythe'. He was one of the pioneers of early aviation and founded, developed and later owned the Supermarine Aviation Company, a chief designer being R.J. Mitchell. Scott-Paine sold his shares in the company in November 1923, believing that the future of commercial aviation lay in flying boats, and became a partner in Imperial Airways. In the mid-twenties, he changed tack, away from aviation and to the development of fast racing boats. He had gone to the US a few years before and was impressed by the marine technology he found. The international races he competed in in the 1920s and '30s, largely against the American Garfield Wood, influenced the development of the RAF boats. Scott-Paine was aware that the American fast boats were making inroads into the British commercial power-boat market and his efforts to counter this kick-started the British inter-war power boat industry.

He developed the 'Puma' multi-step hydroplane, powered by a lightweight converted aero-engine. The steps in the bottom of the hull broke up the drag the water had on the hull, a kind of anti-venturi downforce effect. In September 1927 he bought Hythe shipyard across the Solent from Southampton, with the intention of mass producing affordable, high quality motor boats and the British Power Boat Company was formed at the beginning of next month. Without Scott-Paine's work on fast boat development there would have been no contribution by Lawrence. Scott-Paine's success was fundamental to Lawrence's work.

The RAF were impressed by what Scott-Paine had to show them. He was aware that the RAF was still using the old round bilge type boats for their seaplane tenders. His pioneering work in developing what came to be known as 'hard chine' designs for the world speedboat championships, coupled with his experience at Imperial Airways, had led him to conclude that these would be far more suitable for working with flying boats than the old designs. They were safer, faster, more manoeuvrable and cheaper to design and operate. The 'hard-chine' was the rigid line between the vertical sides of the boat's hull and the rounded underside, or bilge. In Scott-Paine's boats the vertical sides were made of diagonal timber boarding, below the 'chine' the boards changed direction to horizontal.

Lawrence's part in these early developments in power boat design was limited. It was Scott-Paine's unofficial 'apprenticeship' of aero and marine engineering and his later understanding of the aerodynamics of flying boat hulls and speed boat design, plus his unusual capacity for hard work, which led to the development of the RAF 200. Lawrence's contribution came later in the trials of these boats and negotiations for the purchase of the larger 60-foot-plus craft by the Royal Navy. These were later used in a developed form by the Air Sea Rescue Services and the Motor Torpedo Boat crews of the Second World War.[54] One certain influence was Lawrence's celebrity and staff connections in the Armed Forces: Scott Paine, despite his entrepreneurial abilities, did not, initially, possess these contacts.

Notes

1 Still photographs that appear to have been taken from this film appeared in the *Sunday Pictorial* on February 3rd, 1929.

2 Sydney Smith was not actually his surname; though Smith's wife Clare wrote her book *The Golden Reign* using the name 'Clare Sydney Smith'. Sydney William Smith (21st September 1888–December 1971) joined the RAF as a Major in 1918. By 1935 he was an Air Commodore. He learned to fly in 1914 and became a Flying Officer in the RFC that September, in which he became both a Flight and a Squadron Commander. He was awarded the OBE in 1919 and became C.O. of 70 Squadron, Helopolis on Vimys in February 1920, when he first met Lawrence. They met again when Smith was an Administrative Staff officer at HQ RAF Cranwell in 1926. Smith became C.O. of RAF Cattewater, Mount Batten on 15th January 1929, as Lawrence's C.O. and a year later

C.O. of 204 Squadron. On 1st July 1931 he was promoted to Group Captain, and on 2nd October posted to Manston as C.O. In October 1933 he became AOC, RAF Far East and in November 1933 C.O. of Singapore RAF base.

3 *Golden Reign.*

4 Ibid.

5 Yardley's biography recorded this as 29th January.

6 *Hansard.* Quoted as dated 30th January 1929 in the 1938 edition of DG.

7 T.E. Lawrence to E.M. Forster, 5th February, 1929.

8 Quoted from *Hansard* in the 1938 edition of DG.

9 J.M. Wilson quotes the date as 4th February, out of sequence with Garnett's account and the date of T.E.'s letter to Forster.

10 Thurtle's account in *Friends.*

11 Ibid.

12 Thurtle failed to mention this conversation in his 1937 account in *T.E. Lawrence by his Friends.* Even earlier, in March 1927 King George's secretary, Lord Stamfordham had written of Lawrence's illegitimacy, with speculations as to its implications, to Sir Reginald Wingate, formerly one of Lawrence's superiors in the desert campaign.

13 Ibid.

14 T.E. Lawrence to E. Thurtle M.P., 9/02/1929. Barton St, London.

15 Mr. Widdows, office of the Under-Secretary of State for Air, to the Air Ministry, 6th March, 1929. National Archives: AIR.

16 Note to Sir John Salmond from Air Ministry official, 8th March, 1929. National Archives: AIR 1/2702

17 Air Member for Personnel.

18 Minute from Sir John Salmond to J.A. Webster, Air Ministry, 12th March, 1929. National Archives: AIR 1/2702

19 *Brief Outline of my Friendship with T.E. Lawrence,* Air Commodore Sydney Smith. Date should be 1929.

20 *Golden Reign.*

21 This date is based on Air Ministry Meteorological Office reports where the name changed on 3rd October.

22 Source: T.E. Lawrence to A. Russell, R.A.F. Cattewater, 20/03/1929. Courtesy *T.E. Lives* magazine.

23 *Golden Reign.*

24 Tunbridge.

25 Ibid.

26 Lawrence scribbled a margin note against this last sentence to Easton: 'Keep this dark. It might get me into trouble', according to an article by John Theobald in the *Western Morning News,* Plymouth, 10/5/1983.

27 Stanley Weintraub in his book *Private Shaw and Public Shaw,* mistakenly identified this as the 'River Hoe'.

28 'Lady Astor on TE's pillion?' *Western Morning News,* 18/10/1986.

29 Ibid.

30 *The Astors – a Family Chronicle,* Lucy Kavaler, George G. Harrap, 1966.

31 Mack.

32 The source for this was an article in a Plymouth newspaper. Gerald Wasley told the author that Lawrence had his own table in the mess and sat there reading all the newspapers.

33 Quote from Mr. Pieter Shipster's lecture *Lawrence and the Schneider Trophy*, T.E. Lawrence Society 9th Symposium, and Oxford September 2006.

34 *Golden Reign.*

35 Wilson.

36 Source: *Life was a Round of Parties and Dinners*, Gerald Wasley, *Western Morning News*, Plymouth, 25/3/1999. Mr. Wasley has pointed out that the article's title was devised by the Editor, not himself.

37 *Golden Reign.*

38 B:LH

39 The well known photograph of Lawrence in the *Biscuit* with a lady who is not Clare Smith is on p101. Some sources caption her as Lady Astor. It was in fact Lady Cantalupe. The same day they appear to have visited Picklecombe Point on Mount Edgcumbe, Plymouth where a group photo was taken.

40 *Life was a Round of Parties and Dinners*, Gerald Wasley, *Western Morning News*, Plymouth, 25/3/1999.

41 Until his dying day Bruce believed 'The Old Man' existed, but it is generally accepted it was Lawrence masquerading as his uncle, who arranged for the beatings to take place.

42 See *John Bruce and the* Sunday Times, p286.

43 Interviewed in 1985 for the BBC2 Omnibus film 'Lawrence and Arabia' his brother A.W. Lawrence stated 'He hated the thought of sex'.

44 T.E. Lawrence to W.F. Stirling, 28/06/1919. Bodleian Library.

45 Knightley and Simpson.

46 T.E. Lawrence to C.F. Shaw, 26/03/1922.

47 Mrs. H. Beaumont to 'Leo', 15th September 1969. RTC Bovington Camp Library Archives.

48 Friends, p..252.

49 See *John Bruce and the* Sunday Times, p286.

50 T.E. Lawrence to F.N. Doubleday, 18/09/1930.

51 Knightley and Simpson p. 200.

52 *The R.A.F. Air Sea Rescue Service 1918-1986*. Jon Sutherland and Diane Cannell. Pen and Sword. 2005, Chapter One. Since the crash occurred a few miles from landlocked Beauvais this is inaccurate.

53 S.K. Wood later died in the Blackburn Iris crash of 1931.

54 John Harris, in his book on the Air Sea Rescue Service *The Sea Shall not Have Them* (Hurst and Blackett, 1953) recorded that 13,269 lives were saved by RAF Air Sea Rescue in World War Two.

CHAPTER NINE

The Schneider Trophy, Hythe and the Blackburn Iris Crash

The Schneider Trophy races were instituted in 1913 by Jacques Schneider, the French Minister for Air. The first was held in April 1913 at Monaco on a course of 150 sea miles (172.62 miles). From 1913 to 1926 eleven different races were held in seven different locations: Monaco, Bournemouth, Venice, Naples, Cowes, Baltimore and Hampton Roads. Many well known names contributed to the success of the series, including the talented Jimmy Doolittle, R.J. Mitchell and General Italo Balbo. It was a race that was intended to promote long distance, reliable, passenger carrying flying boat services and a number of rules governed the conduct of it:

1) It was an international seaplane challenge, the holders of the trophy having to organize and play host to the succeeding contest.
2) The course was not to be less than 173.75 miles flown either in a straight line, a broken line or on a closed circuit.
3) A maximum of three aircraft from any one country were allowed to compete in each contest.
4) The competitors had to be entered by the relevant national Aero Club.[1]
5) Any nation that won the competition three times in five years would win outright and take the Trophy.[2]

As the contest developed it became the paramount test of the fastest waterborne aircraft in the world. The most successful entrants were Italy and the US, both winning three times, whilst Great Britain won twice and France once. In 1923 the Americans entered a government-backed military service team, contributing to the competition's prestige. The Italians and British subsequently followed this precedent.

The competition made reputations and broke them. It played a key part in developments in aerodynamics, engines, fuels and high speed flying in the 1920s, the planes eventually being designed specifically for the race. But it was also deadly, eleven men dying during the competitions.[3] F.R. Banks, who was an adviser to Napiers in 1927 and an expert on high speed fuel mixtures, assisted Rolls-Royce in the 1929 and 1931 competitions. He later commented that he had never before nor since 'been involved in an operation which sparked such individual and collective energy and sheer enthusiasm.'[4]

From 1913 until 1927, excluding the War years, the competition was held annually, hosted by the national Aero Club of the country who had won the competition the previous year. As such it was, in the beginning, a competition administered by civilian organisations. Both Italy and the US hosted the competition twice. In 1927 Britain entered a specially trained RAF team at Venice, the High Speed Flight, which won for the third time. However, since this and Britain's two previous wins were not successive it had to win in the subsequent two competitions to take the trophy home. Two years later, in 1929, Britain's Royal Aero Club hosted the Schneider Cup at RAF Calshot on the Solent. For the first time two years of preparation was allowed, largely owing to the demands of the Italians who needed time to develop new aircraft. In 1927, they had adopted the American method of 1926 and concentrated on one aircraft and one manufacturer. But in 1929 they used the 1927 British method of employing four separate manufacturers specifically to produce designs for the contest.

Lord Trenchard had monitored Lawrence's movements in the ranks of the RAF with great sympathy. Trenchard would later be known as 'the father of the RAF', being largely responsible for the formation of a unified Air Force in 1918. As such, he shared with Lawrence the belief that success in any future conflict would be determined by air power. However, he was not a fan of the Schneider race and in 1929, when Chief of the Air Staff, he opposed it for three reasons: with

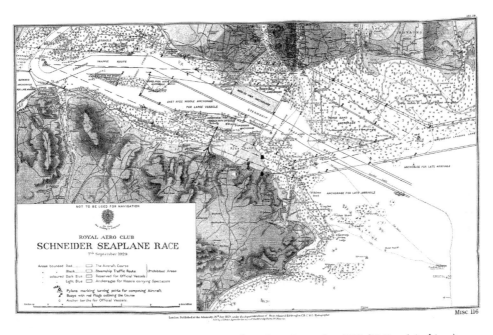

Map of the 1929 Schneider Trophy Race Course, the Solent, September 1929. (National Archives)

accommodation for foreign teams and guests and more sophisticated technology, the 1929 race would cost ten times that of the 1927 one; because such competitions could only result in complications and diplomatic incidents; and he disliked the 'ace' mentality, believing the glamour attached to the race could have a bad effect on his officers.[5]

Despite having allowed the Air Council to organize and finance the 1927 Schneider race, Churchill was not prepared to support another one, despite the RAF's opinion that there were enough technical and commercial benefits to justify participation. Nevertheless, on 7th October 1927, Sir Samuel Hoare, the Minister for Air, asked the Air Council if they were ready. Trenchard then requested the Royal Aero Club to appoint a committee to discuss the next contest: if the R.A.C. would be responsible, he said, the Air Ministry would lend the aircraft. The R.A.C. said they could not run the race without the direct assistance of RAF pilots and ground personnel; that was how the 1927 race was won. A new Schneider Cup Committee was formed, appointed by the Royal Aero Club and composed of its members, officers of the Royal Air Force, and associates of the Society of British Aircraft Constructors. The Chairman was Colonel M. O'Gorman and the vice-Chairman Squadron Commander J. Bird. As a senior officer in the Directorate of Staff Duties at the Air Ministry, Wing Commander S.W. Smith O.B.E. was nominated as one of two Air Ministry representatives, along with Major J.S. Buchanan O.B.E.[6]

At the beginning of 1928 Churchill softened his opposition to Air Ministry support and gradually full government backing became assured. At the end of January C.D. Bullock, the Personal secretary to Sir Philip Sassoon, contacted Trenchard, telling him he had written to the Chancellor saying that in the 1928/1929 programme he proposed to incorporate 'the necessary measures for developing further types of machines and also for producing a new engine if possible'.[7] Sassoon would not increase the expenditure the Chancellor had already agreed to, but: 'The Chancellor and other Members of the Cabinet, with whom the Secretary of State has discussed the question, have all pressed the view that the Air Ministry should spare no endeavour to secure another victory in 1919 [sic][8] and that, in particular, we should undertake responsibility for developing the necessary machines and engines.'[9]

On 25th February 1928 the Air Ministry decided to go 'full steam ahead with developments of machines and engines'[10] for the Cup. This was after Churchill's failure to respond to numerous Air Ministry entreaties in January; the Air Ministry assuming his agreement would be confirmed 'subject to ordinary routine action with the Treasury'.[11] This was an extremely irregular leapfrogging of Churchill's authority by Trenchard, in view of the costs of entering the competition. Fortunately, the same day Sam Hoare was able to tell the C.A.S. of Churchill's support: the Air Ministry should press on with aircraft and engine development. Three days later, in compliance with the R.A.C's. stipulation, Trenchard wrote to both parties asking them to respond at their convenience so he could 'take up the question of the formation of a new High Speed Flight'.[12]

In the spring of 1928 Smith started surveying prospective courses for the competition. That May he flew an Avro biplane from Ireland to Morecambe and spent three days surveying Morecambe Bay. He flew to Calshot in a Supermarine Southampton flying boat and traversed the area from the Solent to Weymouth. The next day he surveyed from the Isle of Wight to Selsey Bill, and the Solent.[13] Morecambe Bay was attractive because it would result in a saving by using the facilities provided by local authorities. However it would mean considerable extra expenditure for the Air Force itself, since there were no RAF establishments locally.[14]

The first suggestion that Calshot should be used for the 1929 race was made by the Royal Aero Club Schneider Committee in July 1928. The problem with using a site on the Solent was that rigorous shipping control would be necessary and so the co-operation of the Admiralty was essential. Because it was an area associated with large-scale Naval reviews the case for Government hospitality was strong, and a high degree of central government control was required.[15] If the Royal Aero Club was unable to meet the financial requirements the Government would be forced to do so. This had a direct bearing upon Sydney Smith's involvement because it meant all the administrative arrangements came under Air Ministry control. The Royal Aero Club would still be responsible for refereeing and race conditions.

By the first week in August 1928 the Air Ministry still did not have the Chancellor's authority to enter an official RAF team. At the foot of the Air Ministry letter explaining this was a pencilled request that Wing Commander Smith and his Air Ministry colleagues on the Schneider Committee, as a preliminary to drawing up the programme asked for by the Secretary of State, should confer with Holloway[16] and Evans at the Air Ministry.[17] This indicated Sydney Smith's high-level involvement at a very early stage, before Treasury permission was received. The choice of Calshot as a site necessitated the administration of the race by the Air Ministry: if Calshot had not been selected, Lawrence might not have been involved at all.

In July 1928 Smith took part in the King's Cup Air Race. This was a long distance air race from Hendon Aerodrome to the aerodrome at Brooklands. The first day of the course had six control points: Norwich, Castle Bromwich/ Birmingham, Hucknall Aerodrome/Nottingham, Leeds, Newcastle upon Tyne and Glasgow. Pilots had to fly 1,069½ miles in two days, stopping overnight at Renfrew Aerodrome, Glasgow. From Renfrew they would fly south on Saturday 21st July making four stops before Brooklands and also turning at the Solway Firth and Bristol.

These were still the pioneering days of flight, before Civil Aviation Authority regulations and air traffic control restrictions ruined the fun. There were 38 entrants, mostly flying the popular de Havilland Moth biplane. Other aircraft included an SE5a, a Cierva Autogyro and two Avro Avians. Entrant number 14 was a Major A.A. 'Bert' Nathan with a de Havilland Cirrus Moth, but the pilot was Sydney Smith. Nathan was a close friend of Smith and he would later fly in one of his Moths with Lawrence when he was at Mount Batten.

Sydney W. Smith at the time of the Kings Cup Air race of 1928 in which he flew a D.H. Moth owned by Major A.A. Nathan. From a Bradford newspaper, where his father was a local industrialist. (RAF Museum)

A De Havilland Cirrus Moth of the same type as Sydney Smith flew in the King's Cup Air Race of 1928 owned by Major Nathan. Nathan's Moth, G-EBYV , in which he flew with passenger Lawrence, was similar but with interchangeable wheeled or floated undercarriage. (Via Thetford)

On 17th July, before taking part in the race, Smith traced out part of its course to just beyond Hucknall. The race proper was due to take place on Friday 20th and Saturday 21st. Other luminaries entered were F/O R.L.R. Atcherley in a Gloster Grebe, who later flew in the 1929 Schneider Cup, and Capt. Hubert S. Broad, a test pilot for Supermarines, in another Moth.

Smith started 6th in the race at 8.56 a.m. Visibility was good with a Force 1 wind varying from west and south. Around London strato-cumulus covered 8/10ths of the sky with a base of 4000 feet. He covered the 99 miles to Mousehold Aerodrome at Norwich in just over an hour. At each control point there was a compulsory stop of 30 minutes and he restarted at 10.36 precisely. The Moth must have picked up speed as the air warmed up and fuel weight decreased; he travelled the 130 miles to Castle Bromwich, Birmingham in 61 minutes, arriving at 12.37 a.m. and at 13.07 he took off for Hucknall where he arrived 43½ miles and 36 minutes later. At Hucknall it went wrong. Smith waited the half an hour before starting up at 13 minutes past 2 but some time after 2.36 he crashed. He noted in the log book: 'Collided with an Avian due to bad ground organisation, machine crashed and had to abandon race.'[18]

After the King's Cup Race was over, visibility was good enough on the warm cloudy afternoon of Wednesday 29th August for Smith to take a Supermarine Southampton flying boat piloted by Squadron Leader Lloyd against the westerly wind for a return survey flight from Calshot to Cattewater.[19] Churchill's sanction was still being sought for the Treasury to meet the expenses of the RAF team,[20] but by the beginning of November Air Ministry staff had concluded that no special Treasury authority was required 'for anything in connection with the High Speed Flight', the costs of the Flight being covered by the budget for its machines.[21] The overall costs for this were later set out in a December communication from the Air Ministry to the Treasury. These were agreed upon by Churchill in accord with Sam Hoare and were for the Flight and its engines. The letter included a disclaimer that the costs would be incurred anyway for improvement of the RAF's aircraft, even without the Schneider Cup Race. The total expenditure for four new machines was projected as £50,000.

Reconditioning of existing aircraft £5,000.
Engines £43,500.
Spares £50,500.
Repairs £2,500.
Contingencies £2,500.

The total expenditure for 1929 was projected as £164,000, plus £62,500 for the programme itself.[22] That same month the Schneider Committee received the Air Ministry's agreement on Calshot as the site of the race.

In the spring of 1929 Smith's and Lawrence's work on the project began in earnest concerning the administration of the race from the Air Ministry's viewpoint.

Calshot Spit was a small dog-leg of land on the west side of Southampton Water, dominated at one end by a large Martello Tower with five or so large hangars and other buildings clustered around the end of it. The RAF area was where all the competing aircraft were to be based. By 1927 it was a centre for courses of instruction for airmen in boat building, marine engineering and training crews for motor boats. This came under the authority of Coastal Area[23] and was the home station of 201 Squadron that operated Supermarine Southampton flying boats. The Air Ministry's accommodation for the Schneider aircraft was a large arched-roof shed divided into four equal compartments. These provided for hangar space, technical stores and offices.[24]

Sydney Smith, who was a key member of several Air Ministry and external Schneider Cup committees, attended a meeting held at the Air Ministry on 6th February 1929. This was for the Air Ministry and Royal Aero Club to discuss the division of responsibilities for the race.[25] Discussions had been going on for several months before this. Under the Chairmanship of Trenchard representatives of the Navy and the Royal Aero Club were present, as well as the RAF. The latter was represented in two guises, the Air Ministry and the Air Officer Commanding Coastal Area. This meeting resulted in a nineteen-point allocation of responsibilities, the Air Ministry's portion indicating the kind of work Lawrence and Smith would have been responsible for from the beginning of February 1929:

1) Accommodation of foreign V.I.P.s at Cowes;
2) Information re. the composition and arrival dates of foreign teams;
3) Notification to foreign teams of accommodation etc. before and after arrival;
4) Official Government banquet arrangements;
5) Issue of special passes to Calshot visitors;
6) Press arrangements at Calshot;
7) Invitation to 250 Government guests to view the contest from H.M.S. *Argus*;
8) Issue of notices declaring the course a prohibited area to all aircraft other than competitors;
9) Special communication facilities at Calshot.[26]

Smith and Lawrence would have had to ensure all these requirements were met by Saturday 7th September, race day. In March, Churchill was working on the 1929 Budget at Chartwell. The financing of the High Speed Flight had by now been approved and in April they arrived at Calshot from Felixstowe for training and research.

Smith had to go to London regularly in his capacity on the Committee. Lawrence told Graves that he could not take his annual leave until after the Schneider Cup as he was 'doing clerking and correspondence for our C.O. who is the big noise on that.'[27] This letter confirms what a high level of responsibility Smith's position carried. It also suggests Lawrence must have sat in on the first meeting at the Air Ministry of the D.O.S.D.[28] Schneider Committee of 6th May. The Chairman was Group Captain A. Fletcher. Squadron Leader A.W. Smith (sic), listed section E.6., was one of four service officers and five civilians co-opted to attend. In fact only eight men showed up: six service officers and two civilians. Squadron Leader A.R. Boyle, a Flight Lieutenant Jones, and a Group Captain E.R.C. Nicholson of Calshot, were also present.[29] One civilian was C.P. Robertson of the Air Ministry's Press section. The Committee considered a 16-point agenda, which included accommodation of distinguished guests, visiting aircraft, foreign teams etc., supply of boats for policing the course and attending foreign and British teams, Air Ministry and Royal Aero Club officials.[30] Also considered were facilities for the RAF to view the contest; marking and buoying arrangements, provision of communication facilities, general signal arrangements, press arrangements, notices in connection with civil aviation, first aid and fire fighting, passes to enter Calshot and meteorology. All this came under the Air Ministry's remit.[31]

Smith made a return flight from Cattewater to Calshot and back on Tuesday 7th and Wednesday 8th May. It was a fairly cold, damp day at Cattewater but visibility was very good with blue skies and Cumulo-nimbus at 4000 feet. A 16-m.p.h. wind blew from the south south west. Smith had decided to make the most of having a genius on his door-step and employed 'Shaw' as his personal private secretary. He realised that, since the race had become considerably more professional[32] than in its earlier days, he would need an extremely capable assistant to cope with the heavy workload of reports and correspondence anticipated. This could not be done without Trenchard's permission: Trenchard reluctantly agreed as long as Lawrence was kept out of the limelight. Smith recalled:

> Since it had been decided to hold the race in the Solent the course had to be designed and marked and the R.A.F. station Calshot was allocated as the base for the competing aircraft.[33]
>
> . . . With all the work entailed with its attendant reports and correspondence, I obtained permission from Sir Hugh Trenchard to employ Shaw as my personal secretary during the period of preparation and eventual operation of the Schneider Trophy race. He accompanied me at all meetings and was invaluable in recording proceedings and the compilation of subsequent reports.[34]

Lawrence described his work as 'a cross between a clerk and a deck-hand on an R.A.F. Motor-Boat',[35] telling Liddell Hart he had only done an ordinary Aircraftman's job until the Schneider Cup.[36] Although the Sydney Smith archive in the Houghton Library at Harvard contains copies of the official minutes and correspondence for the 1929 Schneider Cup there is little mention of 'T.E. Shaw's' involvement, since he was not a member of the various Schneider committees or working groups. As Smith's secretary he undoubtedly sat in on the meetings but only as a recorder or stenographer. But he did prepare much of the correspondence and many of the reports issued under Smith's signature. Consequently the name 'Shaw' occurs only very occasionally. One letter however does survive signed by him. For the duration of the proceedings Smith and Lawrence had an office on board a privately owned motor yacht, the *MV Karen*.[37] This had been lent to the Schneider team by Major Colin Cooper, who was a millionaire friend of Smith's.[38] Air Vice-Marshal Sir Charles Lambe, Officer Commanding Coastal Area,[39] the officer in overall charge, also lived on the *Karen* at the front whilst Lawrence had a hammock at the stern with the rest of the crew.[40] Lawrence personally signed a letter requesting a berth.

Evidence of Cooper's later generosity to Lawrence, as thanks for his help with the contest, can be found at Clouds Hill today. In the downstairs Book Room is a model of a small two-person motor boat. This is a tiny replica of a Biscayne 'Baby' speedboat, manufactured in the US by the Purdy Boat Co. that served as a tender to the *Karen* and was owned by Cooper. Whilst the Schneider contest was taking place Cooper allowed Lawrence to ferry personnel to and from the yacht in it. Despite a badly malfunctioning engine T.E. greatly enjoyed the task and offered to strip the Purdy boat's engine down and service it. Cooper decided to give the boat to Lawrence for his help in the contest. Also, his wife disliked him driving the boat at speed. It was subsequently taken back to Batten and marks the first significant involvement Lawrence had with fast motor boats. His later maintenance of its engine represents the start of his expertise as a mechanic. Professor John Mack considered that in the spring of 1929 Lawrence taught himself to be an expert mechanic by overhauling the Biscayne 'Baby' speedboat.[41] This is not quite right. Lawrence did not overhaul the boat until it was given to him in September 1929 following the Schneider contest,

Calshot Spit facing south 1929, where Lawrence and the High Speed Flight were based. Gerald Wasley is of the opinion that Lawrence was more likely to have been quartered here than on the *M.V. Karen*. (Via Smith)

The *M.V. Karen* owned by Major Colin Cooper who loaned it to the RAF for the duration of the 1929 Schneider Trophy arrangements. Lawrence and Smith used an office on the boat. Clare Sydney Smith said that Lawrence was on board on 7th September to report on the race. Italian and British racers are moored out in front. (Via Barker)

and it was only much later, after working on the maintenance of the engines for the RAF tenders and armoured target boats at Hythe and Bridlington, much more complicated systems, that he became anything approaching an expert mechanic.

The RAF High Speed Flight consisted of 42 people, including R.J. Mitchell and 21 ground crewmen hand-picked from each RAF fighter squadron. The final selection for aircrew was Flying Officer R.L.R. Atcherley, Flight Lieutenant D. D'Arcy Greig, Squadron Leader A.H. Orlebar, Flight Lieutenant G.H. Stainforth, and Flight Lieutenant A.H.R. Waghorn. Lawrence became particularly friendly with and enamoured of the legendary Orlebar, or 'Orley' as he was known: one of the most famous pilots in the service. Orlebar was 32, eight years younger than Lawrence and had served in the First World War, being wounded at Gallipoli. In 1916 he joined the R.F.C. and when the RAF formed was granted a permanent commission as a Flight Lieutenant. He graduated from the RAF Staff College in 1926 and was employed in the Air Ministry's Directorate of Organisation and Staff Duties, where he may have met Sydney Smith, a senior officer there from January 1927. At the beginning of 1928 'Orley' was posted to Felixstowe where he became C.O. of the High Speed Flight.[42]

Between Tuesday 16th April and Wednesday 14th August 1929 Smith made at least six flights to Calshot concerned with the administration of the race. He also went by night train with Lawrence to London, Smith travelling first class, Lawrence third. After arriving Lawrence would go to the Union Jack Club for a wash and shave, later meeting Smith at the Air Ministry. At the ensuing committee meetings Lawrence acted as a stenographer, and would grin if Smith disagreed with anything. The Wing Commander would say: 'Shaw, have you made a note of this?' 'Yes, sir,' Lawrence would reply. He would then scribble a few notes and passed them surreptitiously to Smith with almost a conjurer's dexterity, the words suddenly appearing under Smith's nose. With a perfectly straight face Smith would peruse 'Shaw's' irreverent suggestions on how to get the committee to alter a decision.

The committee meetings Lawrence and Sydney Smith attended had their lighter moments. On Wednesday 24th July one was held at the Air Ministry under the Chairmanship of the Chief of the Air Staff to consider progress.[43] A missive from the Italian Aero Club was discussed that asked a number of idiosyncratic questions that caused some amusement. The letter from Torino asked, word for word:

Question No.1 – Is it advisable to come from a French port on a steamer?

No.2 – Shall we have to pay any fees for anchorage on the starting point?

No. 3 – Can we rely on some sure mean of transport at the starting line from Portsmouth to Southampton, if we reach this two ports from London, instead of by ship from a French Port?

No.4 – Can you confirm exact programm of the contest?

P.S. We ask you to wire answer to each question, or to some of them, because we must decide before Tuesday the choice of our itinerary.[44]

At one of these meetings Lawrence met Charles Pennycook 'C.P.' Robertson who later helped him in his altercations with the press.[45] There were attempts at 'putting one over' on the Committee by Lawrence and Smith. Clare Smith recalled one occasion where a Treasury official was particularly reluctant to help them. Presiding was an Air Commodore with an official from the Treasury opposite him, Sydney Smith on his right and C.P. Robertson on his left. Just before commencement of the meeting 'a small, unobtrusive looking airman quietly walked into the room'. He sat down behind Smith. A few minutes into the discussion Robertson realised the anonymous clerk was actually 'Lawrence of Arabia'. The Treasury official remained ignorant of his identity and behaved recalcitrantly. When the proceedings had finished and Smith and Lawrence had left, Robertson turned to him and asked why had adopted such a difficult attitude with Colonel Lawrence in the room? 'Colonel Lawrence!' questioned the official, 'Where was he?' Robertson told him he was the small airman in the background taking notes. The official was taken aback, stating that if he'd known 'they could have had what they liked [as he would have been] so engrossed in watching him.'[46]

The Schneider Cup was the most important air race in the world, up to a million people turning up on the day to watch it. It was a genuine source of international pride. In 1929 it was a 50-kilometre course up and down the Solent from Calshot to Hayling Island, with four changes in direction and six circuits. Floating flags had to be arranged to set out the course width and all shipping on the day had to be co-ordinated.[47]

The arrangements on Saturday 7th September for the arrival and departure of guests were worked out to a strict itinerary with meticulous efficiency. Special flow charts were drawn up to show the times of arrival of guests by rail from Charing Cross Station and by road, proceeding via Portsmouth Harbour Station and thence by tug to the viewing ships *Vita* and HMS *Argus*. The return was even more complicated, involving numerous RAF, R.A.C. and naval boats, all to a strict timetable, to meet train connections.

Special routes were mapped out by the Royal Automobile Club[48] who had charge of the roads in conjunction with the police. Each car was provided on the day of the race with a special label to indicate it had to go to one of four destinations: Hayling Island; Southsea and Portsmouth; Gosport and Stokes Bay; or Lee on Solent. V.I.P.s travelling privately by road had to display a special badge or distinguishing flag on their car for identification. This was all the responsibility of the Air Ministry.

The area surrounding the course became prohibited from midnight on 4th/5th September until the end of the proceedings and the course had to be clear by 1pm on 7th September. 38 naval boats and 30 motor-yachts would patrol the course, with a naval officer in charge of each boat. A destroyer would control shipping at each approach. As well as the RAF first aid boats, four ships would act as Emergency First Aid Stations and all patrol craft including the RAF boats would come under the orders of a Master of Patrols, who had a system of visual and w/t communication with them, enabling officials on Ryde Pier to see when the course was clear.[49] All of this was required for a race lasting only four hours.

On 16th August Lawrence was still based at Plymouth, moving 'uneasily between Calshot and Cattewater' but his H.Q. was still at Cattewater, 'much the better place'.[50] Before the race commenced Smith was responsible for taking various V.I.P.s on tours of the course. On Friday the 23rd he and Squadron Leader Martin flew Sir Hugh Trenchard from Mount Batten to Calshot on an afternoon survey. The same day Lawrence told Graves: 'Tomorrow I am to move to Calshot for 15 days. Busy up to my eyes.'[51]

The move to the Solent heralded a greatly increased workload for the Air Ministry team. Lawrence's ability to see through to the essence of a problem enabled him to make suggestions for corrections to Smith's communiqués that were readily accepted. He adopted the same slow, meticulous methods he had used for drafting *Seven Pillars*, writing and rewriting memoranda until he was satisfied. Sometimes in the office they would work well into the night. When this happened Smith would bed down on the office table and Lawrence on the floor. He later told Alan Dawnay he had hardly slept or eaten at all during the competition.

On Friday 27th August, a warm, cloudy day with good visibility and a 17 m.p.h. south westerly wind, Smith and Pilot Officer Williams took A.V-M Lambe and the Secretary of State for Air Lord Thompson over the Solent. A week later Smith, Williams and Flying Officer Worthington took Lambe and the Prince of Wales around. There is no indication that Lawrence had any part in these flights. On the same day Lawrence told Graves: 'We work from seven in the morning till eleven at night here. I hope it will end soon. This Calshot is a hell of a place for mails.'[52]

Smith later posed for photographs with the Prince of Wales, and the High Speed Flight in front of a Gloster racer. The Flight had seven aircraft on the Calshot dispersal area: two Supermarine S5s with Napier Lion engines from 1927, two Supermarine S6s, designed by R.J. Mitchell, with specially developed Rolls-Royce 'R' or 'Race' engines, one Gloster IV from the year before and two Gloster VI 'Golden Arrows', so named after their all-gold fuselages. The technology of these aircraft was remarkable but they were dangerous aircraft to fly. In 1927 one of the winning pilots for that year, Sam Kinkead, an R.F.C. ace, was killed when he misjudged his height due to some mist over the water. The plane went into a dive. The controls were probably slack, and it crashed straight into the surface. Partly as a consequence of this, at the request of the Air Ministry, a series of quarter-scale wooden wind tunnel models were made of both the Supermarine and Gloster designs for the 1929 competition. The interference between the floats and the rest of the model was specifically tested on the Supermarine model, as well as testing of the wings, floats and fuselage independently.[53]

R.J. Mitchell, the Supermarine designer now celebrated of course for the Spitfire, was a locomotive engineer whose genius was an ability to forget all precedents

Sydney Smith posing with the RAF High Speed Flight and King Edward VIII at Calshot in September 1919. (L. to R.) Waghorn, Stainforth, Orlebar, Edward VIII, d'Arcy Grieg, Atcherley, Smith, Moon the engineering officer, and 'Nobby' Clarke, Farnborough technical officer. Behind them is a Gloster Golden Arrow. (Via Smith)

and start on something completely new. But he was not so talented at developing his ideas. Consequently, all his solutions were made workable by colleagues. He also copied the ideas of others: the engine oil on the S6, for example, was cooled by passing the hot oil through five pipes running down the port side of the fuselage. They went into an oil tank in the fin, (in front of the rudder), where the cold oil was then pumped back up the starboard fuselage side back into the engine. This idea was borrowed from a pre-war French Antoinette aircraft. The whole wing surface on the S6 acted as a radiator and there were three coin scoop air intakes on the bottom of each wing tip. On the front wing the centre of gravity was located at one quarter the chord width back from the leading edge. This was standard on all British racers and the optimum position. Fuel in the floats was located only in compartments at the centre of each float to prevent the aircraft's handling changing as the compartment emptied.[54] These were just a few of the highly innovative ideas used on the Schneider racers.

Also serving at Calshot at that time was Squadron Leader Ira T. Jones, later the author of *The King of Air Fighters*, the biography of Mick Mannock. Jones was another who thought T.E. should never have enlisted in the ranks, T.E.'s incrutable manner occasionally bordering on insubordination. Jones sensed that many officers who tried to put down Lawrence were jealous and suffered from an inferiority complex. He remembered how Lawrence attended a dinner party one evening where a number of politicians and officers were present who objected to his presence in

Quarter-scale laminated wooden wind tunnel model of a Supermarine S6 made at the request of the Air Ministry for the 1929 competition, following a British fatality in 1927. (National Archives)

the ranks and tried to give him the 'cold shoulder'. Lawrence retold the story the following day imitating their mannerisms hilariously. 'It was really funny and if those who attempted to slight him thought they had succeeded, then they lived in a big fool's paradise.'[55] He was in the midst of writing Mannock's biography and Lawrence obligingly gave him a list of relevant titles and authors on a menu card when he asked for help.

The winning British entry in 1929 nearly did not fly. On the night before the contest Flight Lieutenant Waghorn's S6a was found to have traces of aluminium on one of the spark plugs. This meant the piston was 'picking up' metal from the cylinder sleeve, with a danger that it could get worse. The problem was that Contest rules specified that once an engine had been installed it could not be wholly extracted. However, the Schneider Committee members at Calshot agreed some components could be removed and replaced on site. Another problem was that the cylinders on the Rolls-Royce 'R' engine were cast as a block of six, and removal of a cylinder block was a highly skilled job.[56] Fortunately a large number of personnel from the Special and Experimental Departments of Rolls-Royce had been invited to view the contest and were staying overnight at various establishments around Southampton. [57] After a few nerve-wracking hours a team was assembled and, working all night, managed to replace the block. Waghorn was kept ignorant of the potential disaster until after the race.

One episode in that year's competition had long-term repercussions for Lawrence. General Italo Balbo, Italy's Under-Secretary for Air, was overall leader of the Italian team. There had originally been four countries competing for the 1929 Trophy: France, Italy, Great Britain and the US. However, the French and Americans dropped out early on and Italy had already lost one of their team in a fatal accident, the causes of which were uncertain. They pressed for a postponement, but were refused.

Despite Wing Commander Smith's reassurances to Trenchard, Lawrence did not stay out of the public gaze. The press had been briefed specifically by C.P. Robertson not to photograph Shaw, and they agreed to comply. Trenchard, probably on the day he surveyed the course, saw Lawrence talking to Nancy Astor and told D'Arcy Greig, 'Keep your eye on that damned fellow.' On the day of the race Balbo asked Lawrence to get the Italian slipway cleaned of some green scum that had built up and Lawrence saw to it. Lord Thompson, visiting the site, noticed a British aircraftman cleaning the site and demanded of 'Shaw' why this was happening. At that point a press photographer, unable to resist the temptation, coughed and pressed his shutter, photographing Lawrence and Thompson together. The *Daily Herald* photographer, James Jarche, later remarked 'If one man was going to have that photograph we all were. So Aircraftman Shaw was photographed from all angles. The photographs appeared all over the world.'[58] But not in England. Neither of Jarche's papers, the *Daily Herald*, nor the *Daily Express* ran the famous photo: the obvious inference being that the Air Ministry had censored it. The French and Italian press would publish the photo, but not in 1929.[59]

Thompson was very upset. He drew Sydney Smith's attention to the fact that he had seen Lawrence in conversation with Balbo and Sydney Smith commented:

> I knew well that it was in fact the first and only occasion Lawrence did talk to Balbo during that period. Lawrence had told me however that he had known Balbo, and when the latter knew that he was at Calshot with me, he seemed naturally anxious to meet him again. However, I explained the views of the C.A.S. to Shaw and no further conversation took place.[60]

For the race it was a warm day, the average air temperature being around 64 degrees Farenheit, with a blue sky, no more than a quarter cloud cover and good visibility. (That same day Churchill commenced his tour of the United States, having crossed over the border from Canada.) At Calshot Lawrence went on board the *Karen* to watch the fun. For the British, Waghorn and 'Batch' Atcherley flew S6a's and D'Arcy Greig flew an old S5. For the Italians, Dal Molin flew a Macchi M-52 and their pilots Cadringher and Monti flew M-67s. Waghorn won with an average speed of 528.87km/h and Dal Molin came second. D'Arcy Greig finished third. Atcherley was disqualified for flying around the inside (port side) of a marker

The photo *Daily Mail* photographer James Jarche took on 7th September 1929. He suggested this showed Lord Thompson, (a tall thin man), talking to Lawrence during the Schneider Trophy. Although Jarche stated many photographers snapped the confrontation, none of these appeared in any British newspaper that year. Lawrence had been asked by General Balbo to clean the Italian slipway and instructed an RAF 'erk' to do so. Thompson was wearing a dark suit at Calshot and cannot actually be seen. The woman to the left of Lawrence may be Nancy Astor. (Science and Society Picture Library)

pylon, despite it being painted in Lawrence's primrose yellow with black checks. The usual reason given is that his goggles blew off in flight, but it may have been the S6a's visibility. The cockpit on the S6a was so narrow the pilot could not face forward comfortably. In flight and taxying he had to look with one eye out of the port side of the windscreen to see forward. Because the aircraft was always turning to port around the circuit, the exhaust pipes on that side of the engine were sensibly transferred to the starboard to increase port visibility.[61] This resulted in a decrease in starboard visibility and may have contributed to Atcherley's error. Lawrence's relief at the completion of the competition was expressed to Robert Graves a week later: 'Ouf! I'm glad the Schneider Cup is over. Too much like work.'[62]

For the 1931 final Schneider contest Lawrence was only involved indirectly and Sydney Smith not at all. T.E.'s responsibility was the supervision of the testing trials of eight RAF 200 seaplane tenders at Hythe from February to July 1931, to be ready for the competition that September.[63] The main British aircraft of 1929, the Supermarine S6, was renamed the S6b in 1931 and incorporated a more powerful Rolls-Royce 'R' engine. One major change in 1931 was the abandonment of the aircraft seaworthiness trials,[64] reducing the extent to which the new Scott-Paine tenders would have been used.

In the event the '31 race nearly didn't happen. By 30th October the Air Ministry had decided not to enter an RAF team. It was felt, firstly, that previous government

In 1929 over a million people turned out to watch the Schneider Trophy race. The crowds at Southsea Pier gasp as an Italian Macchi MC-67 passes overhead at around 360 mph. Schneider Trophy machines were at the cutting edge of technology in the 1920s. (Via Smith)

intervention had contributed to changing the character of the race, away from Jacques Schneider's original intentions; and secondly, the earlier justification for the large amount of public expenditure involved – the need for the accumulation of sufficient data for the development of high speed aircraft – had now been met. These considerations, plus the depression, persuaded the Government to refuse support. Consequently, two years before the race was due, on 30th October 1929, the Air Ministry sent the following communiqué to the Royal Aero Club:

> Sir,
>
> I am commanded by the Air Council to inform you that the policy of the Government with regard to future Contests for the Schneider Trophy has been under consideration, and that it has been decided that a Royal Air Force team will not again be entered for this trophy. British participation will in future be left to the Royal Aero Club and private enterprise.[65]

It was only after the widow of a millionaire shipping magnate, Lady Houston, agreed to contribute £100,000[66] that the government relented. Not only this but the Italians, who had devoted great energy and ingenuity towards the race – producing some unique and innovative designs – were forced to withdraw. One design in particular, the Macchi MC-72, was fascinating, featuring two engines in tandem and contra-rotating propellers.[67] Unfortunately this suffered a fatal crash and the team, as with the French, had to abandon their entry. Thus the 1931 race was won by default for Great Britain by Flight Lieutenant John Boothman and after three successive 'victories', the permanent award of the Schneider Cup.

What significance did the Schneider Cup have in Lawrence's life? The fact that the Air Ministry's administration for the competition was carried through successfully despite numerous artificial and natural obstacles is an indication of Lawrence' and Sydney Smith's determination and commitment. 1929 was a vast, complex undertaking for them, requiring a high degree of organisation. In 1931 the situation was different. The inadequacies of the seaplane tenders in 1929 had caused the RAF to reconsider their role. Lawrence spent the first six months of 1931 in intensive activity supervising the trials of these new tenders. The Schneider work, particularly in 1929, was an important step in T.E.'s transition 'from ink to oil'.[68] As previously stated, he told Liddell Hart he had only 'done an ordinary Aircraftman's job until the Schneider Cup'. But it seems Lawrence was fairly well immersed in technical work by September 1929 and his transition to mechanics was probably more accelerated by the Blackburn Iris crash of 1931 than the 1929 Schneider work.

Major Nathan's Moth

Following the' Balbo incident' at Calshot Lawrence's future in the RAF was again jeopardised. He made a gross misjudgment a few days after the 1929 race by asking

Trenchard if he could accompany Sydney Smith's friend, Major Nathan, in his Moth on a European tour. Nathan was the owner of the D.H. X Cirrus Moth Smith had crashed in the King's Cup Air Race in 1928. The itinerary included France, Italy, Switzerland, Germany and Holland. Trenchard, as C.A.S., initially agreed to this, but the project was vetoed outright by Thompson. At a meeting at the Air Ministry on the 16th September, Trenchard told Lawrence he could not go on the European trip saying that he had come very close to being dismissed. He was to 'stop leading from the ranks and confine himself to the duties of an aircraftman'. Furthermore he was banned from leaving England, barred from flying in any service aircraft, and was not to speak to any 'great men' or women.[69]

In November T.E. was invited to a banquet by his friend at the Air Ministry Press Section, C.P. Robertson, but refused to attend partly because he didn't have a dress suit, but also because of the unstable nature of his appointment: he was the 'airman-on, provisionally on condition I do nothing *different*. Any slip and it's *outside*.' He explained that Calshot had been spoilt by the powers-that-be accusing him of being too prominent and 'cursing him back and forth'. He was only prevented from being sacked by the intervention of a 'very important person, the master of all of us.'[70]

The well known photograph of a Moth seaplane (below) shows Lawrence, his large head facing aft, standing on the float clutching a bracing wire. The Moth

Major Nathan's D.H. Moth Seaplane G-EBYV in the Channel Islands with Lawrence on the starboard float. He was forbidden by Thompson to fly in it on a proposed lengthy European trip with Nathan, or to fly in the seaplane at all. David Garnett went to great lengths researching a story of Lawrence and the Moth for his *Letters* (1935), which later proved to be unfounded. (Via Brown and Cave)

was owned by Nathan and the aircraft had the registration number G-EBYV, the photograph taken during a trip by Nathan and Lawrence to the Channel Islands. When off duty the pair often also used to travel in it up and down the Devon and Cornwall coast.[71]

In December 1929 Nathan wrote to Smith saying that he was going to get rid of G-EBYV and change it for a cheap ex-Gypsy Moth he had found at De Havillands. He thought it would be more economical to buy a new aircraft than fit the new engine G-EBYV required. He planned to fly it down to Mount Batten the following week and have floats fitted. Sydney Smith wrote back and the letter is of interest because it mentions Lawrence's responsibilities:

Headquarters,
RAF Base, Mount Batten,
Plymouth
14th December, 1929

Dear Bert,
I got your letter on my return to Mount Batten, I think however we talked about all the points you referred to and we now hope for fine weather so that you can get down here comfortably.

I have made arrangements for meeting you and Shaw will be in charge.

You will find some indication of the direction of the wind, possibly a smoke bomb, it will be let off when you are over the landing ground.

Shaw has just told me that the Moth propeller has again been discovered packed up with some stores in the workshops, I cannot understand how this was done and I am awfully sorry. Shaw gave some instructions for this to be sent off some weeks ago, however it was dispatched yesterday.

The delay in sending this propeller no doubt accounts for the small bill which De Havilland's continually send me, however I have now informed them that the propeller has now been returned so that now they will possibly credit the amount.[72]

Nathan had ordered an airscrew for a Cirrus Mk II Moth from de Havillands some time earlier and it was sent to Mount Batten while repairs were made on his own propeller. This propeller does not appear to have been used by Nathan. Smith wrote to de Havillands at Edgeware, Middlesex on the 17th informing them of this.

Dear Sir,
I have to inform you that a Moth (Cirrus Mk. II) Airscrew, supplied by you to the order of Major A.A. Nathan of 25, Moor Lane E.C. and sent to this base as a replacement airscrew while repairs were being were being carried out upon his own, has now been re-packed in case and put on rail addressed to you, carriage forward. The case has been marked as from Major Nathan.[73]

It seems that the propeller was for G-EBYV but was never used. In 1937, whilst David Garnett was researching his proposed collection of Lawrence's letters for Cape, he came across the story of Lawrence's use of Nathan's Moth. He had been told that in 1930 Lawrence carried on a semi-serious but amusing correspondence with the Air Ministry's Civil Aviation Department regarding a licence to fly the Moth owned by Nathan. The correspondence went on for months.[74] Garnett wanted access to it for the purpose of his book. He was in contact with a Mr. Thomas Jones of the Pilgrim Trust, London, who had contacts with the Air Ministry. Jones asked Colonel Sir Donald Banks, if he could investigate the case, and Banks passed the request onto the Air Ministry's Chief Registrar. The Registrar looked into the matter, spending 'considerable time and energy in doing his best to trace the papers'. Banks reported the results to Jones: 'He sent me a list of the people whom he has consulted and I must say that for the length and completeness it is impressive, but the result, I am afraid, of his investigation is that no trace can be found or even any recollection in any one's memory of the existence of any such correspondence.'[75]

Garnett had drawn a blank. Jones sent him the details of the Registrar's efforts, and began to feel guilty of wasting the Air Ministry's time. However, Garnett then heard that Lawrence had had a dressing down from Sir Sefton Brancker in relation to the Moth. Brancker had said something like: 'Why, are you the ruffian who has been making more trouble than all the private owners put together?'[76] Garnett was given Nathan's name and the registration number. He then realised that his initial understanding of what happened was incorrect:

> The machine was G.A.-A.L.J.[77] Given to me as G.H. A.L.J. which I take it is wrong. The owner was Major A.A. Nathan and the machine was lent by Air Commodore Sydney Smith for a time and was flown by both Nathan and T.E. who put floats on her. The correspondence was trouble about an airworthiness certificate, and the letters were concocted by T.E. to delay matters as long as possible and to pull the Air Ministry's leg.[78]

Garnett was hoping any letters the Ministry might unearth would 'throw light on Lawrence's impishness and also his flying experience'. Sydney Smith, when contacted later, suggested the date of any letters would be from April 1929 onwards, querying if a log book existed. Donald Banks then wrote directly to Sydney Smith, who was by then an Air Commodore in No. 1 (Bomber) Group, Abingdon, explaining the developments. They'd had some difficulty in tracking the plane as the registration marking was wrong. Eventually, however, they succeeded in establishing that the marking was G-EBYV. This was the aircraft owned by Major Nathan and piloted on occasion by Sydney Smith. There was no trace that Lawrence ever flew it. (It was at one time the subject of negotiations between Smith, Nathan and the Department of Civil Aviation in connection with the fitting of floats and the renewal of its airworthiness certificate). Banks could find no connection of Lawrence with these discussions.[79] Smith replied on 9th March:

Shortly after my posting to Mount Batten, a friend of mine, Major A.A. Nathan, lent me his Moth which I transferred into a float plane. At the end of the year the land undercarriage was replaced and the Moth was flown to De Havilland's Works for its annual examination by the A.I.D. It was here that the difficulty arose, as apparently the aircraft construction was not intended for use on the water, and unknowingly I had contravened certain regulations. About this time Nathan wanted to take the aeroplane away with him on leave, and I was naturally anxious to get it serviceable for him as soon as possible. I discussed the matter with Brancker at Calshot, and it was following this talk that I wrote the letter, a copy of which I have attached.[80]

Banks then closed the matter by writing to Garnett. He enclosed a copy of the Chief Registrar's conclusions which were more illuminating than his letter: 'The difficulty was to ascertain the identity of the aircraft . . . but Mr. Searle of the A.I.D. succeeded by appeal to the Inspector, now at Manchester, who carried out the inspection.'[81]

When the Moth was eventually identified and related correspondence inspected none was found relevant to that required. The report stated the aircraft was G-EBYV (not G-AALJ) owned by A.A. Nathan and Sydney Smith was the pilot. There did not appear to be any request by Lawrence to pilot it: 'There was talk of prosecution for irregular flying . . . it is reasonable to assume that if any unregistered pilot had flown it the point would at least have been mentioned if known.[82] The A.I.D. was concerned about the unauthorised fitting of floats but neither Nathan nor Smith replied to Air Ministry letters, their only remarks being verbal when the aircraft was examined by the A.I.D. Inspector, or to Sir Sefton Brancker. The conclusion was that no letters of the character Garnett hoped for were written to the Air Ministry.

Although Garnett did mention Nathan's Moth in *The Letters of T.E. Lawrence* he finally had to admit his attempts to get to the truth of the story were fruitless. Nathan 'had some trouble about an airworthiness certificate and Lawrence used to tell a long, comic story about a correspondence which he conducted with the Air Ministry on the subject, under Major Nathan's name.'[83] By taking advantage of the regulations for land planes being different from sea-planes he was able to postpone an expensive A.I.D. inspection for months. Garnett was unable to find the relevant correspondence but managed to include one letter in his 1938 collection that mentioned a Moth indirectly. It was to F.N. Doubleday on 2nd September 1930 and concerned the flight of a de Havilland Moth over Rudyard Kipling's back garden. Although Doubleday was a friend of Kipling, Kipling did not like Lawrence, so the 'salute' may not have been appreciated. Lawrence wrote: 'I flew over Kipling's garden last Saturday, and again yesterday, on my way back here from Folkstone. We tilted the Moth[84] up on one wingtip and spun round and round over his garden. I wonder what he said: I can guess it nearly.'[85]

Henry Field

In 1928 a well known anthropologist, Henry Field, sought out Lawrence's help. Field was an American who was educated at Eton and New College, Oxford. He was born in December 1902 and graduated in 1927. After Oxford he was appointed Assistant Curator to The Field Museum of Natural History, Chicago and later participated in many of the Near East expeditions the museum made, becoming well known in Arabia in the late 1940s and early 1950s.

Some time in March or April 1929 he contacted Lawrence at Mount Batten (then still RAF Cattewater) sending him an article he had written. Lawrence replied on Friday 26th April 1929:

Dear Mr. Field,

I'm very grateful for your little article. Your work in the Syrian Desert should be very interesting. It's always, I think, in the lava regions that one finds the best ruins (and the best grass, when it rains), and to date them, somehow, would be very interesting.

They are more difficult than sites in Europe – for there is no patina to go by, on flint: flints colour in less than 20 years, as Woolley and I found in Syria. Do you know our sketchy little volume 'The Wilderness of Zin,' written for the Palestine Exploration Fund in 1914? It was got out in a hurry for reasons of politics, and is bad. There's also the snag that the Bedouin today is eolithic, when lazy; and palaeolithic when he wants a decent flint to trim his toe-nails.

If you can go into the Gara district, a lava field 80 miles S.E. from Wejh, in the Hejaz. Ibn Saud would probably let you, if you approached him through Philby,[86] who's a

Henry Field c. 1928.
(Field Museum)

good scientist and lives at Jidda now. The Harret el Gara is full of circles and grave-cairns, of black dolerite.

I'm afraid I haven't anything on the castles of the Middle East. The rumour must have come from a thesis I wrote for my Oxford History degree on the Crusader castles of Syria. It was an elementary performance, and I think it has been destroyed or left behind somewhere, in the course of my life. At any rate, I haven't a notion where it is – but a strong memory that it was worthless.

I'm afraid our Thlaithukwhat tracks will be in the desert for generations. As for the 'kites', I fancy a big tribe like the Rwalla might put them up, when pasturing all their camels together. A quite low wall is an obstacle for a camel, and the herdsmen could sleep safely in the open side, while the beasts grazed. Herding camels is an awful business, and people like the Ghassanide 'kings' must have been much more organized than Nuri Shalaan's crowd, and prepared to put their herdsmen to more trouble than he can afford.

If ever you are in England write to me here, or ring up someone at the Air Ministry, if you know anyone there, and let us meet. But I warn you that the mountain may have to come to Mohammed. The Air Force does not give its slaves great leisure.

Yours Sincerely,
(signed) T.E. Shaw
(Colonel T.E. Lawrence)

Do you know that many of the tribal wasms are Hiniyari letters.[87]

The Wilderness of Zin, a Biblically derived title, was ostensibly an archaeological survey of the Sinai Desert and the area north of Akaba on the Red Sea up to Petra. It was carried out in January and February 1914 by Lawrence and Leonard Woolley, under the orders of D.G. Hogarth of the British Museum, for an organisation called The Palestine Exploration Fund. Actually it was a secret military survey done for Kitchener under the direction of Captain Stewart F. Newcombe of the Royal Engineers. The presence of the archaeologists was intended to give it credibility in the eyes of the Turks. The area was important because it represented the border between Egypt and the Ottoman Empire and previous surveys by Kitchener were incomplete. Field must have assumed that Lawrence had knowledge of Middle East castles because of his degree thesis on the relationship between Crusader Castle architecture and the castles of Europe. The 'worthless' thesis got Lawrence a First. Copies of this document, as with the Palestine survey, have now been published, but in 1929 they were still locked away in the archives.

Field went to see Lawrence in 1930. He was interested in the Middle East, and had with him a map of the Sinai Desert. The original source for this story was an article by George Williams in the *Evening Herald*, Plymouth, on 13th August, 2005. This stated that Field carried a number of uncompleted maps of the Sinai Desert and 'Empty Quarter' supplied from the *National Geographic* magazine, by a man named Milne. Gerald Wasley explained that Williams made this up, causing a lot of confusion. Only one map was used. Milne was at that time one of the leading cartographers in England at the National Geographic Society.[88]

Field probably thought that Lawrence's knowledge of the Sinai peninsula, where the P.E.F. team spent six weeks in 1914 mapping the tracks and watering places, would enlighten him on the archaeology of the desert. This letter from Lawrence to Field is dated November 13th:

> Dear Mr. Field,
>
> I hope you are colossally rich so that the coming all the way to this misery of Plymouth (the last or first town of England according to your hemisphere) will mean nothing to you. I'm a fraud, as regards both the Middle East and archaeology. Years ago I haunted both, and got fairly expert: but the war over-dosed, and nine years ago I relapsed comfortably into the ranks of our Air Force, and have no interests outside it since. Nine years is long enough to make me out-of-date, but long enough to make my views quaint and interestingly archaic. I have forgotten all I knew, too.
>
> I'll meet your 4.48 train at North Road, which is Plymouth station. You will have to do the recognizing. Look out for a small and aged creature in a slaty-blue uniform with brass-buttons: like an R.A.C. scout or tram-driver, perhaps, only smaller and shabbier.
>
> Our camp is a few yards by water, and seven miles by road; you will be for a hotel, I expect. There are many, all bad. Or perhaps you are going back the same night? That will increase your misery. It rains here, always.
>
> Yours Sincerely,
> T.E. Shaw[89]

Lawrence also sent an undated telegram, probably after Field had arrived in England:

21 9.4 PLYMOUTH T 26

> FIELD, BAGGRAVE, GADDESBY –
> AM HIDEOUSLY OUT OF DATE ORIENTALLY BUT IF YOU THINK
> TRIP WORTH WHILE AM FREE EVERY EVENING FROM FIVE TILL
> TEN – SHAW[90]

Field was put up in the Duke of Cornwall Hotel, Plymouth, by Lawrence whilst they discussed the map he had brought with him.[91] Lawrence had been interested in the exploration of the 'Empty Quarter' for some time. He had written to Sir Hugh Trenchard on Friday 12th July 1929 suggesting that the new airships, R100 and R101, could be put to good use if they flew over Southern Arabia:

These Airships: one or two of them have trial trips soon. Some say to the States, others to Karachi . . .

Well, by going just a few miles out of their course to the southward they can pass over the Ruba el Khali, the so-called 'Empty Quarter' of Arabia. This is a huge area of many hundred thousand square miles. No European has ever crossed it, nor any Arab any of us has actually questioned. All the Geographers refer to it annually as the great unsolved question of geography.

Now, I want the trial trip of the airships to settle the Ruba el Khali.[92]

One report has it that Lawrence told Field to fly out to India and return on the R101 as an observer: the dirigible was to be rerouted to fly back across the Ruba el Khali.[93] Apparently Sefton Brancker, Director General of Civil Aviation, wrote to Field that this had been agreed.[94]

The R101 left Cardington, despite forecasts of bad weather, on 4th October 1930, on her maiden voyage to India via Egypt. In the early hours of the morning of 5th she crashed near Beauvais, France. There were six survivors and 48 killed, including the Minister for Air, Lord Thompson and Brancker. Nancy Astor had a seat on the airship but cancelled it. Lawrence earlier asked George Bernard Shaw to suggest to Thompson that he, with his extensive knowledge of Arabia, would be a useful addition to the crew. Thompson replied on 24th July 1929 that he would consider the matter but that T.E.'s 'passion for obscurity makes him an awkward man to place and would not improve his relations with the less subtle members of the crew'.[95] Any possibility of his involvement was vetoed after his falling out with Thompson at the Schneider competition that September.

Bertram Thomas and the Empty Quarter

Henry Field eventually presented the map he and T.E. prepared to the Explorer's Club in New York,[96] and it was used for many years afterwards.[97] Needless to say he did not make the R101 trip. The Ruba el Khali was conquered by an Englishman, Bertram Thomas, the following year. On 10th March 1931 T.E. wrote to Sir Edward Marsh:[98]

> Bertram Thomas, our agent at Muscat, has just crossed the Empty Quarter, that great desert of Southern Arabia. It remained the only unknown quarter of the world, and it is the end of the history of exploration. Thomas did it by camel, at his own expense. Every explorer for generations has dreamed of it. Its difficulty can best be put by my saying that no Arab, so far as we know, has ever crossed it.[99]

Thomas was a 38-year-old civil servant from near Bristol who had served in the Mesopotamian campaign during the War. He had already undertaken a number of expeditions in Arabia including, in 1928, a 600-mile camel journey along the coast of Southern Oman. He crossed the Ruba el Khali with fifteen camels and forty Bedouin in just over two months, leaving Salala on the south Arabian coast in mid December 1930 and arriving at Qatar in Muscat in late February 1931, covering a distance of just over 700 miles. He asked Lawrence, at Jonathan Cape's instigation, to write a preface to the book he had written about it called *Arabia Felix*. Lawrence initially declined. He wrote a series of letters over the next six months to Thomas explaining his reasons. On 10th June he arranged to meet Thomas at the Union Jack Club, London (after a long delay in replying as he had missed any letters whilst detached at Hythe) but he had to cancel because of RAF work.

On 3rd August the British Power Boat Company yard was burnt down and T.E., since he was not needed at Hythe, went back to his old haunt at Barton Street. Despite working all hours on the *Odyssey* he still found time to write to Thomas recommending that no preface be included. The danger he felt was that an introduction by a celebrity could only serve as a distraction and would obscure the quality of the book itself. Any poor quality work might sell in the first edition, but further sales might actually be hindered by a prestigious preface. He had experienced the same trouble with 'eminents' offering to preface *Seven Pillars* and was glad he refused. He wrote to Thomas that only in poor conditions ('misery, anger indignation and discomfort') could good literature be produced, and he was tired of writing.

He went on holiday with the Smiths for a few days from August 17th at Thurlestone. Thomas, who was due to sail to America, apparently misunderstood or simply ignored T.E.'s previous letter that thundered against prefaces and Lawrence agreed to read the proofs, which at that time were unfinished. At this

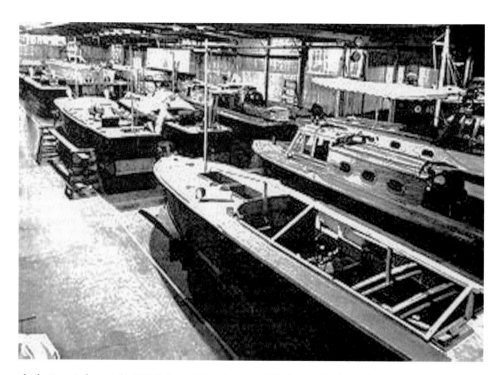

The hull workshop at the British Power Boat Company, Hythe in 1939. (Rance)

point in his life Lawrence had little left of the desire for writing he displayed as a young man. *Seven Pillars, The Mint* and the *Odyssey* had all drained his creativity. He agreed to read Thomas's proofs eagerly: if the work was 'impossibly bad' he would try and write a preface, if it was 'hugely good', then Thomas would be so proud of it that he would 'utterly spurn and despise the idea of a preface'. He concluded that prefaces were 'the fruits not of vanity but of over modesty':

> Let me have your first batches of copy as and when they are ready. No help, no revision, no pains taken, will make a poor draft into a good book: everything lies on your first conception, upon the excitement running into your hand as you write. But it will very much delight me to read it as it comes.[100]

Lawrence was forced to leave Barton Street when his leave was cut short by the Air Ministry in August. A consequence of Sydney Smith's promotion to Group Captain was that he would be sent to command another RAF base and on 2nd October he was transferred to Manston, Kent, a station on the coast that would later play a front line role in the Battle of Britain.[101] At the end of October Lawrence drove Clare Smith from Mount Batten through Somerset and the New Forest to follow her husband to her new home at Pouce's Farm, Kent. He remained there for a fortnight. He was reluctant to return to Plymouth, but when he did, he did not reply to any of her letters for a long time. It may be that he thought it prudent to ease away from the attachment.[102]

By 21st November he was back at Hythe. He had read Thomas's book but had been unable to complete the preface because of work. He was however reassured by what he read. He felt a 'great release and relief at knowing that the book was good enough'. He felt it was 'exceedingly well told' and would 'live for generations'. He told Thomas he was a fortunate man; and that the Foreign Office was displeased with him.[103] It seems that at this point Lawrence decided the book deserved his help: the scepticism and caution he had expressed earlier had disappeared. His attitude though was different to his feelings for C.M. Doughty's *Travels in Arabia Deserta*, for which he had devotedly written an 11½-page introduction in 1922.

At the end of November he visited the Smiths at their new home at Pouce's Farm, Manston, where they inspected a First World War dugout. The following week he was at Hythe with Bradbury, where he would remain until the following Easter. His mother and youngest brother were staying at Clouds Hill.

He posted the introduction on to Thomas at the beginning of December. He had made only one copy of the introduction, which he sent to Charlotte Shaw for GBS's vetting, like all his work. He wrote to Thomas again on 7th December advising against Cape's request but seeing it as the company's salvation:

> I got your doubled letter . . . and wired back that I'd get something done by the end of last week: and did. I hope you have had it. A poor lame thing: but the only reaction stirred in me was the sense of thankfulness that it was alright. Misery, anger,

indignation, comfort – those conditions produce literature. Contentment never – so there you are. It will need your censorship and the proper spelling of all the people's names: and anyhow it is a poor thing. But it will save Jonathan's face at least.[104]

On 8th December Charlotte told Lawrence GBS was 'going to work over it a little'.[105] Lawrence as always mocked his own work, describing it as 'piffle'. His final advice to Thomas was: 'Don't worry. By the way I haven't had any telegrams from you so you probably aren't worrying.'[106]

Clare Smith recalled Lawrence was working like a 'navvy' that January and concluded he had little time for correspondence. Although she sent many letters to him his replies were only intermittent and on the many occasions she asked him to come to Manston he told her his work and other circumstances prevented this. This may be further evidence of his withdrawal from the relationship, for fear of upsetting the Smiths' marriage. His efforts with the 28 h.p. Meadows-engined dinghy had been voted 'the goods'[107] by E6 and he was consoled. He had no idea of Thomas's opinion of his introduction as all his letters were held at Mount Batten, but Cape were not doing well and he hoped that Thomas's book would rekindle their fortunes.

Arabia Felix, with Lawrence's poetic introduction, was published by Cape in London, and Scribners in New York, in 1932. The preface, which contained compound words and phrasing reminiscent of both *Seven Pillars* and the *Odyssey*, was better written than the introduction to Doughty of a decade before:

> Thomas shocked me when he asked for a foreword to his great journey-book, not because introductions put me off (he may as reasonably enjoy them, perhaps) but because he had recourse to me. It took some while to think out so strange a lapse.
> . . . Few men are able to close an epoch. We cannot know the first man who walked the inviolate earth for newness' sake: but Thomas is the last; and he did his journey in the antique way, by pain of his camel's legs, single handed, at his own time and cost. He might have flown an aeroplane, sat in a car or rolled over in a tank. Instead he snatched, at the twenty-third hour, feet's last victory and set us free.[108]

Bertram Thomas died in Cairo in 1950 after writing several books on his travels.

The Blackburn Iris Crash

On Wednesday 4th February 1931 a Blackburn Iris III flying boat crashed in Plymouth Sound, an event that is well documented. Only with this disaster did Lawrence's great achievements in the Marine Craft Section begin when, for the first time, Smith and Lawrence's earlier fears of the inadequacies of the RAF's seaplane tenders were painfully confirmed.

The Iris III was the largest aircraft in the RAF, weighing over 20 tons, with a wingspan of 97 feet, a length of just over 67 feet and a height over 25 feet. It was powered by three Rolls-Royce Condor in-line piston engines, supported on metal struts between

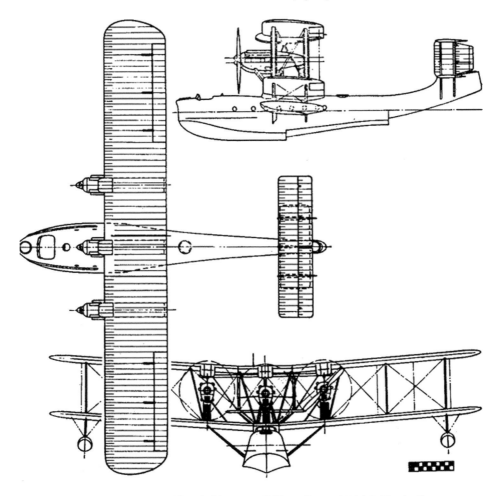

General Arrangement Drawing of the Blackburn Iris III Flying Boat c. 1931 (via Thetford)

the two wings. The normal crew was six, all but one stationed in exposed positions on top of the fuselage. The pilot and co-pilot were in an open cockpit directly in front of the wings, and three gunners were in turrets open to the air, one at the very nose of the hull, one directly behind the wings and one at the tail.

Within the hull was a small compartment for the engineer with two porthole-type windows and an observation hatch, directly behind the cockpit. It was here that the remaining six RAF men were probably located before the accident.[109] The Iris III had an all-metal hull and superstructure. From Lawrence's observations after the accident, the wings and hull appear to have been divided into semi-watertight compartments. 209 was the only squadron equipped with the Iris III.

Despite their 'stick and string' appearance to modern eyes, flying boat design was a sophisticated science by 1931. Extensive experimentation had gone into such aspects as noise, use of salt water distillation apparatus, long distance W/T communication, water pressure measurement on planing hull bottoms, and anchor testing.

Extensive performance trials had been carried out in 1929 on version II. This is the only archive data available on the Iris's performance and, as the aircraft were very similar, is quoted here. These trials reported that the aircraft's flying qualities were exceptionally good: the controls were light and responsive, and, the rudder was light when its servo-motor was on. Control at low speed was good, and there was no tendency to wing-drop at stalling speed, since elevator control was lost before aileron control. The Iris was easy to fly in calm weather, when it could be flown hands-off for long periods. It was also reasonably easy in rough weather, the metal hull proving remarkably resistant to accidental damage.

There was a problem, however, with servo-rudder control. One report stated that when engine speeds dropped from 1650 to 1600 rpm, servo-rudder control was lost almost instantly, without forewarning. Also when gliding in, as happened at Mount Batten, with the engine throttled back, the servo-rudder was ineffective at speeds below 65 knots.[110] In 1929 a series of two-engined flight tests were conducted on an Iris II. In clear weather, with the centre engine stopped it was found that it would hold its height with a normal load, but with an outboard engine off it would not maintain height with a load greater than 25,000 lbs.[111]

All this suggests that the crash at Mount Batten of such a stable, responsive aircraft could only have been the result of poor piloting. But it may be that loss of rudder control as the aircraft dove was the reason for the crash. If an outboard engine had failed, and the aircraft was overloaded with a crew of 12, this could also have contributed to the accident.

February 4th was a warm sunny morning. Visibility was up to 14 miles and an 8- to 12-mph wind was blowing from the north. It was generally cloudy with a layer of low stratus at 4,000 feet. Several aircraft were circling the sound. It was Lawrence's morning break and he and Clare Smith were having 'elevenses' at a place they called the 'Lido', a turfed hollow they had made below the Martello Tower.[112] Clare would go there most mornings. They had been sitting there for about ten minutes.

> ...Tes[113] and I sat in our Lido and looked over the glassy surface of the sound, which seemed an endless mirror, stretching away for ever. Two or three flying-boats were up as usual, practising firing at targets at sea. Presently one of them began to circle downward as they always do before landing. As she circled over the breakwater Tes said: 'That boat looks queer.'[114]

They were shocked to realise that, despite gliding down from a respectable height, the aircraft was making no attempt to flatten out. Directly before them it nosed straight into the water, with hardly a ripple on the surface. The flying boat slowly surfaced, but there was no sign of the crew. Clare was terrified her husband may have been piloting it as he was due to fly that day.

I looked at Tes. His face was taught and set – his body alert: all his relaxation had gone.

'Tes, do you think it's Sydney?'

'No, decidedly not; but I must go and see what can be done.'[115]

They ran down the hill: Lawrence to the breakwater, Clare to her car. Lawrence burned with energy in life or death situations like this. Sydney Smith was on the other side of the promontory and Clare drove over. To her it seemed like hours, but was, in fact, only minutes and she saw her husband was facing her on the slipway. Lawrence meanwhile had run down to the breakwater. Clare's face, in her husband's words, was 'as white as a sheet'. None of the men on the east side of the base knew a tragedy had occurred. Lawrence appeared, running towards them.

'I've got a boat standing by, sir.'

The three of them ran back to the west to see, sticking out of the grey flatness of the Sound, the silver tail of the Iris, framed by the angular rock mass of Drake's Island behind it.

'How many are there in her?' asked Sydney Smith.

'I think twelve, but two have come up.'

The two men jumped into a seaplane tender and roared out to the wreck. For the first time they had their suspicions confirmed – the tenders were too slow.[116] It took them four minutes to cover 700 yards. At the wreck Lawrence took over. Clare Smith later described his reaction to the tragedy:

> Tes became master of the situation. His gift of quick, crystal clear thinking and natural leadership made his authority instantly acceptable to everyone there . . . Each time Sydney's orders followed Tes's suggestions, which were given quietly and respectfully and in such a way that he could accept them without a shade of resentment.[117]

After some discussion they hailed a trawler, the idea being to get a hawser around the tail and stop the boat sinking. Lawrence dived in but the aft cockpit entrance was jammed by an inflated dinghy. His idea was to get some kind of sling round her. The salvage boat went back to the dockyard and the Admiral sent out hawsers and diving equipment. Although they desperately tried to salvage her she was impossible to lift, so the hull was dragged back to the Mount Batten slipway.

Six men had dived into the confined space of the crushed hull. Lawrence released the dead body of Wing Commander Tucker from the controls as the aircraft gradually began to break up, air escaping in belches as the hull and wing compartments collapsed. Those who survived were Corporal Barry, who came up in an air bubble; the injured front gunner Flying-Officer Riley who dragged himself out; and seriously injured aircraft captain Flight Lieutenant Eley. Flying Officer S.K. Wood was brought up but later died from shock and exposure. Of the nine dead, only Tucker, Wood and L.A.C. Rutledge were recovered. Six bodies were never seen again, sucked down into the darkness with the lower part of the shattered hull.

Lawrence and Clare Sydney Smith. Examination of her biography of Lawrence, *The Golden Reign*, suggests she was infatuated with him.

At the Public Inquest that followed less of the truth came out than in the official Air Ministry Inquiry. Because this was not open to the press it was not covered by the report that appeared on Saturday 24th February. Flight Lieutenant M.H. Ely, swathed in bandages as he lay on a couch in the Plymouth Royal Naval Hospital, gave evidence at the inquest on the 21st. He stated that Tucker had knocked the controls from his hands as he made a second appeal to be given control. A number of witnesses confirmed that Tucker had been inexperienced on flying boats, but had many hours on land-based aircraft, being under instruction at Mount Batten.

After the Coroner summed up, the jury's unanimous decision was that Tucker's determination to take control of the aircraft, despite his co-pilot's wishes, and his inexperience, caused the accident. The final verdict was 'error of judgement'. In future, it was recommended, any C.O. should have full flying instruction. Lawrence, called as a witness, was described in a newspaper report as 'a short, compact figure, in the neat, well fitting uniform of the service', with his highly polished buttons. He punctiliously added 'sir' to all his replies. He also injected a gentle touch of humour into the sombre proceedings when asked if he did any flying and replied, 'No, but I used to, sir.'[118]

He had heard recommendations by other RAF men not to fly with Tucker. 'Had I been ordered as a matter of duty to have flown with him I would have done so, but not for choice.'[119] He told the court the crash had occurred 600 yards south of the Mount Batten breakwater in 26 feet of water. The tail had come up, the wings had crashed straight into the water and then folded back. The hull dove straight to the bottom and the tail inverted, only a few feet remaining above the surface.

Tucker's blunder caused great bitterness at Mount Batten. Lawrence wrote to Charlotte Shaw:

> It was due to bad piloting, on the part of the man who (as we all know) should never have flown with passengers. He would not be convinced of that. Fortunately he died with the rest.[120]

With his usual ability to see through to the cause of the problem, Lawrence identified the high-ranking RAF officer as the culprit. Three separate reports had been made to the Air Ministry concerning Tucker's 'unfitness to fly'. All of these arrived at the desk of Air Marshal Webb-Bowen and were ignored. The Air Ministry enquiry that followed was not open to the Press but Lawrence hoped to bring the responsibility down on Webb-Bowen's shoulders, without getting himself into trouble.[121] He was conscious that the court may castigate Sydney Smith and made great efforts to prevent this, receiving a lot of help from friends behind the scenes in putting his case, particularly Nancy Astor. Bernard Shaw, hearing of his plight, likened his position to 'the sentinel in Macbeth who, having seen Birnham Wood start to walk, could say only "I should report what I saw, but know not how to do it."'[122] He exhorted him to adopt the role of a 'simple aircraftsman'[sic]:

> Nothing but an eyewitness's police report can be expected from you. However, as you will probably insist on conducting the enquiry, and as you will want to save your ambitious commander from being sacrificed, the future, in my vision, is on the knees of the gods.[123]

As an afterthought he recommended that Lawrence pray to be sacked; and there was a danger that this might happen if he was seen to press his case too hard. T.E. told Charlotte Shaw he had facts enough that, if published, would prevent a repeat of the incident.[124]

Lawrence had been made Clerk to the Court, and so far agreed with its findings.[125] On March 2nd he told Nancy Astor, being extremely thankful for her help, 'I *think* the battle is won.' He said Sydney Smith had made great efforts to ensure his men told the truth at the inquest. Behind the scenes efforts by the likes of Lady Astor were well concealed. Reforms would later begin to take place. The press held sway and the bench was sympathetic: 'The Coroner was a perfect pet. He asked all the nibbly, difficult, hurtful questions, so innocently and so smoothly that everything came out.'[126] At the funeral the people of Plymouth turned out in their thousands to honour the dead.

The accident galvanised Lawrence. The incident had far more effect upon him than the Schneider Trophy races did and his work on fast boats after that began in earnest, particularly on Air-Sea Rescue. One of the most disturbing things about the incident, apart from the foolishness that caused it, was the time of four minutes it took for an RAF tender to reach the crash. Lawrence and Smith had been thinking faster tenders were needed for some time, and with a faster launch more men might just have been saved. Early in January 1933 there was another Iris accident. By that time however, thanks partly to Lawrence's endeavours, the launch covered 0.875 of a mile in almost 2 minutes: twice as far in half the time, four times faster. Only one life was lost. This was some indication of how successful Lawrence's work with the Meadow-engined RAF 200 was.

Thus another chapter in Lawrences's astonishing life drew to a close. The extremely complex co-ordination of a multitude of subordinate tasks for the Schneider Trophy had passed off without any major problems, and the High Speed Flight took their second, unexpected, victory. The 1929 Schneider Cup also led to the use of the Biscayne Baby speedboat, host of his earliest mechanical work. A.A. Nathan with his passion for Moths had taken Lawrence for trips in one to the Channel Islands and along the Devon coast. This opportunity to fly in his leisure hours was an enjoyable experience, and indicates that his second RAF period was not so blighted by privations as he liked to make out.

He continued to share his Arabian experiences with other authors and explorers, in each case with reservations. Bertram Thomas had achieved what he himself had wanted to do for years, and produced a work he personally approved of, which accounted for his change of heart about the introduction. He found however, that the help he could give the anthropologist Henry Field was very limited, his letters giving no clear idea of what interchange occurred between them. Finally, we find Lawrence 'leading from the ranks' again in February 1931, displaying his natural analytical ability and leadership in the Iris rescue. But was it because the disgust he felt for himself was so deep-seated that he still could not accept any official promotion?

Notes

1 In Britain's case this was the Royal Aero Club. The complex allocation of responsibility explains the frequently fraught relationship between the R.A.C., the Air Ministry and the government.

2 *Technical Aspects of the Schneider Trophy and the world speed record for seaplanes*. Dr. E.Bazzocchi, *Aeronautical Journal*, 2/1972.

3 None of these deaths however took place during the actual competitions themselves, but in trials. Britain suffered two deaths during speed trials, Sam Kinkaid in 1927, and Gerry Brinton, a naval officer, in 1931.

4 *Memories of the Last Schneider Trophy Contests*, Air Commodore F.R. Banks, Journal of the Royal Aeronautical Society, 1/1966.

5 Trenchard was consistently opposed to R.A.F. participation in the Schneider Cup throughout his tenure of office and not solely the 1929 race.

6 Source: Memorandum from AVM Sir John Higgins, Air Ministry to Mr. Harold Perrin, Secretary, Royal Aero Club. Sydney Smith papers, Houghton Library, University of Harvard.

7 Personal Secretary to Secretary of State to Chief of Air Staff, 31/01/28. National Archives: AIR 2/1303/. In this memo lay the genesis of the Spitfire. R.J. Mitchell, who had designed the winning S5 of 1927, abandoned the Napier Lion engine he had used in this and opted for a purpose-designed 'R' or 'Race' engine designed by Rolls-Royce in 1929. The technological developments that were used in the aircraft that bore it, the Supermarine S6 and its successor the S6b, had a great influence on Mitchell's design of the Spitfire, as did the 'R' engine on Rolls-Royce's Merlin.

8 Date should be 1929.

9 Personal Secretary to Secretary of State to Chief of Air Staff, 31/01/28. National Archives: AIR 2/1303/.

10 Source: S.H. (Air Min.) to Under Secretary of State and Chief of Air Staff, 25/02/ 1928. National Archives: AIR 2/1303/.

11 Ibid.

12 H. Trenchard to A.M.S.R. and Secretary of State, 28/2/1928. National Archives: AIR 2/1303/. The 1927 High Speed Flight had been disbanded by the RAF after the last competition.

13 Wing Commander Sydney Smith Flying Log Book, Sydney Smith Archive, RAF Museum.

14 Air Ministry letter to the Secretary of State, 7/8/1928. File *S7289 Schneider Cup Race 1929 arrangements*. National Archives: Treasury Supply Dept: Reg. Files (S Series) T 161/275/.

15 Ibid.

16 Mr. B.E. Holloway CB was a Principal Assistant Secretary at the Air Ministry.

17 Air Ministry letter to the Secretary of State, 7/8/1928. File *S7289 Schneider Cup Race 1929 arrangements*. National Archives: Treasury Supply Dept: Reg. Files (S Series) T 161/275/. This was presumably to allow the Air Ministry to monitor the administration of the programme.

18 Flying Log Book of Wing Commander S.W. Smith, 20/7/1928.

19 Flying Log Book of Wing Commander Sydney Smith, Sydney Smith Archives, RAF Museum.

20 W.F.N. to S. of S. 15/10/1928. National Archives: Treasury Supply Dept: Reg. Files (S Series) T 161/275/.

21 W.F.N. to Mr. Holloway 1/11/1928. National Archives: Treasury Supply Dept: Reg. Files (S Series) T 161/275/.

22 W.F.N. to A.P. Waterfield, Treasury Chambers, Whitehall. 6/12/1928 National Archives: Treasury Supply Dept: Reg. Files (S Series) T 161/275/.

23 In 1929 R.A.F. Coastal Area was a defensive zone around the coastline of the UK. As such, although it operated flying boats and reconnaissance aircraft in support of the Royal Navy for attacking enemy ships and protecting British waters, it had a more limited range than Coastal Command, which succeeded it. 204 Squadron, which Sydney Smith commanded in 1930, was part of No. 10 Group, Coastal Area.

24 Arrangements for the Schneider Trophy Contest, 1928/29. National Archives: AIR 2/1303/.

25 P. Shipster.

26 Ibid.

27 T.E. Shaw to Robert Graves, Cattewater, 5/5/29. RG-B.

28 D.O.S.D. Directorate of Staff Duties.

29 Arrangements for the Schneider Trophy Contest, 1928/29. National Archives: AIR 2/1303/. According to Pieter Shipster the minutes of the meeting do not show Jones or Nicholson attending, whereas a Group Captain E.R.C. Nanson from Calshot and a Flight Lieutenant Jukes were present.

30 This came under Navy, Admiralty, and RAF jurisdiction: 'Wing Commander Sydney W. Smith of R.A.F. Station Cattewater' was mentioned particularly in this context.

30 Arrangements for the Schneider Trophy Contest, 1928/29. National Archives: AIR 2/1303/.

32 From 1927, after the debacle of 1926, the RAF formed the High Speed Flight. This followed the precedent of a military team set by the Americans in 1923, 1924, and 1925.

33 *Recollections of T.E. Lawrence*, Air Commodore Sydney Smith, 1963, Sydney Smith archive, RAF Museum.

34 Ibid.

35 T.E. Shaw to B.E. Leeson, R.A.F. Cattewater, 18/4/1939, MB.

36 B: LH.

37 Some reports are wrong about the size: it weighed 101.49 tons.

38 This was not unusual. A number of wealthy people lent their boats or tenders to the race organizers. Gordon Selfridge put his motor boat *Misconduct* at the disposal of the Schneider Committee. He did much work with it, with Lawrence as a passenger. *Misconduct* was destroyed in the B.P.B. Co. fire at Hythe on August Bank Holiday, 1931.

39 Air Vice Marshal Sir Charles Lambe KCB CMG DSO commanded Coastal Area from July 1928 until October 1931.

40 *Golden Reign*. Pieter Shipster questions this, suggesting it is more probable the Air Ministry personnel were accommodated at RAF Calshot.

41 Mack, p. 379.

42 Arrangements for the Schneider Trophy Contest, 1928/29. National Archives: AIR 2/1303/.

43 In his capacity as an RAF representative on the Committee Sydney Smith should have attended this.

44 Arrangements for the Schneider Trophy Contest, 1928/29. National Archives: AIR 2/1303/.

45 Clare Smith: 'He afterwards became a great friend and was instrumental, in various ways, in keeping him from too much publicity – for which Tes often told me he was most grateful.'

46 *Golden Reign*.

47 According to A.B. Tinsley, who later served with Lawrence at Calshot, one of Lawrence's tasks at the 1929 Schneider cup was assisting in the 'laying out of circuit markers and location of rescue craft'.

48 Not to be confused with the Royal Aero Club.

49 Arrangements for the Schneider Trophy Contest, 1928/29. National Archives: AIR 2/1303/.

50 T.E. Lawrence to A.S. Frere-Reeves, Cattewater, 16/08/1929. R.A.F. Museum.

51 T.E. Shaw to Robert Graves, Cattewater, 23/8/1929. B: RG.

52 T.E. Shaw to Robert Graves, Calshot, 3/9/29. B:RG

53 National Archives DSIR 23/3014.

54 Conversation with Solent Sky Museum technical staff, 2006.

55 Friends.

56 The 'R' engine was superior to the Napier Lion engine of the S5 – but the Lion had its cylinders in three banks. The fuselage was thus shorter, affecting the centre of gravity. The cylinders on each side of the 'R' were cast as a block in 1929.

57 *Memories of the Last Schneider Trophy Contests*, Air Commodore F.R. Banks, Journal of the Royal Aeronautical society, January 1966.

58 J. Jarche, *People I have Shot*, 1934.

59 P. Shipster.

60 *Recollections of T.E. Lawrence.* AV-M Sydney Smith, 1963. Sydney Smith Archive, RAF Museum.

61 Solent Sky Museum technical staff.

62 T.E. Shaw to Robert Graves, Cattewater, 13/9//29. RG-B.

63 See chapter 10 on the RAF 200, p148.

64 *Technical Aspects of the Schneider Trophy and the world speed record for seaplanes.* Dr. E.Bazzocchi, *Aeronautical Journal*, 2/1972.

65 B.E. Holloway, Air Ministry, to the Secretary of the Royal Aero Club, London, 30/10/1929. National Archives AIR 2/1303/.

66 £55,000 of this went to the aircraft and £33,000 to the engines. National Archives AIR 2/1303/.

67 One of the curses of the seaplanes was that high engine torque would tend to press one float down into the water during take off. Use of a contra-rotating propeller eliminated this.

68 Quote from Mr. Pieter Shipster's lecture 'Lawrence and the Schneider Trophy', T.E. Lawrence Society 9th Symposium, Oxford September 2006.

69 George Bernard Shaw, to his great chagrin, was not included amongst these.

70 T.E. Lawrence to C.P. Robertson, Mount Batten, 22/11/1929. I.W.M.

71 It was Nathan who owned the 'little house at Thurlestone' where Lawrence stayed with the Sydney Smiths in the summer of 1930 and the photograph he dubbed 'The Judgement of Paris' was taken.

72 Wing Commander Sydney Smith to Major A.A. Nathan, Mount Batten, 14/12/1929.

73 Wing Commander Sydney Smith to de Havilland Aircraft Co. Ltd., Mount Batten, 17/12/1929. National Archives: AIR 1/2693.

74 Mr. Thomas Jones, The Pilgrim Trust to Colonel Sir Donald Banks, Air Ministry, London, 25/11/1937. National Archives: AIR 1/2693.

75 Sir Donald Banks to Mr. Thomas Jones esq., Air Ministry, Kingsway, London. 6/.12/1937. National Archives AIR 1/2693.

76 David Garnett to Colonel Sir Donald Banks, Huntingdonshire. 26/1/1938. National Archives AIR 1/2693.

77 G-AALJ was in fact flown by Amy Johnson. Moth G-EBYV was within days shipped overseas. Source: Gerald Wasley.

78 David Garnett to Colonel Sir Donald Banks, Huntingdonshire. 26/1/1938. National Archives AIR 1/2693.

79 Sir Donald Banks to Air Commodore Sydney Smith, London, 15/2/1938. National Archives: AIR 1/2693.

80 Air Commodore Smith to Sir Donald Banks. Uxbridge, 9/3/1938. Sydney Smith added 'Shaw was not a pilot'. National Archives: AIR 1/2693.

81 *Chief Registrar's Report*, Air Ministry File No. 110a, Air Ministry, Kingsway, London. c. 3/1938. National Archives: AIR 1/2693.

82 Ibid.

83 *Introduction to Part Five: Flying Boats*, 1938 DG.

84 Gerald Wasley suggests this may possibly have been Sir P. Sassoon's Moth.

85 T.E. Shaw to F.G.N. Doubleday, Mount Batten. 10/9/1930. DG.

86 Hilary St. John Philby. He replaced Lawrence as Chief Political Representative in Transjordan in 1921. Father of Kim Philby.

87 T.E. Shaw to Henry Field, Mount Batten, 26/4/1929.

88 Gerald Wasley. Communication with author, December 2006.

89 T.E. Shaw to Henry Field, Mount Batten, 13/11/1930.

90 Bodleian Library, Special Collections and Western Manuscripts.

91 *Plymouth Evening Herald*, 13/08/05. 'He was the hardest nut I ever had to crack' Field commented later. T.E. told him he found it irksome to recall events he had spent nine years trying to forget. Field asked him to draw in the topography of northern Arabia on the map, which he attempted, now in more ebullient mood, on the next day, Sunday.

92 TES to Sir Hugh Trenchard, 12/VII/29. DG, p. 662-663.

93 A name from C.M. Doughty.

94 Dennis McDonnell, T.E. Lawrence Studies List, 3/4/2005.

95 Lord Thompson to G.B. Shaw, 24th July 1929. Additional manuscript MSS 45904, British Library.

96 The mapping Field and Lawrence discussed had nothing to do with the 'Empty Quarter'. Lawrence did tell Field he would like to fly over the Empty Quarter in the R101, but there is no evidence they discussed this at Plymouth. Source: G. Wasley.

97 G. Wasley, correcting *Plymouth Evening Herald*, 13/08/05.

98 Marsh was private secretary to Asquith 1915–1916 and Churchill 1917–1922.

99 T.E. Lawrence to Edward Marsh, 10/3/1931, Mount Batten. DG.

100 T.E. Lawrence to Bertram Thomas, Plymouth, 22/08/1931.

101 Smith's posting to Manston followed the death of its former C.O. Wing Commander Roy M. Drummond D.S.O., O.B.E., M.C. Drummond served as the station C.O. from June 1931 to October 1931. Manston had earlier suffered an outbreak of cerebrospinal meningitis that was contained after the camp was put in complete isolation. The C.O. had major surgery twice but this failed to save him and his ashes were scattered over the camp, a memorial plaque being placed in Manston village church. (Source: *Tinsley*. Tinsley thought Smith's predecessor was a Group Captain. This may have been Group Captain R.C.M. Pink O.B.E., C.O. before Drummond).

102 The historian Gerald Wasley has made a special study of Lawrence's time at Mount
   Batten. He concluded that Clare Sydney Smith fell deeply in love with Lawrence
   whilst he was there. The Smiths' marriage became threatened. See footnote 100,
   p217. Richard Digby-Smith, *Western Morning News* reporter and a former friend of
   Robert Graves, also confirms the infatuation of Clare Sydney Smith for Lawrence.
   He considers the Clare Sydney Smith 'involvement' as very different to T.E.'s more
   identifiably platonic relationships with Charlotte Shaw and Florence Hardy.

103 T.E. Lawrence to Bertram Thomas, Plymouth, 21/11/1931.

104 T.E. Lawrence to Bertram Thomas, Hythe, 7/12/1931.

105 T.E. Lawrence to Bertram Thomas, Hythe, 9/12/1931.

106 Ibid.

107 Ibid.

108 Foreword to *Arabia Felix*, T.E. Shaw, Jonathan Cape, 1932.

109 The exposed positions of the air-gunners and the overloaded conditions in the
   passenger compartment must have made some contribution to the crash.

110 Source: Marine Aircraft Experimental Establishment report F/21F. National Archives
   file AVIA 19/499.

111 Two Engined Flight Tests of Iris II N.185. 14/03/1929. National Archives file AVIA
   19/499.

112 The tower was built hundreds of years earlier as a defence against expected attacks by
   the Dutch.

113 The Sydney Smith's nickname for Lawrence.

114 *Golden Reign.*

115 Ibid.

116 This deficiency was one of the primary motivations for Lawrence's later work with
   Scott-Paine.

117 *Golden Reign.*

118 *Western Weekly News*, Saturday 24th February, 1931.

119 Wilson.

120 T.E. Lawrence to C.F. Shaw, 6/2/1931. Letters: Brown.

121 He had 'met' Webb-Bowen before. In December 1929 he told C.P. Robertson he had
   not seen Webb-Bowen, whom he referred to as one of the RAF 'gods', but [heard]
   'over from one side (the safe side) of a wall while he inspected the other.' T.E.
   Lawrence to C.P. Robertson, Mount Batten, 30/1/1929.

122 G.B. Shaw to T.E. Lawrence, London, 8/2/1931. LTEL.

123 Ibid.

124 T.E. Lawrence to C.F. Shaw, Mount Batten, 6/02/1931. There appears to be no record
   of whether Lawrence did publish his findings. His other RAF and *Odyssey* work
   probably prevented this.

125 T.E. Lawrence to C.F. Shaw, Mount Batten, 16/02/1931.

126 T.E. Lawrence to Lady Astor, Plymouth. 2/3/1931.DG.

CHAPTER TEN

Power Boats: the RAF 200

Lawrence's most important work with the RAF began in February 1931, shortly after the flying boat crash in Plymouth Sound. He became involved in the trials and development of a new type of marine craft that would revolutionise the RAF's seaplane tender work and power boat design in general, leading eventually to a new form of aircraft target boat to improve offshore bombing, and to craft that would be the workhorses of the Air Sea Rescue services and motor torpedo boat forces in World War Two.

Department E.6, the Marine Craft Section (M.C.S.) of the RAF, was created in 1918, shortly after the RNAS and R.F.C. had been amalgamated to form Trenchard's Royal Air Force. Amongst the senior officers attached to E.6 was a former RNVR Lieutenant and R.F.C. Captain, Flight Lieutenant W.E.G. Beauforte-Greenwood, who was to play a significant part in Lawrence's later life. In section E.6 of the Department of the Air Member for Supply and Research, in 1932, (formerly section E.10 (a)), were three staff: Beauforte-Greenwood, Flight Lieutenant H. Norrington and Flight Lieutenant H.E.E. Weblin. Beauforte-Greenwood was in Room 366 with Norrington and was Head of the provision branch for marine craft, moorings, sea targets, anchors and buoys, spare parts, accessories and special marine stores; also the design and trials of new types and survey and repairs. He was a Member of the Institute of Marine Engineers and an Associate Member of the Institute of Naval Architects. He had been with the Section since 1918.

Norrington was responsible for the inspection of marine engines and electrical equipment under construction and repair; and for the trials of marine craft. In the adjacent Room 367 was his Technical Assistant, H.E.E. Weblin, a retired Royal Navy Lieutenant Commander. Weblin was in charge of the laying and inspection of moorings and sea targets.[1]

During 1931 most of Lawrence's work with E.6 was testing the new RAF 200 seaplane tender. From February to June a series of new boat/engine combinations were trialled using both the original Brooke and later Meadows-powered engines. The reports for these were sent to the Officer Commanding Coastal Area, A.V. M. Lambe, signed by an officer, but the style was obviously Lawrence's. As it was largely through Sydney Smith's efforts that Lawrence became involved in E.6's work, Beauforte-Greenwood wrote to Smith in May 1931 to say that it would

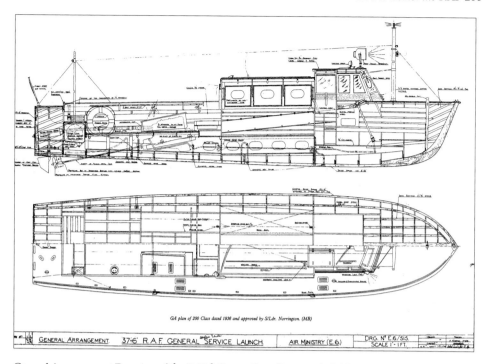

GA plan of 200 Class dated 1936 and approved by S/Ldr. Norrington. (MB)

| GENERAL ARRANGEMENT. | 37·6′ R.A.F. GENERAL SERVICE LAUNCH | AIR MINISTRY (E.6) | DRG. Nº E.6/515. SCALE 1″=1FT. | |

General Arrangement Drawing of the British Power Boat Company's RAF 200 Seaplane Tender (RAF Museum)

The caption in the Scott-Paine archives identified this man as Norrington. Paul Tunbridge however identified him more accurately as Flight Lieutenant Beauforte-Greenwood. Photograph probably taken at Hythe c. 1931. (Southampton City Council)

have been impossible to make the progress they had without T.E.'s help. When Lawrence retired, Beauforte-Greenwood and Norrington presented him with a pair of silver candlesticks in appreciation of this work. They were inscribed 'from B-G and Norrie' and can still be seen at Clouds Hill today.

T.E. and his colleagues worked slavishly on the sea trials for seven months and at the beginning of August 1931, eight new launches were awaiting their Schneider Trophy role in Scott-Paine's boatyard. But the fire there on 3rd August burnt out all but one of them and the work was destroyed. It had been a Bank Holiday[2] with the lowest tide for months and the coincidence convinced Scott-Paine an arsonist had been at work. Despite the setback, he completed seven replacement boats by September, delivering them within the terms of the RAF contract, but too late for the Schneider race.

There were a number of serious attempts to discredit Scott-Paine's work, one reason why he is a relatively obscure figure today. In March 1938 in the House of Commons, Reginald Fletcher, a naval officer in the pay of rival companies, castigated his work with lies and half-truths. Fletcher was an expert on naval affairs and launched an extraordinary attack on him during a debate on the Navy Estimates. The Vosper Company had produced an MTB ostensibly superior to the British Power Boat Company's and Fletcher accused him of using under-powered, unsuitable power-plants. It was an untrue slur but this and the success of Vospers and Thorneycroft in the Second World War contributed to Scott-Paine's eclipse.

The twin Brooke engined RAF 200 on the eastern slipway at Mount Batten, 18th March, 1931, the day after she arrived from Hythe. A biplane floatplane can just be seen behind her, in front of the northernmost seaplane hangar. (National Archives)

Hubert Scott-Paine, probably at the British
Power Boat Company yard, Hythe c.
1931. He was a redhead, which earned
him the nickname 'the Red Fox of Hythe'.
(Southampton City Council)

First Trial: RAF 200 with Two Brooke Engines; Stokes Bay, February

Scott-Paine realised that using American marine engines would always prevent
self-sufficiency for his boatyard and throughout 1930 he had scoured England
for an alternative powerplant. He eventually found one at Meadows Ltd. of
Wolverhampton, who were producing a 100 h.p. tank and motor car petrol engine
half the weight of the Brooke.[3] To adopt this for Scott-Paine's use the Meadows
engineers had to bed it at 17 degrees to the horizontal and redesign the oil-feed and
other systems. Scott-Paine told the Air Ministry of the new engine and Beauforte-
Greenwood indicated they were interested. The deaths of the nine crewmen in
the Blackburn Iris crash acted as a stimulus. As Lawrence and Sydney Smith had
been aware that there was a performance problem with the RAF tenders for some
time, Beauforte-Greenwood, who had already met Lawrence, suggested Mount
Batten would be a suitable test location; partly because of T.E.'s presence but also
because of the base's distance from competitors in the Solent. Before this could be
formalised an acceptance trials team of Lawrence and Corporals Bradbury, Heward
and Staines, all from Mount Batten, was dispatched to Hythe for assimilation.

Whilst receiving instruction T.E. met Scott-Paine for the first time, who
was three years his junior. The boatyard and its innovatory designs deeply
impressed Lawrence, who was happy to work there. On 19th February
Beauforte-Greenwood, Norrington and Flight Lieutenant Jinman[4] with three
other officials took part in the initial trial of the original Brooke-engined tender

A production line at the Henry Meadows Factory, Fallings Park, Wolverhampton, c. 1934. The installation of the Meadows tank/car engine converted to marine use in the RAF 200 transformed it into an effective package for the RAF. (Southampton City Council)

in Stokes Bay, near Portsmouth. The trial, on a flat, swell-less sea, lasted about three hours; 37 gallons of fuel were consumed, and a mean speed of 28.806 knots[5] was attained.[6] E.6 agreed to supervise the Meadow engine's testing, whilst simultaneously the original 200, with the Brooke engine, was given its sea-trials at Plymouth.

Second Trial: Two Brooke Engines; Plymouth, March

The new RAF 200 was run daily from 18th March until 1st April. Lawrence drove the boat a number of times.[7] 18th March was the first break in bad weather. Earlier in the month there had been heavy snow throughout England, the 6th to the 10th being exceptionally cold. Lawrence's piloting ability has often been commented on, the boat did not roll and even in winds of up to 20 m.p.h. the deck was kept dry by skilful steering. On one run a spring broke on an exhaust valve and the heavy Brooke engines were throttled back, averaging 20 miles per hour as a consequence. Normally, however, she maintained a fairly even speed, only lost when boring into a head-on sea.

Scott-Paine's innovative design performed beyond all expectations. The 37'6" length of the 200 class launch was a compromise between an existing 35' length and one of 40' suggested by him. It had an innovative hull design with a pronounced bow flare that threw the spray wide out from the boat, enabling it to glide through

RAF 200 in Plymouth Sound on 21st March, 1931, with Aircraftman Shaw at the controls. Plymouth Hoe citadel is in the background. (National Archives)

Flight Lieutenant Jinman.

26th March 1931. Aircraftman Shaw at the helm of the Brooke-engined RAF 200's first trial in Plymouth Sound, with a fellow M.B.C. man in the cabin. Drake's Island lies in the right centre background with Mount Edgecumbe and Picklecombe Point in the distance. Clearly visible is the wake created by the V-shaped cut-water below the bows. (National Archives)

the water like a speedboat. The bottom of the bows had a concave 'vee' cut-water, the angle of which flattened out towards the rear until at the stern it was almost totally flat. This enabled it to slice through the waves with little turbulence, pushing the water behind it. The stern simply planed over the surface with minimal drag. Even the steering wheel was thoughtfully designed to be horizontal to reduce arm-strain. The forward section of the moulded rubber 'hard chine' had an angled fillet at the bottom that slotted into the horizontal planking of the bilges. This, together with the flat stern and her unvaried planing angle, prevented her from rolling. As speed increased 'they rise out of the water and run over its face. They cannot roll nor pitch, having no pendulum nor period, but a subtly modelled planing bottom and sharp edges.'[8]

Unlike established hard chine designs, the deep cut-water prevented the boat from 'hammering' into waves. Most of the time there were 10-foot broken seas, but she cut and planed comfortably across these and 'only shipped solid sea once'. With a big swell at right angles full speed could still be maintained and even before a 10-foot swell it was not difficult to keep her steady and compass courses were easily held.

On 26th and 27th March the RAF 200 was tested in Plymouth Sound 'towing loads and boats and testing her pull,'[9] followed by a few coastal trips. She ran fairly silently on all the runs and was impressively stable, apart from in very bad weather. The 26th was a cold, cloudy day with a Force 4 wind blowing from the east-north-east. There was a medium swell on a calm sea. The engine running

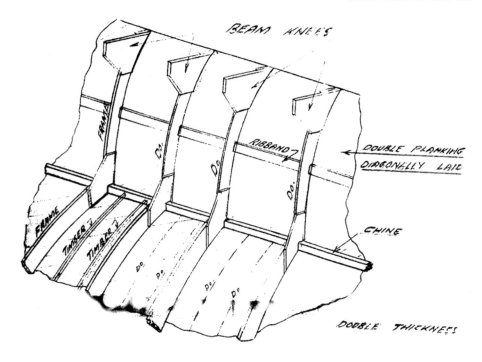

Diagrammatic Representation of the 'hard chine' on a 63-ft. Scott-Paine boat. Titled 'Arrangement of Framing and Planking as proposed by J.S. White and Co.' Prepared for the RAF Marine Craft Section Ref. E6/191. Date 3/9/1935. (National Archives).

was almost vibrationless, the large exhaust silencers rendering the boat nearly inaudible. The only real problem the trial team experienced was the diminutive manganese-bronze rudder which made the boat's turning circle without engine assistance large. Although compensated the rudder had only around 20⁰ range in either direction, which was not enough. In order to turn into the wind and tow at slow speeds it had to be supplemented by engine power. With engine assistance the craft could turn in its own length even fully into the wind.

RAF 200 was taken out of the water on 1st April for hull examination after 50 hours running time and was found to be in perfect condition. A report issued on 2nd April concluded she had behaved extremely well in all weathers and all the duties normally performed by marine craft were carried out successfully. It was felt she was 'a cleaner sea boat' than anything the RAF had yet employed, and 'her sturdy construction qualified [her] for really hard work',[10] showing a vast improvement over earlier RAF marine craft. She returned to Hythe.

Third Trial: Experimental Open Hull with One Meadows Engine; Hythe, April
Lawrence and Bill Bradbury were again despatched to Hythe, this time to observe the installation of a Meadows 'Power' engine in a 28-foot mock-up open hull. They shared the same digs in Myrtle Cottage, Hythe; a small red-

brick terraced cottage within a few minutes walk of the boat yard. It was owned by a Mrs Biddlecombe whose husband worked for Scott-Paine and she ensured the two airmen were happy, Lawrence having his own room. This was accommodation regularly used by the boatyard's RAF personnel and over time a stock of old service clothing accumulated in it. Because Lawrence was so short he found most of it unusable. He wrote to Pat Knowles' brother Dick: 'Just now I am wholly M.B.C.[11] for the R.A.F. is at last trying to get some marine craft of modern design, a need I have been urging on them . . . for 18 months.'[12] He told Graves that the Air Ministry's selection of him was 'poetic justice' describing the job as 'quite worth doing . . . Very difficult, engrossing, and very exhausting'.[13]

 They were testing an open hulled 28 footer fitted with a Meadows engine. He made little mention of B-G's or other people's involvement; it was as if, for the first time in years, he sensed the importance of his own contribution. The weather was very poor and still wintry, with high north and north-east winds making the Solent extremely rough: ideal conditions for a trial. Air Ministry reports for Tuesday the 28th recorded cumulo-nimbus obscuring the sun, low temperatures, high humidity and intense rain. That day a report to the Ministry was filed at Mount Batten:

> Five hours after the engine's installation in an experimental hull the Power Boat Co. handed it over to two airmen from this Station to test. They ran it for the 45 further hours necessary to complete 50 hours full throttle test. It was then taken out of the water for examination. No defects were found upon the most careful inspection.[14]

What a contrast in duties for Lawrence. At that time at Batten he was a clerk in the workshops, typing out technical correspondence to be signed by the C.O. One morning in June, when hut orderly, he had been reprimanded for leaving 'dull brass door-knobs'.[15]

Ivor Jones of Pennington, Hampshire, was a fitter in the engine shop at Farnborough during the First World War. In 1930 he read that Scott-Paine was looking for engine fitters at the Power boatyard and they took him on as chief mechanic for the RAF 200s. He remembered watching Lawrence on a proving trial: Jones was in the stern, looking after the two Meadows engines and Lawrence was at the helm with an Air Ministry official. They had to collect Winston Churchill from Southampton docks and transport him to a battleship in the Solent. Lawrence steered the boat directly beneath the warship's mooring ropes and was later charged with breaking regulations but explained that he had taken the shortest distance between two points, to avoid wasting the time of 'such an important person'.

Jones recalled he had 'a striking character, with a face as though it was chiselled out of sandstone. He was a most unassuming and quiet man.'[16] The writer F. Yeates-Brown described an incident that occurred some time in 1930

Lawrence amidst a crowd of reporters after a half a statute mile trial run, probably in the boatyard at Hythe, c.1931. Motor Boat Crew electrician Jack Barker, who worked with Lawrence at Hythe, said he always wore a No.1 hat, a peaked cap. (Southampton City Council)

Scott-Paine piloting with Lawrence behind him observing. This was probably on the trial of the 28-foot experimental open boat with the single Meadows engine that took place on 4th April 1931 at Hythe. The cockpit arrangement discounts it being either a target boat or a seaplane tender. (Southampton City Council)

Lawrence and another aircraftman behind Air Ministry officials in the experimental open boat trial of 4th April 1931. (Southampton City Council)

Lawrence alone at the helm of an experimental open boat on the open sea. Corporal Bradbury possibly took the photograph in 1931. (RAF Museum)

Stationary, somewhere on Southampton Water. (RAF Museum)

when Lawrence noticeably lost his equilibrium. They had arranged to meet in Plymouth but Lawrence did not show up and Yeates-Brown found him down at the Cattewater cradling a dynamo in his arms, scowling like a fiend. He felt paralysed by the 'air of cosmic menace' that T.E. exuded, as did T.E.'s two quaking companions: 'His temper seemed like lightning; full of the possibilities of destruction . . . I believe that I saw then, for the first and only time, the power in T.E. that had brought his Arabs to Damascus.'[17] It emerged that they had spent two hours, partly submerged in water, trying to find a fault in a launch's ignition system.

Fourth Trial: RAF 200 with Two Meadows Engines; Hythe, May

At Hythe RAF 200 had had her engine bearers and hull strengthened to accommodate the two new 100 h.p. Meadows engines. At that time T.E.'s eyes were so inflamed with salt spray he was not able to see to work on the *Odyssey*. It was a long and tiring day, from 6a.m. to 8 p.m. They tried alleviating this by relaying on the work, but often Bradbury had to work with him.

On Tuesday 4th, the representatives of the British Power Boat Co. and Meadows arrived for a further 50 hours of trials. The next day, the 200 with two Meadows engines – nos. 7487 and 7488 – replacing the two Brookes was launched from Hythe slipway. She was tested daily for the next 21 days and a number of problems were uncovered: some were dealt with immediately, but others required later modification. Beauforte-Greenwood was impressed with Lawrence's contribution; this was the first time he had actually worked with T.E.

The lighter Meadows engines allowed much easier handling. Advantages included the starter motor being removable in five minutes against the Brooke's six hours; the Bendix drive could be freed in 10 seconds, as against the Brooke's six hours. The dynamo could be removed in three minutes – the Brooke took the obligatory six hours, after engine removal! The water pumps could be removed or replaced in three minutes whilst the Brooke took a notably brisk four hours. Gears could be reached and adjusted in 15 minutes – the Brooke had no adjustment. The Meadows powered boat could travel more easily through a heavy breaking sea with a strong opposing wind. Beauforte-Greenwood later commented that 'The simplicity of handling and accessibility of internal fittings seemed to fire him [Lawrence] with a keen desire for the success and further advancement of these types.'[18]

The May weather was unsettled: wet and dull with thunderstorms, especially near the end of the month. For 21 consecutive days from Wednesday 5th May Lawrence kept a record of the trials. They had a lot of trouble with overheating and 'hot spots' on the two engines. On the second day the propellers were changed to a reduced diameter, the pitch on the original ones being too severe for them to reach their peak of 300 revs. Through poor cooling water circulation hot spots appeared on the front ends of the cylinder blocks. A lot of these problems seemed to have been caused by poor manufacture. On the fourth day, for example, it was found the valve clearances had been taken up, so the engine heads were removed and all the valves ground in. When reassembling the head the holding down studs broke off if screwed down too tight, so nickel steel ones had to be used to replace them. On the fifth day a propeller blade ripped off and bent the bronze propeller shaft. It was from a defective batch, normally only used for test runs, and a new shaft and propellers were fitted. T.E. suggested bearing and piston friction was causing the problems with propeller performance

On Monday 11th May Beauforte-Greenwood, Norrington and Jinman sat in for an official test with RN Commander Dunlop. At Calshot a 30 m.p.h. wind was blowing from the south west. Visibility was very good, the surface of the sea being calm but with a heavy swell. Eight personnel were on the boat at one time including two fitters. The trial was abandoned when the right-hand engine seized after 20 minutes and it began smoking badly. On dismantling it was found the small ends of the piston rods had seized up solid, knocking a hole in the right piston head. It would seem that, since the engine was actually designed for a motor car to silent run, the pistons had only been given three thou. clearance and a modification to six thou. was suggested. There was also only a very thin separation between the two cylinders making them both suffer from overheating. The right-hand engine was replaced with the one used in the experimental hull in April.

On 15th May Beauforte-Greenwood wrote to Sydney Smith: 'I can assure you that the help which has been given, together with the reports, have been most useful and resulted in bringing us up to date and at least 4–5 years ahead of the Admiralty. Such an advance would have been impossible without the aid

Scott-Paine in the foreground, in the background (left to right) Bradbury, unknown, Beauforte-Greenwood, Lawrence, Norrington. Probably taken on 11th May 1931 on the slipway at Hythe. (Southampton City Council)

which you have readily given us, and I thank you very much indeed.'[19] He described T.E.'s cheery optimism during some of the harsher sea trials as being encouraging. His reserved character and benevolence had endeared him to many. With his practical suggestions and remarkable amount of technical knowledge he was of great benefit to the service. B-G thanked Sydney Smith, saying Lawrence was determined to 'help solve the many and varied difficulties that had to be overcome'.[20]

On May 16th a 'hot spot' caused 'popping back' on the right-hand engine again. The water circulation in the exhaust manifolds was restricted in places and a bypass to avoid dead water on the front of the cylinder block was arranged. 'Popping back' continued for the next four days until the 20th when Beauforte-Greenwood and Wing Commander de Courcy took out Air Commodore Bigsworth and Group Captain Nanson. A moderate swell on the otherwise calm sea, and a 17 m.p.h. wind from the north north-east did not disturb the trial. The 'popping back' persisted at full throttle so the carburettors, plugs, auto-pulses and fuel pumps were changed. On the 21st things began improving: Beauforte-Greenwood and de Courcy took out Air Vice-Marshal Lambe, C.O. Coastal Area, Bigsworth, a Wing Commander Huskisson and three others. A force 4 wind from the south-east east blew around them, and a moderately heavy sea without swell rocked the boat.

The engines ran smoothly, but in the evening the left-hand motor began 'popping back'. T.E. was beginning to find the job stressful. Scott-Paine's technicians were at their wit's end trying to keep RAF 200 running whilst Lambe's Coastal H.Q. staff were inspecting. As a Supermarine S5 flew up and down the Solent behind him T.E. wrote during a lunch break:

> This job has been beyond a joke lately. Only today we have found and cured the main trouble, I fancy. For half an hour we had absolutely a perfect run. . . . this afternoon we go out to see if the cure is permanent. Nothing radically wrong with the engines you understand: but minor defects have to be put right as they occur . . . Disastrous work this specialization in R.A.F. motor-boat design.[21]

The 'minor defects' were mainly obstructions in the petrol system causing weak mixture, overheating and pre-ignition. It was also found that there were faults in the water pumps and circulators, and the pistons were too tightly fitted. The reason these cooling problems did not appear in the single-engined experimental hull was because its petrol supply was gravity fed and a natural cooling of the engine, caused by the open hull, obscured the defects.[22] The fuel lines on the 200 were dismantled, the tank cleaned and a new filter fitted in the intake.

On Sunday 24th, the final day of the trials, a new electrical system was installed for a trial run, and the boat remained steady at full throttle. A few more modifications (notably a gear box alteration to make the forward and reverse gears more positive)[23] were necessary before the final tests were done and the boat was handed over.[24]

Lawrence wrote up his second report on Monday 25th May. The British Power Boat Co. and Meadows representatives had watched the entire proceedings and suggested a number of improvements: although the engines ran well, they were noisier than the Brooke at full throttle. A report on the tests made to Coastal H.Q., written at Batten on 28th, appears to be the official presentation to Coastal Area of an earlier report Lawrence drafted with a different signatory. The RAF 200 passed its Hythe trials with distinction.

Fifth Trial: RAF 200 with Two Meadows Engines; Plymouth, June

June 1931 was not a good month for sea trials: it suffered a long spell of unsettled, cool weather with widespread fog in the English Channel and unusually heavy rains in the north. On Saturday 6th RAF 200 was again at Hythe. Beauforte-Greenwood took the boat with Lawrence and the three Corporals back to foggy Batten in a heavy swell, on the way racing another boat, which had to turn around after shipping water. They called in at Calshot. T.E. told Lady Astor the trip took seven hours. The sea was rough, a gale blowing at 40 mph., and they did not arrive until 7 o'clock in the evening.

Lawrence wrote from Batten to John Campbell, an employee of the Henry Meadows factory, Wolverhampton, about the trip. He explained that they had

The first RAF 200 in Southampton Water off Hythe, now fitted with two Meadows engines. All these photographs appear to have been taken on the same day. Scott-Paine is in two of them. Lawrence, Bradbury, Beauforte-Greenwood, Norrington, Jinman, and Commander Dunlop R.N. also attended. (Southampton City Council)

This appears to have been taken just off the British Power Boat Company yard at Hythe with Hythe Pier in the background. (Southampton City Council)

RAF 200 during the course of the Meadows engine trial. (Southampton City Council)

In this photograph two figures, probably Jinman (with cap) and Scott-Paine are examining the starboard engine. The covers (called 'coffin lids') of both Meadows engines are raised. The presence of the figure in the dark uniform, probably a Royal Navy officer, seems to confirm that the occasion for these six photos was the fourth period of trials of RAF 200 on Tuesday 11th May, 1931, when the starboard engine broke down and the trial had to be terminated prematurely. (Southampton City Council)

Beauforte-Greenwood and Norrington in discussion, sitting on the cabin roof. (Southampton City Council)

What appear to be, (left to right) Jinman, Lawrence and Dunlop waving at the camera before the starboard engine failed. (Southampton City Council)

hours of rough water, but, unlike on 5th May, the propellors were replaced with larger screws, 14 x 13s, having an inch greater diameter, which gave 200 more revolutions per minute. The engines were quieter and the performance faultless. The former timber boxes which contained them in the stern were replaced with new 'coffins' that were a better fit. Reverse gears were also good. The importance of this work for the Schneider competition in September seemed then to be uppermost in his mind: 'I think all our troubles are over. We keep the boat here for about two weeks and then she goes up to Calshot for training crews for the 8 new ones that are to take part in the Schneider arrangements. So that's all right.'[25]

On the same day he wrote to his friend G.W.M. Dunn [26] (who had known him since 1929) telling him that the work in April, May and June had been almost exclusively for boats to tender the Schneider race: 'Like me your main life chokes the side issues.'[27] That the trials had been specifically aimed at producing tenders for the Schneider Cup shows how seriously the Air Ministry now regarded the competition. If the RAF was victorious that year it would be their third successive victory and they would have won the Cup outright.

Following the success of the trials in May and June, Scott-Paine was able to go ahead with building eight new RAF 200 seaplane tenders for the Air Ministry. Beauforte-Greenwood told Sydney Smith on 13th May 'we have ordered eight launches which will be ready for delivery by the end of July, in time for the Schneider Trophy'.[28] Lawrence told Beauforte-Greenwood that he was concerned that any 37½-foot. tenders without experienced crews may suffer 'battle-scars' at the Schneider Trophy and he preferred a Mount Batten crew.[29] By August the completed boats were in the British Power Boat Company yard waiting for the race: but on the 3rd, the fire.

Lawrence's final report was submitted on Wednesday 17th June, the day the boat with the Meadows engines went back to Calshot. T.E. wrote from Batten to Beauforte-Greenwood the next day:

> Here is an advance copy of the last notes upon R.A.F. 200.
> I see that in all I have written you almost a book upon the boat and her engines. It has been interesting and difficult, and, therefore I am grateful to you for giving me the chance of doing it. This is the third good job I have had in the R.A.F.
>
> You have been very kind in appreciating our work, and the letter received from Coastal Area about Corporal Bradbury should do him good in his trade. I feel particularly pleased about the whole affair, because it has meant our getting so good a boat so quickly.[30]

Towed Target Trials: Plymouth, July

In addition to developing the high speed craft Lawrence was also responsible for new methods of production in the factory and became concerned with experimental use of RAF 200 for target towing. In May Mount Batten had received a very large air-firing target but the water resistance on it was so high that speeds exceeding

8 m.p.h. were not advisable. In June the station was also allocated a 'fog signal-station towing-board' from No. 1 Stores Depot for urgent trial.[31] This was a naval fog-buoy, or 'splash target', designed to throw up a large tower of water behind it, one Lawrence described as 'like all the Trafalgar fountains rolled together'. The principle was that the splashes would show the location and distance of the towing ship in foggy conditions.[32] The only day suitable for testing was misty and Plymouth Sound was full of shipping. The board was towed up the Tamar and tested off Saltash, where the swell was less than in the Channel:

> The target, a cross between a surf-board and a plough, was launched by one man over the stern and let out without difficulty to the full 600 yards. It towed smoothly and straightly, and took nothing appreciably off the speed of the boat. By 15 m.p.h. almost the whole of the very light towing wire had risen to the top of the water, and I think quite a sharp turn could have been made without its sinking or fouling the bottom, had open water been available. Speed was raised to 20 m.p.h. and the tow still followed perfectly, throwing up fans of spray many feet in hight [sic] and wider than a house. The weather was too thick for air observation, but so large a splash should be visible from 1000 feet. Speed was then built to 28 miles per hour at which the target took off from a wave top and leaped high into the air before alighting with a jerk . . . that parted the wire.[33]

This trial was 'promising' but had to be broken off inconclusively when 200 returned to Calshot.[34] Lawrence felt it was successful and it led to him thinking about other forms of floating targets, eventually leading to the British Power Boat Company's Armoured Target Boat.

Lawrence tried using the Biscayne 'Baby' as a towing boat. He wrote to Beauforte-Greenwood on Tuesday 14th, a day of continuous rain and a heavy sea swell:

> Here is a final report, so far as present arrangements go, on the surf-board target. It is very good for its proposed job, I think, the only difficulty being spotting, which is best done from the aircraft, the fixed base-line of 600 yards giving to the observer a good chance of guessing his shot's real position.[35]

At least one flying boat pilot from 204 Squadron had a disagreement with Lawrence over this, PO Thomas Quintus Horner. Mr Horner's widow told the author that Lawrence was known to be a very difficult person in some circumstances: 'The ordinary airmen on the station at the time were (understandably) very resentful of [his] many privileges, private room, and no restrictions on his lifestyle in Plymouth, where he mixed with the elite Lord and Lady Astor and their friends. The station commander must have had a difficult time.'[36] T.E. had asked if it was possible for a flying boat to bomb the target on trials. Pilot Officer Horner refused to comply because of the absurdly low speed. Horner found Lawrence an 'impossible man' if he couldn't get his way, and declined to co-operate. Lawrence hoped to use the *Biscuit* motor boat to tow the target: 'Lawrence, then the owner of a speed boat,

Lawrence in July 1931, using the Biscayne Baby *Biscuit* motor boat for experimental target towing in Plymouth Sound. This was around the time of his altercation with the 209 Squadron flying boat pilot Thomas Quintus Horner. It was partly the success of these trials that convinced the RAF to develop an independent target boat. (Pilsborough via RAF Museum)

The first Armoured Target Boat, probably taken at Hythe. The boat had three Meadows engines. The protection offered to the crew by the armoured hood is visible. (Southampton City Council)

was anxious to use it towing targets for squadron training. This did not prove to be practicable and he and my husband had a somewhat heated altercation on the matter.'[37]

On Saturday 25th July Lawrence took 28 days leave. Around that time two significant events occurred: Sydney Smith's promotion to Group Captain and the fire at Scott-Paine's on August Bank Holiday. As well as seven RAF seaplane tenders burning out, Scott-Paine lost all but three of his racing fleet. This meant Lawrence's work at Hythe had ended overnight. He spent most of his holiday back at Barton Street translating the *Odyssey*. He was hoping to continue doing this until the end of August but his leave was cut short. Despite working manically Scott-Paine was unable to finish his replacement tenders in time for the Schneider competition and Lawrence's next task, testing them at Hythe, was postponed. He spent the autumn back at Batten on more mundane duties.

As the Depression ground on, by 1931 things had become increasingly difficult for the Treasury. In order to restore public confidence and balance the budget, changes in taxation and expenditure were made. When the Cabinet split in August over whether to introduce tariffs or make a 20% cut in unemployment benefit the Labour government resigned. The new National Government, a coalition under Ramsay MacDonald, abandoned the gold standard and in September launched cuts in public spending. A 10% cut in Armed Forces salaries ensued.

This had a terrible effect in the ranks, although Lawrence, who had some private means, was less affected than most. In the Royal Navy, the ships of the Atlantic Fleet were in open mutiny for two days, 15th and 16th September, at Invergordon, Scotland, where in some cases the cuts had been as much as 25%. This was soon corrected. For Lawrence the immediate effect of these cuts was simply more circumspect use of his Brough and the *Biscuit*, and trips to Clouds Hill being less frequent. It also meant he was less able to assist friends like Robert Guy who continued to write to him for help.

In October, Group Captain Sydney Smith contacted the Air Ministry and enquired if it was feasible for Lawrence to be transferred to Smith's new base at Manston, Kent. An official at the Ministry, J.M. Pope, replied on 21st October:

> Dear Smith,
> Since you spoke to me the other day about the possible transfer of Shaw from Cattewater to Manston we have given further very careful consideration to your suggestion, and in all circumstances it has been decided it would be inadvisable to move Shaw from Cattewater. I am sorry, as I know you will be disappointed, but I am afraid there is nothing I can do to help.[38]

This was an extremely sad period for both Lawrence and the Smiths. Clare must have written to him questioning the decision, for on the 27th he replied to her explaining its logic:

I am sorry to be so slow in answering. First there was the uncertainty about myself, which turned into a wandering Jew for some days: and then the feeling that after all I might press my roots in again. The reason I would not ask to move was because I knew it would be refused. There is a definite instruction laid down (by S. of S.) against my posting to any station in the London district. Kent counts, I think, as a home county, Margate being a seaside branch of London.[39]

He told them later that it was not the Chief of Air Staff's but a government decision that prevented him moving near London, made some time before and stamped on his documents. On 7th November he was back at 13, Birmingham Street and wrote to Arthur Russell:

Yesterday I was in the Isle of Wight, boat-building, and am just back. Tomorrow I spend in Hythe and Thursday and Friday in London.[40]

When in London he would stay overnight at the Union Jack Club, Waterloo Road, where he gave his name as '353173 A/C Smith, H.E., RAF', for obvious reasons. On the night of Saturday 11th he hoped to be again at 'the Hill'. The cottage was in a filthy mess and probably would remain so for a while, but he still loved it. Russell had visited the cottage earlier but missed him and had left a note with Mrs Knowles. On the morning of Monday 13th Lawrence had to report to the Air Ministry for three days work.[41] By the 21st he was back at Hythe and was by then reading Bertrand Thomas's *Arabia Felix*, but had little time to spare for it: the new 18 h.p. Power-Meadows marinised engine needed testing for some new 16-foot ferry boats, also used as bomb and fuel carrying dinghies. They had been out on Southampton Water day and night. He told explorer Bertram Thomas 'If you or it had been a con-rod, how technically I should have balanced you and summed up.'[42]

They were driving all hours and were dirty, tired and salt-ridden. The new boat's open hull they found was not robust enough for the engine and needed strengthening. He envisaged another 10 days at Hythe. He told Clare Smith that the Meadows engine had done 70 hours non-stop and was performing like clockwork and he and Bradbury had loaded it with a ton of iron ballast and driven it back and forth across Southampton water at its top speed of 22 mph.

The Power-Hyland System

In December 1931 he began work on the trials of a new engine control system, the Power-Hyland system, rather like a primitive gear-throttle link on a modern 'automatic' car. It meant he would have to work at Hythe, where he arrived mid December. Apart from a few days off over Christmas, he remained there until the following summer.

He was up to his 'eyes and ears in it'.[43] They were testing a 16-foot dinghy for Scott-Paine's yard with a new 28 h.p. Power-Meadows engine. He told a friend that it required 'testing, modifying and inventing'[44] and during the course of the next three weeks he sent three reports on the work to section E.6 telling Beauforte-Greenwood in mid January that things weren't working quite as well as they'd hoped:

> Each edition registers an advance, definite but small. I see probably one or two more changes yet. Mr. Scott-Paine is unwilling to have anyone from Calshot see all the trouble we are having. So he, Leonard and me are the crew, normally: and I have not yet called upon W/Cmdr. Watkins for a coxswain. I will do as soon as the boat is ready for running tests. These yard exercises, which is what we have done so far, make one unnecessary, really.[45]

In his next letter he said that Watkin, his coxswain and an engineer, would probably be coming up from Calshot to watch that Monday's trial of the system in RAF 202:

> We have now tried two alternative safety 'gates' for the gear-engagements, & have decided that the best position is on the cam-pulley,[46] for that renders them independent of wiring up adjustments. I can explain when you see the job.
>
> Now the next move is to reproduce the successful R.H. engine on the L.H. engine: and then to link up and test. This can be done on Monday's tide (p.m.) and I have warned W/Cmdr. Watkin, who will probably come himself to see the installing, & bring his coxswain & engineer. From Monday onwards for at least a week Cpl. Jordan & I will be juggling with the boat, getting it right, or getting ourselves right to it.
>
> It has been difficult, & sometimes disappointing – but now I prefer it[47] to the independent gear and throttle control of the old boats. I think its sweeter & simpler control will much more than make up for the slight extra complexity of fitting, & for the cost. We can draft special fitters' instructions to assist the installation & maintenance. I find the boat easier to drive, now, than the older boats were.
>
> The time-lag is 1¾ seconds, at fastest possible operation, to come from astern into ahead: and 3½ seconds from ahead into astern.[48] Using the gears 'gentlemanly fashion', entirely without snatch, it takes 3½ seconds astern to ahead and 5½ ahead to astern. To accustom oneself to this time-lag is the only lesson peculiar to the Hyland.[49] A week should do it easy, in every case . . .
>
> You will understand of course that this first set is to be scrapped, eventually. There is a redesigned telegraph on paper: new wiring to go in, and changes in cam-slide, pulling and link-up. Only the principle is settled, now, thank goodness. You will be pleased when you try her next.
>
> Will you please tell F/Lt. Norrington that I had a very useful half-hour with his paint expert? I think the new paint worth trying. It closely resembles the Smith racing green, which lasted 9 months on my hull.[50]

Pinchin Johnson, a firm of paint manufacturers from Silvertown, London, were suppliers of marine paint, whose operations in the south of England were from a small office and warehouse in Southampton. Apparently Lawrence was in contact with the firm about paint supplies. The son of a former representative of the firm recalled in 1986 that his father had received a telephone call from the British Power Boat Company in 1931 whilst he, then a 12-year-old, happened to be in the office. 'Do you know who that was?' his father said, replacing the receiver. 'Lawrence of Arabia'.[51] Author Paul Tunbridge recorded that one of the tasks Lawrence particularly enjoyed at Hythe was painting the boats on the slipway, a series of braziers being arranged around each boat to heat the paint.[52]

20th January was too foggy for tests. That evening in Myrtle Cottage he wrote again to B-G. They had done 15 hours of trials with 202, the first new tender since the August fire. The day before, Watkin and a Flight Sergeant from Calshot had tried their hand for the first time. The reverse had been engaging too suddenly and Watkin 'bumped' it eight times, 'stalling the engine one time in two'. He later confessed he had not mastered the operation. Lawrence wrote 'I was able to agree with him'. Watkin's more experienced Flight Sergeant found the system easy, doing 68 beautiful changes with only one 'bump'. Corporal Jordan, with only ten days coxswain experience on the RAF 200, drove it uninterrupted for over half an hour. Lawrence commented, 'It is clear to me that the instructional boat, at least, must have some spring preventors, to save the reverses from becoming scrap iron in a month. After training there will be no need for it.'[53]

In February Lawrence was still at Scott-Paine's. On the 5th he told Clare that he had been commissioned to write 'a handbook upon the 37 ½ foot R.A.F. cruiser by Sunday night. As this is a month's job I shall be very much in need of your prayers!'[54]

Lawrence worked prodigiously during this period. By Tuesday the 15th he had finished testing a new dinghy, and the Power-Hyland system. Seventeen new RAF 200 tenders were due to be handed over to E.6 at the end of February and he was also testing an experimental boat.[55] He had written over 15,000 words for the RAF 200 handbook by mid-February. The Air Ministry expected him to motorcycle to Redhill with the completed work that weekend, and go to London with it on the following Monday, 21st February. But the book of 'about 40 pages' was not completed until around 6th March, so he may not have made these journeys. They were testing 16 boats, one a day normally, occasionally two, in order to finish by Easter. He wrote to Frere-Reeves on the 11th:

> You have caught me just as the official trials of a batch of motor boats are beginning. We have to do two boats a day – which means dawn till dark – for the next eight days. Did I tell you that now my job is testing new motor boats for the R.A.F.? An interesting, difficult, tiring job, which I enjoy when it goes well.[56]

He knew that if any of the RAF 200s went wrong they would have to work over Easter to fix them. The 'entire fleet' was due to leave on the 23rd, 'all I have to do is ensure that every one is ready on the day.'[57] A 'Provisional Issue of Notes' for *The 200 Class RAF Seaplane Tender* was deposited at the Air Ministry between the 6th and 16th March 1932.

A Trip to Scotland

He was searching round for ways to advertise the Marine Craft Section's new pride and joy. An old friend from All Souls days, Geoffrey Dawson, was editor of *The Times*. Dawson had been with *The Times* since 1922. He wrote to him, 'Dear G.D. . . . Today it struck me that as editor you might be interested in the new type of motor boat that we have been producing for the R.A.F.'[58] He explained that the Blackburn Iris crash a year previously had pinpointed the need for fast rescue boats. The Admiralty, he said, was being slow to change, unaware that in the US and Italy fast petrol-driven craft were heralding the future. The Air Force, however, with hints from him, was more open to new ideas, exploring the new science in the teeth of protests from the Admiralty. They had produced 'an entirely new type of seaplane tender', cheaper and more efficient than anything bought before. 'Why don't you send your marine man down to see them? On Tuesday and Wednesday next (29 & 30) we have ten to a dozen of them cavorting about Southampton Water.'[59] Dawson sent his aeronautical correspondent, Shepherd, who produced two very detailed reports, praising the boat's qualities, which pleased Lawrence immensely.

The whole of April 1932 was wet and cool, a change only occurring on the 16th with high pressure to the North and North West. This was the day of the second report in *The Times* under Shepherd's name, covering a now legendary trip from Calshot to Donibristle in Scotland. The sunny Scottish weather arrived too late for Lawrence, and dull, rainy conditions persisted during the trip. This journey was arduous and described by Lawrence as 'an exacting test'. The boat, RAF 210, under the command of Flying Officer Rogers, had Lawrence, apparently Shepherd, and at least one other crew member on board. It was accompanied by RAF 215 and RAF 217 as far as Felixstowe. These were three of the 18 new seaplane tenders that Shepherd had reported on earlier. Lawrence himself piloted 210 occasionally. They trip totalled 742 miles through heavy, choppy seas.

> . . . Crossing the Wash the boat met heavy, short seas which actually broke over its bows, rolled aft over the wheelhouse and spilt in tons of spray into the after well. Again, north of Berwick, similarly bad conditions were met, yet the boat suffered no damage, the crew never even had to put on their oil-skins.[60]

The trial was completed in 35 hours 10 minutes. They suffered worse weather than anything previously experienced by an RAF 200. It was the sea rather than the winds that was exceptional.

> All along the South coast there was a following sea with a heavy, four foot swell that, fortunately, was not breaking. The effect of the swell was . . . to force the boat to swing slightly off its course as it ran down each wave.[61]

The trip proved the precision of the steering. It was geared to be very limited in range and light in operation. As 210 ran from Folkstone to Dover in the dark, her bows threw out two thin lines of spray that 'gave the curious impression of red and green streamers in the boat's running lights'. There was a heavy swell on a calm sea, the relative humidity was low and a light wind blew from the north-west. At the helm Lawrence was surrounded by sophisticated equipment. Above his head, in the enclosed wheelhouse, were three-quarters of an inch of 3 ply sheet mahogany surmounted by a doped canvas cover. In front of this were an electric horn and a flexibly mounted spotlight that shone directly ahead. Before him two wipers swept rhythmically in a semicircle on a vent screen. Behind him the cabin portholes were of toughened glass. Because the boat needed constant rudder correction in rough seas the steering wheel was set horizontal, allowing a man to stand for six or seven hours without feeling any arm strain and the small, high tensile manganese brass, rhombus shaped rudder was designed to withstand extremely high pressures. To get to the stern a man had to walk through two small wooden doors with portholes on each side past the two Meadows engines set at an angle of 17 degrees to the floor.

At Felixstowe on the 13th the air pressure was 1014 mb and the air was very cold with a light north-westerly wind. This changed to a strong south south-westerly by the 14th, veering around to a very strong south-easterly by the 15th. The heavy rain did not hinder visibility too much. RAF 210 left Felixstowe just before two o'clock and Yarmouth was reached approaching evening. Next morning, probably the 14th, they set off for Grimsby. Across the Wash they encountered huge waves driven by a 45-mph north-westerly wind that crashed over the cabin and left them in darkness. It was impossible to maintain a true course without meeting the seas head on, and, because they were afraid of running out of fuel before Grimsby, the boat turned near Blakeney for Kings Lynn. Here they refuelled, then followed the coast north to the Humber. They arrived at Bridlington at low tide, a thick mist preventing them from entering the harbour. Next morning towards Sunderland there was a big swell and near Berwick-on-Tweed it was like rounding the Horn. The swell was so high that day that when they entered a trough the coxswain was unable to see over the next wave-crest. The seas were rough all around Britain and 500 miles off the coast of Land's End the liner *Empress of Britain* was floundering in a heavy Atlantic swell, as was the White Star liner *Olympic*, 300 miles from the Lizard.

The following day a N.E. swell reduced the boat's speed to 18 m.p.h. and it shipped water continuously. Crossing the Firth of Forth there was still a big swell from behind. RAF 210 was still travelling at 18 m.p.h. when they reached Donibristle. For the whole trip the wheelhouse remained dry.

The day after its arrival at Inverkeithing and the handover to the station authorities, the boat was used without any further work being done to her.

On 21st April Lawrence wrote to thank Dawson for *The Times* articles: they were 'admirable', but he could not understand how Shepherd, without taking notes, just 'looking calm and listening easily', could produce such accurate 'notices'.[62] The 200 series was extremely successful and still being produced in 1940, having the specific advantages over the old boats that it could achieve fast speeds with minimal fuel costs and fewer crew members.

The year 1931 was one of the most active and hardworking for Lawrence since the War. At last in the testing of the fast RAF tender he had found a new vocation and sense of fulfilment, where his multiple talents found a worthy application. The RAF 200 was far in advance, in terms of speed, reliability and seaworthiness, of anything the Marine Craft Service had operated for many years, its genesis having nothing to do with the British boat industry, but originating in fast boat races in America. It was almost completely a result of Hubert Scott-Paine's vision and luck in approaching E.6 at an opportune time when they were searching for faster, more reliable craft. Largely as a result of his contoured hard chine design the 200 was able to operate in the roughest of seas and in the most inclement weather conditions. The design suited the RAF's requirements admirably, particularly when it was recast for the large 63-foot Air Sea Rescue boats of World War Two.

T.E.'s contribution has been exaggerated by some of his biographers. He had very little to do with the 200 tender in its early stages, most of his work with E.6 being the testing of the new Power-Meadows engines, which took the boat in leaps and bounds past the restrictions of the old Brooke engine. The marinisation of the Meadows engine at Wolverhampton proved a remarkable success in view of the problems its redesign for marine use involved. Lawrence was almost entirely self-taught and had no formal training in marine architecture – he misunderstood how far the developments of the 'hard chine' boats could go.[63] He and Beauforte-Greenwood mistakenly believed that the hard-chine principle could be applied to much larger designs. It was only later, in 1934, when he was able to use his powerful connections in the services to influence their acceptance, that the larger boats began to appear in the RAF and Royal Navy.

The limited success of the towed target trials of July 1931 revealed deficiencies in both the seaplane tenders and the floating targets for this purpose, and it was these shortcomings that eventually led to the redevelopment of the RAF 200 as an armoured target boat, a remarkably successful hybrid, the development of which occupied Lawrence for the remainder of his RAF service.

Notes

1 Air Ministry: *List of Staff and Distribution of Duties*, October 1934 & May 1926. Ministry of Defence Air Historical Branch archive.

2 In 1931, unlike modern times, the August Bank Holiday was on the first Monday in the month. This wasn't changed until 1971 when a Banking Act decreed that the last Monday in August would be a holiday.

3 The Henry Meadows firm had originally been founded in 1920 to manufacture 3-speed gearboxes, but in 1922 went into petrol engine production. The 'Type 6' engine, used on the RAF 200, was a six cylinder, 4.5 litre automobile engine originally used in Invicta and Lagonda cars.

4 Mount Batten's engineering officer.

5 J.M. Wilson stated 'almost seventeen'.

6 *Report on the Official Trial*, 19/02/1931, by B-G, Norrington, Jinman, Lt. Callomore, and Messers. MacCarthy and Godsel.

7 At least twice, on the 21st and 26th March. National Archives: AIR 5/1372.

8 T.E. Lawrence to Robert Graves. Ozone Hotel, Bridlington. 4/2/1935. Published in the *Evening Standard* as part of an obituary 20/5/1935.

9 T.E. Shaw to C.F. Shaw, Mount Batten, 26/3/1931. BL Add. MS 45905.

10 *Report on the 37½ ft. Seaplane Tender* to Air Officer Commanding, Coastal Area: R.A.F. Mount Batten, 02/04/1931. National Archives AIR 5/1372. It is possible that this partly quoted report was written by AC1 Shaw himself. According to J.M. Wilson, although it was signed by Squadron Leader K.B. Lloyd of R.A.F. Mount Batten, it was drafted by Lawrence.

11 Motor Boat Crew.

12 T.E. Shaw to R. Knowles, Mount Batten, 19/04/1931. Letters: DG.

13 T.E. Lawrence to Robert Graves, Mount Batten, 21/04/1931.

14 *100 H.P. 'Power' Marine Engine: Running.* Report to Air Officer Commanding Coastal Area, Mount Batten, 28/04/1931. National Archives: AIR 5/1372.

15 T.E. Lawrence to G.W.M. Dunn, Plymouth, 10/6/1931. Letters: DG.

16 *Daily Echo*, Southampton, 1963.

17 Story from *Lymington Advertiser and Times*, 1963.

18 *Notes on the Introduction of RAF high-speed craft*, W.E.G. Beauforte-Greenwood, 1935.

19 Beauforte-Greenwood to W/Cdr Sydney Smith, 15/5/31. *The Golden Reign.*

20 Ibid.

21 T.E. Lawrence to Clare Sydney Smith, 22/5/31, *The Golden Reign.*

22 *'Power' Engines in 37½-ft. Seaplane Tender.* Report from R.A.F. Mount Batten to Air Officer Commanding, Coastal Area, Royal Air Force. 28/5/1931. National Archives: AIR 5/1372.

23 This deficiency was almost certainly what led to the installation of the superior Power-Hyland control system the following December.

24 RAF Mount Batten to Air Officer Commanding, Coastal Area: *'Power' Engines in 37½ ft. Seaplane Tender: Diary of Tests.* 28/05/1931. National Archives: AIR 5/1372.

25 T.E. Lawrence to John Campbell. 10/6/1931, Henry Meadows Ltd., Fallings Park, Wolverhampton. I.W.M.

26 Dunn was an intelligent aircraftman who found T.E.'s range of knowledge remarkable, later contributing to *T.E. Lawrence by His Friends.*

27 The RAF 200 trials restricted the work T.E. could do on Book XXI of the *Odyssey.*

28 Flt. Lt. W.E.G. Beauforte-Greenwood to W/Cmdr. Sydney Smith, 13/05/1931.

29 T.E. Lawrence to Flt. Lt. W.E.G. Beauforte-Greenwood, Mount Batten, 18/06/1931. DG:L.

30 Ibid. David Garnett appears to have misinterpreted this report as being the book Lawrence submitted to the Air Ministry on the RAF 200 in mid-March 1932. In fact the phrase 'in all' in the second sentence appears to suggest it was the last of the series of four trial reports he submitted to the O.C. Coastal Area in 1931, the other three being on 2nd April, 28th April and 28th May. Source National Archives: AIR 5/1372.

31 Source: National Archives AIR 5/1372.

32 Lawrence thought the 'fog board' a 'strange device'. It could double as a towed target.

33 Report from RAF Mount Batten to AOC, Coastal Area, RAF, c. July 1931. Source: National Archives AIR 5/1372. This report, signed by a Wing Commander, was almost

certainly prepared by Lawrence. See also Lawrence's letters to Beauforte-Greenwood, Appendix III on Edward Spurr, p335.

34 In fact RAF 200 only got as far as Portland, owing to the large-ship crew having 'got cold feet' in small boats, Lawrence thought.

35 T.E. Lawrence to W.E.G. Beauforte-Greenwood, 14/7/1931, Mount Batten. DG.

36 Diane M. Horner: letter to the author, 2005.

37 Ibid.

38 J.M. Pope, Air Ministry to Grp. Capt. S.W. Smith, RAF Manston, Kent. 21/10/1931. RAF Museum, Sydney Smith Archive.

39 T.E. Lawrence to C.S. Smith, Mount Batten, 27/10/1931. *The Golden Reign.*

40 T.E. Lawrence to A. Russell, Birmingham Street, Southampton. 7/11/1931.

41 Ibid.

42 T.E. Lawrence to Bertram Thomas, 28/11/1931.

43 T.E. Lawrence to C.F. Shaw, 28/11/1931. BL Add MS504.

44 T.E. Lawrence to F. Manning, Hythe, 2/1/1932.

45 T.E. Lawrence to W.E.G. Beauforte-Greenwood, 11/01/1932.

46 The 'Cam Pulley' was part of a servo-motor operating under oil pressure that allowed the controls to be finger light. It connected to a disc valve on top of the cylinder head of a double ended piston, operating the gears under hydraulic pressure. The pulley also connected indirectly to a single lever in the wheel house that was located in a fitting resembling a ship's telegraph. This enabled the throttle and gears on each engine to be each operated by one lever. Thus there were two levers in the 'telegraph' casing, one for each engine.

47 The Power-Hyland system.

48 The two levers on the 'telegraph' fitting had a quadrant between them with 'Neutral' engraved on a segment nearly an inch wide. On another narrow band in front of this was engraved 'Slow Ahead'. On a third band behind 'Neutral' was 'Slow astern'.

49 This was probably similar to the delay that may ensue before the clutch bites on a modern automatic car, particularly when the oil supply is low.

50 T.E. Lawrence to Flt. Lt W..E.G. Beauforte-Greenwood, Hythe, 15/01/1932. (Correspondence in private ownership.)

51 Recalled by Ronald D. Knight in the T.E. Lawrence Society Newsheet No. 3, April 1986.

52 Tunbridge.

53 T.E. Lawrence to Flt. Lt. W.E.G. Beauforte-Greenwood, Hythe, 20/01/1932.

54 T.E. Lawrence to Clare Sydney Smith, Mount Batten,. 5/2/1932. *Golden Reign.*

55 *Golden Reign.*

56 T.E. Lawrence to A.S. Frere-Reeves, Hythe, 11/3/32.

57 T.E. Lawrence to A.S. Frere-Reeves, 20/3/32.

58 T.E. Lawrence to G. Dawson, 22nd March 1932. DG.

59 Ibid.

60 *The Times* 16/4/1932.

61 Ibid.

62 This appears to be another example of T.E. hokum. In fact he had ghost-written the reports himself as it 'avoided farcical exaggeration.' Shepherd may not have even been on the trip.

63 They were thinking to destroyer size, where the hard-chine, sharp cut-water and planing stern would have been unworkable.

CHAPTER ELEVEN

Armoured Target Boats

Until the summer of 1931 bombing training at sea had been inefficient and inaccurate for the RAF, relying upon stationary targets, or upon those towed by larger vessels. In March 1932 the Air Ministry asked Beauforte-Greenwood if a boat could be designed with sufficient armour to withstand 8½-lb. practice bombs. The Director of Training, Air–Commodore Mitchell, that month commissioned E.6 to produce a towed or W/T[1] controlled target-boat.[2] B-G recalled in 1935:

> The problem was to provide sufficient protection for the crew, machinery and petrol tanks, in a boat which could travel at least twenty knots against bombs when dropped from a height of 10,000 feet, with a striking velocity of 890 ft. second, approximately. I was to base my calculations upon the fact that 1 inch mild steel would be proof against an 8½ lb. bomb dropped from the height above mentioned.[3]

In order to solve the problem he went to the Woolwich Arsenal. The material he sought had to be light in weight but strong in compression. He discussed with the staff any gunnery experiments they had conducted that corresponded in terms of weight of projectile and velocity to his requirements.

> I concluded that [an] armour plate called Hadfields Resister, manufactured by Hadfields Ltd. of Sheffield, was the most likely type and sufficiently light weight to meet our requirements. I at once examined possibilities of a type of boat which we could use and the weight of armour which would be necessary for protective purposes.[4]

The RAF's experience of attacking ships was extremely limited. The Fleet Air Arm was yet to be formed and fleet duties were still the responsibility of the Air Force, thus certain RAF squadrons were being trained and equipped specifically for maritime strike operations, and these later became part of Coastal Command. There was no way of practising effectively on moving targets because, until the RAF 200, the Air Force simply did not have a launch powerful enough. Previously targets had been stationary floating pylons and target boats towed by other ships, a method with obvious limitations (and high running costs), the towing vehicle being more or less an extension of the target.

To take the armour a sufficiently strong, light and compatible boat was required. The only one suitable, B-G concluded, was the British Power Boat Company's RAF 200 and a collaboration began amongst him, Scott-Paine, Lawrence and Captain Nicholson of Hadfields for the modification of the hull to determine 'the most suitable type of and shape of armour'. With the help of Tommy Quelch, Scott-Paine's main designer, a final design was arrived at, basically the RAF 200 series with the upper hull cut down and armour plating introduced. Mock-ups were prepared, the boat's superstructure being trimmed forward and aft so that the altered centre of gravity, caused by the extra weight, was as low as possible to maximize stability. The hull had to be strengthened and a third Meadows engine installed to accommodate these new loads. To support the armour special troughs were fitted, filled with ballast on the trials, the prototype boat on one occasion attaining 30 knots. Fore and aft bulkheads, the engine, fuel tanks and the cockpit were protected by the Hadfields 'Resister' armour, designed and installed by the British Power Boat Company staff to allow for easy removal and access to the machinery.[5] Its surface on the top of the boat was painted a bright yellow, probably the primrose yellow Lawrence selected at Mount Batten in 1929. An armoured hood was also fitted behind the crew to protect them from blasts from the rear.

Photographs of these boats show that the bows were of a 'whale-back' design that Scott-Paine later used on the 63-foot Air Sea Rescue Launch. The crew's quarters were unenclosed, set further aft, much smaller and more cramped than on the 200, the coxswain, some reports say, having to sit on the engine casing. In May 1932 the Air Ministry ordered two of these prototype launches from Scott-Paine. An unusual material used on the boats was a substance named 'Onazote'. This was an expanded rubber[6] substance, ten times lighter than cork, which lined the inside of the hull, keeping the boat afloat if holed. In 1935 Lawrence kept a series of maintenance notes at Bridlington on armoured boat A191: 'Onazote and floors lifted. Hull painted inside and out in accordance with specification, also equipment and armour.'[7] When the eight or nine pound inactive bombs punctured the surface normally only a small hole resulted and the crew was supplied with special conical plugs that could be banged into the aperture in seconds to prevent the craft sinking.

The armour plating around the three engines also fitted down the sides of the boat, above the hard chine and was screwed and bolted onto the superstructure. Lawrence's maintenance notes for 1935 stated 'New castellated nuts to side armour, with brass split pins. Two coach screws put in.' The hull was divided into compartments to further reduce the possibility of sinking and Hadfields also designed fore and aft bulkheads of armour plate.[8]

Scott-Paine added box girdering and additional strapping to carry the extra weight. Of A191 Lawrence wrote 'Decking strengthened (forward) with intermediate beams and brass brackets. Two new planks on S.[tarboard] bows': the planks down the side of the hull above the chine were set at a diagonal and cut to standard lengths for ease of production.

All glands repacked. All skin-fittings examined. P.[ort] propeller bracket straightened. One new self-boiler. New rudder. Propellers repitched. Shafts trued. Three new coupling keys. Folk-end in place of ball joint of steering arm. New cam pin in cross shaft of steering, to which large hand-greaser was added. Two new canvas waterproofing sleeves. New clips and P.R. tubing throughout.[9]

Clearly, the craft required much more attentive maintenance than on normal duties. This was because of the unusually high levels of stress and vibrations suffered during the bombing when fittings were knocked out of place. A lot of Lawrence's work at Bridlington was to do with this kind of maintenance, whether of a direct or a supervisory nature. Even the rudders and propellers were cast, high tensile manganese bronze, an extremely strong material. Propellers were of 14-inch diameter and set at a pitch of 13° to the horizontal, with a cutlass rubber bearing. The shafts were of 1' diameter Tungum metal.

The introduction of these boats was a great step forward for the RAF as the use of a small and inexpensive mobile target in place of a battleship and its attendant destroyer (with a crew of several hundred men), resulted in huge financial savings. The target boats, according to Liddell Hart, were beautifully suited to the task, being 'almost too hard to hit, in comparison with a ship.'[10] As a result of their introduction the bombing efficiency of the RAF improved remarkably.

A former pilot in Arabia, Donald Siddons, an ordained minister who had been with Lawrence at Akaba, sent a note to Donibristle that Lawrence missed picking up by only a day. Lawrence wrote to him, saying that he had only been in Scotland for a few days where he had handed over a new type of motor boat (presumably RAF 210).

> ... It must be strange, from the safety of a ministry, to look back upon Akaba. My path has been less progressive. Today I am an airman of ten years standing, but only an A.C.1 for all that. My job is overseeing the building of boats for the service of a boatyard here. I have been a year on the job, living in this cottage near the works as a billet.[11]

Jack Mitchell Barker had joined the RAF in June 1931 aged 19 and trained at RAF Cranwell as a wireless and electrical technician. In June 1932 he was posted to Calshot where he was surprised to learn that he was M.B.C., not knowing what 'M.B.C.' was, or that the RAF had a boat section. He began working on the Armoured Target Boats, radio equipment on the boats being a long wave Transmitter/Receiver with a tuner unprotected outside the armour plating that was connected to an aerial on the mast. One day Barker was inspecting an aerial when a very short airman, with an old fashioned uniform and an old cap perched oddly on top of his head, approached. The small man climbed into the boat without introducing himself and started asking questions about the radio equipment. He was well spoken and appeared to be 'genned up' technically.

When he asked Barker if he thought the system would work alright, Barker told him it depended on what the boat was going to be used for. The man said it was to be bombed on a bombing range off the Yorkshire coast using 6½-pound practice bombs. He answered all the questions Barker (who had joined the RAF to fly, not to be bombed) asked. Barker told him he thought it would be OK, but they had to fine tune the tuner, which was connected to a receiver and W/T as there was a danger that the force of any impact on the hull would knock the tuning off and they would be unable to send Morse messages. When his interrogator walked off and climbed upon a very large motorcycle, Barker asked a deck hand who came aboard who the little aircraftman was. 'A/C1 Shaw' the hand replied. 'A/C1 Shaw? Who's that?' 'Lawrence of Arabia.'

Barker was amazed by the way 'A/C1 Shaw' was able was able to tell senior ranks what to do, or cajole them into his way of thinking. He persuaded a Flight Sergeant to release Barker from a dinghy lamp making duty on one occasion. At the end of Barker's period at Calshot, an Air Commodore arrived by flying boat to inspect work done on an armoured target boat. Barker looked on in bewilderment as his C.O., a Group Captain, stood aside whilst Lawrence chatted to the officer.

Human target

In June 1932 Lawrence delivered two armoured target boats to Bridlington to be fitted with armoured decks, and another two prototypes in July, the first trials taking place on the 11th. Three days later he arrived with a further two prototypes and spent the following five weeks fixing five boats and, until early September remained fairly settled. That summer had witnessed marvellous weather and he spent most of it conducting the running trials of two of the new A.T.B.s at Hythe, particularly adjusting for overtiming. However, at the end of August articles began to appear in the press, specifically the *News Chronicle* and *Sunday Chronicle*, dramatizing his role in the testing of these new launches and sensationalizing the occasion when he had personally driven an A.T.B. whilst it was being bombed and an 8½-lb practice bomb hit it.

> **Human Target for Bombs: Men Risk Death in Speed-Boats**
>
> Using heavily-armoured, unsinkable speed-boats, Aircraftsman Shaw – 'Lawrence of Arabia' – and two other R.A.F. men, have risked their lives as human targets for bombing planes, it was revealed yesterday.

This sensationalism was criticized in Air Ministry reports. The sensitivity was all the greater because a World Disarmament Conference was taking place at the same time in Geneva, attended by the League of Nations, the USA and the USSR. The Air Ministry had to place a ban on any press coverage of target boat trials. It was a ban Lawrence and his colleagues resented, perhaps misunderstanding the Air Ministry's motives.[12] Lawrence was returned to normal duties at Plymouth. The Air Ministry felt obliged to withdraw him from the eyes of the press, and concocted a cover story that the 'current programme of construction of new marine craft' had been completed and only repair work and repeat orders were being carried out at Hythe, so the retention of Shaw at the British Power Boat Company yard 'could no longer be justified'.

From 29th August to 5th September 1932, after a few days at the Air Armament School at RAF Catfoss, Yorkshire, Lawrence took seven days of his annual leave visiting the annual Malvern Festival and also Birmingham, where he saw George Bernard Shaw's play *Too True to be Good* playing for the first time.

Letters to Weblin: the language of the 'rude mechanic'

He now wrote a series of letters to Flight Lieutenant Weblin of E.6. These began shortly after the *News Chronicle* article appeared and the first was written from Myrtle Cottage on Tuesday 6th of September. It is included here to give some idea of how far Lawrence had assimilated himself into the role of an RAF mechanic. As previously stated Weblin's official role with E.6 was the laying and inspection of moorings and sea targets, although the letter suggests his work went far beyond this. At this time, although the armoured boats were in service, he was still working on the RAF 200. Beauforte-Greenwood was on leave. Lawrence was very much in control of the work and his striving for efficiency provoked criticism of the staff as well as the equipment, much of the latter being inadequate or unnecessary; even

British Power Boat Company's 18-foot round bottom 'Inboard Dinghy', with an inboard engine. The propeller shaft passed through the stern of the hull requiring a watertight seal or 'stern gland' to accomplish this. Lawrence probably worked on this shortly before he wrote his first letter to Flight Lieutenant Weblin. (Via Symonds)

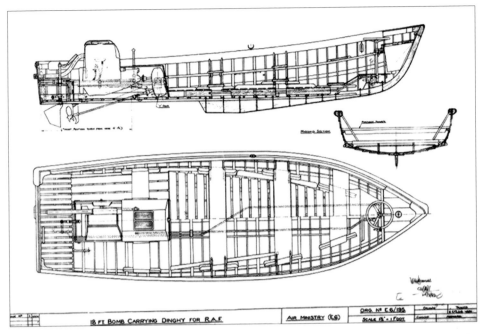

Air Ministry (E.6) drawing of an 18-foot Bomb Carrying Dinghy c. 1936. This was used to carry up to 12 tons of bombs to moored flying boats at bases such as Mount Batten and Felixstowe. (National Archives)

his oilskins were Sydney Smith's old cast-offs. He was due to be transferred to Mount Batten, but was still interested in the work at Bridlington. The Chief of the Air Staff, Sir John Salmond, made it clear following the *News Chronicle* articles, that his involvement was not on.

Dear Flight Lieutenant Weblin,

Dinghy stern gland. There is no neck-ring in this. They were added to the larger boat's stern glands when the moulded packings came in, to reduce the pressure on them. With piece packing, such as you are now using, no neck-ring is needed. It does no harm, but is not worth the cost of fitting. You will find the dinghy all right without, when properly packed. If it goes on leaking, then suspect alignment, or a bent shaft. Those phosphor bronze [propeller] shafts are very soft, and bend upon any excuse. I wanted to condemn the lot but could not, as the Admiralty had specified them expressly.

I have sent off today nearly a pound of 3/16' square packing. Should last you quite a long time.

I am surprised at the S.[tarboard] engine of [RAF] 207 going before the S.[tarboard] of [RAF] 206, and wonder what is the matter. It does not sound like bearings: I suspect some pinion trouble. However we will know soon.

The odd screws sent with the stern tube locking plate screws were a mistake. Please tell Cpl. M. to throw them away. They were made up by the B.P.B. Co. in error, and the other set-screws were my substitute for them made by myself. I did not know I had sent them.[13]

He thought the new armoured boats were 'going through it', although they had not yet been hit: the RAF aircrews were bombing either 'very well or very low'. He thought it good that at the rate they were improving the boats 'might be hit any day'. In this letter he did mention an improved design he had thought of for a splash target, that he had earlier mentioned to Beaufort–Greenwood: 'I have an idea for a 10–30 knot spray-throwing surf-board, not weighing much and offering far less water resistance.'[14]

He told Weblin he had been transferred to Mount Batten because of the *News Chronicle* article, joking that it also said he had designed the *Schneider Trophy* aircraft.

The Hyland clutch mechanism on the A.T.B. enabled the Meadows engine's gear and throttle to operate on a single system. Scott-Paine's yard manager Stuart Barker reported the boats at Calshot were in a filthy condition: Lawrence found one with an engine with a 'kick like a mule' which was a quarter of an inch out of line. Weblin complained about advertising matter on the Hyland plates and Lawrence told him Barker was 'looking into the blue print matter'. It took ten days to complete the work.

> . . . F/Lt Norrington is coming here tonight, and I shall ask him how the Bridlington establishment stands. Till Captain Beauforte-Greenwood comes back E.6 can only go on half throttle . . .
>
> My oilskin I took out of the dinghy, where it was covering the engine that last wet Sunday. I had torn my old 'skin across the knee in climbing into a flying boat: so put it on the engine cover and adopted the new one. It is quite new, no name in it, and very long, right down to my heels. Cpl. Olley said he would change the U.S.[15] one easily. I tried the other un-numbered skins in the digs to find a shorter one, but failed. I'm sorry [if] it is yours. Did yours go in the dinghy? Perhaps it was used for the Mayor's party the day before. My old one has 'Wing Commander Smith' written inside it.[16]
>
> I am glad the Kernoozer engine works. It should do, for we took pains with it – but there is always doubt. It has a very good oil-pump anyway. Both Meadows and the B.P.B. Co. are testing oil pump after oil pump, in the effort to reach real efficiency and quietness. Some of them scream the shop down, and others take twice as much h.p. as the best. Some heat the oil to 100°C in a few minutes. Apparently there is a great deal to learn about oil pumps. They are trying all makes and sorts, aero and car and boat, with the widest differences showing up . . . I am sorry about the manifold washer . . .[17]
>
> We will get the coil dissected and find out the cause. Or perhaps I mustn't say 'we' now. All the same it would be nice to know what it is. I shall miss this factory work; but the leisure of Plymouth, where I will only do deck hand, will be great: and I'll be able to read books again. So it's swings and roundabouts.
>
> Yours Sincerely,
> T.E. Shaw[18]

Shortly after this letter was written he was posted to Calshot for ten days specifically to adjust the Hyland clutches on three armoured target boats which were badly needed for bombing tests with H.M.S. *Ark Royal* and *Valiant*.[19] These boats were in extremely poor condition and the work was not finished until 16th September when he wrote another letter from Plymouth to Weblin, who was still at Bridlington. By this time Lawrence had been transferred permanently to Mount Batten, stating specifically it was the Chief of the Air Staff (C.A.S.)[20] who ordered it, and that he would be unable to help Weblin out.

There was no official communication to Weblin from the Air Ministry of Lawrence's movements, Weblin only hearing the news when Norrington informed him, suggesting how casual T.E.'s employment was. Although ten days had passed he still was unaware whether the Bridlington bombing trials were having any success:

> I hope the boats have behaved themselves, and that the armoured boats have been hit
> – once in the wood and once in the armour!

Lawrence took three more weeks of his annual leave, returning to Mount Batten a month later. The Oxford University Press's trade edition of the *Odyssey* had been published and was selling well. At Batten he was back working on engines in the Marine Section and Weblin and the rest of the Marine Craft Unit had, by 15th November, moved down by boat to Felixstowe:

Dear Flight Lieutenant Weblin,

I owe you for two letters. I am very sorry. Only in life at Plymouth there is nothing to write about. There are 35 of us in five boats, and everybody wonders what can be found to do, as a pastime. Very unlike Bridlington . . . but the work is not better done, for lack of that sense of urgency.

That voyage back sound[s] like too much of a good thing. My Wash experiences have been uniformly bad. If the day is windless and sunny, without a ripple on the sea, then I shall strike straight across. If there is a cloud, or a 5 mph breeze then I shall go to Hunston, and via the Boston Deep. That way is like navigating a tropical lagoon: water like a calm deep river always.

The Hyland clutch complication is very serious. Nobody seems able to get the hang of it. Yet there is a plain explanation and course to follow. Of course it takes quite a time to get a wrong right: but they are easily kept right. Sometimes I think of putting the whole A.B.C. of it on paper.[21]

I have seen your clutch-plates. That is something new. None of ours here has worn out at all. I think they can only wear by slipping. B-G suspects the metal, but I think not. Also I saw the photographs of the hits on the armoured boats. That 45° angle of incidence is rather formidable. Another six feet forwards and it would have got the engines, and probably killed the crew with fragments. They will have to put a steel apron from the back of the roof, downward.

He then considered the quality of the staff at Hythe. A fitter named 'Wills' was 'no good', there being only one first class fitter in the whole Company, a man named Leonard Tilbury.[22] There was a very young fitter who, despite tending to be lazy was 'not at all bad'. Scott-Paine's second-in-command, Stuart Barker, apparently knew very little and, like his boss was a hard taskmaster. As a consequence Scott-Paine had lost a number of good men.[23]

> You have had two camshaft bearings go. That is something quite fresh and important. The new piston, oil pumps and auto-cleans are coming along. We at Plymouth are putting the auto-cleans on the hull, with a rubber joist in their pipes. On the gear cover they are a perfect nuisance, and altogether impossible, for they make clutches inaccessible.
>
> I wonder how long the slipway will be before it is fit for use. Next season you'll need it. They are tiresome about things.

At Felixstowe Weblin was supervising a gang of twelve fitters, who, Lawrence suggested, would keep Weblin's hands full all winter. At Mount Batten they had just successfully serviced two Meadows engines, and T.E. was trying to persuade the Air Ministry to supply a Meadows tool kit as the other fitters kept using his tools.

> Our hulls have stood up perfectly, here – though Bridlington conditions are much worse than any others in the R.A.F. It is a pity the engines are not as good as the boats.
>
> I saw your report in the Air Ministry. The dinghy and 25-foot refuellers wouldn't stand Bridlington Bay! They talk of fitting 150 as your depot ship. It might work well. The armoured boats are generally praised, and many more are to be built, eventually, if Geneva pleases.[24] We all depend on Switzerland now-a-days!
>
> To take out a damaged cutlass bearing, drill out the grub screws, and then screw a 1-inch tap into the bearing till it twists: and then pull!
>
> I'm sorry they put me out of action, so far as boats are concerned: for that Bridlington was amusing . . .
>
> My regards to Mrs. Weblin. I hope she finds Felixstowe all right as a winter resort. I fear it must be precious cold.[25]

Fall Out with Graves

Robert Graves first met Lawrence at All Souls in 1919. Graves had run a small shop at Boars Hill after his time at Oxford but this had proved unsuccessful and Lawrence assisted him financially after he ran into debt. Up until the publication of *I, Claudius* Graves had had nothing, but following the success of the 'Claudius' books he had offered on at least one occasion to return Lawrence's generosity. By September 1930 they were still corresponding but the relationship had deteriorated: Graves had observed a noticeable change in Lawrence, rather, two changes. One was his accent: whether feigned or not, the intonation had been transformed from

Oxford English to garage-English. Lawrence now had the accent of 'men who drove lorries'. Second: more shocking and vulgar, to Graves' mind, was a row of what T.E. termed 'practical' gold front teeth. 'Common-clay vulgarity: no All Souls fellow could possibly have showed up with a mouthful of gold like that.'[26]

Lawrence, on his part, took an intense dislike to Graves' partner, Laura Riding. Graves adored her both physically and intellectually and Lawrence feared their sensual relationship would destroy Graves' poetic life.[27] Years later he wrote:

> Being a mechanic cuts one off from all real communication with women ... No woman, I believe, can understand a mechanic's happiness in serving his bits and pieces ...
>
> Laura saw me too late, after I had changed direction. She is, was absolutely right to avoid communication with me. There are no faults on either side, but common sense, the recognition of a difficulty to be too difficult to be worth surmounting, when there are so many other rewarding activities in reach.[28]

The change in Graves and Lawrence's relationship filtered through into their correspondence. Early in 1931 Graves had sent him some examples of his and Riding's poems, but Lawrence only had time to glance at them, then 'descended to *Tit Bits* and *Happy Magazine*, which seem to go with speed testing and water sports'.[29] By 1933 they had not met for a long time. Graves was not convinced by Lawrence's low-brow stance. Lawrence had once been his equal intellectually; now he was posing as a blue collar worker. Graves failed to realise how far Lawrence had stepped out of his world and into another with which he himself was not familiar. The bourgeois poet-adventurer had become one of the proletariat. 'Come off it, R.G.!' wrote Lawrence. 'Your letter forgets my present ... I'm now a fitter, very keen and tolerably skilled on engines, but in no way abstract. I live all of every day with real people, and concern myself only in the concrete.'[30]

This change in Lawrence, whether forced or not, hurt Graves deeply. It made him question how sincere he had previously been: 'Had all the past interest in my work been just another kind of game?'[31] he asked. But Lawrence did not mince words: the 'ancient' self-examining T.E.L. of Oxford and *Seven Pillars* was 'dead ... Not regretted either. My last ten years have been the best of my life.' Contrast this with his later description of the life of the mechanic as 'concrete, superficial, and everyday.'[32]

Was Lawrence genuine? Many think he came out of the RAF a more fulfilled person. The down to earth language he used reflected his new assumed persona. In May 1934 he used the expression 'this other bloke'[33] to Liddell Hart and on 8th June 1934 he wrote to Bradbury 'For the love of Mike, get me back the remains of my tool kit.'[34] These colloquialisms were not the language he would have used with Churchill or Phillip Sassoon; but was he simply 'slumming it' or are these changes unconscious, authentic? He had also become less introspective than when younger.

Graves remained unconvinced. At the beginning of 1933 he sent Lawrence some 'critical work' he and a number of other writers had produced. T.E.'s reaction is fascinating; does this read sincerely, or is it posturing?

> I have read it and your letter again carefully: and I'm damned if I have the foggiest idea what it and you are driving at. Further, I'm prepared to swear that did the Air Ministry similarly word their instructions issued in A.M. W.O.'s, not a station in the R.A.F. would comprehend. [35]

This letter marked the breakdown of the Lawrence and Graves relationship: it was never mended. Graves failed to recognize – or refuted – the fact that Lawrence lived in a different world to him: a harsh, pragmatic one with no place for the abstract. He thought Lawrence was 'playing silly', putting their 'seriously practical thought on an obscure abstract level'.[36] Lawrence replied: 'Well, there we are. I only wish I was playing silly: for it is not good to be unable to straighten out that stuff.'[37]

   Graves kept in contact, nevertheless. At the end of the year he wrote, thanking T.E. for an earlier reading of a proof copy of *I, Claudius*. He found Lawrence's criticisms difficult to deal with: Graves had written a 'popular' historical study, keeping 'within the limits of personal integrity' as far as he could, but Lawrence did not see Claudius as 'an essential book', and Graves thought Lawrence was looking for things in it that were not there, finding himself 'unsatisfied', without knowing why. Graves shows Claudius in an age of disintegration which he found impossible to reintegrate, where 'every moral safeguard of a religious or patriotic or social sort had gone West'. Claudius's efforts to right this disintegration only serve to provoke it. Perhaps Graves' fictionalizing of history frustrated Lawrence; but it is also likely that some of the processes in the book reflected those of his own life: an underlying disintegration that he spent years trying to reintegrate, in many senses successfully during the RAF years. The attempted abandonment of the intellectual, donnish self in favour of of a humble, working class image cannot have been without a great deal of painful introspection. So perhaps Claudius's failure to 'heal' or ameliorate the body politic seemed to give the lie to, or undermine, Lawrence's own self-healing The attempted shedding of the sophistication and intellectual complexity of his younger life was a keystone of T.E's rebuilding. At the end of this letter Graves described the relationship between them as 'still unsatisfactory'. He said things might improve if T.E. became his own master again.[38]

'Putting the RAF fleet on New Lines'

Lawrence was meticulous in keeping the motor boat Coxswain's log. He would jot details of the previous few days work on small pieces of paper, and then sit for hours at night writing them up. Each boat had a log book for the hull and one for each of the three engines. At Bridlington, where there were ten armoured boats and a dinghy, this amounted to over forty log books. Every one of these had to be filled in, covering the results of tests. The entries were signed 'TE Shaw AC1'. After Lawrence died some of the books mysteriously disappeared.

Although he had neither a First nor a Second Class Coxswain's certificate Lawrence drove all manner of boats. This was totally against King's Regulations, which stated he had no authority, as an aircraft hand, to have anything to do with boats under any circumstances.[39] Between April 1932 and November 1934 he moved irregularly between Bridlington, Hythe, Catfoss, Mount Batten, and the Meadows factory at Wolverhampton. William Wilson, a painter for Scott-Paine in the 1930s, commented on Lawrence's work at that time: 'He spent long hours at night, after a long day on Southampton Water, testing these boats and had little time left for his books and music, of which he was so fond.'[40]

His posting back to Plymouth initially acted as a palliative since the work at Scott-Paine's had been arduous. He began to relax, but soon became dissatisfied with the routine duties. In March 1933, he considered invoking the release clause of his contract to return to Civvy Street. He explained his reasons to Trenchard:

> I'm not being turned out. Coastal Area are very obstructive, and won't let us do anything from Batten, in the way of boat testing or equipment. The savour of living here in Batten is not what it was. So I put in to go as from April 6 – unless my services are for any purpose specially required.[41]

One of the 'help-mates' that assisted him, under the influence of Sir Philip Sassoon, was Sir Geoffrey Salmond, who succeeded his brother, Sir John Salmond, as the Chief of Air Staff in April 1933. Lawrence told Trenchard that he had seen Sir Geoffrey Salmond 'who will sit in your chair . . . and explained myself fully: so I must leave it at that.[42] Salmond's daughter, Anne Baker explained:

> Perhaps some instinct had told Lawrence to come that day to see Geoffrey. He also asked him if he could be given more interesting work in the RAF as, although his work on the flying boats had fascinated him, and he had been of great help in the Schneider Trophy races, he had now been offered work he felt was uninteresting . . . It was typical of Geoffrey that, although so ill, he managed over the next few days to recommend Lawrence for more interesting work in the RAF telling him also how much the RAF appreciated him.[43]

Lawrence felt that the work he had done with Scott-Paine of 'putting the R.A.F. fleet on new lines' was, after 18 months, only 'half-finished'. Salmond discussed the matter with Lawrence's C.O. and then wrote two letters to Phillip Sassoon. the Air Ministry issued a memorandum in April:

> Lawrence of Arabia has decided to stay on in the Air Force. As he knows a good deal about motor boats he has been given a fairly free hand to go around various motor boat firms in the country.

His new RAF contract of 2nd May stated his duties:

a) Generally to watch the Air Ministry's interests at contractors' yards during the construction of marine craft, various types of bombing target, moorings, engines and equipment;

b) Assist in the trial reports and notes on running and maintenance of various types of craft;

c) Assist in the production of craft and equipment generally and in particular the high speed vessel for crashwork, life saving and also salvage of boat planes.[44]

Lawrence's time with armoured target boats at Hythe, Calshot and Bridlington had been stimulating, introducing new challenges, some of them hazardous, after the RAF 200 work. Lawrence's return to station duties at Mount Batten had frustrated him. However, the demanding work on the Hyland Clutch system took his mechanical expertise in a different direction. His letters to Flight Lieutenant Weblin show how varied the work was and how responsible he felt for it. He became painfully aware of the restrictions caused by the Geneva Conference and could not have been blind to the increasingly hostile situation in Europe, which made the work important. From 24th April 1933 he was officially posted to the Marine Aircraft Experimental Establishment at Felixstowe[45] from where, and at other smaller boatyards, he worked mainly on developing armoured target launches until March 1935.

Well known photograph of Lawrence taken by Liddell Hart at Hythe in 1933. This was one of a series taken by Liddell Hart and his wife, the occasion being a visit by Liddell Hart to question Lawrence for his biography. It was taken at the B.P.B. Co. yard.

The Marine Aircraft Experimental Establishment, Felixstowe

Lawrence was stationed at Felixstowe for only a short period from April 28th until May 15th 1933, his only other appearances being brief visits.[46] He was employed generally in the boat section at the Commanding Officer's discretion but was not a permanent member of a boat crew, being required to wear plain clothes at any contractors' yards, but uniform at an RAF unit. The Department of the Environment estimated he could be kept fully employed for nine months in a year. At Felixstowe he was to be 'available to be sent to contractors' yards under the orders of the D. of E. direct', and 'employed at an RAF unit as it may seem expedient', in both cases his C.O. being notified previously.[47]

The M.A.E.E. had been part of the Admiralty originally but was taken over by the Air Board in January 1917.[48] It went into the Ministry of Munitions in 1918 and the Air Ministry in 1920, its initial purpose being to research and develop water-based aircraft, equipment and air-sea rescue apparatus for service needs.[49] It was originally based on the Isle of Grain but transferred to its new location in 1924. This was mainly for reasons of economy and efficiency: Felixstowe was not as subject to tidal change as Grain and its sheds were closer to the sea. Also, communications had been poor at Grain, the only land access being by rail. 150 staff were sacked and £20,000 a year saved.

Aerial view of the M.A.E.E., Felixstowe in the 1940s facing north east indicating the three seaplane hangars and marine craft shed.

Felixstowe is located on the Norfolk coast at the mouth of the Stour and Orwell rivers, facing the North Sea. The M.A.E.E. was based near the dock on the west side of a spit of land projecting into the estuary directly opposite Harwich. Across the station's seafront were three tall steel seaplane hangers numbered 1, 2 and 3 and on the south side of these the 'Old Station' consisted of eight alphabetically marked sheds. The only steel one of these was 'G' shed originally housing Porte/ Felixstowe flying boats during World War One. From 1927 to 1931 it was the home of Orlebar's High Speed Flight.[50] The base was a famous seaplane station during World War One. After the Armistice it was not completely closed, becoming a care and maintenance unit. As such there was already a permanent camp there when the unit transferred.

Aircraft design was still in its infancy and the sky was the limit in terms of experimentation. The M.A.E.E was at the cutting edge of this in the 1920s and '30s and came directly under Air Ministry administration. Its Commanding Officers were Group Captain G.R. Bromet from 1928 to 1931 and Group Captain A.J. Miley from 1931 to 1936.[51] The Officer Commanding the boat unit was Lawrence's old friend from Batten, Flight Lieutenant W.H. Jinman. [52]

T.E. would have worked in G shed, the Marine Craft Shed, then housing the new Armoured Target Boats. This was in the heart of the establishment, where acceptance tests and trials on motor-boats and dinghies, necessary for flying-boat operations, were performed. In the early days of flying boats these had been hired from private firms and were very expensive. The shed, with all the other buildings apart from the hangars, was in urgent need of replacement, having been constructed during the First World War.[53]

Occasionally, when based in the southeast, he would call unannounced on the Churchills at Chartwell for Sunday afternoon tea. Winston's daughter Sarah remembered him arriving on his motorcycle from a nearby RAF station. The noisy, extrovert Churchills were silenced by his soft voice and beguiling personality:

> He was a small, slight man, and his fine head looked almost out of proportion . . . we would all listen in pin drop silence to what he had to say. I remember my father sitting back watching him with half a smile, and letting him run the conversation.[54]

In May, 1933 Lawrence was detached from the M.A.E.E. to various other bases in England. These included Mount Batten, the Isle of Wight and Hythe.[55] At Hythe he lodged alternatively at Myrtle Cottage and at Southampton. On April 26th 1933 he was ordered to the boatyard of John Samuel White and Co. Ltd at Clarence Yard Wharf, East Cowes, to survey the construction of five of a new type of 56-foot pinnace fitted with twin Gardner diesels. The pinnace (a name derived from pine) was a round-bilged, steam-driven, ship's tender used for heavy duty work such as aircraft towing and weapon recovery.

In the second week of May he was at Felixstowe for a few days. Liddell Hart wanted to talk to him there about the forthcoming biography but missed the connection. Lawrence made a trip to Nottingham, no doubt to visit the Brough works at Haydn Road, either to have his bike serviced or to check up on the progress of its replacement. He returned to Scott Paine's yard at the beginning of August 1933 and from the 14th worked under contract at Hythe on the testing of nine 8/28 Power Meadow engines for the Wolverhampton factory. (These were petrol driven engines that powered, amongst others, the 18 ft. 'inboard dinghy' that he worked on from July to August 1932 at Bridlington. The inboard dinghy's engine was fixed into the hull as opposed to an outboard engine that rested on the stern. This explains the function of the 'stern gland' Lawrence referred to in his letter to Weblin, which acted as a watertight seal, its packing allowing the propeller shaft to pass cleanly through the rear of the hull). A claim for £633.12 for the engine work was submitted to the Air Ministry on 6th September. He sent the completed test report sheets to Wolverhampton on 5th of October.[56]

Intermittently from the end of July 1933 until November 1934 Lawrence lived in a terraced red brick house at 13 Birmingham Street, Southampton, which he found very cold in winter. He told Churchill in the second week of December 1933: 'I work all day on R.A.F. boat building and reach evening tired: partly because my room in Southampton grows colder and colder as the winter deepens. It sends me quickly to bed.'[57]

Over a period of six years from March 1929 Liddell Hart conducted a series of interviews with Lawrence, initially for an entry in the *Encyclopaedia Britannica* on guerrilla warfare. However, in October Liddell Hart was approached by Cape to write a book that would supplement the picture presented in *Revolt in the Desert* and correct the misleading account in Graves' book. Over six years he conducted at least 14 discussions with Lawrence about his career, with many more contributions in the form of replies to written queries. *T.E. Lawrence in Arabia and After* was published by Cape in February 1934. It was serialised in the *Sunday Chronicle* in January.

On December 3rd 1933 the two old soldiers met to talk at Clouds Hill. Lawrence looked forward to the time he would spend there after his retirement. This time their discussion centred on garbled reports in the American press of T.E.'s 'human target' work with Armoured Target Boats. One English newspaper copied this coverage and Liddell Hart intimated it might politic to refute its bogus claims. An article appeared two weeks later in the December 15th issue of the *Daily Telegraph*[58] by 'Capt. Liddell Hart, *The Daily Telegraph* Military Correspondent'.[59]   In fact much of Liddell Hart's article was prepared from a 'detailed questionnaire' he sent to Lawrence. The article is one of the few surviving descriptions of armoured boat work.

> Certain lurid stories have recently appeared in America that Aircraftman Shaw (Col. Lawrence of Arabia) has been playing the part of a human target for aircraft with live bombs. These stories have been dismissed over here as being too fantastic for belief.
>
> Thus it is time that that the facts should be recorded – of a very important R.A.F. development which has markedly improved the efficiency of air bombing at sea. In it Aircraftman Shaw has played a part, but only a part.[60]

Most of the article came from Lawrence's notes and the questionnaire itself. It described how 8- or 11-lb cast iron practice bombs, with smoke-compound filling, were dropped by dive-bombers from 15,000 to 1,000 feet. There was no concussive effect upon the crew. Once, when a bomb fell on the armour plate, it went unnoticed, there being little shock or noise. But the noise of a water impact was terrific.

If an unprotected part of the hull was hit, the bomb went straight through and out of the bilges; the only danger being the crew's feet getting wet as they plugged the hole. This work, although not desperately dangerous, could be tortuously tiring: two-hour shifts for up to 12 hours a day were the rule. The men were confined to a cramped, constricted cabin abutting the engines.

These trials were a resounding success. The boats were faster than the old marine targets like H.M.S. *Centurion*, and one high altitude bomb in five generally hit home. (Liddell Hart pointed out that the success rate at Jutland was one shell in 50). Lawrence only crewed during an early trial and was exposed to little danger. One oblique reference confirms that he helped to some extent early in Beauforte-Greenwood's researches.

> The idea of using small and inexpensive mobile targets apparently originated in the training directorate of the Air Ministry. The suggestion of using an armoured boat with a crew, instead of a towed or wireless controlled target, came from the branch which deals with the production of speed-boats for the service of marine craft.[61]

Jack Barker, a W/T technician, recalled travelling up from Calshot to Bridlington with Lawrence for the summer bombing exercises in 1933. They were in an armourless safety boat that resembled the armoured boats. Lawrence was on board but got off at Dover to visit the Air Ministry, making his own way up north. Barker remembered alternating shifts on the trials at Bridlington with another crew. The attacking aircraft were Fairey Gordons of 14 Squadron. Although T.E. appeared fairly regularly, Barker never saw him outside work hours. In September 1933 the bombing exercises were terminated.[62]

For most of 1934 Lawrence spent his time at Hythe with occasional trips to the Meadows factory at Wolverhampton. He was still receiving outraged letters containing cuttings of the *Sunday Chronicle* articles from friends, but maintained a dignified silence. The armoured boats were by then receiving their engines but it was not until the middle of May that the 'Power' engine was satisfactorily tested, its performance far surpassing that of its predecessors.

Seven of the twin engined RAF 200s at Hythe had been finished by 28th January, and Meadows passed 15 engines, three for each of five target boats, which were now proving to be faster than the tenders. One engine was being passed a day. T.E. spent the first three weeks of February at Meadows, overseeing the work on these boats. He then travelled to Plymouth, London, Southampton, the Brough works at Nottingham, and back to Hythe by the end of February.

Three-man crew of a target boat during a bombing trial, probably in Bridlington Bay. Gas masks, crash helmets and ear defenders were disagreeable encumbrances. Despite his involvement creating a sensation in the press, Lawrence was only bombed once. (Via The Fleece Press)

Armoured Target Boat A191 on trial, probably near Bridlington, December 15th 1933. A191 was serviced by Flight Lieutenant Manning at Bridlington on the day of Lawrence's funeral. (*Daily Telegraph*)

On the last day of February 1934 Henry Williamson was due to sail for the United States on the liner *Berengaria* from Southampton docks. Lawrence took a launch across from Hythe in order to see him off. They met on the boat's gangway, Lawrence awaiting him patiently by a bulkhead, commenting quietly, 'Is it you? You've changed. You're not so tall.' Williamson thought his brick red face and head looked uncannily like Wagner's. They had only met once before, in 1928, when T.E. motorcycled up from Plymouth to Williamson's home in north Devon in an old wartime black rubber minesweeping suit. He stayed for a few hours and returned after they had taken lunch and discussed motorbikes and the merits of *All Quiet on the Western Front.*[63]

On 3rd May he wrote to George Brough telling him he had missed him at the Nottingham factory when he had called in to inspect the progress of his new motorbike, George VIII. 'It looks most promising – and most expensive. I shall be broke but happy. Please take your time over it.'[64] George VII had done 20,000 miles but was still 'running splendidly'. He had broken the speedometer drive which had the surprising effect of raising his top speed by 6 mph.

Phillip Bailey of Wimborne, who was 11 at the time, recalled seeing Lawrence outside the Brough works in Haydn Road:

> I was in a shop within sight of the Brough works. The shopkeeper pointed out that George Brough was in conversation outside the works with 'that there Lawrence of Arabia', who was seated on a Brough bike. After a few moments, the two men shook hands; Lawrence started the bike and took off like a rocket down Haydn Road. The shopkeeper watched Lawrence and the bike disappearing down the road, shook his head and remarked, all too prophetically, 'Daft bugger, he'll kill himself on one of them bloody things.'[65]

At the end of March Lawrence was sent to Northwich, Cheshire for the acceptance trials of a small cargo vessel, the RAF Auxiliary and Recovery Steamship *Aquarius*. In early April he had just returned from a blustery trip to Devonport when a man rang the doorbell of his digs in Birmingham Street claiming to be from the French Consul, but upon examination his card identified him as a *News Chronicle* reporter. He was sent packing. The following week Lawrence again appeared in the papers after demonstrating Scott-Paine's boats on Southampton Water.

The Navy had allowed him to go on the maiden voyage of the *Aquarius*, from Cheshire to Liverpool and then on to Plymouth via the Irish Sea. The ship was a 'tiny, ugly little thing', but of excellent quality, he observed: 'It is the only instance I have yet seen of two quarts having been successfully inserted into a pint pot.'[66] When the ship arrived at Plymouth, from where she was due to sail to Singapore, there were no orders for her. Any delay would mean she could be caught in the Far East's monsoon, but Lawrence saw a solution. He rushed to Mount Batten to ask Fullerton for help. The chief Pilot for Plymouth came on board and within a few

View of Lawrence's digs at 13 Birmingham Street, Southampton with the plaque that was later erected outside it. It was demolished after World War Two to make way for a bus station. He told Churchill it was extremely cold in winter.

minutes the diminutive ship was steered into her berth. She was a 270-ton vessel but by some skilful trick this was reduced to 112 tons to allow for the payment of dock dues. She received a new tarpaulin, topped up with oil and water and the dockyard staff checked the steering, which was jammed. *Aquarius* proved to be faster than expected. By 8th May she had reached Gibraltar and within six weeks was almost at Singapore.

After she sailed Lawrence spent the 8th to the 15th of April helping to demonstrate high speed boats on the Solent for the British Power Boat Company The press assailed him as always, trying to get into the Power yard, but he refused to talk to them. In early May he arrived back at Hythe, receiving a letter on the same day from Douglas Carruthers, an Arabian explorer he had sent some maps to in 1922, which he used for his book *The Desert Route to India*.[67] But Lawrence had expelled Arabia from his thinking and no longer wished to discuss the subject.

There remained five new target boats for him to run in, taking 20 hours each. He was particularly impressed by the new Sea Lion engine being employed by Scott Paine, which was a marinised version of the Napier Lion aero engine. On 24th May he wrote to Clare Sydney Smith in Singapore that he was back at the Power Yard building boats: 'Scott Paine's new designs are very promising. His Sea Lion, in

197

particular, looks like becoming a reliable engine, and if so we shall use it for the larger and faster boats which the Air Staff . . . are determined to have.'[68]

He was still working on five armoured boats at Hythe. One of them was due to be sent to Singapore for trials. He was aware that the seas around there contained some peculiar acids known to attack the copper sheathing normally used on these boats below the water line. He proposed a type of stainless brass named Tungum, also used on the RAF 200's rudder, which might effectively resist the erosion.

The Marine Craft Section had been contemplating building a further 12 boats and Beauforte-Greenwood was approached on 2nd July by the Associated Equipment Company of Southall (AEC), who manufactured a high speed heavy oil engine, asking if they would be considered for the supply of the necessary units.[69] Norrington replied in the affirmative.

Admiral Boyle and the Meeting at Devonport

In March 1934 the Royal Navy's C in C Mediterranean recommended the introduction of fast motor boats for his fleet, but the Materiels Department of the Navy disliked Scott-Paine's novel construction techniques, the Admiralty Naval staff was unable to identify any operational requirements for them and the Naval Constructor's Department thought them flimsy, too expensive and difficult to maintain. Lawrence was disturbed by this reluctance of the Admiralty to try out the boats. It is difficult to pin down exactly what he did to get things moving in Scott-Paine's favour, but he did go to see Admiral Boyle, Commander of the Home Fleet, at Hythe. This is significant because it was within months of him being invited down to Devonport with Scott-Paine to talk to Admiral Fullerton and his staff about Scott-Paine's ideas.

'Ginger' Boyle, 12th Earl of Cork, Baron Boyle of Marston was 67 years old. He joined the Navy at the age of 13 in 1886. He was a small man with a shock of red hair and very fit, but short tempered, an ever present monocle his trademark. Boyle was a formidable disciplinarian but well liked by the officers and men who served under him. Churchill admired him and later described him as 'an officer of the highest attainments and distinction.'[70] He was made a Knight of the Bath in 1931 and an Admiral in 1932. In March 1933 he took up command of the Home Fleet.

Lawrence's decision to see him must have been a painful one. During the War Boyle had been senior officer in the Red Sea Patrol, and in June 1916 led the opening bombardment of the Arab Revolt against the Turkish-held fort of Jeddah. During the subsequent months he and Lawrence worked closely together. The problem was that Boyle disliked Lawrence. In 1916 he had been offended by his off-hand, apparently rude manner. He was

> . . . a little astonished when a small, untidily dressed and unmilitary figure strode up to me on board the ship I was temporarily commanding and said, hands in pockets and so without a salute: 'I am going over to Port Sudan.'[71]

Lawrence's account of this first meeting concurs:

He [Boyle] had done much in the beginning of the revolt, and was to do much more for the future: but I failed to make a good return impression. I was travel stained and had no baggage with me. Worst of all I wore a native head-cloth, put on as a compliment to the Arabs. Boyle disapproved.[72]

Consequently he cannot have felt all that well-disposed towards the Admiral in 1934. However he arranged to meet him at Hythe, to get things moving for Scott-Paine.

In April Admiral Boyle had 'wangled one [boat] for six months out of Air Ministry, for himself.'[73] This was because Boyle became tired of seeing Lawrence streaking past his Admiral's barge in an RAF speedboat! (Lawrence was actually having trouble with this boat. From 1st August to 31st October the Scott-Paine works tested and repaired the engine of his Biscayne Baby. Renewals and adjustments to the engine were necessary, new copper panels fitted to the plywood doors and running trials held. They billed him £11.2s for this in November.) [74] In a letter to Clare Smith T.E. expressed some doubts about the wisdom of the larger boats:

Scott-Paine's new designs are very promising. His Sea Lion, in particular, looks like becoming a reliable engine, and if so we shall use it for larger and faster boats which the Air Staff (rather against my judgment) are determined to have.[75]

Admiral Sir Eric Fullerton was another influential friend. In September 1934 he gave in to Lawrence and Scott-Paine's lobbying and also tried out a custom-built Admiral's Barge with three 100 h.p. Meadows engines, based upon one of Scott-Paine's 45-foot designs.

The Admiralty went on being mulish about Scott-Paine's motor-boats, and I lost patience and thought it might be rather a rag to force one down their throats. And also it would buck the Navy up to have a modern boat set against their primitive junks. So I pulled string after string, and all the bells rang, till finally Scott-Paine and I were asked down to Plymouth to explain these new boats.[76]

On October 11th he was invited down to Admiralty House, Devonport with Scott-Paine and his trusted assistant Bill Sheaff, to demonstrate the Admiral's barge and talk about their ideas. Although the meetings could have been awkward Fullerton and his wife were extremely kind and put them up for two nights at Admiralty House, Mount Wise.

The following day Scott-Paine, with Lawrence in attendance, presented his ideas about fast military boat development. Up until that time they had only worked on the smaller 37½-ft RAF 200 and armoured target boat designs, but Scott-Paine's ambitions were for faster, bigger boats in the 60- to 70-foot category. He described his plans for a 60-foot armed Motor Torpedo Boat

(M.T.B.) emphasizing standardization: if the Navy could confine itself to a 16 to 60-foot boat range, using six standard boat sizes, two sizes of plank, and one engine, it would be able to use a limited amount of standard electrical-mechanical equipment and the engines could be replaced in two hours. His vision was for an MTB able to operate away from its parent station, unlike the Coastal Motor Boats of the First World War, and he offered to turn the yard at Hythe over to the Navy for experimental purposes. Halfway through the meeting another of Lawrence's friends from Arabia, Viscount Eyres-Monsell,[77] pulled into Plymouth in his yacht.[78] Although things had been going well, the presence of Monsell swung the decision in Scott-Paine's favour.

Seven months later, in April 1935, just over a month after Lawrence left the service, the RAF put out a tender for a 60- to 70-foot High Speed Seagoing launch. An outline specification was prepared. The Air Ministry required their own resident inspector and a 10-hour bench test should be performed of the proposed engine supervised by the Air Ministry inspecting officer. By October 1935 a number of firms had tendered for this including Vospers, Thorneycroft and the British

Left to right: Lawrence, Scott-Paine, Viscount Monsell and Admiral Fullerton on 11th October, 1934 leaving the Admiralty Building, Mount Wise, Devonport. The occasion was Scott-Paine's presentation to the Board of the Admiralty of his ideas for fast motor boats and a 60-foot torpedo boat. This was one of the fruits of Lawrence's representations to Admirals 'Ginger' Boyle and Fullerton earlier that year. (Southampton City Council)

Power Boat Co. Scott-Paine's tender was submitted on 24th July for a 64-foot launch with three 500 h.p. 'Power Napier Sea-Lion' engines. On 4th October, Air Marshal H.C.T. Dowding,[79] representing the Air Member for Research and Development, recommended, after careful perusal of all the tenders 'from the technical point of view', that Scott-Paine's scheme be accepted. Construction of the 'hard-chine' design should commence without delay, it being urgently required for service trials.[80] These designs eventually developed into the Type Two 63-foot 'Whaleback' High Speed Launch used by the Air Sea Rescue service in the Second World War. Scott-Paine's designs were also built under licence by the Electric Boat Company (Elco) in the US during the War.[81] One of these was the 78-foot PT boat, of which Lieutenant John F. Kennedy's PT109 was one. By July 1935 over 30 different types of fast motor boats had been delivered to the Royal Navy.

An Impersonation

Early in May 1934 Basil Liddell Hart heard of a man passing himself off as 'Aircraftman Shaw, formerly Colonel Lawrence' who intended to conduct a business transaction with a friend. After asking a few questions and inspecting a letter his friend had shown him, Liddell Hart's suspicions were aroused. He wrote to Lawrence, who replied to him on 17th May from 13 Birmingham Street:

> Now about this other bloke . . . If you see the blighter do rub into him that I have never signed myself as Lawrence since 19 twenty something. He is years out of date. In fact he doesn't sound the right sort of man at all. Do you feel that I ought to do something? It is rather hard to catch him by post. However there is Eliot; the Hon. E. Eliot. He is a very balanced solicitor.[82]

Eliot looked after Lawrence's legal interests in *Revolt in the Desert*. Although he couldn't afford extra legal expenses, Lawrence felt Eliot may see this new 'Lawrence' as being an infringement of his trust property, the *Revolt* trust owning the property in that name. If this was so Eliot 'could ask the bloke to stop his games, and charge his trouble to the fund.'[83] Lawrence wrote to Eliot from Southampton:

> . . . the second happening was an alarm by Liddell Hart, offering me proofs that I was being personated in London. I took it coldly and declined his proofs, for never a week passes without my receiving a letter from some poor woman or other, distraught with the fancy that the airman she walked out with in 1920 or 1930 something was me. Clearly personation is a common event – but as a sop to L-H, who is sincere and serious, I suggested he should try to interest you in his talk. Please take it very calmly. If I don't call myself T.E. Lawrence, I see no reason why others should.[84]

Eliot informed Lawrence that a man named Rogers was masquerading as him. Rogers had persuaded the proprietor of a firm in the Strand that he was Lawrence and that he had very considerable knowledge of Arabian affairs and mechanics.

Eliot's fear was that unless the negotiations were stopped Rogers could do great harm to Lawrence's reputation and to the proprietor's business dealings. As Rogers had not as yet apparently committed any offence the police were unable to act.

George Henry Rogers's impersonation of Lawrence had gone back at least as far as July 1931. He had previously served in the Army as a driver, finished his service and then gone on the road travelling. Some time after that he was employed as a motor engineer. He then went into selling. After several jobs he decided on a commission with an agency. It occurred to him that Lawrence's name would be useful in the commercial world. He then met Orton, a salesman, and through him, H.W. Jenny. Jenny was the principal of 'The British and Continental Advertising Service'. He was completely taken in by Orton and Rogers, even to the extent of allowing Rogers to use his firm's headed notepaper. He gave Rogers models, drawings and confidential information on a mechanical invention called a 'horoscope' designed by Paul Schatz.

Rogers had also been in contact with a Mr. F.C. Owlett of Vauxhall Bridge Road, London. On 29th July 1931, using headed paper of the firm 'Ultra-Vision', advertising and illumination specialists, of 97 Leather Lane, London, he wrote confidently:

> Dear Owlett,
> Phoned Dr. Norman and made definite appointment for Friday evening 8 o'clock. That's that. Waited at Lyons [Coffee House] until 5 p.m. Anyhow thought I would write you – excuse letter heading – asking you to meet me Thursday morning (30th) at Lyons in Queen Vic. St. Will wait until 11.15 am. Will be there myself about 10.30 a.m. Rice believes I am not in town on Thursday at all.
> Yours Sincerely,
> T.E. Lawrence[85]

Nearly three years later, on 30th April 1934, Rogers again wrote to Owlett. He again used the headed letter paper of Jenny's firm:

> My dear Owlett,
> I should be pleased to see you tomorrow, Thursday, at the above address, any time between 11 a.m. and 1 p.m. or 2 p.m. and 4 p.m.
> If you will be so kind as to give me a call there, I have several things I would like to discuss with you.
> Yours faithfully,
> T.E. Lawrence[86]

Rogers tried to gull others including, Dr. H.G. Norman of Peckham Road, London. Dr Norman later told Edward Eliot that although he was at first rather doubtful, he was taken in by Rogers' impersonation. He came to the conclusion at a later date that Rogers was mentally disordered, and that he had actually persuaded himself that he was the person he pretended to be.

Eliot's plan to expose Rogers was to get Lawrence to call on the firm when Rogers was known to be there. Eliot and the police would accompany him. Lawrence replied to him on 8ᵗʰ June:

> Dear Eliot
> I suppose there is no help for it but coming up to Lon[don] isn't so easy. We are in the midst of a batch of target boats, and busy from morning till night. However: any day this coming week, except Saturday, can be made free. Send me a wire to this address or write well beforehand . . . I can see that it ought to be stopped.[87]

He ended the letter with an admonition: 'Don't take it too seriously. If only the poor wretch could take my war name and all that it connotes!' He wrote to Eliot from Birmingham Street informing him he would reach his offices at noon exactly on the 13ᵗʰ and would be in uniform for 'greater verisimilitude . . . Let's hope we get some drama!' The confrontation with Rogers duly took place at Dr. Norman's offices at 442/443 the Strand. The exchange that occurred was not, in the event, terribly dramatic:

> 'How long have you been using my name?'
> 'About 12 months.'
> 'How many people know you as Colonel Lawrence?'
> 'I was introduced by a man named Owlett but neither of them believed me.'
> 'Who is Owlett?'
> 'He is a literary man.'
> 'Where did you come across Dr. Norman?'
> 'That was over 12 months ago at Camberwell House. Dr Norman introduced me to him.'
> 'Has he treated you medically?'
> 'No.'
> [Eliot]: 'I want a list of the names and addresses of all the people you have held to be Colonel Lawrence.'

Rogers then reeled off a list. He told the police, Eliot and Lawrence that he had never attempted to do anything dishonest, always holding Lawrence's name in esteem, and tried to live up to it. He had been tempted several times to write to Lawrence asking for permission to use his name but did not. He made a signed confession. On 14ᵗʰ June Lawrence wrote to Liddell Hart:

> I was in London for a few hours yesterday: with Eliot and two Bow Street experts we interviewed [name omitted], my imposture and persuaded him that he was not me. To my relief, he agreed at once. Had he stuck to his statements I should have begun to question myself.

I owe you many thanks for putting me back on his track. He was a little worm of a man. The game had been going on for some time, and had extended from the zoo to Ward Lock, the publishers. Comically enough, he has been under observation as a case by the specialists of a mental institution, still under my former name. We arranged for him to write to his various victims and explain that there had been a personation. I am not flattered at the thought that he got away with it successfully. An obviously feeble creature with the wrinkling face of a chimpanzee.[88]

After the confrontation Rogers wrote letters of apology to all those he had wronged. Despite questioning the man's mental stability, Dr. Norman was not unimpressed by the diminutive hoaxer. He wrote to Eliot: 'I hope the young man will take the lesson to heart. I think he has got quite sufficient intelligence and initiative to do things on his own.'[89] Jenny, in contrast, was shocked by the exposure. He wrote to Eliot on 23rd June, 1934:

> I have heard from my Swiss friends who, not unnaturally, were dumbfounded by the news. Their chief concern is that steps must be taken to safeguard the invention against possibility of abuse, having regard to the fact that Rogers obtained access to models, drawings and confidential information under the pretence of being Colonel Lawrence.[90]

Eliot had written to Lawrence that he felt sorry for Jenny,

> But at the same time he must be so simple as to be almost dangerous and I need hardly say that it will be necessary for you to be extremely guarded in any letter which you write to Jenny should you refer in any way to the invention.[91]

Eliot told Jenny that, as far as he and Lawrence were concerned, the object had been accomplished and that it was up to Jenny to deal with any adverse result the impersonation may have caused, to protect himself and his Swiss friend.[92] Lawrence followed Eliot's advice:

> First I have to thank you for so admirably handling that business in London. I feel that I took advantage of your kindness most unwarrantably. That you should be the King Pin of the city solicitors makes it all the worse. However we could hardly leave the little man alone.
>   I am returning to Mr. Jenny his horoscope with thanks . . . and being entirely non-committal about his invention. The poor child.[93]

Dr Norman took the opportunity to ask Lawrence if he would sign a copy of *Revolt in the Desert*. Lawrence was averse to signing his books, but promised to send him a signed note. He didn't, and four months later Norman, still wanting a souvenir of the meeting, contacted Eliot reminding him of the promise.

The G.H. Rogers episode is only one of many attempts to capitalize on Lawrence's name and reputation. These took the form not only of impersonations, but of many bogus eyewitness and personal accounts and even complete published biographies that were clearly sheer fantasy to those who actually knew Lawrence. That he was able to confront Rogers and resolve the matter in a patient and gentlemanly fashion, without humiliating the man, exemplifies T.E.'s humanity. In later years his brother Arnold was to encounter the problem many times; and in 1968 the constant probing and half-truths would oblige him to reveal the dark side of T.E.'s life that had remained concealed for over 30 years.

Corporal Bradbury

One of Lawrence's closest working friendships during his last days at Hythe when he was under the auspices of the M.A.E.E. was with Corporal Bradbury. They shared the same lodgings at Myrtle Cottage and often worked together on the 37½ seaplane tender, armoured boats and Scott-Paine's dinghies. Bradbury, with Arthur Russell and Pat Knowles, was one of the pall bearers at Lawrence's funeral, representing his service in the RAF. After leaving the RAF as a sergeant, he went to work for Scott-Paine, supervising the works at Poole.

Bradbury and Lawrence worked well together with E.6. According to Bradbury, Lawrence never referred to any part of a boat in the correct terms: the stern was always the 'thick end', the bow the 'thin end', port was left and starboard right. [94] There had been a suggestion by the Air Ministry that it would need two civilian Technical Officers to replace Lawrence. To allow Bradbury to take up his position Lawrence hoped that any civilians would be too expensive. There was still a great deal of work to be done on the armoured boats and he anticipated his replacement would have at least two years of extremely varied work to complete:

> The fitting side of it (metal-work and engines) is the leading job, and any bright fitters will soon mug up the allied-trade accessories, such as hulls and layouts and equipment generally. [95]

Lawrence's prospective work was not solely confined to Air Ministry contracts: Scott-Paine had jobs from all over the world. In the pipeline were a Junkers Diesel (500 hp) engine; Monel and Tungum propellers; pinnaces for Navy cruisers, an armed 45-foot boat for Chinese customs, [96] and tugs for the War Office.

Lawrence's letters to Bradbury are full of precise technical terms: any engine he did not know he would strip down to the last nut and bolt until satisfied. There had been problems with a lack of appropriate equipment. On a boat trial to Plymouth there was some trouble with the engine and Lawrence did not have the right tool so he pulled out a spark plug, took it to bits and used the casing to bend a screwdriver to the required shape. This feat has been acclaimed by some as a sign of improvisatory genius, but, as anyone who has worked in a machine shop will tell you, it is not unusual for mechanics to make tools up for a job when there is no suitable one available.

The Marine Craft Unit, Bridlington

Long before Lawrence served at Bridlington its bay was used as a bombing range by the RAF, hosted by an unremarkable Yorkshire fishing port facing the biting westerlies of the North Sea, a place that would have been long forgotten by history but for Lawrence. Bridlington was a remote northern town as far removed from the deserts of Arabia as one could possibly imagine. Lawrence of Arabia's presence there ensured it a unique place in Air Force history.

He probably arrived some time between Monday 1st October and Thursday 15th November 1934. His Coxswain's Log Book of 1934 records his work as starting in October. The appointment was semi-formal and lasted until the final day of his twelve years of service in February 1935. It was at his own instigation that he took the work on: initially he was the only Airman at Bridlington and his position, authorised by the Air Ministry and still under the control of E.6., was that of a technical liaison man between Scott-Paine, Beaufort-Greenwood and the maintenance and development section at the M.A.E.E.

The Marine Craft Unit at Bridlington was, before December 1935, only open in the summer. It relocated in the winter months to Felixstowe and usually re-opened in the spring, serving RAF Catfoss, an armament practice camp to the south-west which itself was responsible to the Air Armament School at Eastchurch. Bridlington was a lobster fishing port; consequently the tiny harbour was full of floating lobster pots that made navigation for the RAF occasionally irksome. The crews were billeted in Mrs Hilda Blanchard's Ozone Hotel a hundred yards or so north of the harbour, now the premises of the Royal Yorkshire Yacht Club. The original commander of the unit was a Squadron Leader Snow but, at the end of December 1934, he was replaced by 24-year-old Pilot Officer F.J. Manning, who commanded the unit from January to March 1935.

The airmen at Bridlington were so involved with their work that they had little time to get to know one other; the unit in early 1935 consequently had little cohesion. On 15th November Lawrence wrote from his two-roomed billet on an upper floor of the Ozone Hotel to his old friend Sir Philip Sassoon:

> Dear Sir Philip,
>
> I'm glad you got back well and hope the trip proved worth it. This isn't a letter because I don't want anything. It is notice that E.6 have changed my job, there being ten R.A.F. boats in Bridlington for overhaul by contractor and someone needed to represent the Air Ministry on the details, as they arose. It means a lot of work and continual attention; probably I shall be here till that lamentable day next February when the R.C.A.F.[sic] leaves me behind on its March to glory.
>
> If ever you feel that you want a nice place for the winter – give Bridlington a miss. Without the work it would be impossible.[97]

Sassoon's secretary, Russell, replied to say Sassoon was ill with influenza, but wondered if Lawrence would come to lunch on Tuesday, 27th November at his London home in Park Lane. T.E.'s comments on Bridlington raised the question of whether he would prefer to spend the winter elsewhere. Lawrence replied to Sassoon the following day:

> He says you are in bed with influenza. I hope it isn't bad. One expects that sort of thing after two sudden changes of weather. When Air Routes to the Far East are in general use, there will be an enormous mortality amongst winter passengers.[98]

Because of the boat work, the 27th was too early. Three weeks at least were needed. Despite his comments about Bridlington it was his own decision to take the job on:

> My 'complaint' is against the foulness of the North Sea in winter and the excessively northward positioning of the British Isles. I should like to swap them for the Azores.
> Please assure Sir Philip that I'm perfectly happy here, and shall be till February. After that we'll see.[99]

He also wrote to Lady Nancy Astor at the end of November. He discussed the work of C. Day Lewis, the sudden death of Mrs Knowles, and his plans for December. He also mentioned a certain lady:

> Mrs. — wrote to me ever so often at first. I have sent two notes back. Am I a beast? But she wants something which I want to keep, and she ought to understand it. There are Untouchables, thank Heaven, still, despite the Gandhis of this world.[100]

There were no written records of how Lawrence was to carry out his RAF tasks. Everything was done informally and arranged verbally. He was ordered to wear plain clothes at all times and his duties were to assist in the development and testing of the new type of marine craft that were about to come into service. The King's Regulations stated that no one was allowed to drive coxswain boats unless they had at least a Second Class Coxswain's certificate, or a superior qualification, but Lawrence's Air Ministry authorization overrode this.[101]

T.E. refused to take any educational exams to avoid being promoted. His only promotion was AC2 to AC1, in 1927[102] and he remained an Aircraft Hand, the lowest form of unskilled work in a technical service, until he retired. But Pilot Officer Manning reported 'everyone from the Air Ministry to Catfoss', including all the coxswains and fitters 'looked upon him as some very superior being,'[103] because of his technical knowledge and his ability to short circuit official channels to get things done.

By the third week in January 1935 about 30 new airmen had arrived in Bridlington to replace the civilian workers. They came in dribs and drabs of three or four a day for some time. This was a permanent posting as it had been agreed that the M.C.U. would become full time. There were five Armoured Target Boats and five RAF 200 seaplane tenders in a garage on the harbour front. All the maintenance and manouevring of the RAF boats was done by the Moorings and Marine Craft Service contractor Ian Deheer, who owned the Britannia Boatyard in Bridlington. The boats arrived at Bridlington railway station and were transported on trailers through the streets to the harbour front. Deheer oversaw this with Lawrence's help.[104]

Since the crew of each boat consisted of coxswain, deck-hand and wireless operator, 30 men were needed for ten boats. There were also 10 hangar tradesmen. A large amount of specialist equipment was required: on the A.T.B.s during bombing practice crews had to wear protective helmets, gas masks, and ear defenders as the situation was very hot and noisy. At the end of the south quay in the harbour was a small hut where the duty airman would log in all unusual occurrences and the weather. When Lawrence was duty sentinel he would fill in half a page on the wind, the weather, the sky, the moon, the distance that could be seen, and what the harbour activity was. It was signed 'T.E. Shaw AC1'. This log book later disappeared.[105]

The standard RAF Motor Boat Coxswain's Log Book in 1934 was 'Form 218'. These were progress reports for the boats and had to be signed every four weeks by the Camp Commandant of the nearby No. 1 Armament Training Camp, RAF Catfoss and the Officer Commanding Marine Craft Depot, Bridlington. That for A191 still exists for the period 27th May 1934 until the end of December 1935. Many of the entries by Lawrence recorded simple maintenance tasks.

> Boat taken to Alexander Garage for reconditioning according to Air Ministry contract. Armoured roofs removed. Engine roof sent to Hadfields for insertion of hinged hatch. Engines removed and sent to Hythe.[106]

A191 was one of five armoured boats Snow told Manning about as he handed him over command of the unit in the Buffet at Paddington Station. At that time they were still under repair by the contractor in various garages around Bridlington but most of the engines were overhauled at Hythe. For A191 all three engines were removed for servicing and sent back to Scott-Paine rather than to the Meadows factory. The removal of a Power-Meadows engine from a boat normally took an experienced fitter about 45 minutes. Lawrence thought it was not a difficult engine to fit 'granted training in its habits'. He considered a ten-day course at Meadows would be enough and wrote a description of the process in his handbook of the RAF 200. All electrical connections, oil pipes and reservoir had to be removed first. The exhaust pipe was then removed, the fitting of which varied from boat to boat. The left-hand engine was a closer fit than the right and had to be winched out first with slings under the gearbox shaft and fly-wheel casing. The armoured bulkhead was positioned and removed using a winch, the whole semi-circular structure being lowered in one piece.

Mr S. Hughes of Bournemouth was one of those working with T.E. on armoured boats at Bridlington in 1935. He recalled that Manning had complained 'He got posted to me and life hasn't been all that easy for me since!'[107] When Lawrence found anything wrong with the engines he had a habit of writing direct to the Air Ministry and *then* discussing it with Manning. Hughes recalled how the airmen in his unit at Bridlington used to find pound notes in their blankets. He remembered an inspection held for those who had not been on parade for some time. Lawrence was very untidy, with dirty boots, when he turned out. He was ticked off for this and the following day appeared immaculately dressed with 'acres' of decorations.

Ian Deheer and Lawrence would work closely together during the manoeuvring of the boats through the Bridlington streets to the harbour. Although Manning felt Deheer could have done this easily himself, Lawrence was 'one of those busy little men who had to be there all the time'. Both Deheer and Lawrence would supervise the launching, whereupon the senior fitter, Sgt. Camden, was then 'busy with the other fitters getting the engines tautened down and it was in this particular field [Lawrence] felt that his prime responsibilities rested, and would daily take one to sea in order to do the test running.'[108] He was still getting his equipment from the British Power Boat Company, and on 21st January paid them £3.15s for a Smiths 12 volt 85 amp battery, noting 'Splendid' on the invoice.[109]

Pilot's-eye view of an Armoured Target Boat, possibly A191, in Bridlington Bay, late 1934 or early 1935. Electrician Jack Barker recalled that Fairey Gordons were used at Bridlington for bombing exercises when he was there. (RAF Museum)

He was 'dodging about like a flea with a bad conscience,' he said, watching the boats under repair. 'My time runs out a month hence, and I shall be very sorry. The work passes my time and the last twelve years would have been long without it. Yes I shall be really very sorry.'[110] The recipient of this letter, Tom Beaumont, sold it to the *Daily Express*, its news value being that it was the first indication of the date of Lawrence's retirement. Shortly before it was published, on 17th February Lawrence wrote to C.P. Robertson, the Air Ministry's Press Secretary calling him his 'Publicity Deflector'. He pointed out that that for 'Ceepee' it would be 'like another half day a week . . . or a rise in pay', when he left the service.

> My movements. 'Out' on March 11th I believe; and with discharge leave and things, I ought to have gone after duty today. Unfortunately I am not quite finished up here: the first of the ten boats I have been overhauling completes on Monday, for launching: and the last launches on February 26th.
> I want to see the job through, more or less: not the final tidying, but the essence of it.[111]

By February 15th, 11 days before he was due to leave the service, the Meadows Power engines were well established on the Hythe production line and had their own tool set. That day he wrote to Bradbury, who was still down there, from the Ozone Hotel, Bridlington, his mind again on the job: 'Also if possible a new or part-worn Power adjustable spanner, as asked for by Sergeant Cambden, also a set

Target Boat A191 at top speed (30 m.p.h.) probably late 1934. E.H. Symonds suggests this was taken at Felixstowe with Lawrence piloting. A191 was the last boat Lawrence worked on in 1935. The photo illustrates graphically how impossible it was to set the three Meadows engines in reverse. They were fixed at 17 degrees to the horizontal: any reverse screw on full throttle would have dragged the boat under. Neither of the wireless aerials normally present is visible here. (RAF Museum)

of Power gauges, as supplied in tool kits. I think that is all unless you can see some of those worm-driven water hose clips lying about.[112]

On 25th February he wrote another letter to Tom Beaumont. He had told him on the 31st he couldn't employ him as a valet. Now he was aware Beaumont had sold him out: Beaumont had been offered £20 for one of the letters. T.E. suppressed his anger:

> I've been away, and the letter wasted, and, tomorrow I leave here (and the R.A.F. finally). Your contribution sent the press men scurrying about Bridlington: but vainly. . . . If it's true you got a good offer for my letters by all means take it! They are your property but the copyright . . . remains mine always. Sell them cheerfully but for the Lord's sake don't let the pressmen read or repeat them, it's pretty beastly to have them snooping around the place.[113]

It was too late. He had only an irritating reception at Clouds Hill to look forward to. Beaumont's behaviour on this occasion was not out character. Years later he told a friend of J.M. Wilson's that he would say anything about T.E. 'as long as he was paid enough'.

Lawrence photographed by Ian Deheer on 19th February, 1935, the day of his leaving the RAF, leaning his bicycle against the harbour wall at Bridlington. There is a view different to the one generally published where his left hand is on his left knee. It proves that Deheer took at least two photographs of the occasion, and probably more. (The Fleece Press)

The Equipment Officer and Civil Adjutant at Catfoss, Flight Lieutenant Reginald G. Sims, with his wife, became one of Lawrence's most devoted admirers. Sims had corresponded with him earlier whilst stationed in Iraq. Manning, who knew Sims, said of the hero worship: 'I've never come across two people who were so overwhelmingly devoted to Shaw. At times it was overpowering, particularly the devotion of Mrs. Sims.'[114]

In February 1935, Sims asked Manning over to Hornsea for supper as Eric Kennington the artist was visiting him from London. He was collecting Shaw and could pick up Manning at the same time. Sims' car duly appeared: Manning sat in the front and Lawrence in the back, as was proper. It would be 'unthinkable' Manning thought 'for the positions to be reversed!'[115] The relationships changed the moment they got in the car: Sims became 'almost overwhelmingly subservient to Shaw . . . the Service relationships had been abandoned.' This extraordinary devotion is in evidence in an interview Sims gave in 1955:

> We fortunate ones who knew him . . . well know how his presence at a Unit, promptly caused events to move at a speed, and with a zest previously foreign to any occurrence. He shed a spirit of brotherhood and joyous exhilaration just by being there. That God-given gift of being able to lubricate with humour even the dullest task, and the chance that one's work may be praised by Mr. Shaw as most airmen called him, effected results that no actual organisation could accomplish.[116]

Manning was slightly less smitten. The fact that T.E. had been a Colonel 'did not come into the equation at all'. The other airmen dismissed the Arabian affair as a Beau Geste type of escapade, it receiving 'no special points'. It was the Shaw they knew that concerned them. If he could 'do his stuff', was 'gritty' and 'co-operative', that was all that mattered. The answer, Manning said, was that 'he did pull his weight and he was companionable, even if at times he wasn't startlingly hilarious.'[117]

On 23rd February 1935, a Saturday, Lawrence entered the final entries in his Coxswain's Log Book for A191. These notes are confined to one boat and so do not cover all the work he did during that period. They are written in a far more precise and confident hand than those made at Uxbridge:

> Sealing rubber fluid along gunwales under armoured roof-edging, for watertightness.
> Fire extinguishers and pipes tested. W/T equipment installed by Kidbrooke party.
> Engines and armour replaced.
> Boat taken to harbour for running trials on 23-2-35.[118]

Three days later, on Tuesday 26th February 1935, he prepared for his final departure.[119] First he was interviewed in the C.O.'s office, the 'interview before discharge'. He had been in the RAF for ten years, and for five months at Bridlington. Now was the first and only time Manning, with Lawrence's service records on the table, ever saw him in uniform. He was required to ask him several questions about whether he might need help resettling in 'Civvy Street'. They discussed personal plans and Lawrence said he was going to cycle to Bourne. After he had changed Manning, Deheer and a few others saw him off:

> He was in his familiar rig – scarf, sports jacket, flannel trousers, sitting on his bicycle, and leaning against the harbour wall . . . He gave a half smile, and a half wave of the hand and he was on his way. We never saw him again.[120]

There were no fanfares for him and no cheering crowds, but it was as T.E. would have wanted. His brother recalled that he 'had aged noticeably' by 1935, being fatter in the belly with a double chin and tinges of grey. He had achieved more in his later years than he could have possibly dreamt, and certainly found more fulfilment than he ever did at Bovington. It was a life he chose for himself. Although the value of his contribution to the development of fast boats has received little recognition, it helped save hundreds, perhaps thousands of lives during the Second World War. This occurred largely due to Lawrence's high level contacts in the services and his extremely efficient background work: he took the opportunities as they came and made the most of them. At the same time he had written one of the most important books about Arabia since Doughty, with the help of friends such as the Garnetts, E.M. Forster and the Shaws.

Nancy Astor wrote to him on 7th May inviting him to visit her country home at Cliveden for a social gathering, but there were more serious undertones to the invitation: the government was due to reorganize. She told him 'I believe . . . you will be asked to reorganize the Defence forces.'[121] Lawrence was not interested – at that moment. His RAF work, his confrontations with the press, and trips back and forth to London had left him physically and emotionally exhausted. He replied emphatically:

> No wild mares would not at present take me away from Clouds Hill. It is an earthly paradise and I am staying here till I feel qualified for it. Also there's something broken in the works as I told you: my will I think.[122]

The log records that the boat 191 was launched at 1830 hrs on 21st May 1935, then towed to mooring. Manning would have been unaware that three hours earlier, at Moreton in Dorset, Lawrence's body was lowered in a simple timber coffin into a freshly dug grave near St. Nicholas Church. When he left the service he had but ten weeks of his life left to live.

It was Manning who, as the Officer Commanding the Bridlington Marine Craft Detachment, was responsible for signing the final entry in the Log Book of A191. He signed it off on 27th May 1935. The final passage contained a series of simple tasks T.E. would have approved of: 'Deck painted yellow . . . Bilges cleaned & painted . . . Bilge pump repaired.'

Notes

1 Wireless Telegraphy, i.e. wireless controlled.

2 Note from T.E. Shaw to B. Liddell Hart, December 1933. *B-LH*.

3 *Notes on the Introduction of RAF high-speed craft*, W.E.G. Beauforte-Greenwood, 1935. Various sources for this report give it a number of different titles including *Lawrence of Arabia and the RAF Marine Craft Connection*. It appears to be originally from an Air Ministry file now in the National Archives. This is the most reliable transcript later published as *Notes on the Introduction of RAF high-speed craft* in Vol. 1 No. 1 of the Journal of the T.E. Lawrence Society, spring 1991.

4 Ibid.

5 *Lawrence of Arabia and the RAF Marine Craft Connection*, Beaufort-Greenwood, 1935.

6 *Speed Target Boats for RAF Bombers*, B. Liddell Hart, *Daily Telegraph*, 15/12/1933.

7 R.A.F. Motor Boat 191, Coxswain's Log Book.

8 Ibid.

9 Ibid.

10 'Speed-Boat Targets for RAF Bombers', B. Liddell Hart, *Daily Telegraph*, 15/12/1933.

11 T.E. Lawrence to Rev. D. Siddons, Myrtle Cottage, Hythe. 26/ 04/1932. I.W.M.

12 There was an awareness amongst certain parties in Britain that the Nazis were building up for war, but there was still a wave of public support for disarmament. There was in the view of Churchill and others a need to continue with a subtle rearmament policy in Britain, as represented by projects such as the Armoured Target Boat trials, whilst concealing them from public view. Any advertisement of the involvement of a well-known figure like Lawrence would have created great difficulties.

13 T.E. Lawrence to Flt. Lt. H.E.E. Weblin, Hythe. 6/9/1932. Bodleian.

14 Ibid. This might relate to Lawrence's ideas on the air-cushion principle. See Appendix III on Edward Spurr for references to planing surf-boards, p335.

15 Unserviceable.

16 Sydney Smith left Mount Batten the previous October.

17 Weblin had previously written to T.E. informing him that in an engine's running trials, which Lawrence fitted with another airman, a part was found to be missing and that the corporal in charge blamed him.

18 T.E. Lawrence to H.E.E. Weblin, Hythe, Southampton, 6/09/1932. Bodleian.

19 A.B. Tinsley recalled that Lawrence's influence whilst at Calshot resulted in the abolition of an order for all airmen to carry rifles as they journeyed to and from Base. After Lawrence left, a number of insensitive changes occurred that persuaded many airmen to apply for posting.

20 The Chief of the Air Staff was Sir John Salmond, who had replaced Lord Trenchard on 1/1/1930. He served until 1/1/1933 when he was promoted to Marshal of the Royal Air Force, and replaced by his older brother Sir Geoffrey Salmond on 1/4/1933. 'Geoff' died on 27/4/1933 and Sir John was temporarily reappointed.

21 A piece of T.E. paper play. He had already written a very detailed description of the Power-Hyland Control System in Chapter Eight of his handbook of the RAF 200.

22 Mentioned in a letter of 11/01/1932.

23 Through resignation, including one of his early chief designers.

24 The International Disarmament Conference then taking place at Geneva.

25 T.E. Shaw to H.E.E. Weblin, Mount Batten, 15/11/1932. Bodleian.

26 B:RG.

27 Wilson.

28 T.E. Shaw to Robert Graves, 4/2/1935. RG-B

29 T.E. Lawrence to Robert Graves, 21/04/1931. RG-B

30 T.E. Lawrence to Robert Graves. Plymouth 24/1/1933. RG-B

31 B:RG.

32 T.E. Lawrence to Robert Graves. Plymouth 24/1/1933. RG-B.

33 T.E. Lawrence to B. Liddell Hart, Southampton, 17/05/1934.

34 Ibid.

35 T.E. Lawrence to Robert Graves. Plymouth 24/1/1933. RG-B

36 B:RG

37 T.E. Lawrence to Robert Graves. Plymouth, 28/2/1933. RG-B.

38 Robert Graves to T.E. Lawrence, Mallorca, 11 or 12/1933. AW-L.

39 Manning.

40 *Daily Echo*, Southampton, 1963.

41 T.E. Lawrence to Sir Hugh Trenchard 20/3/1933. Trenchard Papers.

42 Ibid.

43 *From Biplane to Spitfire,* Anne Baker. Leo Cooper, 2003.

44 Extract from Lawrence's personal file, Bodleian Reserve Collection.

45 Source: AIR 1/2698.

46 On 27th April Wing Commander Ryan, representing the Officer i/c Records, informed Coastal Area H.Q. that a signal from Mount Batten concerning A.C.1 Shaw, addressed to the Marine Aircraft Experimental Establishment advised that the 'above named airman is reporting to Felixstowe by road p.m. on 28.4.33.' National Archives: AIR 1/2698.

47 A.M.S.R. directive, D. of E. to Air Ministry, 2/5/1933. Bodleian Library: Special Collections and Western Manuscripts. MSS Eng. d. 3343-5. Whilst on detachment duties he was entitled to a special subsistence rate (typically 30/- a week).

48 Originally the Marine and Armament Experimental Establishment.

49 National Archives: AIR 1/2698.

50 Symonds.

51 Ibid.

52 Jinman commanded the section from 1931 to 1937 when he was promoted to Squadron Leader. He was eventually posted to Whitehall and awarded the O.B.E.

53 National Archives AIR 1/2698

54 *Churchill, Vol. V* , Martin Gilbert.

55 Tunbridge.

56 Memo from T.E. Shaw to Meadows Engineering Co., Wolverhampton. Hythe, 5/10/1933. Private ownership.

57 T.E. Lawrence to W.S. Churchill, 13, Birmingham St., Southampton, 12/12/1933. DG. 13 Birmingham Street was knocked down in May, 1951 to make way for an extension to the bus station.

58 'Speed Boat Target for R.A.F. Bombers', *Daily Telegraph*, Friday, December 15th, 1933.

A variety of nautically related events were happening in the *Telegraph* that week. That very Thursday the same pages announced that future circus master Bertrand Mills had taken out an insurance policy with Lloyds of London. He had offered a large some of money to anyone who could capture the Loch Ness monster and hoped to safeguard against a successful reply. The day before, a proposal to construct an aeroplane landing ground above central London's River Thames, halfway between Blackfriar's Bridge and Southwark Bridge, was reported.

59 A year later, in December 1934, Liddell Hart was appointed Military Correspondent and General Defence Adviser to *The Times*.

60 *Daily Telegraph*, Friday 15/12/1933.

61 Ibid.

62 Interview with Jack M. Barker by Graham and Christine White, November/December 1996.

63 From *The Genius of Friendship*. H. Williamson. The Henry Williamson Society, 1988.

64 T.E. Lawrence to George Brough, Birmingham St., Southampton, 3/5/1934. MB.

65 Mr. P. Bailey, Wimborne Minster. Letter to the author, 2005.

66 T.E. Shaw to Clare Sydney Smith, Clouds Hill, 24/05/1934. *Golden Reign.*

67 T.E. Shaw to Douglas Carruthers, 2/5/1934. DG.

68 T.E. Lawrence to Clare Sydney Smith, Clouds Hill, Dorset, 24/05/1934. *Golden Reign.*

69 AEC to Squadron Leader Beauforte-Greenwood, Air Ministry 02/07/1934. National Archives AIR 2/1484.

79 Quote from *The History of the Second World War. Volume One*: *The Gathering Storm*, Winston Churchill.

71 *My Naval Life*, Earl of Cork and Orrery, Hutchinson, London, 1942.

72 *Seven Pillars*, Book 1, Chapter 16.

73 T.E. Lawrence to Paymaster-Captain Archibald Cooper, Birmingham St., Southampton, 08/04/1934. DG.

74 British Power Boat Co. invoice to Aircraftsman Shaw, Hythe, 9/11/1934. Bodleian Library Special Collections Western Manuscripts, MS Eng. c. 6742.

75 T.E. Lawrence to Clare Sydney Smith, Clouds Hill, Dorset, 24/05/1934. *Golden Reign.*

76 T.E. Lawrence to Clare Sydney Smith, Bridlington, 15/11/1934. *Golden Reign.*

77 Eyres-Monsell was then the First Lord of the Admiralty.

78 Lawrence, in his November letter to Clare Sydney Smith, suggested Eyres-Monsell's appearance was a coincidence, but this may have been another example of T.E. hokum.

79 Later Air Chief Marshal Lord Dowding, chief of Fighter Command in the Battle of Britain.

80 National Archives AIR 2/1484. The first 64-foot hard chine High Speed Launch, RAF 100, was handed over to RAF Manston in 1936. Source: *Symonds*.

81 Rance.

82 T.E. Lawrence to B. Liddell Hart, Birmingham St., Southampton, 17/05/1934. DG.

83 This refers to the Lawrence's Anonymous Education Fund Trust that Eliot was administering.

84 T.E. Lawrence to E. Eliot, Birmingham St., Southampton, 24th May, 1934. MB.

85 G.H. Rogers to F.C. Owlett, London, 29/7/1931. Bodleian Library Special Collections Western Manuscripts, MS Eng. c. 6738.

86 G.H. Rogers to F.C. Owlett, London, 30/04/1934. Bodleian Library Special Collections Western Manuscripts, MS Eng. c. 6738.

87 T.E. Lawrence to E. Eliot, Southampton, 06/06/1834. Bodleian Library Special Collections Western Manuscripts, MS Eng. c. 6738.

88 T.E. Lawrence to B.H. Liddell Hart, Southampton, 14/06/1934. DG.

89 Dr. H.G. Norman to E. Eliot, London, 20/06/1934. Bodleian Library Special Collections Western Manuscripts, MS Eng. c. 6738.

90 H.W. Jenny to E. Eliot. 23/06/1934. Bodleian Library Special Collections Western Manuscripts, MS Eng. c. 6738.

91 E. Eliot to T.E. Shaw, London, 19/06/1934. Bodleian Library Special Collections Western Manuscripts, MS Eng. c. 6738.

92 E. Eliot to H.W. Jenny, London, 25/06/1934. Bodleian Library Special Collections Western Manuscripts, MS Eng. c. 6738.

93 T.E. Lawrence to E. Eliot, Southampton, 26/06/1934. Bodleian Library Special Collections Western Manuscripts, MS Eng. c. 6738.

94 Friends.

95 T.E. Lawrence to W. Bradbury, Hythe, 8/6/1934. DG.

96 This was the first of Scott-Paine's large 45 foot hard chine boats, an armoured customs launch for the Chinese Maritime Customs to combat smuggling in Chinese waters. It was delivered as the *Kuan Wei* in March 1935. Source: *Rance*.

97 T.E. Shaw to Sir Philip Sassoon, Bridlington, 15/11/1934. National Archives AIR 1/2703

98 T.E. Shaw to Sir Philip Sassoon, Bridlington, 20/11/1934. National Archives AIR 1/2703. Refers to Sassoon's championing of Far Eastern air routes.

99 Ibid.

100 T.E. Lawrence to Lady Nancy Astor, Bridlington, 26/11/ 1934. MB. Malcolm Brown in a footnote to his Letters of T.E. Lawrence identifies this lady as the wife of an RAF officer. In the introduction to a recent reprint of *The Golden Reign* however, he is more specific. She is Clare Sydney Smith. By then Clare's daughter, 'Squeak', had passed away: any danger of upsetting the family had passed. Gerald Wasley made a study of Lawrence's life at Mount Batten and concluded that Clare was deeply in love with him. This was to such an extent that the Smiths' marriage was almost on the rocks. Lawrence refused to have anything to do with her for a period after she left Batten. Only after she persisted in writing from Manston and Singapore did the correspondence continue.

101 Manning. This qualification stemmed from the RNAS men who had followed their boats into the RAF.

102 RAF Museum. Other sources contradict this. In April 1931 Lawrence described himself to Dick Knowles as 'clerk A.C.II in workshops'.

103 Manning.

104 *Cats and Landladies Husbands.*

105 Manning.

106 *R.A.F. Motor Boat 191, Coxswain's Log Book.* RAF Museum.

107 Mr. S. Hughes recollections. *Bournemouth Echo,* 13th May, 1964.

108 Manning.

109 British Power Boat Co. invoice to T.E. Shaw. Hythe. 21/1/1935. Bodleian Library Special Collections Western Manuscripts, MS Eng. c. 6742.

110 T.E. Lawrence to T.W. Beaumont. Ozone Hotel, Bridlington, 31/01/1935. I.W.M. Dept. of Documents.

111 T.E. Lawrence to C.P. Robertson. Ozone Hotel, Bridlington. 13/02/1935. I.W.M. Dept. of Documents. This letter is one of five letters to C.P. Robertson that Phillips, the London auction house, offered for auction in November 2001. Of these, two, the first and the last, were sold to the Imperial War Museum for £8,800.

112 T.E. Lawrence to W. Bradbury, Bridlington, 15/2/1935. DG.

113 T.E. Lawrence to T.W. Beaumont, Bridlington, 25/02/1935. I.W.M. Dept. of Documents.

114 Manning. Gerald Wasley concluded that Mrs. Sims' infatuation with Lawrence was to such an extent that by March 1935 the Sims' marriage was on very rocky ground. Source: conversation with author, November 2006.

115 Ibid.

116 *T.E. Lawrence – His Last R.A.F. Years*, Air Commodore R.G. Sims, Hornsea, Yorks., 1955. Air Historical Branch 3 (RAF) Ministry of Defence,

117 Manning.

118 *R.A.F. Motor Boat A191. Coxswains Log Book*. RAF Museum.

119 The M.A.E.E. had the problem of filling out his discharge papers. He told C.P. Robertson: 'I shall not tell Felixstowe what day I go until I'm gone.' T.E. Lawrence to C.P. Robertson, Bridlington, 13/2/1935. Imperial War Museum. Department of Documents.

120 Manning.

121 Lady Nancy Astor to T.E. Shaw, 07/05/1935. MB.

122 T.E. Lawrence to Lady Nancy Astor, Clouds Hill, 8/05/1935. DG.

PART THREE

Tragedy at Clouds Hill

CHAPTER TWELVE

Out of the Service

After leaving Bridlington Lawrence cycled south, taking a very leisurely route passing through Hull, Market Rasen and Lincoln before continuing to the RAF College at Cranwell. Here he met Rupert de la Bere, his friend from the 1920s, who showed him around the Cadet College. He had intended to visit the author Frederick Manning at Cambridge but de la Bere told him Manning had died that February. The Australian Manning was the author of *Her Privates We*, the remarkable account of his experiences as an infantryman in the war, which Lawrence deeply admired. They had corresponded for some time.

On Friday 1st March he stayed overnight at his brother Arnold's house in Cambridge, devoting most of the time to playing with his niece: it was the last time they would see each other. The following Sunday he called on John Buchan at his home three miles outside Oxford. They had had a mutual friend in D.G. Hogarth and shared similar views on literature and the Empire. Buchan's wife Susan, Lady Tweedsmuir, recalled the meeting in her biography of her husband: Lawrence seemed to her to be happy, and more charming than ever, fit and hard, but there were deep lines on his forehead and around his mouth and he seemed much older than before. She discussed his household arrangements at Clouds Hill with him: 'His fuel of rhododendron twigs, his pots of jam on the shelf.'[1]

From Oxford he cycled to Clouds Hill, his fitness allowing him to ride 115 miles in two days; normally he covered over 60 miles a day. He arrived at the cottage to an unwelcome reception from hordes of press, many of whom were freelance reporters. Rather than provoke a confrontation he set off immediately for London.

He arrived in London and found lodgings as Mr. T.E. Smith at 3, Belvedere Crescent, south of the Thames.[2] 14 Barton Street was up for sale, as Herbert Baker had suffered a heart attack. During the subsequent week he made urgent enquiries as to which newspaper agencies and individuals he ought to contact to prevent the press intrusions. He did not appear at Clouds Hill until the 15th. Whilst in London he may have contacted Captain Knight of MI5. A house in Dolphin Square SW1 played host to an obscure subsection of B-Branch, the operations department of MI5, that, certain unsubstantiated accounts report, Lawrence had been asked to work with. B-Branch was charged with monitoring foreign immigrants, left and right-wing subversion and, in particular, 5th Column activity.[3] It operated externally to MI5 H.Q. and was run by a counter-intelligence officer and former member of the British Fascists, Captain Maxwell Knight.

On the 18th T.E. was back in London. The day before at Clouds Hill the reporters returned and he punched one in the eye. During this second time in London he tried to resolve the situation with the press. He visited the Newspaper Society offices at Salisbury Square House, EC4 and spoke to the General Secretary, E.W. Davies. Lawrence realised that the solution to the problem lay not in banning the reporters but in banning the stories they published. Despite Davies' sympathy he decided he would eventually have to go higher. On the 19th he sought the aid of Churchill:

> Dear Winston,
> I wonder if you can help me? My R.A.F. discharge happened about three weeks ago and I've since had to run three times from my cottage at Dorset (where I want to live) through pressure from newspaper men. Each time I've taken refuge in London, but life here is expensive, and I cannot go on moving about indefinitely.
> My plan is to try and persuade the press people, the big noises, to leave me alone. If they agree to that the free-lancers find no market for their activities.[4]

The Chairman of the Newspapers Proprietors Association (N.P.A.) was Esmond Harmsworth. Although Lawrence had met him in Paris in 1919 the chances of Harmsworth remembering Lawrence were unlikely. Churchill had once mentioned he knew Harmsworth and Lawrence asked for an introduction. Not being one for inactivity he wrote to Harmsworth direct and complained of the hounding. He had been compelled to ask the police to patrol Clouds Hill and feared being the subject of local gossip. Could the Press Association alleviate the situation? Although some of the reporters were freelances, he said, even those found outlets in the big papers. A denial of further exposure would comfort him greatly.

On the 20th he called in at the studio of Captain Scott's wife, Lady Kennett. Lawrence was an acquaintance of Apsley Cherry-Garrard, who had been on Scott's last expedition. Lady Kennett was a sculptress and was fond of Lawrence, but found his complaints about the press and his depression caused by the second American edition of the *Odyssey* not selling very demanding. The slump had drained the buyers market for expensive books in the US.

On 24th March, a Sunday, he cycled 20 miles south to visit Churchill at his home in Westerham, Kent. He was always a welcome visitor there. Winston was conscious of Lawrence's poverty (or apparent poverty) and still insisted, as he had after the Cairo Conference, that T.E. had merely to wave his hand to receive any diplomatic position he wished. But Lawrence, who had come to despise worldly goods and the trappings of power, refused to be persuaded. The visit had been to thank Winston for his help with the Press Lords, but Churchill had been hoping 'the defence of his country' would be T.E.'s subject.

On the evening of the 26th Lawrence was back home in Dorset. Fortunately, there was no press: evidently they had backed off after he went to see their Directors. He now settled down to prepare for retired life, pottering about like 'any old retired Colonel', writing a letter to George Brough about the performance of his bike:

I've only ridden the ancient of days twice this year. It goes like a shell and seems as good as new. The push bike is reality though. I came down from Yorkshire on it and have travelled much of the south of England on it in the last three weeks.

The loss of the R.A.F. job halves my income, so that my motorcycling would have been much reduced for the future, even without this 30 m.p.h. limit idea. I had half thoughts of a touring side-car for long jaunts, with the push bike for leisure and local trips, but we shall see. The old bike goes so well that I do not greatly long for its successor. If only I had not given up my stainless tank[5] and pannier bags and seen that rolling stand! But for those gadgets my old 'un would still be the best bike in the S. of England. Good luck with your fan![6]

Leaving the R.A.F. meant ending an extended period of interesting work and also losing the comradeship he valued so much. He did return to at least one RAF base after he retired. Anthony Tinsley reported seeing him a few weeks before his death, probably in mid April, at the Army Co-operation base at RAF Old Sarum. Looking out of an office window Tinsley saw Lawrence standing in the middle of the aircraft park talking to Dick Knowles, Pat's brother, who was then in the service. Lawrence stood talking amicably in full motorcycle kit, his gloves dangling from one hand. It was the last time Tinsley saw him.[7] Dick Knowles was later killed at the beginning of the Battle of Britain in May 1940, as a fighter pilot.[8]

Despite buying Clouds Hill in 1929 Lawrence was still living on very limited means. Although the world could have been at his feet, he declined to accept its prizes. He spent the short remainder of his life in obscurity.

Clouds Hill friends

Clouds Hill is the name of the hillside one mile north of Bovington upon which both the Knowles' bungalow and Lawrence's cottage stood. Lawrence paid for the rebuilding of his cottage initially by selling his dagger from Arabia, and later from the proceeds of his *Odyssey* translation. He began renting it in 1923 and finally bought it in 1929, helped in his restoration work by Sergeant Knowles and Arthur Russell. Knowles did the roof, the window frames and sash bars on his own. He also made the larger dormer window, which Russell and Shaw copied. A purlin has been cut to install the window in the upstairs bunk room. This second upstairs room was sheathed in sheet cork and had a port hole as a window, and the 'larder' or food room was lined with aluminium foil. The ceiling height on the stairs is so low that Lawrence fitted two leather pads to prevent his friends suffering concussion. This shouldn't have worried T.E., who was only 5'5½". (Ken Payne, a local friend, remembered seeing him looking up at his cleaning lady, Laura Day, to talk to her.)

When Lawrence returned to Clouds Hill in March 1935 almost all his friends from the 1920s had left Bovington. Arthur Russell was posted to Perham Down, Tidworth in 1924 and retired from the Army in 1930. He went to work for the Red House Group. In 1932 he began working as a coach driver for Bunty's in Coventry

Lawrence on his Brough SS 100 'George VII' at Clouds Hill, photographed by Pat Knowles' son Bill between the beginning of June and the end of August 1934. Bill had just returned from visiting Lulworth Cove, Dorset, with his mother. Lawrence's comment was 'It will be a long time before you catch me with a camera in your hand.' Behind are the rhododendrons described as 'claustrophobic' by Margaret Montague. The bike still has the stainless steel petrol tank and side pannier bags that Lawrence later gave to the Brough works to be used on 'George VIII'. Lawrence's left hand can be seen operating the exhaust lifter lever (required to reduce compression on starting): this was well inboard of the end of the handlebar. (Via The National Trust)

and often offered to put Lawrence up at his house. T.E. in return volunteered to act as ticket collector on his coach.

Alec Dixon left the Tank Corps in 1926 and went to the Far East to join the Straits Settlement Police in Singapore, eventually becoming a Detective Inspector. He wrote a book about this – *Singapore Patrol*. He stayed there for four years, leaving only because under new regulations, advancement to the higher ranks would be for university graduates only. Later he travelled to Kenya, Tanganyika and Borneo, and eventually returned to Singapore as a journalist. In 1933 he went back to England, joining R.E.M.E. as a draughtsman. He was a talented artist and later had paintings exhibited by the Royal Society of Miniature Painters.

By the end of February 1926 E.S. 'Posh' Palmer had left the Tank Corps. Palmer had money and marital problems after the Army and T.E. tried to help him, commanding him in 1934 to visit Clouds Hill as there was no gas oven there (Palmer had intimated suicide). At the end of 1933 Palmer was living with his wife in Cheshunt, Hertfordshire and working as a gardener. From here he wrote a number of letters to Lawrence in 1933 and 1934.[9] He died some time before 1985.

A.E. 'Jock' Chambers was out of touch with Lawrence in the 1930s but after a long search T.E. managed to find him working as a postal sorter in Paddington. From here in 1934 Chambers sent him a series of letters that continued right up until the month T.E. died.[10] On 31st January 1935 Lawrence wrote to Pat Knowles from Bridlington: 'Chambers (Jock) has made a life-like noise again, and asks if he can spend his leave (April 22–May 11) in the cottage. I have said yes, with me or without.'

Lawrence sent Chambers a parcel of books on the day of his accident. He had also bought him a wedding ring. In 1962, when the BBC was filming its first Lawrence documentary, Chambers appeared at Clouds Hill on a bicycle towing a home-made trailer. 'Jock' Chambers died in 1986.

Pat Knowles and Billy Bugg were two of the few remaining in the Bovington area by 1935. Bugg, the handyman from Bovington, whose grandfather had fixed the small window in the west wall of Lawrence's cottage after father and son failed, owned the Garrison Cinema and 'Bugg's Café' in the camps. Bugg refused to discuss his relationship with Lawrence.

Pat Knowles had returned from seven years in Canada in 1930 and was waiting to marry his fiancée, a local girl named Joyce Dorey. He went into the building trade, working his way up from Foreman to Clerk of Works for the Ministry of Defence. From 1930 to 1935 he undertook a number of tasks on the cottage preparing for T.E.'s retirement, working on the water tank and ram pump. By 1934 they were planning a joint venture printing and hard binding special editions of *The Mint*; but it wasn't to be. So only a few of T.E.'s old friends from the 1920s remained near 'the Hill'. However, he still maintained irregular correspondence with many of the others, often inviting them to stay there. Despite his eccentricities he remained a loyal friend and inspiration to many of them.

Notes

1 *John Buchan by His wife and Friends*, Susan Tweedsmuir, Hodder and Stoughton, 1947.

2 This area, now called Belvedere Road, today lies immediately south of the London Eye.

3 Richard M. Bennett.

4 T.E. Lawrence to W.S. Churchill, London, 19/03/1935.

5 The stainless steel tank was removed from 'George VII', GW2275 around the beginning of 1935, and returned to the Brough works for fitting to the new Brough 'George VIII', which was never completed.

6 T.E. Lawrence to George Brough. Clouds Hill. 5/4/1935.

7 Tinsley.

8 His grave now lies directly behind Lawrence's in Moreton cemetery.

9 See Appendix VI, p353.

10 See Appendix VI, p353.

CHAPTER THIRTEEN

Monday, 13th May 1935

The day of the crash was a fine day. As ex-Corporal Frank Gordon put it: 'Sunny. Wasn't wet, 'cos otherwise we wouldn't have been stood in the road talking to him.'[1] That day in the Pacific two destroyers of the American White Fleet collided off Pearl Harbour and six crewmen were killed. Lloyd George was guest of honour at the 99th annual dinner of the Newspaper Society. The previous week had seen the Silver Jubilee celebrations. The Home Fleet was visiting the Thames and had been illuminated on the Sunday evening. The Ministry of Transport reported a substantial increase in the number of road accidents for the week, 132 deaths. The number of people injured was 4,966, the highest casualty figures since the imposition of the 30 mph speed limit in built-up areas earlier in the year.

Lawrence woke up early and, seeing smoke rising from Pat Knowles' cottage, walked across to have breakfast with him. Afterwards they spent some time together sorting the post. Lawrence had to send a parcel of books to 'Jock' Chambers. He also intended to send a telegram to Henry Williamson. at Filleigh in North Devon. Williamson had sent a long letter to Clouds Hill three days earlier: 'I'll call in anyway on Tuesday unless rainy day, probably around 1-2 p.m. noon.'[2]

That morning Lawrence and Pat Knowles had already planned a lunch of bread, cheese and pickled walnuts, with Joyce Dorey as the hostess. For some reason, Lawrence was anxious about Williamson's visit. He 'felt that it would be well to come as soon as possible as he might not have time to spare later.'[3] It was Pat who suggested Williamson come the next day. Lawrence agreed. Williamson much later said he had wanted to talk to Lawrence about Anglo-German relations, and the wording of the telegram has often been misinterpreted as indicating Lawrence was eager to respond.[4]

After they had finished sorting the post Lawrence went back to his cottage to work on the motorbike. The Brough Superior had been laid up for months in the small garage nearby. Three days earlier he had purchased a pair of brooms from the Dorchester ironmongers 'Thurmans', and he went off with them tied to his motorbike, another Brough Superior, the handles on the petrol tank and the broom ends on the saddle, 'like a black cat about to take off over the moon'.

Brough Superior SS100 GW2275, believed to be the one Lawrence crashed on. Owned by John Weekly it was found in 1965 rusting away in a back garden by Leslie Perrin of Portsmouth and purchased for one pound. Today it has been valued somewhat incredibly between one and two million. Much of the damage the bike suffered in the 1935 crash was still visible decades later. The pipes of the twin offside fishtail exhausts are badly dented, and the offside front of the fuel tank was also dented, now replaced by a welded hemisphere. (Author)

At about 11.00 a.m. he kick started the Brough twice, standard procedure from cold. The whole series of preliminaries of starting up the Brough took a few minutes.[5] It was unusual for motorcyclists to ride with a helmet in those days but he sometimes wore a leather flying helmet. On the opposite side of the road

Pat Knowles was sowing some seed in his garden . . . It was a bright cheerful day with a strong wind blowing from Clouds Hill towards the camp. He remembers the wind in particular because it was blowing away the fine tilth of his seed bed. He did not see Lawrence leave because a hedge blocked his view of Clouds Hill.[6]

Knowles heard the Brough move off. The journey to Bovington took only a few minutes. Lawrence loved speed. After negotiating the three small bends and changing down twice to take the two larger dips he crested the last rise to take the final long slope towards Bovington. As loose gravel crunched beneath the John Bull tyres and telegraph poles flew past on his left, soldiers in the summer tented camp on the moor to the east must have heard the distant purr of the Brough's motor. The JAP engine was warming up and the needle on the Jaeger speedometer began to climb as the Brough accelerated downhill. He changed back through two gears, sliding the wooden gear knob forward through two gates before releasing it with his right hand, a more awkward process than a modern foot change.

He continued accelerating down the Tank Road. He had done this journey many times before and knew when to gently decelerate. A few soldiers recognized him. He passed off the sprayed gravel surface and onto the metalled apron of the camp. As he approached the northern entrance he changed back to first, applying both the brakes. Passing the rail head on the left and the Driver and Maintenance School and workshops on his right he went into the camp beside the Royal Army Service Corps yard. He gradually reduced speed and motored towards the shopping area in Bovington village. He passed the Post Office on his right and H. Smith'sthe newsagents and Dodge and Company, the camp butchers on his left.[7] A few hundred yards further downhill he turned left into the Red Garage.

The garage's owner, H.A.R. 'Roy' Reiffer, had taken it over at the beginning of the 1920s and built a number of lock up garages, one of which T.E. rented from 1923 to 1925 during his time in the Tank Corps. Reiffer's two mechanics, the Runyard brothers, were the sole maintainers of Lawrence's Broughs, apart from the manufacturers.

Up the road, outside Dodge and Company, two teenage boys were putting orders into the front basket of a butcher's bicycle. They had agreed to meet at the

View of Bovington main street facing south, mid-1930s. Left to right: Smith's general store, Charlie Way's shoe shop, the butcher's Dodge and Co., Speed's hardware store, the Red Garage, C.W. Payne's barbers. Bovington Post Office was on the right, set back from the road. The old Smith building still exists. (Via Marriott)

shop at 11.00 a.m. The 14-year-olds Frank Fletcher and Albert Hargraves planned to cycle north up the Tank Road to go bird nesting after Hargraves had delivered his orders.[8]

Up at Crown Hill Camping Ground Corporal Ernest Frank Catchpole of the Royal Army Ordnance Corps was tired but still working, having been on duty for a number of hours. With spring manoeuvres there were a large number of soldiers of many different units at the camp. One account has Catchpole clocking out of the guardroom at Bovington Camp at 11.10 am and beginning to walk his dog across the heath in the direction of Knowles's cottage. But local historian Rodney Legg, who has made a meticulous study of the events of that day, is adamant that Catchpole was actually working up at the Camping Ground, probably erecting tents or fixing equipment.[10]

In the Corporals Club, near the Guard room, Corporal Frank Gordon and Quarter Master Sergeant Instructor 'Nobby' Noakes of the Royal Tank Corps were relaxing. Lawrence picked up his parcel of books and walked across the road, back up to the Post Office, and picked up his mail. This was always tied up and sealed because of its possibly secret military nature.[11] He wrote out the telegram to Williamson at 11.25 am and the Postmaster Bill Williams stamped it:[12]

> Williamson Shallowford Filleigh Lunch Tuesday wet fine
> cottage 1 mile North Bovington Camp
> Shaw.

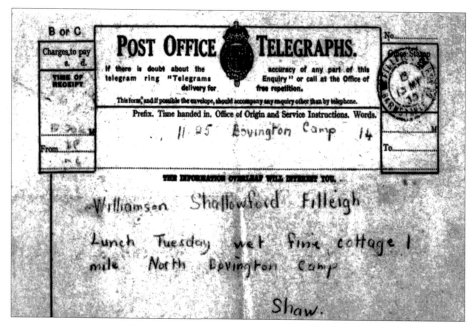

Lawrence's telegram of 13th May 1935, showing clearly the posting time as 11.25 am. The telegram was stamped by the Bovington Postmaster, Bill Williams (Henry Williamson Society. Now in private ownership.)

He also posted Chamber's books, which were addressed uncertainly to 'The Sorter? Paddington D.O. London W.' He went to the butchers and bought pork chops. Standing beside the counter was Albert Hargraves. Hargraves recognized Lawrence and offered to deliver the chops for him to Clouds Hill. Shaw accepted, saying he had some errands to run and had to go to Wareham before returning home.[13] He had to be going as he had (according to Stratton) to report to Catterick Camp in North Yorkshire at 5 pm.[14] Although he had been known to travel long distances at high speeds, over 100 mph sometimes, this is highly unlikely if he was to meet Williamson at Clouds Hill the next day. It may have been one of his habitual vagaries, a kind of white lie to get moving.

William 'Bill' Bugg then saw him come out of the local ironmonger's with a paintbrush which he said was for the window frames of the cottage. He bought a screwdriver from a shop in Bovington's main street, probably just down the hill from Smiths the newsagents.[15] He walked slowly back to the Red Garage. According to the ex-Royal Armoured Corps officer, biographer Michael Yardley:

> Lawrence left the Post Office and walked back to the petrol station where the pump attendant, Walt Pitman, asked if he needed any fuel. Lawrence replied, 'I'm alright, thanks,' climbed back on to his bike, started it up and began the fateful ride back towards the cottage.[16]

This is unlikely. Godfrey Runyard, one of Reiffer's mechanics, could not recollect anyone by the name of 'Walt Pitman'. And Reiffer's own account contradicts it. In 1970 he deposited a manuscript in the archives of the Imperial War Museum entitled *Recollections of Life in the Tank Corps and T.E. Lawrence*. The gist of what he recalled three and a half decades later was that Lawrence asked him to put a couple of gallons of petrol in the Brough. His two mechanics had already gone to lunch, and he was the only person around. Lawrence sat astride the bike as it was being filled up and told him he was going home for dinner. He paid from the saddle, kicked the bike over and roared off.[17]

There is also some confusion as to the sequence of events that followed. In the 1950s BBC Radio interviewed Albert Hargraves for their 'Voices of Dorset' series. In his strong Dorset burr, Hargraves mentioned the Wareham errand. One possibility was a visit to Percy Spillar, who lived in a cottage next door to St. Martin's Church. He had been repairing the church roof since April. Wareham is about six miles from Bovington.[18] There are two ways one can go there from Bovington Camp: south through the camp, past Wool, or north up the Tank Park Road, turning right at Clouds Hill. If he did go it seems likely he went by the shortest route: southwards. There is corroboration: Mike O'Hara, the curator of Wareham Museum, told the author that years ago he was in conversation with the late George Gover of Wareham. Gover was working as a shop assistant at Sansom and Speed, an ironmonger's in South Street, Wareham. He met Lawrence that morning when he came into the shop. He bought two tins of paint. As he knew one of the proprietors Mr Speed quite well, he went through to the back for a chat and a cup of tea. This suggests he spent at least five minutes in the town.

It would have taken Lawrence six to ten minutes to reach Wareham. The whole journey would have taken at least 15 minutes, possibly twenty, meaning he would have got back to Bovington at 11.40 a.m. at the earliest. On 14th May, the medical specialist Captain Charles P. Allen told a *Daily Sketch* reporter that T.E. Shaw and Hargraves were received at the Bovington Camp hospital at about 11.45.[19] This casts doubt on the Wareham story.[20] Hargraves meanwhile had picked up the two chops with the rest of his orders. He took them out to the waiting Fletcher and they loaded up the butchers' bicycle. Some time after this they began cycling out of the camp towards Clouds Hill.

As Lawrence was driving back through Bovington village he passed the camp gates at Rhine Road, where there was a small group of soldiers. Lawrence recognised a couple of them from his days in the Tank Corps. He swung the Brough around and rode back to talk to them. They were chatting generally for a short time when 'Nobby' Noakes and Frank Gordon came out of the Corporals Club. Gordon recalled: 'he last thing he done was, pulled his driving glove back over his watch and said, "Well, folks, I want to be in the Smoke for one o'clock if I can and I must get a move on because I want to change first." With that he kicked

Frank Fletcher at the time of the accident aged 14. (via Marriott)

Burt Hargraves, aged 14, photographed at Bovington Camp on the day of the Inquest, shortly after coming out of the Camp hospital. Edited from a Pathe News film. (ITA via Marriott)

his bike into gear and roared off.'[21] The earliest this could have been was just after 11.45 am with the Wareham trip, otherwise perhaps 11.35.

At the end of the metalled surface area of Bovington Camp in 1935 was a rough, potholed tank road, later named King George V Road, going northwards up a fairly steep incline. This passed the cottage after just over a mile. It was undulating with areas of dead ground and to the east of it, for most of the 1920s, lay a large Tank Park, full of rusting, wrecked British tanks, dumped on the moor after the end of the War. The road was built to enable salvage contractors to access the Park at the beginning of the 1920s. The author heard three different accounts of the surface. Corporal Frank Gordon described it as soft tarmac: anything that dug into the surface would leave a mark. Arthur Russell was certain that the road was a flat gravel one of local conglomerate about 14 feet across. John B. Connolly, another Tank Corps soldier, recalled the road as having been surfaced using the technique of spraying with tar and throwing stones on top.[22] This is a cheap finish, the tar being susceptible to any extremes of temperature. By 1935 it had been through fifteen summers and winters without resurfacing and it would have been fractured and shattered in many places. Arthur Russell confirmed this: 'It was a very narrow road and just that Dorset gravel, rough and pot holey.'[23]

Corporal Frank Gordon, one of the last R.T.C. soldiers to see Lawrence alive on 13th May 1935, photographed (right) with a Rolls-Royce staff car in the 1930s. (Author via Gordon)

The old Tank Road leading north-west to Clouds Hill from Bovington Camp. On the left is the R.A.S.C. yard, behind it the D & M (Driving and Maintenance) School. On the right are the old Detention Barracks and the Sergeants Mess. The steep slope (of the sprayed tarmac road covered with gravel) is easily visible, as are the roadside telegraph poles and the trees of the Frampton Estate on the hillside around Clouds Hill. (Via Marriott)

The Return to Clouds Hill[24]

Lawrence drove the Brough out of the camp and after dropping down past the tank hangars, cleared the metalled surface inside the camp and began accelerating up the sprayed gravel incline of the Tank Road. One account has it that shortly before his accident he slowed the bike down to wave to a lady on the left hand side of the road and asked how she was.[25] By this time the two boys, Fletcher and Hargraves, had crested the top of the incline and were out of sight. They were cycling abreast, the taller boy, Hargraves, on the inside. By the time he was halfway up the Tank Road the wind was blowing from the north-east towards Bovington, carrying the sound of the Brough away from the boys.[26] It was starting to cloud over.

Corporal Ernest Frank Catchpole had been working all morning at the Crown Hill Camping Ground, the summer camp on the east of the road. This was a collection of small bell and ridge tents that served the troops out on manouevres on the moors. All sorts of units could be found there. The popular image of a lonely moor and a solitary rider colliding with two butcher's boys appears to be false. Roland Hammersley, unofficial historian of Bovington Camp, was sure that there were dozens and dozens of troops in the vicinity of the site. Frank Gordon mentioned that there were troops doing manoeuvres on the moors. However they would, he said, have been hidden in copses along the road.

Just to the east of the second dip in the road was a first aid marquee or Casualty Clearing Station erected to serve troops out on manoeuvres. It was not uncommon

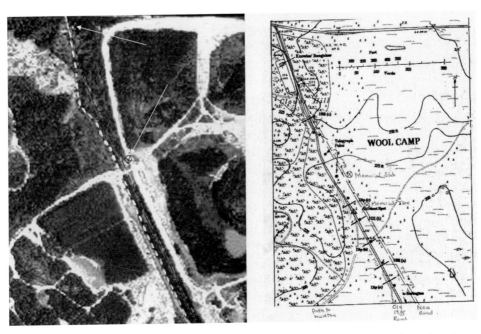

Comparison of a modern aerial photograph of the Clouds Hill road and an old map of the Tank Park road in 1935 with the course of modern King George Vth Road superimposed upon it. The course of the old road can be seen snaking through the undergrowth in the aerial view. (Marriott/author)

Looking north up the modern King George Vth Road in 2005 towards Lawrence's cottage at Clouds Hill from the position of the memorial tree (right). (Author)

for Carden-Lloyd carriers, small two-man tanks, to tip over on the slippery slopes. According to Frank Gordon there were no trees at the scene of the accident, unlike today. The ground has now been churned up by tanks on either side of the road but it was flat then. The big tank jump that exists to the east of the road now was flat ground. The Casualty Clearing Station was located on the far side of the jump from the road, and, because of the open terrain, it had a clear view: 'They got what they call a Casualty Clearing Station that if there was any accidents say, they were brought there before they were transferred to the hospital.'[27]

In the area of Clouds Hill, after cresting the top of the incline there were three dips in the the Tank Park Road and two intervening rises. The third dip was almost unnoticeable, but the first two were deep enough to conceal a car, motorcycle or cyclist and hide from view any traffic to the north. On the left of this was a steep earth bank, overgrown with gorse, heather and small pine trees. On the right lay the Crown Hill Camping Ground. The first dip in the road was 650 yards from Clouds Hill, and the second 510 yards. The third dip was 380 yards distant. The first hill was 580 yards from the cottage and the second 440. The road was 18½ feet or so wide. The road had three bends in it. As one travelled south there was a pronounced bend to the left passing the boundary to the Frampton Estate on the left in which Clouds Hill cottage lay, and W.D. fence on the right. After it swung back to the right, there followed a much shallower curve to the left as the road began descending to Bovington.

As Lawrence approached the top of the hill in 3rd gear he would have been travelling at around 55 mph. Pat Knowles later stated that every time Lawrence returned he would change down to negotiate the dips. This time however, no-one heard him change gear.

There has been a difference of opinion as to the impact point of the crash. None of the witnesses at the inquest state specifically where the collision occurred. Corporal Catchpole said 'level with the [Crown Hill] camp'. Fletcher told the inquest 'opposite Clouds Hill Camp' and Hargraves' signed deposition said the same. Neither Catchpole nor the two boys made any mention of the dips and rises in the road. Crown Hill Camp was just near the present-day tank jump to the east of the road, south-east of the existing memorial tree.

Rodney Legg specified the impact point as 'on the Bovington side of the brow of the incline', that is the long northerly incline out of Bovington Camp. Paul Marriott puts it on the crest of the rise between the second and third dips, as one travels north. The author considers Marriott's location as the most plausible, mainly because Hargraves had to be in one of the dips to be concealed from Lawrence. Marriott also presents photographic evidence of this.[28]

The two boys, by the time Lawrence reached the top of the incline, would have entered the second dip. They were, according to Hargraves' testimony at the inquest, travelling at 'a normal pace', with both hands on the handlebars, and riding in single file. Hargraves later said this had been so 'for about 80 yards . . . for . . . about ten minutes.'[29] Fletcher was in front. If they did hear the motorbike (as they said) despite the wind direction, and so changed into single file, they only did so for a short time. By the time Lawrence had entered the second dip the boys were coming out of it.

When Lawrence crested the rise and changed down to negotiate the second dip, according to Catchpole, a private, a black four seater saloon appeared on the opposite side of the road coming up towards him at about 30 m.p.h. Catchpole

Ernest Frank Catchpole (extreme left) at a Christmas dinner party in Tientsin during his service in China c. 1927. His friend Charles Eyles later said he was teetotal and of a sober disposition. (Via T.E. Lawrence Society)

testified that he 'actually saw the deceased pass the car', then the motorcyclist swerve across the road immediately after passing. Catchpole had not seen Fletcher and Hargraves up to that point. He then 'heard a crash and saw the motorcycle', minus its rider, 'twisting and turning over and over along the road.' The two boys later flatly contradicted this, testifying that 'there was no motor car or any other vehicle in the road at the time'. This was the cause of all the controversy.

Lawrence must have seen Hargraves at the rear, and accelerated to go around him. He had no choice but to go right: three large water butts and an earth bank were on the left. But he was too late. He pulled suddenly on the front brake and it snapped.[30] He urgently applied the rear brake, which had not been maintained for some time and may have locked. The bike went into a skid and the front tyre went straight into the top of Hargraves' rear wheel. Lawrence's tyre hit the top of Hargraves's wheel pushing the mudguard into an 'S' shape and folding the wheel itself to the rear of the hub.[31] The Brough crashed over to the right, rotating around the bending right footrest, skidding along the road, and making a semicircular scar in the surface. Lawrence went over the handlebars, his helmetless head smashing against the gravel surface. He rolled or slid, decelerating from nearly 40 miles per hour towards the right side of the road before coming to a halt, already unconscious as his head collided with a tree. The bike continued spinning down the road.[32]

View of the old Tank Park road on the day after the accident, 14th May 135. The pronounced elevated bank can be seen on the left. This was taken from the approximate site of the collision, facing north towards Clouds Hill. (Via Marriott)

The actual location of the crash site in 2005. This view, facing north, is taken from approximately the same position of the view of the old road in the previous picture. Despite a heavy undergrowth of rough grass, heather, gorse and baby pine trees, the dark shadow of the high elevated bank, 29 metres west of the modern King George Vth Road, is remarkably similar to the roadside bank in the 1935 view. (Author)

Hargraves was thrown onto Fletcher by the impact after his right leg was badly gashed by Lawrence's left footrest. The rear wheel of his bike was wrecked and punched into a figure of eight. As he came off the bike his body slid across the gravel surface which severely lacerated the skin of his back and arms. He immediately lost consciousness.

Fletcher was knocked off his bike but remained conscious. He had not looked behind before the crash, and told the inquest 'I heard a motorcycle coming up from behind . . . after Bert's cycle hit me I looked up and saw the rider of the motorcycle going over the handlebars about five yards ahead. He ended up a few yards further down the road than Hargraves. Only one pedal and a mudguard on his bike were damaged. He then walked back over to Hargraves who was unconscious. He could see Lawrence, his head leaning against a tree, covered in blood.

Realizing what had happened Catchpole ran across the moor to the scene. A man on a bicycle came up to Fletcher and told him to get an ambulance. Two civilians arrived at the scene: Bill O'Connor, a local lorry driver moving Army equipment, and Lyle Chapman, Joyce Knowles' cousin. Catchpole arrived with some soldiers, and the cyclist rode down to Bovington. A girl named Joan Way appeared from Clouds Hill as the soldiers were waiting for an ambulance, and a lorry drew up.

Private John B. Connolly, a tank Corps soldier was having an injured knee dressed in Bovington Camp hospital that morning. Shortly after the crash a man ran in and told the medical orderly or officer that there had been a serious accident up the road involving several persons.[33] This must have been the 'man with a bicycle' Frank Fletcher saw. Connolly was then detailed to drive up to the accident scene in a soft-sided Morris Commercial 4 x 4 ambulance with Captain Geoffrey Anderton.

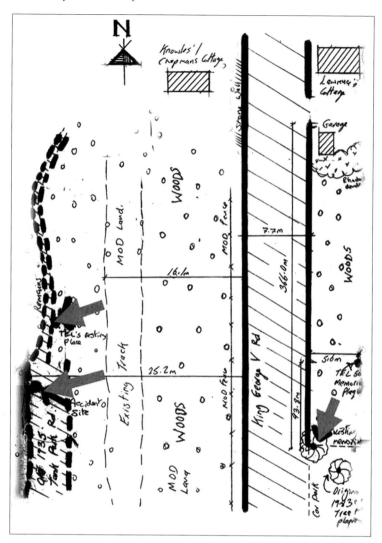

Sketch Map of the location of the old 1935 Tank Park Road and the crash site in 2005. (Author)

Tony Cripps' illustration of how the Brough GW2275 rolled over upon impact, with consequent damage to the bike's fittings on its right side. (Cripps)

Anderton checked Lawrence over and they put him and Hargraves onto stretchers and into the back of the vehicle, Connolly holding the door open.[34] The ambulance was driven down the Tank Road to the Bovington Camp military hospital. Pat Knowles was still in his garden at Clouds Hill when a soldier appeared and asked him to accompany him to Bovington to identify the injured man. He had heard Lawrence rev up moments before the crash but thought that he had stopped to talk to someone.

Anyone examining this account must realise immediately that there are many inconsistencies. Catchpole did not see all the protagonists before the crash. His report was contradicted by the two boys, and Hargraves contradicted himself. If the accident happened at 11.45 am, how did Lawrence have time to visit Wareham, a story confirmed by two separate sources? If Connolly drove an army ambulance to the site, why did a local builder's merchant later claim to be the owner of the lorry Joan Way saw? More inconsistencies like this arose at the subsequent inquest. Then even odder accounts emerged, some obviously untrue, others more persuasive.

Notes

1 Interview with Frank Gordon, former Corporal RTC, May 1985.

2 *The Journal of the T.E. Lawrence Society* vol. 5, no. 2.

3 Quietness.

4 See Conspiracy Theory – 1, p263.

5 The 1962 David Lean film gave a reasonably accurate representation of the events. The initial sequence of the film, the overhead view of T.E. preparing his motorcycle, playing behind the main titles, was filmed in Spain. A Brough was shipped out specifically. Despite being offered the use of GW2275 by its owner, the producers ignored his letters and used a Brough painted with the code UL656, mistakenly that of 'George VI'. A foot change Brough is used, which neither GW2275 nor UL656 were.

6 Knightley and Simpson.

7 The Smiths and Dodge and Company buildings are still recognizable in Bovington today on the left of the brow of the hill before the descent towards the Tank Museum. The Post Office building and Red Garage have long since been demolished.

8 Sid Cooper, whose family lived at North Lodge farm, Clouds Hill said that Hargraves and Fletcher, both of whom attended Bovington School with him, were going to visit North Lodge that morning but never arrived.

9 Knightley and Simpson.

10 Mr Legg, conversation with author, 2005.

11 F.J. Stratton's account.

12 Godfrey Runyard, letter to the author, 2005.

14 Tony Cripps., conversation with author, 2005.

14 F.J. Stratton's account.

15 Photograph in *The Life and Times of Joyce Knowles* by the late Bob Hunt shows Bill Bugg's

daughter Mary in front of a shop/workshop in Bovington where 'T.E. Shaw bought a screwdriver just before the accident'.

16 *T.E. Lawrence – a Biography,* Michael Yardley, Stein and Day, New York, 1987 (originally published in England by Harrap as *Backing into the Limelight.* Yardley was one of the few biographers to examine the sequence of events on 13th May. This report was based on an interview he says he conducted with Pitman in 1981.

17 There are a number of different versions of this story. Helen Beaumont talked to Reiffer at his home in Weymouth in 1967. Reminiscing about T.E he told her that he filled up with petrol at his garage before starting his fatal ride back to Clouds Hill. Godfrey Runyard told the author Reiffer filled up the Brough.

18 Details of this version of events were kindly supplied by Tony Cripps, in 2004.

19 *Daily Sketch,* May 14th, 1935.

20 None of these timings can, of course, be precise. Everything works back to the time Bill Williams stamped Lawrence's telegram – 11.25 am.

21 Interview with F. Gordon, Bovington, May 1985.

22 *The Life and Times of Joyce Knowles.*

23 Interview with author, 1985.

24 The journey David Lean filmed was on a minor road outside Chobham, Surrey. It was extremely uncomfortable for the then unknown Irish actor Peter O'Toole. He was towed along a dirt road behind the camera car, sitting astride the Brough, mounted on a trailer. On one occasion the attachment to the trailer snapped and O'Toole fell off, narrowly escaping serious injury. The main inaccuracy in the crash sequence was that the boys appeared cycling towards Lawrence. This stunt was arranged by Frank Heyden. He surely selected this setup because it was easier to film and more dramatic than what actually happened.

25 Mr Nick Birnie of the T.E. Lawrence Society to the author, 1985.

26 Pat Knowles subsequently gave at least three different accounts of the wind, all seeming to contradict each other.

27 Interview with F. Gordon, Bovington, May 1985.

28 None of their accounts correspond to the newspaper reports of the inquest.

29 To travel 80 yards in ten minutes they would have been cycling at about 0.25 mph.

30 Arthur Russell told the author in 1985 that the front brake, a caliper type, had been broken in the accident.

31 See photograph, p257.

32 The David Lean/Robert Bolt script originally called for Lawrence's goggles to come slithering across the road towards the camera. This proved too difficult to film and Lean replaced it with the idea of the goggles hanging from a twig. This was cut from the 1962 version, but for the director's cut in the 1980s it was reintroduced.

33 This was originally reported in *The Life and Times of Joyce Knowles* by the late E.V.G. 'Bob' Hunt.

34 Captain Geoffrey Anderton, the officer he named as in charge, was a regular soldier of about forty years of age. He was confirmed to have been on the Army List in 1935 by the Bovington Camp archives librarian.

CHAPTER FOURTEEN
The Inquest and After

The inquest into Lawrence's death held on 21st May 1935 has perplexed some historians. The fact that such tight security was devoted to it and yet the inquest proceedings were concluded in only a few hours with disturbingly inadequate conclusions has only served to fuel the speculation that surrounds Lawrence's crash. On 14th May 1935 *The Times* published the following short paragraph:

> MR. T.E. SHAW GRAVELY INJURED.
> MOTORING ACCIDENT IN DORSET.
>
> Mr. T.E. Shaw, who recently left the Air Force after serving his engagement as an aircraftsman, [sic] and who during the war became famous as Colonel T.E. Lawrence, the leader of the Arab irregular forces in the Palestine campaign, was seriously injured yesterday morning through an accident while riding a motorcycle a few miles from Wool, in Dorset. He was removed to the camp hospital at Bovington camp, where it was found that his skull was fractured.

Lawrence lingered in a coma from the 14th to the 19th in the Camp Hospital. Just after 8.30 am on the Sunday, his pulse stopped. He had been unconscious for 140 hours since the crash. On Monday the following report appeared:

> LAWRENCE DEAD
> FATAL END TO CYCLE CRASH
>
> We record with much regret the death which took place yesterday morning of Mr. Shaw, the name adopted some years ago by Colonel Lawrence, the legendary hero of the Arab War.
> Lawrence died shortly after 8 a.m. yesterday in Wool Military Hospital, Bovington Camp. He was 46 years old. Since last Monday he had lain unconscious after a collision between his motorcycle and a boy cyclist near the camp . . .
> Mr. A.W. Lawrence sent the following written message to those in the waiting-room: 'In accordance with his own wishes and those of the family, it is desired that no flowers be sent and that only a few intimate friends will attend the funeral, which will be very simple.'

As part of a statement issued on behalf of the relatives it was declared that because of the severity of the effects of his injury, if he had survived: 'In view of the immense activity and energy of Mr. T.E. Shaw it is felt that this (his death) may be some consolation to those who had entertained anxious hopes of his recovery.' Britain had lost one of her most lauded sons. At the subsequent funeral Churchill wept.

The *Daily Sketch* of Monday 20th listed the attending surgeons and then described the end:

> The crisis of Lawrence's illness was reached late on Saturday night. Sir E. Farquher Buzzard, Physician in Ordinary to the King, and one of the greatest authorities on Neurology and Mr. H.W.B. Cairns, the noted brain specialist, dashed to the hospital.
>
> Mr. Cairns made the journey by car from his home at Arundel – over 100 miles away – in less than three hours. Oxygen was administered. X ray photographs were sent for and Captain C.P. Allen, the specialist, who has had the case in hand from the first, remained almost continually at his patient's bedside.
>
> Shortly before 8.30 am yesterday Captain Allen entered the little hospital waiting room where friends and others were gathered and said simply: 'It's all over now'.[1]

However, Colonel Rupert Noel-Clarke, the Adjutant of the Royal Tank Corps Depot, who was responsible for arranging the military side of Lawrence's funeral, later gave a different description:

> My Commanding Officer, Lt. Colonel P.J. Reeves, O.B.E. and myself waited up in the Officers Mess until the small hours to greet Lord Dawson of Penn,[2] the brain surgeon, who arrived by London taxi cab, his Daimler car having broken down, having been called on for urgent consultation regarding Lawrence's condition. Later Lord Dawson pronounced little hope of recovery.[3]

Surgeons later stated that if he had survived he would have been unable to speak, would have lost his memory and been paralysed. The post mortem examination revealed a severely lacerated brain, a fractured orbital plate,[4] and a nine-inch long fracture extending from the left hand side of the head backwards. This meant the left side of the skull had been cracked open in the crash and the exposed outer face of Lawrence's brain had been dragged across the surface of the road, suffering severe lacerations. He was kept in the mortuary in the camp hospital until the funeral.

The inquest was held on Tuesday, 21st May in the hospital at Bovington Camp. This was a civil inquest held in a military establishment; already a strange affair, and subject to security restrictions that were unusual. Rodney Legg has suggested that the whole proceedings were stage managed throughout and others have described them as badly handled and sloppily conducted.[5]

Mr. Ralph Neville-Jones;[6] the East Dorset Coroner, had greater powers then than he would today, and almost certainly directed the jury towards its final decision.[7] Then there was the evidence of the witnesses: some given by one witness was certainly untrue, but generally believed, evidence from another was on the balalnce of probabilities true, but discounted. Subsequent research has suggested that many people did know the truth, and that they concealed it from the public, and continued to do so for years. Many people were struck by the unnecessarily severe security clampdown. Army personnel were instructed not to talk to the press for fear of breaching the Official Secrets Act. Other personnel, soldiers' wives and police constables were ordered not to say anything. The day following the incident a mounted Military Police guard was stationed at the accident site: no-one was allowed near it.

The security presence that week in the camp was unprecedented. A friend of Nigel Neville-Jones, the Coroner's son, passed through Wool station that week and was surprised by the huge amount of security. Even General Allenby could not understand why such extraordinary precautions were taken. Before the police investigation had started, a Bovington officer issued the false statement that there had been no witnesses.[8]

Examination of newspaper reports from that time and summaries of the incident since then suggest that some form of official cover-up was taking place. All news had to come from the War Office, consequently few journalists bothered to try and penetrate the tangle of contradictions. The hospital was initially instructed not to give out any information. The credentials of any person approaching it were scrutinised. Lawrence was guarded by two plain clothes Special Branch policemen, one sitting by his bed, the other in a cot outside the door. This clamp-down stirred up rumours of official concealment. In order to counter local suspicions of this a *Dorset Daily Echo* reporter was allowed to interview Fletcher, who said that the boys had been looking for birds' nests at Warwick Close, two miles from the camp.

On 15th May the *Daily Mirror* reported Clouds Hill was heavily guarded 'to safeguard vital Air Ministry documents which Mr. Shaw had in his possession'. We cannot assume that these were concerned with military intelligence. Before A.W. and his wife had returned from Majorca, officials from the Air Ministry 'or some other body' had gone through Lawrence's possessions in the cottage.[9] Fifteen letters to John Bruce and one to Mrs Bruce, along with three letters from 'R' (the 'Old Man') to a companion who administered beatings when Bruce was absent were taken, along with a diary in which the beatings were recorded.[10] The letter from Williamson also disappeared. Williamson later claimed it had been taken by the press or suppressed.

A.W. Lawrence commented upon this report to the *Dorset Daily Echo* on May 16th: 'With regard to the stories of Air Ministry officials coming to take secret papers away from the cottage I can only say that a special guard has been sent to the cottage. This has been done to ensure that sightseers should not bother us and to protect my brother's valuable books, which are in the cottage. That is all there is in that story.' In a letter of May 6th 1968, John Bruce wrote to Colin Simpson of the *Sunday Times* alluding to a file at the Air Ministry concerned with Lawrence's activities in the Air Force: 'Dear Colin, thanks for your letter of the 6th. I knew of the Spy File at the Air Ministry, but never thought you would get within a mile of it.' Colin Simpson has since told the author that these were simply documents for an RAF Marine craft. He described Bruce as a liar and a 'shit'. Since much of the work Lawrence did on Armoured Target Boats before retiring were contrary to the spirit of the International Disarmament Conference at Geneva, it would have been in the interests of the Air Ministry to prevent such papers becoming public. On the 16th the *Dorset Daily Echo* reported: 'The day after the accident military and civil police called on the father [of Albert Hargraves] and told him that on no account was the boy to be interviewed by anyone without authority.'

Lawrence's accident is a conspiracy theorist's dream; but the precautions taken were not unusual in view of Lawrence's connections. On the 18th the *Daily Mail* quoted A.W. Lawrence: 'So far as I know he [T.E.] had no connection with any government department, nor was he doing any government work. Whatever Secret Service work he may have done is finished now.' As Lawrence was a civilian there is no legal reason why the case came under army jurisdiction. But as soon as he was admitted to the camp the army took over.

Tuesday 21st May

Before the inquest opened Neville-Jones, accompanied by his officers, visited the little mortuary chapel to see the body. Lawrence lay before the altar in a coffin of elm[11] draped with the Union Jack. As they entered the chapel they would have been surprised to see the robust figure of Sir Ronald Storrs, one of Lawrence's old comrades, standing astride the coffin on a trestle, trying to photograph the corpse with a hand-held camera. A few moments later a small army lorry arrived outside, carrying the Brough, supervised by Arthur Russell. The bike appeared to be only slightly damaged, and beside it was Hargraves' butcher's delivery bicycle, its back wheel buckled and the rear mudguard twisted.

The inquest commenced on Tuesday, 21st May, 1935, two days after Lawrence's death. The *Exeter Express and Echo* that day ran the headlines: 'How Lawrence came by His Death. Swerve to Avoid Pedal Cyclist. Victim's High Speed. Mystery of a Motor Car.' An article was distributed by the Press Association and made the final edition. The proceedings were conducted in a small dining room at the hospital. Only 30 feet long and less than 20 feet wide, a single door led to a small corridor off which the wards full of patients could be seen. Thirty people were crammed into this tiny makeshift courtroom. Neville-Jones was an old soldier, experienced in judicial proceedings, whose son would fill the same position 50 years later. The three witnesses Corporal Catchpole, Fletcher and Hargraves, with Captain C.P. Allen, sat opposite him a few yards away. On the Coroner's right was the seven-man jury, composed mainly of local men,[12] and to his left were the spectators including a few journalists, Professor A.W. Lawrence and his wife, G.D. Ridge (representing Albert Hargraves and the Bovington butchers, Dodge and Co.), Fletcher and Hargraves' parents, at least one policemen, and officers from MI5 and Special Branch.

At 10 am Neville-Jones introduced the case. Arthur Russell thought the proceedings lacked rigour.[13] Amongst the public sat a few RTC soldiers, Pat and Joyce Knowles, A.H.R. Reiffer, F.J. Stratton, the Runyard brothers, Eric Kennington, Corporal Bradbury, Sir Ronald Storrs, Colonel Newcombe and Arthur Russell, all still in a state of shock, and relatively ignorant of events as Catchpole would describe them, although they had a vague idea of what had happened. Russell, in charge of the Brough and Hargraves' bike, had closely examined Hargraves' mangled rear wheel and seen the snapped front caliper on the Brough. Everyone was in a hurry to get the proceedings over: Churchill was expected to arrive by special train for the funeral in two hours and the proceedings had to be completed by then.

As Neville-Jones spoke the solemn chatter died away, and he addressed the jury:

> I very much regret the necessity for calling you together today to inquire into the circumstances that have led up to the death of someone who was known at the time of his death as Thomas Edward Shaw, but who was much better known to the world in general as Colonel Lawrence of Arabia.
>
> The facts are very simple. I do not propose to go through them, but you will gather just what took place from the witnesses. The accident actually occurred on May 13th. Mr Shaw was removed to the military hospital at Bovington, where, despite the skill and devotion of eminent medical men who attended him, and the hospital staff, he died on Sunday last.
>
> The cause of death you will hear from Captain Allen and Mr. Cairns, who performed a post-mortem. I shall call Mr. Arnold Walker[14] Lawrence.

In this opening address, Neville-Jones had prejudiced the court and jury by implying he had already made up his mind as to the verdict.

A.W. 'Arnie' Lawrence took the makeshift stand, introduced himself and gave a brief description of his brother. Two days before he had been at his brother's bedside when he died. The papers described him as 'a tall, sunburnt young man, hatless and in a light raincoat.'[15] He had travelled to the hospital with two friends, arriving at 1.30 pm on 15th May and spent nearly an hour in consultation with the attendant surgeons before leaving in a saloon car with a motorcycle escort. He had arrived earlier that morning with Colonel Stewart Newcombe. A photograph shows him mounting the steps to the building in a light trench coat, tousle haired with a bewildered expression on his face. The balding Newcombe waits patiently behind, staring into the distance, dressed in a dark, crinkled suit. Newcombe had earlier instructed the hospital to release twice daily bulletins on Lawrence's condition.

Catchpole was next to speak, as the most important witness. He had been photographed by the papers earlier that morning. The hordes of press that descended on the camp had already ensured most of the story was public knowledge. He gave his name and rank and took the oath.

> At about 11.20 a.m. on Monday 13th May 1935 I was at Clouds Hill Camping Ground about 100 yards from the road. I heard the noise of a motorcycle coming from the direction of Bovington Camp. I saw the motorcycle which was going between 50 and 60mph. Just before the motorcycle got level with the camp it passed a black car – it was a private car and the motorcyclist passed that safely. I then saw the motorcyclist swerve across the road to avoid two pedal cyclists going in the same direction. I then heard a crash and saw the motorcycle twisting and turning over and over along the road.

In those seconds after the collision the attention of all in the vicinity must have been turned towards the accident. At that moment, travelling at half the speed of Lawrence, the black saloon (if it was there) probably came out of the first dip, crested the final rise, and continued downhill towards Bovington, unnoticed by those distracted by the crash nearby.

Catchpole sat down and Hargraves and Fletcher took the stand. Both boys denied seeing any black car and said they were riding in single file for over 80 yards before Lawrence encountered them. Catchpole, sitting silently in the background, must have been shocked. He must have realized that something was wrong. But he probably discounted the testimony of mere boys and expected the jury to do so. He had already made a written deposition. He knew the police had been told earlier about the car and tried to locate it. He knew it had been mentioned in the *Daily Mail* the previous Saturday. But he also knew neither the police nor his camp superiors would be able to corroborate his sighting.

At this point Catchpole probably suffered a loss of confidence. The boys, positive they had not seen a car, were also certain they had ridden one behind the other. He was called back to the witness stand because of the disagreement. The Coroner assumed he would retract or, at least, alter his statement. Catchpole had obviously been confused. On the contrary, he reaffirmed that he had seen a black saloon, the number of occupants of which he could not see, even adding to his statement this time its speed, about 30 mph. Cross examined by A.W. Lawrence whose identity he knew, he said the car was on the correct side of the road.

Catchpole had had days to change his testimony in the face of the police and his superiors. In the tense atmosphere of the courtroom, filled with police and army officers, and friends and relatives, he reiterated his version. If he was lying he must have had good reason. Perhaps he sought attention, even notoriety. But the more persuasive explanation is that he believed what he said was the truth.

The man who caused all the controversy: Corporal Ernest Frank Catchpole photographed at Bovington on the day of the Inquest, May 22nd 1935. Part of a Pathe News film. (ITA via Marriott).

Catchpole's testimony became notorious after Lawrence's death. He was reported to have had a history of mental instability. Until recently only one former soldier has supplied any information about him. Corporal Ernest Frank Catchpole, Royal Army Ordnance Corps, was based with Section 2, Tidworth on Salisbury Plain in May 1935. He died on 10 July 1940 in Cairo, shooting himself in the head in the Senior N.C.O.'s bunk. He is buried in Plot P, Grave 236 in Cairo War Memorial Cemetery, Egypt.[16] In the 1980s L.M. Foot of Upton, Poole, wrote to Rodney Legg:

> I was also serving with the Royal Army Ordnance Corps at Bovington at that time and was (fairly well) acquainted with Catchpole ... Catchpole ended his own life in Egypt, June-September 1940 (from memory) the reason for which still confounds me ... I took over the Senior N.C.O.s bunk or quarter in which Catchpole met his end and many a time I lay looking at the bullet hole in the ceiling wondering what made him do such a thing.[17]

Some new information has come to light about Catchpole. Charles Eyles served with him in the R.A.O.C. in Tientsin, China in the 1920s. Eyles stressed that Catchpole was 'a reserved, quiet, unassuming chap who kept himself to himself. He was scrupulously honest and truthful and not prone to fantasy ... He was unusual in that he didn't booze or partake of the nightlife as most of us did. Tientsin night life was bars and dance halls. But Catch didn't catch on!'[18] In 1972, at an old comrades' dinner, Eyles learned of Catchpole's suicide. He thought Catchpole was commissioned after Lawrence's death and put in command of an 'exhibition type of Ordnance depot' at Copnor near Portsmouth. This was a wearisome, dead-end job. Rodney Legg thought he was waiting to be transferred to Lulworth Camp before the accident.

The only known photograph of him from 1935 was taken at the inquest in Bovington (page 247). It shows him dressed in a fairly smart trenchcoat and trilby hat, clutching a dark pair of leather gloves, with a light coloured tie and shirt, possibly army issue. He is grim faced with a strong chin.[19] The earlier photos from Eyles' time show a fit, clean shaven man staring straight at the camera. Charles Eyles' description of Catchpole suggests that his testimony might have had more integrity than has generally been conceded.

Catchpole was warned by his superiors not to communicate anything to the press. Most of the cross-examining was done by Inspector Drake of the Dorset Constabulary, A.W. Lawrence and G.D. Ridge.[20] The depositions taken appear to be biased in favour of the authorities.[21] So the contemporary press sources are more accurate. The following dialogue has been extracted from a report in the *Exeter Express and Echo*, 21st May:

Coroner: Did you see any other vehicle?
Catchpole: The motor cycle passed a black car when it was about level with the camp. The car, which was a private one, was going in the opposite direction, and the motor-cycle got past it all right. Then I saw the motorcycle swerve across the road to avoid two pedal cyclists coming from Bovington; it swerved immediately after it had passed the car.
Drake: You cannot describe this car except that it was a black private car?
Catchpole: No.
S.C. Patrick (Foreman of the Jury) to Coroner: We would like to ask the witness whether the two pedal cyclists were riding abreast, and whether there was room for the motor-cyclist to get between the car and the bicycles.
Catchpole: I could not say whether the cyclists were riding abreast.
Coroner: Was there sufficient room for the motor-cyclist to pass between the car and the pedal cyclists?
Catchpole: There would have been if the motor-cyclist had not been going at such a speed.
Ridge: Did you actually see the pedal cyclists before the crash?
Catchpole: No.

The following is a similar reconstruction of the exchanges from a report in the *Daily Telegraph* for Wednesday 22nd May:

Coroner: Did you see anything of the driver?

Catchpole: No, sir.

Coroner: Did the motorcycle appear to be dragging the rider along?

Catchpole: I cannot swear that the driver was then on the motorcycle. I ran to the scene of the accident and found the motor-cyclist lying on the right side of the road. His face was covered with blood which I tried to wipe away with handkerchiefs. I sent to the [Crown Hill] camp for a stretcher. Then an Army Service lorry came along and I stopped the driver and asked him to take the motor-cyclist to hospital.

Coroner: Did you see anything of the pedal cyclists?

Catchpole: One of them was lying some distance down the road.

Coroner: Did you see the accident happen?

Catchpole: No sir.

Drake: You cannot describe this car except that it was a black, private one?

Catchpole: No sir.

Drake: Can you estimate its speed?

Catchpole: It was not going very fast.

Drake: Did you see Mr. Shaw pass this private car?

Catchpole: Yes.

Drake: How far after he passed the private car did the collision take place?

Catchpole: Fifteen to twenty feet.

A.W. Lawrence: Would it have been possible for the motor-cyclist to see the cyclists before passing the car?

Catchpole: It would have been possible if he were on the right [proper] side of the road. The road was straight.

A.W. Lawrence: I would like to ask you whether the car was on its proper side?

Catchpole: It was.

The *Telegraph* stated specifically:

Inspector Drake said in consequence of receiving a statement of a motor-car being in the road at the time, inquiries had been made in the district of a number of people. No other person than Corporal Catchpole could say that they saw a car, and the Lieutenant in charge of the Camp could not say he saw a car.

Fletcher and Hargraves testimony followed, after which Catchpole was recalled.

Coroner: You have heard the evidence of these two boys that they heard no vehicle pass them on the road. Is it possible you were mistaken?

Catchpole: No, sir. I saw the car when I was alone. It was a black four-seater saloon.

Coroner: How far away were you at the time?

Catchpole: About 100 yards. I could not see how many people were in it. It was going about 30 miles an hour.

There were questionable aaspects to Catchpole's testimony. He was 100 yards away from the road, looking from undulating moorland at an undulating road. At the time, the bright sun was near its zenith. In his original statement he implies the incident happened much earlier than it could have done. 'At about 11.20 am I was at Crown Hill Camping Ground.' This was five minutes before Lawrence's telegram was stamped[22] and maybe as much as half an hour before the collision. 'I heard the noise of a motorcycle coming from the direction of Bovington Camp.' This suggests he confused the sequence of events; he does not mention hearing the Brough going *towards* the camp. Catchpole appears to have mistaken the time of the returning Brough for the outward journey. At the Crown Hill Camping Ground he was surrounded by soldiers, both Royal Tank Corps and others, some of these closer to the road than himself. But only Catchpole was called to give testimony. There was a reason for this.

He said it would have been possible for the motorcyclist to see the cyclists before passing the car if he had been on the correct side of the road. So the car did not obscure Lawrence's view. But this contradicts his previous statements that he did not see whether the cyclists were abreast and did not actually see them before the crash. Such imprecision suggests Catchpole was not certain of what had happened, and it almost certainly drained the jury's belief in his story of a black car. He said the collision took place 'fifteen to twenty feet' after the motorbike passed the private car. One concludes from this that Lawrence presumably saw Hargraves immediately he crested the rise after the second dip and as soon as he passed the car (which had a combined collision speed with him of around 80 mph) he swerved immediately to the right. With a distance of fifteen to twenty feet before the collision there should have easily been sufficient room to get around Hargraves. The boys were riding in single file, Lawrence was advancing from left to right across a straight road over 18 feet wide for fifteen to twenty feet, but a collision still occurred. This suggests either the suggested mechanics of the accident were incorrect or the evidence was inaccurate.

Fletcher and Hargraves revisited the subject so many times over the years that the contradictions multiplied. Hargraves died in the 1980s and Fletcher is also dead. The boys said they had been riding abreast since they left Bovington. At some point, they said, they changed to riding in single file. The *Daily Telegraph* of 22nd May quotes Hargraves as saying he had not seen any vehicle and remembered nothing after he heard the motorcycle's engine until he woke up in hospital. He claimed that the boys had changed positions from riding abreast to single file because of the noise of the motorcycle, and had been riding thus for about 80 yards when the crash occurred. In order to confirm that Hargraves was capable of estimating distances, at the suggestion of A.W. Lawrence he was taken outside and judged the gap from a telegraph pole in a field to the courtroom as 80 yards, about right.

None of Hargraves' calculations make sense. As already mentioned, 80 yards in ten minutes is a nonsense. (Fletcher later reported the distance as 100 yards). Even if Lawrence was travelling at a minimum speed of 30 mph, allowing for the rough surface and other delays, he would have travelled the mile from the Frank Gordon group to the accident site in around three minutes. So the cycling in single file for ten minutes does not work. Hargraves did not answer Neville-Jones' question about whether they had heard the motorcycle for as long as ten minutes. It doesn't take a mathematical prodigy to work out that at 30 mph, T.E. would have covered five miles in 10 minutes.

Hargraves said Fletcher overtook him when they changed into single file. He was three feet from the roadside bank. Fletcher said he was 'between one and two yards' from the left side and four to five feet in front of Hargraves.

Again from the *Daily Telegraph,* Fletcher said that no car had passed them and that they had not left the road at any point and thus could not have helped but see one. He had not heard the sound of the motorcycle until just before the crash.

Hargraves at first said that he did not know what happened after he heard the motorcycle. He did not turn round, stayed in position on the left, and could not remember anything. Later he said they changed positions because of the motorcycle noise. Fletcher did not know if Hargraves was behind him at the time of the collision, but he was not beside him. A.W. Lawrence tried to determine if Catchpole's account of the bike swerving to the right across the road was true, but Fletcher did not know. Fletcher said he overtook Hargraves whilst they were in single file, but did not know why. Neville-Jones was unhappy with this and recalled the boy. Fletcher then said he did not hear the motorbike until just before the collision and still did not know why they went into single file.

Richard M. Bennett, who made a special study of Lawrence's crash, felt that 'The idea that the two boys in particular had been interrogated by Military Intelligence and persuaded to change their statements does not gel with the facts.'[23] MI5 did not exist as an independent body in 1935. Only if the event took place on military property would its staff have had the executive powers to investigate an accident or question witnesses. MI5 was a directing agency of Police Special Branch. It would only have been involved if it was a matter of state, not military, security. The Civilian Police would have been called in if any serious criminal activity was suspected.

The two 14-year-olds, well known to play the fool,[24] probably did not know their own minds in 1935. They were uncertain why they went into single file. They were positive that there was no oncoming car and repeated this statement with certainty many times, sticking to the story for the rest of their lives. Ralph Neville-Jones summed up:

> The only conflicting point in the evidence seemed to be that with regard to the car. It did not necessarily mean that the car had anything to do with the accident, but the fact that Corporal Catchpole was certain he had seen it and the boys were certain that they had not, was rather unsatisfactory. Apart from that, I do not think the jury will have any difficulty arriving at their verdict.

After the accident many suspected foul play because of Catchpole's sighting of the car. But the general consensus was that Catchpole had been wrong, and and remained so for many years. In his interview with the author in 1985 Mr Gordon said 'I know nothing about no black car. I know nothing about it, and, as far as I know, none of our people do . . . There was no mention about it at the time.'[25] John B. Connolly, interviewed in the 1980s became slightly exercised over the matter: 'All this talk about black cars annoys me! All cars in those days were black. It would have been odd to see one that wasn't black'[26]

A number of theories arose to explain the anomaly. Catchpole could have seen an insurance man named Montague, who drove through the area often, and who had visited Clouds Hill a number of times. It could have been Montague's car he saw, but on a different occasion. Pat Knowles remembered that 'a small black delivery van went past Clouds Hill at about this time every day, except on Sundays.' Seen from where Corporal Catchpole was standing, the black van could easily have been mistaken for a car. In an article in *First Word in Wessex* in 1968, Colin Graham, of *Dorset County* Magazine, told the story of an airman friend of T.E.'s, possibly 'Jock' Chambers, who went out motorcycling with him a week before the accident. They saw a black car nearby and after the inquest he told a number of people it was being tested by a local garage because the road passing Clouds Hill cottage was particularly suitable. Neither the owners of the car nor the garage ever came forward. The police never traced it. The airman, as with many other witnesses, never testified at the inquest, because, it was reported, the inquest was held in such a hurry.

Mrs Margaret Montague, the wife of the insurance agent Lionel Montague, who spoke out about her husband's possible involvement in Lawrence's death in 1985. She was adamant that her husband had driven the black Hillman. At her home in Wimborne, Dorset, November 1985. (Author)

A Hillman Minx saloon of the type driven by the insurance agent Montague. The five letter registration matches Montague's in terms of age. Montague's car was one of the prime identifiable contenders for the 'black car'. (National Motor Museum)

The funeral service took place in Moreton Church and Lawrence was buried in Moreton cemetery. Arthur Russell was one of the pall-bearers, as were Pat Knowles, Eric Kennington, Colonel Newcombe, Aircraftman Bradbury and Sir Ronald Storrs, each representing a different period in his life. Informal dress had been stipulated and only one man wore a top hat. As the coffin was lowered Gunners Beaumont and Bailey, friends from the Arabian days, shook hands. Beaumont saw a name plate on the coffin, but the newspapers denied it. As the first earth was sprinkled a girl of twelve ran forward and threw in a bunch of violets. Siegfried Sassoon saw a man try to photograph the coffin, and knocked the camera out of his hands. Churchill was there, as was Lady Astor, Lionel Curtis, Augustus John, Basil Liddell Hart and Thomas Hardy. Arthur Russell went off with Pat Knowles after the burial, not feeling comfortable in the presence of the 'big wigs'.

The safety helmet laws passed by the government shortly after the crash were probably influenced by Lawrence's death. Sir Hugh Cairns, the London neurosurgeon who attended Lawrence after the accident, was so affected by the circumstances of his death that he introduced safety helmets for army dispatch riders during World War Two. Many lives were saved as a consequence.

At the end of the inquest even Ralph Neville-Jones had to admit that its findings were 'rather unsatisfactory'. If there had been a black car, who was driving it? Was

Catchpole the only one who saw the accident, and, if not, why didn't others come forward? Some unidentified party had to know the truth.

A Possible Solution

There are so many contradictory statements, wild inaccuracies and false assumptions involved in Lawrence's death. The author would like to point out that all the people he talked to who were alive at the time, Arthur Russell, Godfrey Runyard, and Joe Fletcher (Frank's brother), said it was just an accident.

Joe Fletcher was 12 at the time. He was reluctant to talk at length about it as he had discussed the subject so many times before, but he did say that after the crash Frank came back to their house and told the family what had happened. He did not know the victim was 'Lawrence of Arabia' then. Some time later journalists descended on the house in droves, but not the police or the military. He did not attend the inquest but said the Tank Park Road was not a dirt road but a major, straight road in that area. He said that Lawrence collided with a tree and 'that's what killed him'. He thought there was no 'black car': the reason Catchpole talked of it was because he was mentally unstable. He knew Catchpole had later committed suicide.

Rodney Legg, a well known Dorset historian who has written over 50 books on the West Country, has a suggestion as to why Catchpole was the only mature witness. Legg knew many of the people at the scene of the incident. His findings were that a number of the soldiers as well as Catchpole had seen the black car. Legg said one of the reasons Catchpole was selected as a kind of spokesman was because he insisted that he make an appearance in court. He acted as a representative for a group of soldiers who were witnesses at the accident site. Catchpole emerges as a far stronger character than he is represented in many published accounts. He is generally seen as the lone, mentally unstable Corporal, a weak character whose report cannot be taken seriously. Rodney Legg disagrees. Catchpole was the only man who saw the incident who insisted that the truth should be told, and stuck adamantly to his story.

His reliable source was a retired Dorset police officer that Legg's paper, *Dorset – the County Magazine,* often used as a consultant for its articles in the 1960s and 70s. He had served in the Dorset Police force in 1935 and was involved with the inquest investigations. During the Second World War he had been engaged in counter-espionage activities. The man has since died. He told the magazine that Police Special Branch conducted lengthy interviews with a number of the soldiers at Crown Hill Camp after the accident. Of these only a representative number, three or four, were selected to attend the Inquest and only Catchpole was allowed to speak. Catchpole had been interviewed by the both the Army and the police.[27] Security expert Richard M. Bennett told the author that in 1935 any investigation of a VIP or of a security nature would have been taken over from the Dorset Constabulary by Special Branch. Any interference from the military would have been quickly dismissed.[28]

Catchpole was one of a group of men who had helped put Lawrence on the lorry. A number of these men, soldiers and civilians, corroborated Catchpole's report of the car.[29] John Connolly, the soldier in Bovington Hospital, remembered there were a large number of soldiers at the site but no-one appeared to want to know what had happened. He thought the accident area was a 'death trap' and saw the injured man 'had a terrible injury with the brain exposed'.[30]

Fletcher and Hargraves asserted to the end of their days that they had not seen a car. But they could easily have been distracted if involved in horse-play. Catchpole, representing the men who had seen the accident, was allowed to speak by the authorities reluctantly. They did not want any witnesses who had been at the scene to testify. The police feared they would be judged as inefficient. Despite having spent days conducting a lengthy search, they had been unable to locate the car or its driver.[31]

It seems that the proceedings may have been manipulated by government agencies. None of this is proven or provable. The inquest was rushed through and no other witnesses were called, despite many being available. No further efforts were made to find the driver of the 'black car'. Richard Bennett concluded 'The inquest was certainly not handled in any way that could be considered "normal" for what was apparently a relatively straightforward accident . . . The tight security and reported clampdown on media speculation were, if the reports are indeed correct, quite out of character for a County Inquest.'[32]

Nigel Neville-Jones, the son of the 1935 Coroner, told the author that his father very rarely spoke about the events surrounding the incident and he has no knowledge of any cover up or any attempt to get the inquest over as quickly as possible. The funeral had been arranged for two o'clock that afternoon and Churchill was arriving by special train at 1 pm. The proceedings started at ten and were over by twelve. A less important man – or less controversial – may well have had a protracted series of inquests. Not so Lawrence, and it may be that his supposed involvement in military intelligence hurried things along. In 1935 the authority of the Coroner was greater than today and inquests were a much tighter affair. Mr Neville-Jones' summing up directed what decision the jury should make, using powers that do not now exist. No details of Lawrence's private life were to come to light. It was, in Rodney Legg's opinion, a wholly stage-managed show to the end.

Journalist Colin Graham thought 'there was an accident, everyone says . . . and that, basically, is the only evidence on which everyone seems to agree'[33] Ralph Neville-Jones, addressing the seven jurors, summed up:

The facts are only too clear and that the collision was an accident there can be no doubt. What caused the deceased to run into the pedal cyclist from the rear we shall never know, but the evidence would lead one to think that Mr. Shaw must have been travelling at a very fast speed and possibly lost control of his motorcycle.

The problem facing the jury was trying to understand why Lawrence, on a bright, sunny day in good visibility, lost control. Those present at the inquest got the clear impression that he had collided with something that should have been easily visible. This confounded them. Lawrence was an expert motorcyclist. Something happened that made him lose control.

The second source was the late Roland Hammersley. Hammersley knew Frank Gordon, Arthur Russell, Joan Hughes and many other people concerned with Lawrence's death. He was interested in anything relevant to Lawrence and Bovington, and in the 1980s talked to Albert Hargraves, then in his sixties, of his involvement. What Hargraves said puts a completely different slant on things.

It must be accepted that this is a third hand anecdote, and having undergone a gestation period of over 50 years, its truth is questionable. It is impossible to know how much faith Mr. Hammersley placed in it. Still, it is the most plausible answer yet as to why the collision occurred. We may conclude Hargraves assumed that, because of the time elapsed, he would not be subject to prosecution.

The boys stated at the inquest that they had been riding in single file for 100 yards before Lawrence collided with them. Arthur Russell said the boys were turning around go back to Bovington when Lawrence hit Hargraves and that this was 'touched upon' at the inquest. Neither appears to be true. In fact, Mr Hammersley said, Hargraves told him that what they said at the inquest was not really the way it happened. As they passed the Crown Hill Camping Ground one of them was shouting across to a soldier on duty. Hargraves was riding across the path of Lawrence from the left hand to the right hand side of the road when Lawrence appeared. They were playing the fool, out looking for birds' nests. As Lawrence collided with Hargraves' rear wheel, it was not pulled into an elongated oval, as Arthur Russell had assumed, but pushed into a contorted figure of eight, the shape made when a wheel has been buckled from the side. The offside rod supporting the rear wheel was bent into a parabola from the seat to the wheel hub. This is confirmed by the 1935 photographs of Hargraves' bike opposite.

There may possibly have been another reason why Hargraves was riding from left to right across the road. At the bottom of the second dip in 1935, going off to the left, was a narrow dirt uphill track. One suggestion was that he had cycled up there to collect a bird's nest from the woods and had just re-emerged on the road when the Brough appeared.[34] If the boys had lied about riding in single file this would be a motivation for them omitting to report the black car. Andrew Norman queried 'Is it possible that this car came out of the camping ground entrance after the boys had passed it but before Lawrence had reached it?'[35] This seems highly unlikely. Any vehicles exiting the camping ground would have been military, painted khaki drab.

Immediately after the accident there was a huge security clampdown. Although Lawrence was a civilian, the Army took over all the proceedings. Both Catchpole and the boys were questioned by the Army far more than the police. For Hargraves and Fletcher it must have been apparent that when Lawrence

Hit from the left or shunted from behind? Two views of Hargraves wrecked bicycle after the crash on the morning of the inquest. Russell mistakenly recalled in 1985 that the front wheel was buckled. One can see where the top of the Brough's front wheel has collided with the rear mudguard and pushed it into an 'S' shape. The wheel has been knocked off its hub from the top and to the left. This indicates the wheel was not pulled into an elongated shape by Lawrence's left footrest meshing with it from behind, as Russell assumed. The Brough's front wheel appears to have hit Hargraves' wheel from the right side, confirming that Hargraves was cycling from left to right across the road, and not in line behind Fletcher. (Bodleian via Marriott)

The rear inner tube has come out. The pronounced buckle in the rear mudguard and the offside tubular framing from the saddle to the rear wheel seems to have been punched from the right hand side, rather than pulled out of shape. The front wheel looks untouched. (Bodleian via Marriott)

died on the Sunday they were in serious trouble. Their fathers, who were both soldiers, were not allowed to see them immediately after the accident, and the boys were advised not to discuss it.

It may have been the possibility of a manslaughter conviction that made their fathers tell the boys to stick to the tale of riding in single file for 100 yards. If this was so it would explain their inconsistencies. It was well known locally that the two boys always fooled about in the road. Rodney Legg mentioned that many Wareham people knew they had been looking for birds' nests but kept quiet. The most likely reason for the boys denying seeing a black car, is simply that if the driver of the car was found, he would tell the truth about what had happened. Denial of the car's existence by both boys immediately undermined Catchpole's testimony and the police would not pursue the matter. The other possible reason is that they were instructed to do so.

The boys stuck rigidly to their story throughout the inquest making the circumstances of the accident inexplicable. It is hardly surprising that the jury and Neville-Jones were so confused. No-one had considered that the boys' testimonies could be false. Hargraves was in the centre of the road when the car came across him, Fletcher was nearby. The car would have veered left to avoid the boy then swung back right into the centre of the road. At that moment Lawrence appeared doing between 50 and 60 mph. Some part of the offside bodywork of the car could have clipped Lawrence's right handlebar. This would explain some black paint found on his right handlebar. The Brough reacted by immediately swinging to the right, as Catchpole saw. Sixteen feet later Lawrence went at about 45 degrees into the side of Hargraves' rear wheel.

The driver of the car may have been a visiting VIP or someone important in the camp. What a scandal would have ensued if it had become known that a member of the brass had caused the death of Lawrence of Arabia. An immediate security clampdown ensued. The Army took over all the proceedings, interviewed the boys and told them and Catchpole to deny seeing any car. At the inquest the boys could not remember much of what happened but were unwaveringly certain there was no car. Then the teetotal Catchpole, after he insisted, was allowed to testify by the authorities, but none of the other soldiers who saw the car was permitted to speak. It was assumed when Catchpole was recalled, after the boys' testimony, that he would withdraw his statement. But he did not. He elaborated upon it.

The authorities manipulated the inquest to such an extent that it was over as soon as possible and no other witnesses were allowed to speak. The Dorset Constabulary stated they had been unable to find the car or its driver. Possibly a story was circulated that Catchpole had a history of mental instability. His story began to lose credibility. Five years later he shot himself and no-one knew why. There is no ultimate answer to what happened that day, but almost certainly some of the truth was suppressed. The jury returned a verdict that Mr. Shaw died through injuries received accidentally.

The policeman's story is the first and only evidence the author has heard that the black car existed. Rodney Legg's theories of the cause of Lawrence's crash have been questioned by many, but having heard the story of the black car first-hand from him, and having questioned him about it, the author accepts it. It is the only corroboration that there was a black car and, taken with Eyles' recollections of Catchpole as being a reliable, sober man, it makes some sense. The Roland Hammersley tale may not be true, but it certainly goes a long way to explaining why T.E. collided with Hargraves in perfect visibility and, taken with Pat Knowles' account mentioned elsewhere, we have a number of factors that could plausibly have produced the final result. Some say that Lawrence was bitten by an insect; the front brake snapped, and the rear wheel locked; Hargraves was in the middle of the road; the Brough clipped the side of the approaching car. Some believe that Lawrence looked down seconds before the impact,[36] which would have contributed to his loss of control. Lawrence died because he was riding too fast, because the car was there at the wrong moment on a dangerous stretch of road, and because Hargraves was in the centre of that road.

A final gesture?

When two men working at the Camp, Lyle Chapman, Joyce Knowles cousin, and Bill O'Connor, arrived at the scene, Lawrence was lying on the east side of the road a number of yards north of the impact point, his head resting against a tree trunk. His skull had collided with the tree, cracking it open further, and there were trails of blood and ripped clothing across the road. Chapman and O'Connor approached, whereupon Chapman exclaimed 'Why, it's Mr. Lawrence.' As with most aspects of Lawrence's crash, there are a number of different versions of what happened next. According to Michael Yardley's biography:

> At this point Lawrence, who had appeared unconscious, opened his eyes and, looking directly towards L.C., O'Connor and Catchpole, bought up his hand and held up a finger as if to indicate the number one – then he lapsed back into unconsciousness.[37]

This story was repeated in in a slightly reworded form in E.V.G. Hunt's *The Life and Times of Joyce Knowles*.[38] Pat Knowles stated that he had heard of and believed the 'raised finger' episode in 1938. In Hunt's version Chapman was working quite close to the road. He heard the Brough but did not bother to look until he 'heard the engine racing uselessly'. Chapman and O'Connor then ran to the crash. When Lawrence raised his finger, he moved it 'unsteadily' from side to side. Joyce Knowles' account was almost identical. Yardley later learned the single finger gesture could have been a Moslem one for God. Chapman told him Lawrence was bleeding from nose, ears and mouth.[39] Bob Hunt's explanation was simple: a shaken finger was the sign one gives to a child meaning 'No!' 'Quite clearly he was merely saying my name is not Lawrence.' He was determined to remain 'Shaw' until his death.

Could Lawrence have survived?

As time passed numerous theories appeared about Lawrence's demise. One was that the accident had been faked in order to allow Lawrence to retire in peace to Morocco. Another was that a steel hawser had been stretched across the road to cause the crash. A third, even more bizarre, was that he had ridden into the back of a hay cart pulled by two shire horses. Most of these were nonsense of course, but the author did hear a story of Lawrence's treatment after the crash that differed considerably from the official one. Professor James Malpas[40] was a doctor at the Radcliffe Hospital, Oxford in the 1960s. The story he had been told that Lawrence remained in Bovington Camp hospital after the crash and no diagnosis was made. 'Eventually he was transferred to the Radcliffe Infirmary in Oxford where again no diagnosis of his continued coma was made. He died and at the post mortem a subdural haematoma [haemorrhage] was found which, if it had been recognised and treated might well have saved his life.'[41] Professor Malpas reported that the senior consultants at the Radcliffe Hospital implied there had been a cover up. 'They suggested that Lawrence's care had not been of the best. Unfortunately all the senior participants in that discussion are now dead.'[42] Professor Malpas subsequently consulted the Radcliffe Infirmary who confirmed that Lawrence was visited in Bovington Hospital by the Professor of Medicine from Oxford and that Professor Hugh Cairns took Lawrence's brain to Oxford:

> The transcript of the Inquest and the post mortem report confirm a fracture of the skull but although it recorded extensive brain damage it says nothing about a subdural haematoma, and it seems that even if it had been recognised and removed TEL would still have died from pneumonia. Unfortunately it will never be possible to learn the truth for the brain was destroyed in a fire in 1971.[43]

Suicide

Had Lawrence committed suicide? The story was that Air-Marshal Trenchard, Chief Commissioner for the Metropolitan Police, had arranged that a warrant be issued for Lawrence's arrest to face charges after accusations of indecent behaviour with servicemen at Clouds Hill. When he was in the RAF no action was taken, leading him to believe that, as a public figure, he would not be liable to prosecution. However, a plain clothes police officer visited his cottage after his retirement, and advised him to leave the country immediately or suffer the consequences. If true ,this represents a complete change of heart towards Lawrence on Trenchard's part. There would first have had to have been a complaint to the Home Secretary for Trenchard to have issued such a warrant for execution in Dorset.[44]

John Mack dismissed the possibility that Lawrence had attempted suicide. He realised that the immediate post-retirement period was well known as one of depression, particularly for those who had recently left the armed forces. Lawrence's letters, written after he retired from the RAF, suggested a 'continuing and progressive despair and emptiness'.[45] Men who suffered a severe recent loss, of any kind, were more prone to accidents. A.W. Lawrence's suggestion was that his brother rode at an excessive speed 'to forget himself for a few seconds . . . and that he thus rode into a catastrophe which the normal quickness of his brain might possibly have averted.[46] He also thought that Lawrence sacrificed himself to save others from injury. This was also believed by Dr. Marguerite Roberts, friend of Florence Hardy: 'I feel he could have saved himself if he'd wanted to, but, characteristically he involuntarily sacrificed himself rather than hurt someone else.'[47] Liddell Hart had worried for years about the speed T.E. rode at. In the summer of 1934 he was convinced that 'At the moment when an accident appeared inevitable he would throw away his life on the chance of saving another party.'

Notes

1 See Appendix One, p328.

2 Originally Mr Penn. He became 'Lord Dawson of Penn' later.

3 See Dr. J.R.C. Burton-Brown's entry in 'Personal Remiscences', *Tank Corps*.

4 The orbital plate is the frontal bone structure of the skull that contains the eye sockets.

5 In a BBC *Newsnight* programme broadcast on 13th May 1985, the 50th anniversary of Lawrence's death, John Witherow of *The Times* stated that the inquest was badly handled and the authorities themselves did not know what had happened. Phillip Knightley agreed its conduct was sloppy.

6 Mr. Neville-Jones' Christian name is sometimes recorded as 'Reginald'. The Coroner's son confirmed to the author that his father's name was actually Ralph.

7 Neville-Jones had served as a Major in the Royal Horse Artillery in the First World War, but coroner was a civil appointment. In those times a coroner had the power to imprison. This was Neville-Jones's only famous case:

8 Members of RAC Bovington Tank Museum's Archives Department were unable to comment on the possible ordering of a clampdown because apart from a few chance survivals and outlines, most of the Camp's day-to-day Orders have long since been disposed of.

9 Stuart.

10 Mack.

11 Knightley and Simpson say 'plain oak'. It was made by Herbert and Frank Runyard in the Thurmans' shops in Dorchester.

12 The jury consisted of S.C. Patrick (Foreman), W.G. Bugg, W. Burke, R. Dulleston, G. Mason, Jesse Rawles and Thomas Shaw.

13 He actually described it as 'very airy-fairy'.

14 The 'W' actually stood for Walter.

15 *Dorset Daily Echo*, Thursday 16th May, 1935.

16 Marriott.

17 Legg.

18 The T.E. Lawrence Society Newsletter, no. 73, Spring 2005.

19 The 1935 photographs of Catchpole, Fletcher and Hargraves, the accident site, and Hargraves' bicycle are all in fact stills from a Pathe News newsreel of May 1935.

20 Ridge represented the Bovington butchers Dodge and Co.

21 Marriott.

22 See photograph p228.

23 Richard M. Bennett to author, November 2004.

24 Information supplied by Mr. Ian Handoll in correspondence with the author, November 2004. A former custodian of Lawrence's cottage told him 'it was well known that the two boys were always larking about on their bikes and would almost certainly not be riding in single file as they maintained.'

25 Interview with F. Gordon, Bovington, May 1985.

26 *The Life and Times of Joyce Knowles*, E.V.G. Hunt, Dorset, 1994.

27 R. Legg to author, 2004.

28 R.M. Bennett to author, November, 2004.

29 R. Legg to author, 2004.

30 *The Life and Times of Joyce Knowles*, E.V.G. Hunt, Dorset, 1994.

31 R. Legg to author, 2004.

32 R.M. Bennett to author, November 2004.

33 *The Crash Which Killed Lawrence of Arabia*, C. Graham, *Dorset the County* magazine, summer 1968.

34 A.H.R. Reiffer, the owner of the Red Garage, Bovington, stated in 1970 that the first impression they had at the time was that Hargraves had come from a track on Egdon Heath onto the side of the road.

35 Norman.

36 Conversation with Wareham Museum staff.

37 Yardley.

38 Rodney Legg's *Lawrence in Dorset*, 1988.

39 Yardley declined to identify Chapman, naming him only as L.C., a local teenager. This was at Chapman's request.

40 Professor James Spenser Malpas M.B., Emeritus Professor of Medical Oncology and Honourary Consultant Physician, St. Bartholomew's Hospital, London. Examiner Dept. of Medicine, Oxford University. Member (ex-Vice President) St. Bart's Hospital Medical College, London.

41 Communication from Professor J. Malpas. 17th February 2005.

42 Ibid. 21st February 2005.

43 Ibid.

44 From *The Golden Warrior*, Lawrence James. 1990. Richard Aldington was told this story by Somerset Maugham some time before November 1938.

45 Mack.

46 Friends.

47 Knight.

CHAPTER FIFTEEN

Conspiracy Theory – 1

The crux of any conspiracy theory is the suggestion was that the Brough had somehow collided with the 'black car'. The physical evidence for this was some black paint found on the Brough's right handlebar. Dorset historian Rodney Legg related the story in *Lawrence of Dorset*: two hours after the accident George Brough was called to check GW2275. Although he found no serious structural or mechanical fault he noted there was black paint on the offside (right) handlebar and the petrol tank.[1] After Brough's death his wife Connie confirmed the story to a reporter, Howard Dodsworth, from Tunbridge Wells who told *Dorset – the County Magazine* in 1968 that Brough had not been happy to appear at the inquest, being 'unwilling to perjure himself'. Had he been summoned to give evidence he would have felt compelled to mention that the motorcycle collided with a black-painted object.

On 13th May 1985, the 50th anniversary of Lawrence's death, Brough expert Ronald H. Clark told the BBC *Newsnight* programme that George Brough himself had told him that black paint was found on the inside of the right handlebar. In November 1985 Clark told the author: 'All I explained in my interview was to point out how the black enamel would chafe or chase off into the right hand handlebar as it scraped along the side of the black car. With the front brake on it could not as there's insufficient gap. It can however with the brake off.'[2] Rodney Legg concluded that Brough 'believed to his dying day that his expert evidence had been suppressed and that there was therefore more to the crash than the authorities would admit.[3]

Who would want to kill Lawrence? Forces within the establishment, or those outside it? Lawrence had he been approached about home defence, and he may have been involved with Military Intelligence. Some students of the crash are convinced this has some basis in fact. Lawrence also had friends in two of the most politically influential groups in the land: the 'Round Table' and the so-called 'Cliveden Set'. By 1935 Britain's Home Defence was in disarray. If Lawrence had become involved in Home Defence it would have been in the interests of the enemies of Britain to get him out of the way before any contribution he made became effective.

The Fascists?
Lawrence's connections with Fascism were tenuous and not taken very seriously, at least by him. Henry Williamson, author of *Tarka the Otter*, is the person responsible for suggesting Fascist elements were the centre of a conspiracy against him. He had been

a friend of Lawrence since receiving a heart-warming appraisal of *Tarka the Otter* from him in 1928. Williamson was a supporter of Sir Oswald Mosley. Williamson regarded Hitler as mentally unstable, but felt he had the capacity to accomplish something good for Europe. In the First World War the fraternization during the 1914 Christmas Truce had transformed his attitudes to the Germans and this sympathy remained with him after the war. He became a convert to the Communist cause.

Although Lawrence had no sympathy with the German government, Williamson believed T.E. was one of the few men capable of influencing Hitler. Williamson falsely suggested in articles published in 1936 that he had been going to Clouds Hill on 14th May to ask Lawrence to meet Hitler. The idea of is not as far fetched as it sounds. It was not unusual in the early days of Hitler's Chancellorship for the Führer to meet delegations from abroad. Both a Major in RAF Intelligence, F.W. Winterbotham, and Lawrence's Zionist friend from the Middle East war, Richard Meinertzhagen, an Army intelligence officer, met Hitler personally in 1934.

Whether Lawrence would have agreed to Williamson's suggestion is debatable. Williamson was a writer, not a politician. He did not even meet Mosley until October 1937. When he visited Germany in August 1933 he was deeply impressed by the restructuring of the economy and the new direction the Nazis had given the German people. Lawrence, a man more experienced in diplomacy and the ways of politicians, would surely, with his profound understanding of men's motivations, have sensed Hitler's true intentions and rejected Williamson's proposal.

But there *is* evidence of Lawrence contacting the Nazis. In 1934 he was toying with the idea of writing a biography of Roger Casement, the Irish patriot Britain hanged for treason in 1916. He informed John Buchan in April 1935 that the Government had confiscated Casement's diaries and refused all access to them.[4] In 1985 an Australian television producer, Mal Read, told the BBC that he had found a document showing Lawrence had approached the Nazi authorities about procuring a copy of Casement's diaries. There was also a report that the Nazis had attempted to contact Lawrence. The Swedish historian Erik Lonroth, in a long-forgotten biography of 1956, reported that Hitler's National Socialist foreign affairs representative Kurt von Ludecke had been in touch with him in 1932, but T.E. 'rejected these advances.'

Early in 1934 Lawrence received an invitation from Captain H.W. Lettman-Johnson to join the January Club, a discussion group for those who were interested in Fascist philosophy. It was ostensibly independent of Mosley's B.U.F. 'L-J' was a Scottish landowner and former cavalry officer in the Indian Army who was active in Right wing and Pro-Fascist circles in Britain. He became Honorary Secretary of the January Club in 1934. Lawrence had a poor view of how the Indian Army was run: during the siege of Kut in 1916 he was sent to Mesopotamia to try and 'buy off' the Turkish General besieging the British. He was so shocked by the way British officers treated the native Indian soldiers that he deliberately resisted having Indian Army troops shipped in for the Hejaz campaign in 1917. He replied to Lettman-Johnson twice, once on 1st May 1934 and again on the 17th from 13 Birmingham Street. (His friend the author Francis Yeates-Brown was a leading member of the Club.)

Dear Captain L-J,

When you see Y-B please tell him off from me. He knows I loathe dinners, that I do not possess any joy clothes, that I can seldom afford to visit London. As for orders and decorations – help! They and the ladies would about put the lid on any unhappy evening. No, when I want to make myself miserable, I dress up and go on parade quite free of charge.[5]

This was a light-hearted letter to a sinister organisation. The January Club was formed in 1932 by Sir Oswald Moseley as a front organisation to the B.U.F. Recruited into it – some believe – were several important men. Some sources report Edward F.L. Russell (Lord Russell of Liverpool), who won thee M.C.s in World War One and was Chief legal Adviser to the Nuremberg War Crimes Tribunal in 1945, became a member, and in 1934 Major General J.F.C. Fuller, planner of the 1917 tank attack at Cambrai, military history author and pioneer of the 'Blitzkrieg' theory. Other sources contradict this, thinking that both men declined, Fuller criticizing Mosley's tactics and predicting a decisive defeat for the B.U.F.

Lawrence had some advice for the Club:

It would be glorious to dance on the combined cess-pit that holds the dead *Daily Express, Daily Chronicle* and *Daily Herald*. My dictatorship programme would also uproot all telegraph poles and bury the wires,[6] assume ownership of all sea beaches – and scrag the police.

Yours not very sincerely,
T.E. Shaw

Captain Lettman-Johnson (extreme left) at a dinner held by the Fascist January Club in the Savoy Hotel, London, 1934. Lawrence refused to join his club. (Imperial War Museum)

The second letter, of more serious tone than the first, stressed that one of his reasons for being unable to join was poverty:

> I cannot afford visits to London. Ten shillings is three days pay. Politics in England mean either violent change . . . or wasting 20 years of one's time and all one's strength in pandering to the House of Commons. So I can't afford politics either.[7]

Lettman-Johnson's opinion that contemporary youth lacked 'character and guts', a premise he may have used to try and persuade T.E. to join, did not convince:

> [They] get much more out of life than my contemporaries did, 25 years ago. I should have called them a cleaner and better generation. I don't see how anybody in daily touch with working fellows could have dismal thoughts of England.[8]

He had also obviously observed Mosley's rise with interest.

> I suppose Mosley is doing his best. He is daemonic, and a leader of conviction . . . but the staff work very patchy. Men are only made great by the linked force of their friends . . . What faces you actually is the machine of government; and what ails you is that you don't know where the keyboard is – or so you think.
> No, please don't make me any part of you[r] club. I'm prepared only to serve . . . and I am very tired; even of serving.
> Yours,
> T.E. Shaw

Here Lawrence is engaging in a dialogue with the Fascists, certainly, but the dismissive, even mocking tone is unmistakeable. The conclusion must be that Lawrence had little time for 'The Roads to Fascism'. On 31st July 1940 Lettman-Johnson was imprisoned under Defence Regulation 18B for the duration of the War, as a member of the B.U.F.

It may have been that the Nazi hierarchy was astute enough to realise that T.E., having left the RAF, was a great potential asset to British Home Defence. In that case it would have been to their advantage, at a time when their rearmament programme was gaining momentum, to kill him, knowing through his rejection of the advances of the January Club that he was no Lindbergh to be exploited, still less a potential fifth columnist.[9]

The Zionists?

After the Balfour Declaration, Chaim Weizemann considered Lawrence: 'did not think the aims and aspirations of the Jewish people in Palestine contrary to the interests of the Arabs. . . . Zionism, in his view was morally justified, but would the Jewish people respond to the call?' [To repopulate Palestine][10] In the winter of 1921 Lawrence told Weitzman that he thought the Jews would act as 'a ferment' to bring out the 'latent energies' of the Arabs. Jewish redemption would bring Arabic redemption.[11] Chaim Weizmann was elected president of Israel in 1949. Lawrence was pro-Zionist. It seems he did not believe the Balfour Declaration was a 'conspiracy' to rob the Arabs of the fruits of their victory. There appears to be no supportable reason why the Jews would attempt to assassinate him.

Rodney Legg's Theories

The most plausible agency for assassinating Lawrence, and the one most suggested, was MI5.

Dorset historian Rodney Legg has radical views about Lawrence and MI5 in the 1930s. He holds the opinion that Lawrence's life was a 'grand bluff' and that he had been earmarked to command a united British intelligence service. Intrinsic to the theory is the belief that the black car was operated by MI5 and deliberately collided with Lawrence. He believes that Lawrence was 'the designated head of a new streamlined intelligence service he had planned with the approval of Churchill'.

Legg's theory of Lawrence's involvement with military intelligence finds its source in a quote from Colonel Richard Meinertzhagen's *Middle East Diary*. The eccentric Meinertzhagen had served with Lawrence in the Middle East war. He was a supporter of the Jewish people and had been at the Paris Peace Conference. Meinertzhagen's diary, Mr. Legg believes, records that in May 1935 Lawrence was at the head of a review panel charged with examining and reforming the British Intelligence services. He quoted the diary:

> We worked together in the C.O. [Cabinet Office] on a scheme for a Directorship of Intelligence embracing both political and military aspects and coalescing under one head F.O. [Foreign Office], W.O. [War Office], Admiralty, Air Ministry, Scotland Yard and MI5. Out the thing to Churchill, Amery, MacDonough, they concurred. Involved training college in London and one in the country. It was complete and we were applying for Treasury sanction when T.E. died. I felt I could not go on with it as it was very much his work.[12]

Legg thinks that Lawrence was being prepared for the intelligence community's top job: he was to become 'Director Designate 'of a proposed 'Intelligence Directorate', a Directorate that was being designed to upgrade the Government espionage services onto a war footing and also (he is here quite specific), to 'co-ordinate the general monitoring of German penetration into Britain.'[13]

> Colonel Richard Meinertzhagen's *Middle East Diary*, a highly sensitive and secret document which he entrusted to the care of the Rhodes House Library in Oxford, confirms that in May 1935 T.E. Lawrence was at the head of a review panel considering the entire restructuring of the British secret intelligence services.[14]

Legg told the author that also involved in this were Winston Churchill, Leo Amery,[15] General Sir George MacDonough, Director of Military Intelligence 1916–18, and F.W. Winterbotham,[16] head of the Air Section of the British Secret Service (MI6). In 1930 Winterbotham was working under the stewardship of Admiral Sir Hugh Sinclair and had contacts with Alfred Rosenberg,[17] one of the key Nazi intellectuals. This enabled him to meet Hitler in 1934. He was one of the Nazis' most trusted links to the British establishment and was introduced to other key Nazi leaders in their efforts to promote British neutrality.

There is nothing in any of the books by Winterbotham, MacDonough or Amory to confirm the existence of the Directorate. In Winterbotham's book on his experiences in MI6 from 1934 to 1939, he did write that, contrary to the hopes of the MI6 workers, the senior staff frowned upon the idea of subsuming all the services' intelligence branches into one organisation.[18]

Mr. Legg's conclusions, he said, were formed from seeing contemporary notes and letters held by Kenneth Allsop[19] and Henry Williamson and a Parliamentary file of Captain Somerset de Chere when he was a National Conservative MP. Legg also stated, 'Other material was supplied anonymously and I still do not know who sent me copies of the inquest papers and other documentation. I discussed Lawrence at

Colonel Richard Meinertzhagen, probably taken around the time of the Paris Peace Conferece in 1919. Meinertzhagen worked with Lawrence during the war and at the Peace Conference and Cairo Conference. Many of the entries he recorded in his Middle East Diary have been regarded by historians as absurd. (Via Stuart)

some length with Arthur Kenneth Chesterton, Mosley's henchman in the British Union of Fascists, and with Malcolm Muggeridge (briefly).'[20] These conversations were held in the mid 1960s, so it was impossible to remember them with precision.

Mike Chapman, a military historian who served with the 51st Parachute Brigade as a National Serviceman, was the curator of Lawrence's cottage at Clouds Hill for a number of years. He told the author that he had read an authoritative account that Lawrence had been asked by Military Intelligence to assist in monitoring the immigration of German businessmen into Britain, the fear being that they may be involved in fifth columnist work. By 1935 all cases of suspected German espionage work were beginning to be investigated more thoroughly. The story is that a few hours after Lawrence crashed two plain-clothes policemen appeared at Clouds Hill and confiscated a number of official papers that were lying on his bed. These had been sent to him by MI5 to prepare him for this work.[21]

In May 1935 T.E.'s brother had publicly denied that Lawrence was engaged in Secret Service work or had recently visited Berlin. In a letter to H. Montgomery-Hyde, a lawyer researching Lawrence's life in 1977, A.W. stated that he had flown back from Majorca on the 14th and stayed at Clouds Hill until after the funeral. They saw and heard nothing of the security services. He thought that if they had already searched the cottage 'they would not have left the transcripts of *The Mint* and the hundreds of letters that I found there'.[22]

The security expert and author Richard M. Bennett found no proof that Lawrence had any connection with the Intelligence services in the 1920s and '30s, despite rumours to the contrary. He does not support the premise that Lawrence could have been offered any position in the Intelligence Service in 1935, let alone be a 'Director Designate'. MI5 had been part of the Home Office for many years and did not then exist as an independent body. The original Directorate of Military Intelligence was abolished in 1922 and 'absorbed with minimal staff and even less powers within a Directorate of Military Operations'.[23] However, Richard Bennett did confirm that a fifth column monitoring committee existed in 1935. It was not just an MI5 committee, but a complete sub-section of B Branch, the operations branch. This was Section B5b that monitored left and right-wing subversion. It operated externally to MI5 at Dolphin Square. At its head was Captain Maxwell Knight,[24] a counter-intelligence officer.

Notes

1 Godfrey Runyard who, with his brother Frank, collected the bike after the accident, in 2005 had no recollection of Brough doing this, and said he did not, himself, see any black paint on the bike. This statement was made seventy years after the event.

2 Letter to the author, 21st November 1985. Arthur Russell told the author he found the front brake broken after the accident. The brake lever was seven inches long.

3 Legg.

4 Wilson.

5 T.E. Lawrence to Captain H.W. Lettman-Johnson. 13 Birmingham St., Southampton. 01/05/1934.

6 Lawrence had been having trouble with the telegraph poles around Clouds Hill.

7 T.E. Lawrence to Captain H.W. Lettman-Johnson. 13 Birmingham St., Southampton. 17/05/1934.

8 Ibid.

9 There is another tenuous link with the Nazis. In late 1934 Lawrence was invited by the governor of the Bank of England, Montague Norman, to become secretary of the bank, a post requiring leadership ability but not experience. Although touched by the offer, he declined. Norman was a close friend of Gunjar Schact, Hitler's economic adviser. The relationship Schact and Norman had is highlighted by one notorious incident. When the Nazis invaded Czechoslovakia in 1939 they forced the Czech government to transfer all the Czech funds (six million pounds) that were in a B.I.S. account in the Bank of England to the Reichsbank. Norman could have delayed this, but allowed it to happen. This caused uproar in the House of Commons.

10 Weizemann. *T.E. Lawrence by his Friends*, Jonathan Cape, 1937.

11 Ibid.

12 *Lawrence of Dorset– from Arabia to Clouds Hill*, Rodney Legg, Dorset Publishing Co., 2005.

13 Ibid.

14 Ibid.

15 Leo Amery as an Under-Secretary in Lloyd George's government of 1917 had helped draft the Balfour Declaration. He was First Lord of the Admiralty 1922–24, and Colonial Secretary 1924–29. In the 1930s he was a forceful opponent of the government's appeasement policy, often openly attacking his own party.

16 F.W. Winterbotham, Major. Head of the Air Section of MI6. Author of *The Ultra Secret*, *Secret and Personal* and *The Nazi Connection*.

17 Alfred Rosenberg (1893–1946) was an early and influential member of the Nazi Party. He is regarded as the main author of the key Nazi ideological creeds of *Lebensraum* and racial theory.

18 Winterbotham, p.33. Apart from this brief reference there is no mention of any intelligence 'review panel' in any of Winterbotham's three books.

19 Kenneth Allsop (192–1973), TV personality and author, became a household name on the BBC's *Tonight* programme in the early 1960s. A friend of Williamson, he died of a drugs overdose.

20 Rodney Legg to author, 2005.

21 Mike Chapman, conversation with author, Clouds Hill, 2005.

22 A.W. Lawrence to H. Montgomery-Hyde, 18th June 1977. Bodleian Reserve. Another contradiction: other reports state that a number of documents were taken from the cottage.

23 Richard M. Bennett to author, November 2004. He declined to include the case of Lawrence's crash in his book *Conspiracy: Plots, Lies and Cover-Ups* because he felt the evidence that an actual murder had occurred was insufficient.

24 Knight later became well known as a BBC TV naturalist. He was a member of the British Fascists (BF) before being recruited to MI5.

CHAPTER SIXTEEN

Conspiracy Theory – 2

Colonel Meinertzhagen's Diaries caused an awful lot of trouble and confusion. The quixotic Richard Meinertzhagen enlisted in the Royal Fusiliers in 1899 and served in Kenya with the King's African Rifles from 1902 to 1906, was wounded, mentioned in dispatches and promoted to captain. He was involved in a deception plan during Allenby's Palestine campaign in the First World War that involved leaving behind a blood-stained haversack containing false battle orders, helping the British to take Beersheba. He was severely wounded on the Western Front and also during World War Two at the Dunkirk evacuation. He reportedly met Hitler twice, in 1934 and again in 1939.

A number of historians have expressed doubts about the reliability of the *Middle East Diary*. The *Diary* was reconstructed from Meinertzhagen's 'original' notes over 40 years after the events it described and contained many dubious references. Professor John Mack noticed Meinertzhagen tended to be condescending about his relationship with Lawrence: some of his entries Mack thought seemed fabricated. Both he and others have been disinclined to use the diaries as a source.[2] Fabrications occurred in other areas as well: the ornithologist Meinertzhagen is known to have falsified submissions of new bird species, these being actually stolen and relabelled museum specimens. He was dismissed as Allenby's Chief Political Officer in 1929 for insubordination; his second wife died in a questionable shooting accident in a remote Scottish village in 1928, and his ornithological magnum opus, *Birds of Arabia* is believed to be based on the unpublished manuscript of another naturalist. Meinertzhagen was also known to be violent.

A.W. Lawrence was critical of Meinertzhagen. He stated many people knew T.E. better than Meinertzhagen claimed he did, particularly D.G. Hogarth. Meinertzhagen was, unlike Lawrence, completely self-assured and aloof. A.W. observed, 'During and just after the war, and in the early 1920s, they met fairly often on business. No doubt T.E. found it easy to talk to a man so different from himself . . . like talking to a stranger in a railway carriage.'[3] One American scholar felt 'Meinertzhagen capitalised on the notoriety Lawrence received in the 1950s with the publication of Aldington's biography. Although the diary entries about Lawrence were 'allegedly contemporary with the incidents they relate', they appeared fabricated.[4] Thus it is inadvisable to take any of the eight T.E. Lawrence passages in the *Middle East Diary* seriously. (An American student of Lawrence's life, J.N. Lockman, has made a meticulous analysis of these falsifications, and rather than elaborating on his thesis here Appendix V has been devoted to it.)

Since Meinertzhagen's *Diary* has lost any academic credibility that it may have had, Legg's theories must do also. His theories are based on assumptions that have little to support them and do not stand up to analysis. His suggestion is that Lawrence was being watched by MI5 because of his liaison with the pro-Moseley Williamson, at a time when the British Union of Fascists was becoming more active. This, as already shown, is not credible: firstly because Williamson's empathy for the extreme Right was based partly on fantasies; and secondly, as Legg himself suggests, Lawrence had already been recruited by MI5 to monitor any fifth column activities.

The 'Director Designate' theory is disqualified quite easily: Legg quotes the relevant passage out of context and even alters it. The original passage comes at the end of the second chapter in the book on the Paris Peace Conference. A lot of the quotes in the book are not complimentary to Lawrence, Meinertzhagen describing him as 'a vain little man'. Legg's quoted passage comes at the end of a sub-section in the *Middle East Diary* headed '10.I.1938. Devon.' In his version Legg omitted a number of words that appear in the 1959 Cresset Press edition of the *Middle East Diary* completely altering the meaning of the passage. These words are underlined below. Following a short discussion on Lawrence and guerrilla warfare, the Cresset version has:

> <u>When</u> we worked together in the Colonial Office <u>we worked</u> <u>out</u> a scheme for a Directorship of Intelligence embracing both political and military aspects and coalescing under one head <u>all the</u> <u>little organizations of the</u> Foreign Office, War Office, Admiralty, Air Ministry, Scotland Yard and M.I.5. <u>We put</u> the <u>scheme up</u> to Churchill, Amery and Macdonogh <u>and</u> they concurred. <u>It</u> involved <u>a</u> training college in London and <u>a training college for agents</u> in the country. It was complete and we were applying for Treasury sanction when T.E.L. died. I felt I could not go on with it as it was very much his work.[5]

The inclusion of the underlined words demands a completely different interpretation of the passage. There is no suggestion at all in this version that this took place in May 1935, but more probably that it occurred at the time of the Cairo Conference in 1922 when both men were working in the Colonial Office. There is no mention of the scheme progressing. There is also no mention of an 'Intelligence Directorate', or that Lawrence was a 'Director Designate' of it.

Williamson's intended visit to Clouds Hill was the subject of a second misconception. An old school friend of his, Victor M. Yeates, had written a classic on air warfare, *Winged Victory*, a fictionalized account of his experiences in the Royal Flying Corps. Yeates died of a war-related illness before finishing it and some have mistakenly assumed that Williamson wanted to deliver the book to Clouds Hill to ask for Lawrence's opinion of the manuscript.[6] (Williamson was later to write the final chapter himself). But *Winged Victory* was not the typescript he planned to take to Clouds Hill. Williamson's letter of the 10th May to Lawrence which was thought lost is now in the possession of the Henry Williamson Society. It contains no reference to Hitler, neither does it contain any reference to *Winged Victory*. In fact, Williamson was going up to London to have the steering of his Alvis fixed on the Great West Road and also to visit his publishers, Faber. He suggested dropping off a Yeates manuscript with Lawrence on Tuesday 14th May, and picking it up on returning from London on Friday 17th.

> I am reading through Yeates 60000 fragment FAMILY LIFE. I wish I knew_what I thought of it: read until 2 a.m. two days ago, couldn't put it down . . . Poor chap, he had hell all right: his own family portraits (mother, sisters) are too terrible. I feel exaggerated. He was dying as he wrote; and kicking against the coils still holding him, but not intellectually. It is an awful hard-minded book. Would it interest you to see it? I could leave it on Tuesday and pick it up on my return about Friday.[7]

This cannot refer to *Winged Victory* because Lawrence had already read a published edition. He received an advance copy whilst still at Southampton. On December 31st, when at Bridlington, Lawrence wrote 'How good that he [Yeates] did it in time . . . every mess has a copy.'[8] So Williamson did not arrange to visit Lawrence to discuss a meeting with Hitler, nor to lend him a typescript of the already published *Winged Victory*, but to leave another unpublished work by Yeates.[9]

Lawrence told a number of people he was interested in becoming involved in Home Defence in his later years. Did this make him a target? Lawrence discussed the post of Secretary of the Committee of Imperial Defence (C.I.D.) with Liddell Hart.. The C.I.D. was established in 1902 by PM Sir Arthur Balfour. For a long time there had been a need for an organisation that could flexibly co-ordinate defence: the aim of the C.I.D. was to do this across all the different departments in Whitehall. The Ministry of Defence did not then exist. The complexities of the Boer War, when for the first time troops from many different dominions were employed, showed that the existing Cabinet Defence Committee, established in 1895, was inadequate for the co-ordination required. With the establishment of the C.I.D. the British Army and Royal Navy could be co-ordinated on an empire-wide basis. At the head of this the man responsible for administering the C.I.D.'s relationship with the Government was the Secretary.

In some quarters, even right up to the end it was felt that Lawrence could still do something great. He had expressed an interest in helping to guide defence strategy for a while and Liddell Hart had talked to him a number of times on this subject. Liddell Hart had been offered the post himself in 1932, which did not surprise Lawrence. The Secretaryship of the C.I.D. was a very responsible position. At this time the position was filled by Sir Maurice Hankey, a former Royal Marine Artillery officer. Hankey was recruited into naval intelligence in 1902 and by 1914 had become Secretary of the Navy. He was one of the men responsible for recommending to Churchill, then First Sea Lord, the development of an armoured vehicle to break the trench warfare deadlock. By 1918 he had become Secretary of the Imperial War Cabinet and after the war was appointed Secretary to the Cabinet and Secretary of the Committee of Imperial Defence in 1920. These were all progressively more powerful positions. By the time of Lawrence's retirement from the Air Force, Hankey was both Secretary to the Committee of Imperial Defence and Secretary to the Cabinet.

By 1935 the C.I.D.'s power was actually greater than was originally intended. It had formally served only with advisory powers. By 1935, however, its decisions were normally adopted without requiring Cabinet approval. Because the C.I.D.'s main function was preventing and planning for war, it ceased to operate as an official body in August 1914. The C.I.D. Secretaryship was only a peacetime appointment.

In his book *Great Contemporaries* Churchill wrote that he had hoped Lawrence would get involved in Home Defence after his retirement.[10] Lawrence's feeling about the Secretaryship was that Hankey had more work than he could handle.[11] On 22nd March 1935 he told Liddell Hart that he had received approaches about becoming Hankey's successor. He told Liddell Hart in 1934 that he could not accept Hankey's responsibilities of being Secretary of both the Cabinet and the C.I.D; he would be Secretary to the C.I.D. only.

Hankey was blinded by his own power. He believed he was an institution and could go on forever. The Cabinet, of course, knew otherwise.[12] Although he agreed Hankey was pleasant and helpful, Lawrence felt that neither he nor Liddell Hart were people the Secretary would consider as deputies and, consequently, successors.[13]

It would seem highly unlikely that Lawrence, having served for 12 years in the ranks, would have the strength to go straight into an executive position of such responsibility; most of his strategic knowledge would have been out of date. Final evidence of his commitment, however, came on 12th May 1935, the evening before the crash. He was in conversation with Pat Knowles at Clouds Hill. Knowles recalled that Lawrence said he had mixed feelings about some news he had received. They had planned to start up a small printing press outside the cottage, but this would have to be deferred. He was expecting, he said, to be asked to undertake 'work of national importance, work relating to Home Defence'.[14]

So Lawrence had certainly agreed to become involved in the defence of his country in some capacity, if not with the C.I.D. His conversation with Knowles does not preclude the fifth column monitoring work already mentioned and if this was so, and the Home Defence and MI5 work were actually one and the same, then some time between his leaving the RAF in February and his crash in May, he must have contacted a representative of the intelligence community. Captain Maxwell Knight, already mentioned, operated from Dolphin Square. Knight employed at least 14 operatives, many of whom had strong right-wing sympathies. Many worked on a part-time time basis, and would often meet him in the foyers of obscure London hotels. Amongst these were Ian Fleming and William Joyce (later 'Lord Haw-Haw'). For two periods before his accident from 6th to the 13th of March, and from the 18th to the 25th March, Lawrence had enough free time on his hands, particularly in the first period when there is little record of his movements, to have stopped off for a briefing with Knight or his associates. During the second period Lawrence travelled widely around central London and visited Liddell Hart and Churchill, and on at least one occasion discussed home defence.[16]

At the hub of British commercial and political society in the 1930s were two groups that were made up of the most influential personalities in England: the Round Table group, headed by Lionel Curtis, and the Cliveden Set, headed by Lady Nancy and Lord Waldorf Astor. Both had influence on Government policy in the 1920s and '30s. Several of their members were in communication with Lawrence only a few weeks before he died: Lord Lothian, Geoffrey Dawson, John Buchan, Winston Churchill, R.H. Brand and George Bernard Shaw. The two groups were strongly interlinked.

The Round Table

The main interest in the Round Table in relation to Lawrence's accident is that two of his biographers suggest he was influenced by its ideas and that the organisation, according to some sources, had associations with Freemasonry. The suggestion here is that Lawrence may have been killed as a consequence of this connection.

The Round Table had its roots in the imperialist administration of South Africa in the 1890s. By this time one of the richest and most powerful men in Africa was the gold and diamond magnate Cecil Rhodes. Rhodes had made a fortune with his de Beers Mining Company and became devoted to the expansion and consolidation of British rule in Africa. When he died in 1902, Milner became the trustee of his fortune. Milner, Governor General and High Commissioner, had employed a number of up and coming young men from Oxford University in South Africa to help run his administration, including Curtis, Dawson, R.H. Brand, Lionel Hichens, John Buchan and Phillip Kerr. These were called 'Milner's Kindergarten' by his opponents in Johannesburg, and all obtained influential posts in government and finance after they left South Africa. Dawson was appointed editor of *The Times* in 1916; Brand became a successful banker for Lazard Brothers; Kerr became a political thinker of international repute and inherited the title Lord Lothian in 1930, in World War Two he was made British Ambassador to Washington. Hichins became head of a large shipbuilding firm; Buchan became Lord Tweedsmuir and eventually Governor General of Canada.

Milner inherited the legacy of a 'Secret Society' Rhodes had dreamed of since 1877, devoted to the extension of British rule throughout the world. Rhodes' fantasy never materialised. Between 1909 and 1913, however, Milner, Curtis, Kerr and Sir William S. Marries used the 'Kindergarten' to establish semi-secret discussion groups, known as the Round Table Groups. These were set up throughout the Empire and in the US and were controlled from England. All these men got to know and became close friends with Lawrence after the War, particularly Curtis, Buchan and Geoffrey Dawson. Dawson, with Curtis, Phillip Kerr and Robert H. Brand, were staunch imperialists. Phillip Knightley and Colin Simpson contended that Lawrence before the War absorbed the precepts of the Round Table from D.G. Hogarth and 'and these came later to be his main motivations in Arabia'.[17] Whilst at All Souls under the influence of Curtis, his political views became more sophisticated. He developed a vision of change for Arabia and Asia, more subtle than his basic solutions to Arab nationalistic aspirations during the War; a concept of dominion status that was contrary to the traditional imperialism that influenced the postwar peace conferences.[18]

The rather surprising friendship between Lawrence and Curtis began in London when Lawrence took Curtis to meet Prince Faisal and continued at the Paris Conference. There was a capacity for friendship in Curtis that later evoked some of T.E.'s most heartfelt letters. Lawrence often invited himself to stay at Curtis's home at Hales Croft, Kidlington, where Curtis grew a bed of orange tulips in his honour. T.E.'s vulnerability moved Curtis, and his talents evoked a deep admiration. When Milner died in 1925 Curtis took over the Round Table, committed to Rhodes' principles of Federation and Imperialism. The group 'played a role in British imperial affairs that has never been properly analysed or described'.[19] Phillip Knightley and Colin Simpson thought that the wealth, scholarship, patronage and class consciousness of its followers enabled the Round Table 'to exert considerable pressure on the decision making elite of government'.[20]

In 1920 Lawrence wrote an anonymous article for the Round Table journal entitled 'The Changing East'.[21] This was most interesting because its ideas persuaded Churchill to bring Lawrence to the Cairo Conference in 1921 with the Colonial Office. The article warned of a rising nationalism in western Asia, suggesting how the Empire's governing policies should adapt to accommodate this. The Round Table looked for an 'Imperial Federation', i.e. a federation of the self-governing parts of the Empire. Curtis and the others hoped this imperial policy would be controlled by a new parliament, representative of all the Empire's electors. They came to the conclusion that self-government should be given in stages to India and other states. Their main influence is to be found in drawing a compromise between the out-and-out imperialists and the Labour party radicals. They also strongly influenced reform in India.[22]

The theory that the Round Table was the centre of an 'international anglophile network' is nonsense. It is based on the poorly researched theories of American historian Carroll Quigley.[23] The theory uses the common cod historian's model of 'influence by association': 'A was at school with B, B worked for the same company as C, C was a member of the same club as D, therefore A "controlled" D etc.'[24] The group would have been considered radical by most and this is what influenced Lawrence. The term 'Commonwealth' was devised by Curtis to distinguish his vision from 'empire'.[25] Lawrence was influenced by the theories of the Round Table and agreed with some of them, so any claim that he was a target for its members is fatuous. The members of the Round Table and the 'Set' were in certain cases one and the same. Many 'Round Tablers' were, like the 'Clivedens', appeasers. There were various reasons for this, but mainly because they thought, correctly, that another world war would destroy the Empire. Others, like Curtis and Brand, who often went to Cliveden, were not supporters of appeasement.

The Cliveden Set

Cliveden,[26] the country home of the English Astors, was an estate on the banks of the Thames near Maidenhead with a history going back to 1666. Nancy and Waldorf always denied the existence of a 'Cliveden Set'. Waldorf said it was 'absurd to associate Cliveden with conspiracies for any set of views' and Nancy wrote to *The Herald* national newspaper in the same vein.[27]

The term was an 'ideologically motivated falsification',[28] coined by a left-wing journalist named Claude Cockburn in the 1930s, who overstated the group's influence for personal reasons. He alleged that leading politicians convened at Cliveden to pull strings, and especially to devise means of appeasing Nazi Germany. Although subsequently dismissed as a myth the idea entered the popular anti-appeasement litany of the period.[29]

Lawrence's connection with Cliveden was mainly through Nancy Astor, from 1929 when he was posted to Mount Batten. He often visited Cliveden when he had time off. Other guests he could have met there included many prominent politicians including Churchill of course, Nazis like von Ribbentrop, Kipling, King George V, Gandhi, diplomats like Curzon, soldiers like Kitchener and Sam Hoare. The Astor family was one of the wealthiest families in the country, and, with their American branch, in the world. Nancy became the first female MP in 1919 (for Sutton, Plymouth). Harold Nicholson called Nancy 'a kindly, but inordinately foolish woman' with a subversive influence. In the 1930s he made some astute, critical observations on her gatherings.

> The harm which these silly, selfish hostesses do is really immense. They convey to foreign envoys the impression that policy is decided in their own drawing rooms . . . they create an atmosphere of authority and responsibility and grandeur, whereas the whole thing is a mere flatulence of the spirit.[30]

Robert Vansittart, the Conservatives' Permanent Under-Secretary of State to the Foreign Office, was Lawrence's cousin on his father's Irish side. His support for the Tories' anti-Fascist element was so strong that 'Vansittartism' passed into the English language as a term for extreme anti-German sentiment. He found he had increasing difficulties with the Cliveden Set and protested against their denials of the existence of a conscious pressure group. He noted their spontaneous inclination to criticize France rather than Germany, and to continuously blame him as head of the Foreign Office for any foreign transgression.[31] Lucy Kavaler, who wrote a study of the Astor family, felt there was indeed a Cliveden Set and although it did not possess the degree of power Claude Cockburn suggested, 'Its members unquestionably influenced the thinking of government.'[32] Because they were the Establishment, bonded by their education and background to the highest offices in England, the need to conduct any sinister plot did not exist. Lawrence's affiliation to the group was loose in the extreme, he was not directly involved in politics in 1935 and his visits to Cliveden were social.

In 1934, however, a number of his former friends from All Souls days, among them Round Tablers Curtis and Lothian, worked towards drawing him into an active political role. Despite his initial refusal to respond, in March of that year he did write a remarkably perceptive analysis of home defence for Curtis. It was a no-nonsense criticism that reflected his experience at both the crown and roots of the tree. He said that Beaverbrook and Rothermere were inept, he criticized the application of funds and warned of the threat that German aviation technology would present. His recommendations were for more aerodromes, better equipped aircraft firms, up to date designs, and more intelligent staff. Over a year later, on 7th May 1935, he received the letter from Nancy Astor inviting him to a dinner party at Cliveden: her intention was for him to meet Baldwin to discuss Defence and Curtis and Lothian would also be there. At that time the lobbies of the House of Commons and the newspapers were full of the impending reconstruction of the government. Lawrence declined Lady Astor's invitation, preferring to remain at Clouds Hill. Less than a fortnight later he was dead.

On May 21st, the day of his funeral, the Cabinet held a special meeting that approved the preparation of plans for a sub-committee to accelerate the expansion of the Air Force. This should have set a broad timetable for any future building work. On the same day, it was announced that a contractor had received instructions to proceed with the construction of RAF stations at Waddington, Lincolnshire, and Tern Hill, Shropshire. These instructions must have been in the pipeline for some time suggesting the expansion of the RAF was a foregone conclusion. On May 22nd *The Times* announced that an important debate was to take place in both houses of Parliament that day on Defence. Lord George Lloyd, Lawrence's friend from Arab Bureau days, was to bring forward a motion 'calling attention to the situation in regard to Imperial Defence'.[34] The speakers in the Commons included Churchill and Philip Sassoon. The debate was part of the growing realisation in Parliament of how serious the European crisis was becoming. How much had Lawrence's defence commitments affected the timing?

Despite having many friends within the Establishment, Lawrence's popular, strong, capable, yet unconventional personality may have represented a threat to many entrenched members of the government. At the beginning of the 1920s his views of a 'New Imperialism' were disturbingly new. In March 1934 Lawrence had written his analysis of the Defence problem, criticizing its inept handling, to Lionel Curtis. It would be obvious to anyone in contact with Curtis that Lawrence had thought deeply about home defence. Although threats to his life may have come from the English Establishment, the more likely threat would be from the enemies of the Empire, particularly after his confirmation of a commitment to home defence. The crisis in Afghanistan in 1928 revealed how easy it was for concocted media stories to affect political opinion. Lawrence was still an important public figure.

> I believe when the government reorganizes you will be asked to re-organize the defence forces. I will tell you what I have done already about it. If you will come to Cliveden, the last Saturday in May, you will never regret it. Please, please come. Lionel, Pat, Philip, and, for the most important, Stanley Baldwin. Please think about this.[35]

Lady Astor's letter shows that she had obviously already consulted others about the matter and was probably encouraged to pursue a meeting between T.E. and Baldwin by Curtis and Lothian. Everyone accepted Baldwin would be the new PM. The spring of 1935 was a watershed in Britain's awareness of German military intentions and imperial defence and the expansion of the Royal Air Force were at the forefront of government thinking. Lawrence refusal to attend what could be a meeting with geopolitical significance was because something inside had broken. As previously quoted:

> . . . there is something broken in the works, as I told you: my will, I think. In this mood I would not take on any job at all. So do not commit yourself to advocating me, lest I prove a non-starter.[36]

It was part of Nancy's nature to try and organize other people's lives, which she was now trying to do, but she had obviously misunderstood Lawrence's state of mind. Unfortunately, the precise nature of the job that was on offer never came to light. He forbade Nancy from making any further approaches to Baldwin.

Then, on the evening of the 12th, he told Pat Knowles he wanted to put their printing press project on hold 'for a year or two'; as he was expecting to be asked to undertake work 'relating to Home Defence'. The work would last until mid-1937. It seems that, because he refused to discuss the subject with Baldwin, he had already been approached by another party who had emphasized that the work was important. This may even have been his reason for refusing to meet Baldwin, because the work was secret, so secret that it was not to be discussed at this stage with the future Prime Minister. It could have been MI5, but a man like Lawrence would not have classed monitoring fifth column infiltration as being of such great importance. So the job remains undefined. A week later, this important public figure, who was in the running for contributing to some kind of nationally important work on home defence, was killed. On the 21st Baldwin suggested the trebling of RAF home numbers. The following month he was Prime Minister.

The evidence that Lawrence's crash was an assassination is evanescent. If the powers that be had wanted Lawrence out of the way they could hardly have made more of a botch up. Nobody sensible would have attempted a killing in broad daylight, with dozens of soldiers in the vicinity. Any such plot could not possibly have envisaged the two butcher's boys' involvement. Both Lawrence and the boys were on spontaneous outings. The perpetrators would have to have been waiting in the area for days for a suitable opportunity. But one thing that has always struck the author as odd about Lawrence's crash is the fact that it occurred so soon after he left the RAF. On 26th February 1935 he cycled out of Bridlington harbour. Almost 11 weeks later, he was dead. That short period of time was the first occasion since 1922 that he had been outside the strictures of the forces life: it was his first opportunity in 13 years of returning to the political scene.

Notes

1 *T.E. Lawrence Studies*. 11 July 2004.

2 Despite these views Legg stands by Meinertzhagen as being 'a great spook and a complete hero', standing head and shoulders above his detractors.

3 A.W. Lawrence to Dr. M. Lanes, 4th October 1965, in reply to a letter of 28th September 1963.

4 Article by Professor M.D. Allen, *Arab Studies Quarterly*, summer 1996.

5 *Middle East Diary*. Colonel R. Meinertzhagen C.B.E., D.S.O., the Cresset Press, London, 1959.

6 Paul Marriott mistakenly assumed this.

7 Henry Williamson to T.E. Lawrence. Shallowford, Filleigh, North Devon. 10/05/1935. Williamson's letter was published as part of *The Genius of Friendship* in the *Journal of the Henry Williamson Society*, no. 27, March 1993. The underlined section of this letter was omitted inadvertently from this publication which can only have increased the confusion. Lawrence had already received three letters from Williamson, predating the 10th May letter. These all referred to *Winged Victory*, its contents, and the fragment *Family Life*. For the full text of these see Appendix VII, p355.

8 Letter 551 to G. Wren Howard. 31. XII. 34. *The Letters of T.E. Lawrence*, Cape, 1938.

9 The letter was published in its full form in *The Journal of the T.E. Lawrence Society*, vol. 5 no. 2, spring 1996. J.M. Wilson alludes to this in the official biography, as do Knightley and Simpson, without stating specifically the manuscript's title.

10 Churchill was, at that time, 'a voice in the wilderness'. His changed from one side of the floor in the Commons to the other and the fall of Baldwin's 1929 government left him out of office for 10 years and in the political ante-room. His last official dealings with Lawrence had been at the Cairo conference of 1922.

11 Friends 1955: Baker.

12 B:LH

13 Ibid.

14 Quietness, p.42.

15 Today the whole area has been rebuilt. The present Belvedere Road lies a few 100 yards due south of the 'London Eye', passing in front of the Shell Centre.

16 The idea of a meeting between Maxwell Knight and Lawrence is speculative and cannot be substantiated.

17 Knightley and Simpson. p. 39.

18 Mack.

19 Elizabeth Monroe, *Britain's Moment in the Middle East, 1914-1956*. Chatto and Windus, London, 1963, p.134.

20 Knightley and Simpson. P. 38.

21 RT40, September 1920.

22 Correspondence with A. May, Hon. Secretary/Treasurer of the Round Table, December 2004.

23 *Tragedy and Hope – a History of the World in Our Time* by Carroll Quigley. MacMillan and Company, 1966. Quigley (1910–1977) was a professor of history and international relations at Georgetown University, U.S.A. For many years Quigley's account was uncritically accepted as authoritative. He claimed the RT had exercised disproportionate influence over the American and British governments for much of the 20th century. He cited 20 years of studying the RT's history, including, mendaciously, gaining exclusive access to its documents over a two-year period.

24 Correspondence with A. May, Hon. Secretary/Treasurer of the Round Table, December 2004.

25 Ibid.

26 Pronounced with a short 'i', as in 'cliff'.

27 'The Cliveden gatherings actually represented the diminishing 19th century phenomenon of the political house-party where sumptuous hospitality was mixed with opportunities to discuss politics but not to settle affairs of state.' *The Blackwell Biographical dictionary of British Political Life in the 20th Century*, p. 131, ed. K. Robbins, Blackwell, 1990.

28 Christopher Sykes.

29 '. . . out of this mélange came a predominant impression that a great part of the Cliveden set, Geoffrey Dawson among them, felt that Hitler's demands were "reasonable" and should be appeased. Baldwin and Chamberlain seemed to share this view.' R.G. Martin, *The Woman he Loved – the Story of the Duke and Duchess of Windsor*, p. 234, W.H. Allen, 1974.

30 Sir Harold Nicholson, *Diaries and Letters, 1930–1939, Vol. I*, ed. N. Nicholson, New York, Atheneum, 1966. pp. 396–7.

31 *The Mist Procession*, Lord Robert Vansittart, Hutchinson, London, 1958, pp. 482–3. Vansittart was lukewarm towards Lawrence in this biography.

32 *The Astors*, Lucy Kavaler, George C. Harrap and Co. 1966, p. 220.

33 Baldwin had already had two terms as Prime Minister, in 1923 and from 1924-29. On 26th August 1931 Lawrence, by chance, had met Baldwin two days after he had been appointed Lord President of the Council in Ramsay MacDonald's National Government.

34 *The Times*, 22/05/1935.

35 Viscountess Astor to T.E. Lawrence, 06/05/1935.

36 T.E. Lawrence to Viscountess Astor, 08/05/1935.

CHAPTER SEVENTEEN
Conclusions

There are layers of contradictory accounts about Lawrence's death. Contradictions about what Lawrence did in the camp; where he intended to go, what happened on the road, what happened immediately afterwards; there are even different views on what he was going to eat for lunch. In the absence of the principal witness, Lawrence himself, there can be no final answer. A number of factors contributed to his death:

1 The deteriorating mechanical condition of the Brough GW 2275, combined with its handling peculiarities, and the weakness of the front brake cable.
2 The undulating road surface.
3 Lawrence's love of speed and the possibility of his deteriorating eyesight.
4 The butcher's boys' playing the fool.
5 Lawrence being distracted seconds before the crash.

The evidence that anything other than an accident happened is scanty, but it does exist. The doubt is caused by:

1 The suppression of George Brough's evidence about the 'black paint' that he insisted was there for the rest of his life.
2 The failure of the driver of the 'black car' ever to come forward.
3 Pointers that some kind of 'cover up' or subterfuge had taken place, whether within the police investigation, the surgical services, the conduct of the inquest, or the military intelligence set up afterwards.
4 The peculiar time and circumstances of the accident: close to Lawrence's home and only a few months after he retired, when the European military situation was becoming more threatening and he was about to become involved in home defence.

The circumstances of Lawrence's death built upon the mystique he had created about himself. The media is aware the public loves a mystery. Anything that involves a suggestion of intrigue has selling power. Henry Williamson expanded on this in *The Genius of Friendship*:

> Once started the news-value of the accident increased like a snowball rolled down a white slope. The wealthier newspapers began to compete for sensational material.[1]

One London newspaper, he said, which was often hot on T.E.'s trail, concocted a cock-and-bull story about the accident being 'a trick while he slips out of England on a secret service mission'; 'mysterious heath fires near his woodland cottage, set ablaze by sinister agents of foreign chancelleries' to destroy his 'secret books and papers'. The paper then repudiated these stories with a 'categorical denial'. This was not difficult, since the tales had been made up specifically with such an end in mind in the newspaper's 'own flamboyant columns.'[2]

Colin Simpson concluded that 'The wilder theories of how and why Lawrence died that have flourished during succeeding decades may seem more attractive and in keeping with the spirit of his Arabian career, but the facts do not bear them out. They point to a far more prosaic end for one of Britain's great heroes.'[3] The crash was nevertheless recreated as a full-length murder fiction.[4] The author concludes that the crash had to have been an accident, just as those alive at the time stated. It was only after time and distance separated interested parties from the actual event that the speculation and myth developed. It is accepted that there was a black car, that Catchpole was a reliable and mentally stable witness, and that Bert Hargraves was riding irresponsibly.

Problems with the Crash Location

In March 1979 General Sir John Hackett unveiled a plaque in the Bovington Camp Medical Centre stating that T.E. Lawrence 'died near this spot on 22nd May 1935'. 'Near' in this case gave a very wide margin for error, as the original camp hospital was over 100 yards further east. 'Near' for the commemorative sapling oak planted on 13th May 1983 by Tom Beaumont, one of Lawrence's machine gunners in the Hejaz campaign meant within about 30 yards. The original wooden plaque was attacked by vandals and had to be replaced by a more substantial stone monument. The sapling was moved northwards by a few feet, to its present position.

Some time later the newly formed T.E. Lawrence Society erected a second stone plaque at the approximate site where Lawrence came to rest (they thought). This was located at the bottom of the roadside bank adjacent to a mature tree four or five yards from the edge of the road. Mike Chapman was astounded when he attended the unveiling ceremony, as there appeared to be no logical reason for its location. It is placed approximately 95 yards north of the memorial tree, but still far from the actual crash site. Using references from Marriott's book, this author was able to find what appeared to be the original 1935 road. 'Using this [the old concrete and post wire that denoted the Frampton estate boundary] as a marker the old road was discovered as it wound south [just to the west of the modern road] amongst thick foliage with an elevated ridge as its western banking.'[5]

In the MoD land immediately to the west of the new road two tracks are discernible in the undergrowth. Only the track furthest west has a noticeably elevated ridge as its western banking. The photograph on page 237 shows the old road as it is today, heavily overgrown with gorse, heather, rough grass and small fir trees. Yet a comparison with the view of the crash site facing north, taken in 1935, reveals the high western banking. Jeremy Wilson's explanation for the location of the memorial tree and plaque was that

> Both the tree and the stone are located where they are accessible to the public. The tree was presumably sited by the authorities at a point where parking could be provided at a reasonable cost. The stone was sited at a point then believed to be a bit closer to the crash site, in a place accessible from the car park but less evident to vandals. The wording on the stone does not claim to mark the actual site.[6]

Notes

1 *The Genius of Friendship*, H. Williamson, The Henry Williamson Literary Estate.
2 Ibid.
3 From 'Death of a Hero' by Colin Simpson, *Unsolved* magazine, Orbis Publications, issue 16 of Volume 2. This article attempted to solve the 'mystery' of Lawrence's death. Although Simpson had been assumed to be an expert on the subject, it contained so many errors that it cannot be taken as reliable.
4 *The Murder of Lawrence of Arabia* by Mathew Eden.
5 Marriott.
6 Communication with the author. June 2005.

Left: Philip Kerr (Lord Lothian) reading *Mein Kampf*.
Above right: Communist pamphlet debunking the appeasement policies of the Cliveden Set, 1930s.

PART FOUR

The Commentators

CHAPTER EIGHTEEN
John Bruce and the Sunday Times

In 1923 an uncouth-18-year-old Tank Corps private, whom Lawrence later described as 'the roughest diamond in our hut', shared the same barracks in Macelhayes Road, Bovington with T.E. and Arthur Russell. Forty-five years later he sent an 84-page loose-leaf typescript to the *Sunday Times* that was later published and caused a worldwide sensation, as he knew it would. He claimed that he had administered regular beatings to T.E. Lawrence at Clouds Hill, and other places, in the 1920s and '30s.[1] Arthur Russell remembered him from his time at Bovington:

> Now, there was supposed to be a man named Bruce in there, who had a lot to say about Lawrence afterwards. You may have heard of him. But Bruce never went up to the cottage once with us, he never went down into Bovington Camp, for feeding, with us, so I don't know what went on in his mind. He was in the same hut but the other side.[2]

Russell was amazed by the report that Lawrence had been flagellated by Bruce at Clouds Hill and never suspected they had any kind of relationship.

> It was said that Bruce was at the funeral. I didn't see him. Now you would have seen me because I was one of the bearers. He never approached me, never spoke, why? Was he there? I don't know. Mind you I didn't mix with a lot of people because, when the funeral was over. Pat Knowles and I went back to his place, we didn't go to the house to mix with the others. I mean, they all were big nobs.

From a letter he wrote to Charlotte Shaw in July 1924, Lawrence's opinion of Bruce is hardly warm:

> Kreutzer Sonata being played by Bruce (a Scotsman, inarticulate, excessively uncomfortable). He comes up here often on Sundays, will enter only if I'm alone, glares and glowers at me till I put some Beethoven on the gramophone, and then sits solid, with a heroic order of solidity about him: my room after four hours of Bruce feels like a block of granite, with myself a squashed door-mat of fossilized bones, between two layers. Good perhaps to feel like a prehistoric animal, extinct and dead and useless: but wondering also.

The story of Bruce's flagellation of Lawrence first became public on June 9th, 1968 in the *Sunday Times* in an article entitled *How Lawrence of Arabia Cracked Up*. This was one of a series of four articles entitled *The Secret Life of Lawrence of Arabia* by Philip Knightley and Colin Simpson, part of the *Sunday Times Insight* team. The typescript of Bruce's account of his relationship with Lawrence sent to the *Sunday Times* in March 1968 was an almost exact duplicate of a similar script Bruce had accidentally sent to Lawrence's brother Arnold in February 1967.[3]

The first person to meet Bruce was Simpson, a former Army officer nicknamed 'the Major'. Simpson became convinced of the truth of Bruce's story: 'He claimed he could authenticate all his claims about his relationship with Lawrence but did not want to give away too much until a financial arrangement could be agreed.'[4] The journalists decided to prepare a full length revisionist biography of Lawrence based on what Bruce had told them and other material they had accumulated. This was published as *The Secret Lives of Lawrence of Arabia* in 1969. Leonard Russell, who ran the review section of the *Sunday Times*, described it as a 'gold mine'. *The Secret Lives* was a lucrative, high profile business venture that could not fail. Even before the book had been written, enormous bids were made for it. McGraw-Hill of New York offered $65,000. With all the other offers the gross advances for the book totalled $100,000[5] still unwritten.

In the course of their investigations the *Sunday Times* employed a professional psychiatrist named Dr A.S.D. Leigh[6] as a medical adviser on Lawrence's condition in general and particularly in relation to the beatings. Philip Knightley's reason for employing Leigh was 'to avoid a Layman's conclusion' that could leave him open to attack from critics. The move was prompted by criticism of some of the earlier chapters from Dr John Mack, a psychiatrist at Harvard University, who suggested that the team did not have the psychiatric expertise to understand Lawrence's drives. Knightley suggested paying Leigh a fee of 100 guineas for his help and stated: 'Any advice you give me which will help me reach a conclusion about Lawrence of Arabia's emotional state will be strictly confidential between you and me.'[7] On 19th November 1968 Dr. Leigh replied to Knightly:

> Many thanks for first chapter on Lawrence . . . there's one point you ought to clear up because medically it is wrong and that is the story of the fracture of Lawrence's foot. I am afraid the peroneal nerve does not supply the whole area of the foot with sensory nerves and there is no known injury or damage to that nerve which would cause a total anesthesia of the foot. I don't think it is enough to say that he broke a small bone in the foot for I did that many years ago too and it didn't make me a masochist.[8]

On 4th December 1968 Knightley wrote to Leigh:

> Before I forget I understand that bowel movements have some significance in psychiatry. I have just noticed a piece in *Seven Pillars* expressing admiration for the Arabs because of their infrequent bowel action. He says something like: An Arab

army does not soil its camping places like the British Army does . . . But I would like to see this man because I am going to see Bruce early next week and this is an ideal opportunity for me to put to him any questions you would like answered. He is an old man, he is sick, for complicated reasons this is probably the last time he will agree to see anyone from the *Sunday Times.*

Knightley wrote to the Ministry of Defence:

Dr Leigh has succeeded in compiling a case history of Lawrence from available resources, but it would be of immense help to him if he could see the R.A.F. medical records for Lawrence's period in the Force. In general what Dr Leigh would hope to obtain from seeing the records is guidance for his own conclusions about Lawrence, rather than anything specific.

On the 17th Leigh wrote to Knightley:

I spent the weekend going over Lawrence's medical history and we are never going to get anywhere with it unless we have the original records from both the Army and the R.A.F. As my task is a medico-psychiatric assessment of Lawrence, I am trying to obtain various data about Lawrence's various illnesses.

Dr Leigh was trying to get hold of 'Dr. Marshall's Diary' from the British Museum, reputedly prepared by a medical officer who accompanied Lawrence in Arabia.[9] The Museum denied any knowledge of it. On December 19th 1968 Knightley and Simpson met Bruce at the Grosvenor Hotel, Chester. Knightley reported on Bruce's condition: 'He looks ill. His face is flushed and his cheeks and nose mottled with blue lines. His eyes water. He says he has bronchitis, a heart complaint which prevents him from exertion and emphysema (which he said began after being stabbed in the back in Cairo). He says he does not think he has long to live, but Colin says he looks better than he did six months ago.'

The RAF (Ministry of Defence, Adastral House) was able to send some records to Leigh on 8th April 1969. This is Lawrence's RAF registration form of August 1922:

R.A.F. Form 35 352087. Stamped: 4/9/22.
Examined: London R.D. 28/8/22. Aged 28.
John Hume Ross, Pole Hill, Chingford.
Clerk.
Previous foreign service = nil.
6/6 vision both eyes.
Normal hearing.
2 teeth defective. 6 teeth missing
Ht. 55½ ins. Wt. 122lbs.
Expiration: 30½ ins. Inspiration: 33½ ins.

Two scars left lower ribs.

Condition of nervous system: fine (eyes, hands, tongue).

History of Venereal Disease = Nil.

Vaccination Marks: 3 left.

Mentality: Alert.

Sufficient teeth for mastication.

Fit for General Service.

RAF registration form of September 1925:

R.A.F. Form 35. Date: 7/ Sept.1925 01748

Shaw examined West Drayton 21/8/25 age 31

Previous service: 2 years R.T.C.

6/6 vision both eyes.

No teeth defective.

6 teeth missing

Ht. = 65½ ins.

Chest expired: 32 ins Chest inspired: 35 ins.

Wt. = 128 lbs.

Distinctive body marks, Cicatrices (painful, adherent), fractures:

Four superficial scars left side.

Three superficial scars lower part of back.

Conditions of heart, lungs and nervous system: normal.

Passed fit for service by W. Coghlan F/Lt.

So Lawrence's two defective teeth were fixed during his time in the R.T.C.[10] His increased weight and chest inspiration indicate he was fitter and stronger when he left the R.T.C. than when he joined it. The Army records Centre at Hayes, Middlesex informed Leigh that they were unable to locate the records of Shaw's time in the Tank Corps, but gave his date of registration as 12/3/23 and his date of transfer to the RAF as 19/8/25. In December 1968 Dr Leigh wrote to Dr Lumsden of the London School of Hygiene and Tropical Medicine about the malaria Lawrence picked up in France as a young man: 'Lawrence was a pathological liar so it is very difficult to pin him down on anything, but he claims he developed malaria as a result of a stay in the Camargue when he was 16 – that is in 1904.'

In January 1969 Leigh wrote to Charles P. Allen[11] of Aldenburgh, Suffolk. He had conducted Lawrence's post mortem. Leigh's scepticism about Lawrence's tales led him to ask:

The crucial point is whether he had scars of the alleged bullet wounds on his body and of the bayonet wound he is supposed to have been had inflicted upon him by the Turkish Bey at Deraa and also whether he had any scars of the alleged flogging which occurred then . . . I rather suspect that he had no scars on his on his body but I may be wrong.

There was, apparently, no reply to this letter. Although Leigh was an expert in his field, that very expertise in his work must surely have coloured his attitude to the Lawrence case. His attitude to his vocation is revealed in a slightly bizarre letter he wrote to another psychiatrist, Dr Dingwall of Battle, Middlesex, on 10th January 1969:

> I do the work on obscenity for the D.P.P.[12] and have had, of course, access to their collection of erotica. And I must say that appearing in courts sharpens one's wits v. much. I think I can say that I have more than the usual knowledge of sado-masochism and I know that you will be interested to hear that I have had the only case of infibulation since that one you described in your book.

Dingwall wrote back:

> I read the Bruce papers last night and find them very puzzling. Would the 'old man', if a fantasy, throw any light on the financial dealings? It seems all linked up with some complicated copyright negotiations with trustees etc., but I would suppose from your letter that the others must know of the existence or otherwise of this person. From the book it does not look to me as if Bruce thought that it was a complete fantasy, but if it were it would throw a good deal of light on Lawrence's general behaviour and attitudes.

An article by John Mack, the Harvard Professor of Psychiatry, was published in *The Times* Saturday Review on February 8th 1969.[13] Entitled 'The Inner Conflict of T.E. Lawrence', it attempted to describe the condition that engendered the 'Old Man' character:

> The war left Lawrence an inwardly shattered man . . . Notes written during Lawrence's Air Force basic training in 1922 and letters to a friend in 1923 from the Tank Corps . . . reveal a powerful need for self-degradation and an extraordinarily debased self-regard.
>
> The war experiences, especially the assault at Deraa, also precipitated in Lawrence a complex set of symptoms, including a flagellation ritual and various other forced ordeals he required of himself to extinguish sexual impulses and fulfil a need of punishment while at the same time adding to his sense of degradation.
>
> . . . In order to get another serviceman to carry out the beating while at the same time absolving him of responsibility, Lawrence fabricated a complicated tale about an 'Old Man', a certain uncle (he had no uncle at the time) who demanded his enlistment, the whippings, swimming in the freezing North Sea, and other ordeals as punishment, redemption and rehabilitation . . . Lawrence kept intact the structure of this symptom complex . . . through an elaborate correspondence between himself, the few others he involved in the problem, and the 'Old Man'.

The story of the 'Old Man' had first appeared in Bruce's original statement to the *Sunday Times*. Bruce remained convinced of his existence right up until his death. In a letter to Colin Simpson from Wrexham in July 1968, after the series of articles had been printed, he wrote: 'Congratulations – Philip and you did a wonderful job on Lawrence, your painstaking research has been well rewarded. Please tell me though, why you did not make more use of the old man? THERE WAS ONE regardless of A.W.L. Did you play it COOL for writ reasons?' Earlier in 1968, on May 6th, Bruce had written an elaborate five-page typescript letter to Simpson alluding to a secret file at the Air Ministry that was concerned with Lawrence's spying activities in the Air Force. He also reiterated his belief in the 'Old Man'. None of this letter was ever reproduced in Knightley and Simpson's book.

> Dear Colin,
> Thanks for your letter of the 6th. I knew of the Spy File at the Air Ministry, but never thought you would get within a mile of it --- good for you, did it give you a shock? I'm more pleased about this than you would imagine, because you can have no doubts in your mind, that as far fetched my story looked in the beginning, unbelievable really, your digging must expel any doubts. The old man bothers me still, and I won't have that there wasn't one.[14]

An alternative explanation for the flagellation ritual is provided by a note on one of Dr Leigh's Out-Patient Medical Notes forms for January 1969. This was of a conversation he had on 29 January 1969 with the Lawrence biographer Anthony Nutting[15] who told him Lawrence had told Dr Ernest Altounyan[16] that he was beating himself to prepare for an ordeal. The main body of the May 6th letter recalled an incident so fantastic that no account of it has ever been reproduced in any biography. Here Bruce claimed that he was taken, in 1928, by a man named Eric Stillman, an associate of Lawrence, to India to help Lawrence out. Lawrence, then stationed at Karachi, had told Bruce in a series of letters that 'The senior officers in the camp resented him and life was becoming unbearable, and that the Indian government were keeping a tag on him, because of rumours. Camp officials wanted to get rid of him, but Whitehall officials refused even for him to be transferred up country.' Stillman told Bruce that senior officers in Karachi wanted Lawrence away from the camp; out of India as soon as possible, not saying whether the Indian government or the camp officers were responsible. Lawrence's presence in the country was unacceptable.

Stillman said his contact man in India had absconded. A letter had come via diplomatic bag from Lawrence, from Delhi: he wanted Stillman to take Bruce out with him if necessary. Stillman doubted Lawrence would be willing to co-operate with anyone not known to him. Bruce was briefed for the trip and arrived in Karachi early in May 1928. He would not describe how he got there. He was put up in an hotel and the following day went on a fishing trip out on the Indian Ocean. As soon as they were clear of the harbour Lawrence appeared from below.

When Lawrence learned that Whitehall wanted him up country, he had to get rid of loads of papers, far too much to burn in the camp without drawing attention to himself, because, as far as I [Bruce] was to understand, only the very senior officers knew he was going, and when. A camp lorry took four sacks of papers to a dump, some miles from the camp off the beaten track. These papers had to be looked at before burning, he did the looking, I did the burning. The lorry driver having been sent back.

This story was never recounted in any of Knightley and Simpson's publications – hardly surprising since it is so unlikely. Bruce's letter stated that, as they were burning the papers, some native boys arrived. They gave them some money and they left. But subsequently an older, larger group of natives arrived who demanded money. Lawrence and Bruce paid them. It was not enough and the boys threw objects at them. Then some manhandled Lawrence. He pushed one and they ran off screaming. Some time later two of the boys returned with some men. They shouted at him for striking the youth:

Lawrence tried to explain in Urdu, but they would not have any explanations, and things looked ugly. While all this was going on we kept on burning, till at last we were finished, except what Lawrence wanted to keep. We made to leave, but they surged round us, pushing and pulling, till I got a smack across the mouth with something, I struck out at one of them, and before we knew where we were, we landed on the ground, with fists flying in all directions.

Bruce said that the natives then stole everything they had, even their pants, and threw the remaining papers on the fire. They were left sitting up with their hands tied behind their backs while an adolescent watched over them. Bruce said Lawrence then offered the boy the gold in his teeth and the boy cut their bonds. As they were walking back, two men on donkeys approached whom they overpowered taking their donkeys and pantaloons. They released the donkeys on finding a road and were picked up by some MPs. Bruce had 'hell's own delight' in explaining to the police where he got his clothing. This fabrication did not undermine Bruce's credibility with the *Times* team altogether, as it so clearly could have done, and they proceeded to publish. In January 1971 Knightly wrote to Dr Leigh from the *Sunday Times* offices: 'I beg you to write your definitive psychiatric study of Lawrence as soon as you can so that we can put Mac[k] to the wall once and for all.'[17]

Inevitably during the course of the investigation there was a considerable amount of communication with Professor A.W. Lawrence, T.E.'s brother. It was A.W. who had first allowed them to examine a closed collection of Lawrence's letters in the Bodleian Library, Oxford that were at the time embargoed until 2000. The Professor confessed at a meeting in London that he knew one day Bruce's story would come out, and he was prepared to allow the *Sunday Times* team to investigate, providing the story was treated with understanding and sympathy.

An unusual instruction was written out on a paper napkin in an Italian restaurant in Soho:

The Keeper of Western manuscripts, Bodleian Library.

Dear Hunt,
Will you kindly allow Mr. Colin Simpson to read anything he may wish in the collection of T.E. Lawrence material you are holding incommunicado till 2000.
Yours sincerely,
A.W. Lawrence.[18]

A.W. Lawrence monitored the progress of the research. In June 1968 he wrote to Simpson:

Dear Mr. Simpson,
I have posted back to Knightley the draft of the next article. It is an excellent piece of work. It would be very unpleasant for Mrs. Knowles if the data of Bruce's you are to publish was to include the story of the beating in the upstairs room. (Which she has to show to visitors; the draft I rejected gave a description of the room). If you can please do not refer to the cottage in this connection.

Writing to Dr. Mack in May I repeated what you had shown me about swimming in cold sea under B's supervision, and said it fitted with self-cure for nervous breakdown, adding 'so too, maybe, in the abstract does beating, since it was the accepted treatment for lunatics in Bedlam. (Not perhaps so wrongly as is now generally supposed, if the effect was comparable to that of electric shock???)'. He replied 'You are quite right in your idea about electric shock therapy, for many of the early theories of its efficacy, especially by psychoanalysts, had to do with the idea of cure through beating, although it now appears it has some additional unknown effects on the nervous system.'

In May 1969 Professor Lawrence wrote to Leigh:

You have told me over the telephone that the records at the Ministry of Defence dealing with my brother's first enlistment contradict, by silence, the story of the mass of recent marks on his back given in the *Sunday Times'* third article, based on a statement by Captain W.E. Johns.[19] The records say nothing of these marks but mention only two scars on the left breast. You said that you would ask the *Sunday Times* to omit any reference to this statement by Captain Johns in the book. Do you know whether they have done so?

Although Leigh failed to get a reply from the surgeon C.P. Allen, Dr Alan H. Richardson wrote to him. Richardson was Lawrence's cypher clerk in the Hedjaz campaign of 1916–1918 and had administered medical treatment to him. On 16th July he wrote to Leigh's Harley Street surgery from Bolton:

Now I must make my position quite clear. I was serving in HMS *Humber* as Surgeon-Lieutenant RN but on reaching Akaba I was 'lent' to Lawrence to assist in keeping in touch with the Arab Bureau as well as being in charge of the mixed collection of Arabs, British and Indian contingents making up the entire population of Akaba as far as medical arrangements were concerned.

As far as Lawrence was concerned I was more of a confidential fellow officer than a M.O. I worked with Lawrence and Lloyd [later Lord Lloyd] as cipher officer taking messages direct from the two fellows and sending them off in a special code known only to Lawrence and myself. I did not use the naval ciphers in my sole charge in the *Humber*. On occasion I went up country with the armoured cars or on trotting camels. None of this was medical work and I went well armed on Lawrence's advice. This was uncivilized war and as Lawrence remarked when advising me to 'never be without your revolver', 'you will not find the Genever [Geneva] code in operation in these parts.'

Dr Richardson wrote a second letter dated 22nd July 1969:

Re. T.E. Lawrence's medical condition. Have you ever worked out East? The Britisher is quite a different animal abroad to the home living relation. Mostly he 'knows it all'.

'Doc, I've got another dose of malaria coming on and I'm running out of quinine', or 'My dysentery has flared up again'. T.E. came to me on only a few occasions, boil on the back of his neck and a deep seated collection of pus in the palm of his hand. The sharpest knife I could get my hands on was the treatment. Of course I helped him with simple remedies for excess of sun burn and raw patches after extra long camel rides.

There was simply everything ashore, horrible untreated wounds, dysentery, smallpox, cholera, liver abscesses. Lawrence had his share of pyrexias but no one really bothered about that sort of thing. It was and had to be a tough world. There was only one line of treatment, keep going, don't lie down – you might not be able to get up again! Nobody ever complained, least of all Lawrence. If a man was not tough then he died. So he saw to it that he was tough!!

Bruce's Unpublished Accounts

Not all of Bruce's original statement to the *Sunday Times* went into print. At the end of a paragraph mentioning Lawrence's initial meeting with Privates Russell and Palmer:[20] 'Palmer was Lawrence's choice. He was a gentler kind of chap without brawn, and seemed to have read a little', the following passage did not make it into print:

Lawrence was getting along nice. His new friends were about him most of the time, and others kept their distance, but he was getting careless. His mail was increasing daily, some of which being re-addressed. His motorbike turned up and was admired by all in the camp. Crowds of soldiers came to the hut to inspect it. He was creating curiosity and most certainly making the troops talk. I told him he was digging his own grave, I wasn't far wrong either, his first encounter with authority was not far away. It was on the following Wednesday afternoon. A military funeral was heading towards Wool from the camp, when Lawrence went roaring past three times on his bike. The officer in charge had put him in the guard room and, when he was searched, they found two motor licences on him, one in the name of Shaw and the other Lawrence.[21]

He got away with it, how, I don't know. This gave the troops more to talk about. Then it happened, the press got to hear he was in the Tank Corps and the next day the papers were full of it, and he had to leave camp. He was away ten days and returned as though nothing had happened.

Bruce's account of why Lawrence changed his surname to Shaw differs considerably from that given by Russell:

When he came back from Karachi I asked him why he changed his name by deed poll to Shaw while he was away. He said that when he was double-crossed over 'Revolt' what was there left; he was depending on that money which was given to the R.A.F. fund, because it was his intention to leave the ranks on his return. He would now have to stay at least until 1935. He wanted to get rid of the Lawrence tag, and as the Shaws had been my best friends for years, he would take their name for the rest of his life . . .

Until the day he died he never quite got over the Revolt affair. There were fits of depression and temper, which was quite foreign to his nature and often too. For instance when he came back from Karachi in 1929 I was with him when he threw a small box in the Thames from Waterloo Bridge. I had never seen this box before as it had been sent from Oxford to Barton Street that morning. I understand it contained medals and decorations, but there must have been other things in the box as well. It was 6' x 6' x 4' and weighed about ten pounds. When he threw it over he said 'Goodbye Lawrence'. I asked him why had he done that? He said 'Remember my name is now Shaw, anything I have which belonged to Lawrence, I have no further use for.'

How far are these statements to be accepted as the truth? Arthur Russell corroborates Lawrence threw his medals in the Thames, but probably shortly after he returned from the Paris Peace Conference. Bruce continued:

Some time after this we were in Clouds Hill, we had just arrived, our coats were still on. He went straight to the gramophone records, looked at Elgar's 'Land of Hope and Glory', and smashed it in the fire place. He then took his coat off and sat down at his desk and started writing a letter. I said 'What the hell did you do that for?' . . . 'I have been wanting to do that for years.' Some time later he bought a new one.

There was also Bruce's account of why Lawrence left the Colonial Office. The generally accepted story is that, despite Churchill's entreaties, after 18 months with the department, an emergency appointment in Lawrence's view, he was ready to leave of his own accord in July 1922. John Bruce's story of the events is more tempestuous. While Lawrence was at the Colonial Office the Anglican Bishop in Jerusalem, Dr McInnes, became disturbed at a report in a Zionist publication that Lawrence had pointed out to Chaim Weizmann 'The Anglican Mission in Jerusalem was a hot bed for anti-Jewish propaganda' (Bruce's words). McInnes took offence and demanded an apology from Lawrence. McInnes appealed to Winston Churchill who considered that since the publication had appeared before Lawrence joined the Colonial Office, it was no concern of that department. Lawrence refused to deny the statement. Much of this is recorded in letters 155 and 156 of the complete edition of *The Letters of T.E. Lawrence*. Bruce's version however, was slightly different:

> The Prime Minister sent for Lawrence, and told him he had to bring the matter to a successful conclusion without delay, failing which, he would have to be asked for his resignation. Lawrence was furious, the Prime Minister and he had heated words, resulting in him being told to go, but before it became official, he tendered his resignation to Churchill's secretary the same day, and [this] was published in the press a few days later. Whitehall was aglow with rumours, and speculation which soon reached the city, [but] by then accounts as to what had happened between him and the Prime Minister are unprintable. There is no doubt, Lawrence brought this situation on himself and paid dearly, because he had written to Dr. McInnes and told him he was not fit to brush Dr. Weizmann's boots, nor his.[22] If ever there was a red rag to a bull this was it.[23]

Bruce says the 'Old Man', through his publisher, prevented Lawrence from arranging a contract regarding the copyrights for *Seven Pillars* because he had refused to apologize to Dr McInnes, who had (according to Bruce) already contacted the 'Old Man'. The 'Old Man' called him a cheat, and a liar; told him he had dragged the family name through the gutter. He had turned his back on God, he had insulted a Bishop, insulted King George at Buckingham Palace, he had ruined the life of a great Foreign Minister, (Lord Curzon) and called him a 'bastard', not fit to live amongst decent people. The matter was of such a serious nature that a meeting of the family would have to be called, to see what was to be done with him. The alternative would be for T.E. to place himself in his hands unreservedly, which affected the copyrights etc.[24]

The published account of Lawrence's resignation by Knightley and Simpson simply said 'Lawrence was now ready to say goodbye to the Colonial office. Churchill made several attempts to persuade him to stay on, dangling before him the promise of a glittering career. But Lawrence was not interested.'

On 11th January, 1969, having read Bruce's original page typescript, Dr Dingwall concluded:

Bruce, of course, is not a satisfactory witness. It looks to me as if he embroiders and exaggerates with half-truths and suggestions [that] make it appear that he knows a great deal more than he does. It is certainly a very odd story and I am not sure how the *Sunday Times* and yourself are connected with it and in what capacity. My experience of newspapers is that their 'research' is occasionally v. good indeed but usually v. poor and not worth much from a scholarly point of view.

The stories told by Bruce were unacceptable to many of Lawrence's old friends and disbelieved. Tom Beaumont considered them 'piffle'. In February 1973 he wrote to a friend:

To me the 'Bruce muck' seems absolutely ridiculous. Knowing T.E. as I did I cannot for the life of me even imagine that such things happened. I still say that it is a load of B.

... You must remember Leo that I was in the desert a couple of years and the saying goes 'live with them to know them', so how can I be expected to believe the muck and rubbish written about him.[25]

In October 1969 Helen Beaumont had written to the same ex-Tank Corps soldier: 'The *Sunday Times* said they double-checked it and double-checked it from other sources. When I put it to Mrs Rivington "Is it true?" she said "A.W.L. says it is"'[26]

On 25th September 1969 *The Sunday Times* held a kind of launch party at Thompson House, Grays Inn Road, London to which they invited a number of Lawrence's old friends. L.B. Anwyl was at Bovington Camp with Lawrence in the 1920s and remembered pushing coal around in a handcart with him to the married quarters.[27] Of the *Sunday Times* ceremony he wrote: 'It turned out to be a farce and I was very much involved, as I was the only one present in the room who was aware who Bruce was, and was ready to openly denounce him ... when to my utter amazement he disappeared, and no-one met or spoke to the man who had been responsible for the ruination of my hero's character.'[28]

Helen Beaumont thought his rapid disappearance from the 'do' was more than odd: 'Perhaps he got cold feet and nerves ... I am not clear as to why anyone should tip him off to get out of that reception.' Mr Anwyl met Bruce over a cup of tea the same day at the Tavistock Hotel. He thought *The Times* had deliberately set him up with Bruce expecting fireworks. 'He was locked in his room, and I had to shout and ask him to see me, after he had called: "Who are you? What do you want? Who sent you?" etc.' The two men faced each other defiantly, but Bruce was obviously fearful: 'A strange bitterness surrounded his talk. I could not recognize him but felt he knew enough of Bovington and some of the officers and NCOs to convince me he was there with me.'[29]

After 1969 John Bruce disappeared from the public scene. He had been responsible for one of the most scandalous revelations about a public figure's private life in publishing history. His motivations had been entirely ignoble and unrepentantly financial, and all those involved in the narrative, including Lawrence himself, agreed that he was an entirely unpleasant man. Although many of his claims were untrue, there was a core of truth in the story he told. He had carried his experiences with him for three decades without going to the press, but the author was told he had blackmailed A.W. Lawrence for years.[30] The story he told changed completely the understanding of Lawrence's life and psychology after the war, although hints as to the motivations for his conduct had been made by earlier biographers. The revelation also led people back to Aldington's accusation that T.E. was homosexual, untrue according to all those who knew him personally. John Bruce was a sick man physically and some would say mentally when he approached the *Sunday Times* in 1966. He died in the summer of 1971.

Notes

1 Bruce is mentioned in a number of Lawrence's letters. A.W. Lawrence said in 1985 that he was aware that this had happened immediately after T.E.'s death but said nothing about it.

2 In *The Secret Lives of Lawrence of Arabia*, (1969), Philip Knightly and Colin Simpson quote John Bruce: 'It was the usual type of Army hut. Inside there was a partition in the middle, dividing it into two, but without a door. There were beds on either side and two large stoves, one in each section. Lawrence took the bed which was second to the partition on the top section. I took the bed which was second to the partition on the first section, and on the opposite side.'

3 A full account is given in Dr. John Mack's *A Prince of Our Disorder* (1976).

4 From A *Hack's Progress* by Philip Knightley, Jonathan Cape 1997.

5 $0.6 million-plus today.

6 Dr Denis Leigh BSc, MD, FRCP was a distinguished World Health Organisation psychiatrist and Secretary General of the World Psychiatric Association in 1969.

7 Letter from Philip Knightley to Dr Dennis Leigh, 29th October 1968.

8 Lawrence fractured his fibula during a playground fight at Oxford High School in 1900 when he was 12. He never grew after that accident.

9 'Doc' Marshall was known to Lawrence; see his letter to H.W. Bailey, 4th February 1923: 'British Minister to Hejaz. Lives in Jeddah'. MB.

10 By April 1929 16 of Lawrence's upper and lower teeth had gold fillings.

11 See Part Three.

12 Director of Public Prosecutions.

13 Mack went on to write the Pulitzer-Prize winning psychiatric study of Lawrence, *A Prince of Our Disorder*, presumably as a response to Knightly and Simpson's work. He was killed in a motor accident in London, March 2005.

14 Colin Simpson believed that the Air Ministry file was a specification for an RAF marine craft. When asked what he thought of Bruce, Simpson said he was a 'shit' and a liar. A.W. Lawrence had been paying an allowance to John Bruce's wife for years, presumably to keep Bruce quiet.

15 Former Minister of State for Foreign Affairs, Nutting had published *Lawrence: the Man and the Motive* in 1961. He reviewed Knightley and Simpson's book unfavourably in the press.

16 Dr Ernest Altounyan was a surgeon, the son of an old friend from Syria. Lawrence was in communication with him in 1934 whilst stationed at Bridlington.

17 That there were points of contention, not to say tension, between Knightley and Simpson and Mack is obvious from this letter.

18 From *A Hack's Progress* by Philip Knightley, Jonathan Cape 1997.

19 Johns was the recruiting officer at Lawrence's first registration for the RA. at Henrietta Street, Covent Garden on 28th August 1922. He was never a captain. He appointed the himself to the rank when he authored the Biggles books. There is no mention of Johns' account of the physical examination in the Panther 1971 reprint of *The Secret Lives of Lawrence of Arabia*.

20 Page 190 of the Thomas Nelson 1969 edition.

21 This appears to have occurred early in July 1924. On 27th July Lawrence wrote to Alan Dawnay: 'Lord help us: did I write miserably? Learn the unworthy reasons: (a): being choked off by the Adjutant for impertinence – to wit, passing an officer at more than twice his speed, while motor-cycling.'

22 What Lawrence actually wrote was: 'I suspect you want my denials only to assure yourself and triumph over Dr. Weizmann, a great man whose boots neither you nor I, my dear Bishop, are fit to black.'

23 Quote from pp11 and 12 of Bruce's original statement to the *Sunday Times*. The document at this point is quite sophisticated in its understanding of the political background, suggesting Bruce may have had more than a little help in the drafting of it.

24 Ibid.

25 Letter from Tom Beaumont to 'Leo', 6th February 1973.

26 Letter from Mrs. H. Beaumont to 'Leo', 15th October 1969.

27 In the cold winter of 1923 Lawrence went on a coal hunt for his hut in H Lines. He climbed into a coal yard and purloined a sack of coal for his comrades.

28 Letter from L.B. Anwyl to the Officer Commanding, Bovington Camp, September 5th, 1973.

29 Ibid.

30 Conversation with Colin Simpson, August 2006.

CHAPTER NINETEEN

Edward Robinson: a Bogus Biographer

During the course of the research for this book one of the things that became painfully obvious was that, although there was an initial joy in discovering little known, unpublished accounts of people who had close personal friendships with Lawrence, as the number of these accounts increased, one realised that either Lawrence had a huge number of unrecorded friendships or at least some of these reminiscences were untrue. Since 1935 there have been hundreds of bogus accounts of people saying they met Lawrence or claiming to know him.

J.M. Wilson had a lot to say about this in his introduction to his 1989 biography. Wilson found four main sources of misinformation. First, people who knew Lawrence sometimes found it difficult to distinguish their own recollections from the popular legend. Second, although many in the ranks, like Dixon and Russell, refused to capitalize on their friendship with him, a few, such as John Smith, did trade on it and fabricated incidents and anecdotes to bolster their importance in his life. Third, the desire for 'new' information on Lawrence led some to fabricate ingenious fictions that tied in with well known events. John Bruce is the exemplar, who embroidered his recollections considerably. And fourth, some accounts of Lawrence's life were distorted to fit a pre-conceived theory. This could be said of Lawrence James' 1990 book *The Golden Warrior*. Concerning Lawrence's flagellation at Deraa, James quoted as a source a field diary of a Royal Field Artillery unit at Akaba saying that on the day of the incident Lawrence was on an armoured car reconnaissance, proving the beating never happened. The diary was compiled six months after the event and is contradicted by many contemporary documents. The reason for James' error, Wilson postulates, is that he had already convinced himself the Deraa event was fabricated. In the 1920s, whilst the Lawrence myth was beginning to develop all over the world before the eyes of millions, 'a second, much darker legend was inevitably forming in the minds of certain (however understandably) critical people. The result was a number of scurrilous stories about Lawrence which, decades later, would be credibly quoted.'[1]

A classic example was the story of Lawrence attending a flagellation party in London in 1922 organised by one Jack Bilbo, a.k.a 'Bluebeard'. This was cited by Desmond Stuart in his 1977 book *T.E. Lawrence* and by James. Details of the dubious event were due to be made public by a German magazine. Lawrence supposedly contacted Edward Shortt, the Home Secretary, asking for the deportation of Bilbo and the suppression of the publication. However, according to James, no copy of the letter was kept in Home office files. Colin Simpson was the man who discovered the Bilbo story.[2]

A.W. Lawrence writing to H. Montgomery Hyde in June 1977 said he thought Stewart's biography was 'a fine example of what Kipling called "Higher Cannibalism"'. Simpson told him that a rival newspaper was trying to rush out John Bruce's story ahead of the *Sunday Times* and

> ... turning the public records upside down as the papers of a man called Jack Bilbo are now on the market. A non sequitur, and were there any Bilbo papers? And my reply 'Bilbo put a completely false libellous story about T.E. in a book he published in German (T.E. stopped the translation) some 40 years ago'. Actually over 40 years. I must tell you ... that some items disappeared from the Bodleian collection in 1968 and not all were recovered – verb. sap.[3]

J.N. Lockman in his illuminating little book *Meinertzhagen's Diary Ruse*, discussed the Bilbo case: 'Even without knowing about Bilbo (which an hour in the British Library would have cured), any researcher reading Lawrence's lighthearted letter to his solicitor should have recognised that the case was, almost certainly, not a serious one.'[4]

Ever since Lowell Thomas's *With Lawrence in Arabia* (1922) every biography of Lawrence has had some form of error in it. But the one book that can be regarded as *totally* bogus was 28 years in gestation.

In 1935 the young Edward H.T. Robinson was approached by the Oxford University Press to write a biography specifically aimed at boys. This was entitled *Lawrence – the Story of his Life* and was relatively successful, running into several editions. It contained 250 pages and 32 plates. It was published in the same year as Liddel Hart's approved biography. At the beginning was an introduction by A.W. Lawrence that lent it authority:

> The author of this book was himself an eye-witness of many of the scenes described. I have many of the proofs of the book, and find no errors of fact, while the general picture seems to me as accurate as could reasonably be expected in a book of its purpose.
> July 1935
> A.W. Lawrence

From Robinson's preface:

> Fifteen years ago, to satisfy the curiosity of a small circle of friends, I wrote a two hundred page study of my two and a half years association with Colonel Lawrence and his Arabs. It caused a slight sensation especially when those who read Lawrence's story realized that I had, in fact, understated the adventures ...

I was in a position to watch Lawrence and his fellow officers, and the Arabs, in all their moods, I handled a large number of the dispatches that passed up and down the line.

Robinson said he was asked to write this first book by A.W. who also recommended him to Jonathan Cape to write a second, more comprehensive biography aimed at an adult readership. It was over ten years before the book was eventually published, by which time it had lost A.W.'s and Cape's support. The firm that eventually published the book *Lawrence the Rebel* was Lincolns-Prager of Seymour Place, London, W.1. The first edition came out in the spring of 1946. It had followed a rough road to the presses.

Robinson 's second book, *Lawrence the Patriot Rebel* was about to be published by Jonathan Cape in June 1937. However, Cape did not follow through. Ostensibly this was because Robinson did not fulfil his obligation to secure leave to quote matter that was A.W Lawrence's copyright. It had been found that *Lawrence the Patriot Rebel* contained 'inaccurate transcriptions of British official documents, with new phrases and sentences interpolated. Long passages were allegedly extracts from a diary Robinson had kept during military operations in Arabia 1917-18.'[5] Some copies of Robinson's book were published as jacketless proof copies by Cape in 1938. It was subtitled *A War History by Edward Robinson*. The books contained 399 pages and 53 chapters. In its introduction Robinson wrote: 'This book would have been impossible but for the tolerance and kindness of T.E.'s brother, A.W. Lawrence, and for many reasons my debt to him cannot be repaid.'

Scrawled across the title page of the one book retained by the Bodleian Library is a note written much later in A.W. Lawrence's spidery handwriting: 'The author was proved to be an imposter who had only spent a few days in Heja (at Akaba only?) and this book was suppressed before publication.'

E. H.T. Robinson had spent the 1914–18 war as a clerk in Cairo and his only known personal contact with the Arabian campaign was a short visit to Akaba (probably in charge of a consignment of stores). When hostilities ceased he was stationed at Damascus where (according to Lawrence's driver S.C. Rolls) he made extensive enquiries of the British 'other ranks' who had taken part in the desert war.

Back in England he produced a typescript that he said was produced from shorthand notes made to T.E. Lawrence's dictation at Akaba. These he deposited in the Imperial War Museum. Anyone reading portions of Robinson's final book *Lawrence the Rebel*, large portions of which are based on this typescript, can easily see that the style obviously is not that of T.E. None of the phrasing rings true. In the Prologue of the 1938 proof copy of *Lawrence the Patriot Rebel* Robinson describes his first encounter with Lawrence:

> I had, up to then, seen little of Lawrence but one incident led me into strange paths. I
> had wandered out to the foothills of the Wadi Ithm, from Akaba in order to keep my

eye in with a rifle. Two or three of Lawrence's men went with me, both as company and guard, and, always, a tolerable shot, I was amused – indeed vaingloriously pleased – at showing them what could be done at a fair distance with the aid of sights.

Once comfortably settled, I had reached the 'showing off' stage when a gentle question slewed me round. Lawrence was standing behind me, fidgeting with his sandaled feet, and glancing from my position to my mark, 'That's quite a habit, isn't it?' he queried.

'I thought I'd show them what can be done with a good rifle' I replied.

Lawrence laughed, 'Well, I think I shall be using you'. He hesitated for a moment, and then added, almost shyly, 'if you'd like it.'[6]

The IWM notes were in two parts. The first consisted of eleven pages of shorthand notes on a lined pad. The initial page was headed 1918 and the occasional Arabic proper name appeared in longhand. The final half page was signed 'TEL'. The second part consisted of 17 pages of typescript on foolscap. The IWM recorded this as being 'donated by E.H.T. Robinson, accessioned 20th July 1936' and was given the title *Reports by Lawrence of the Hedjaz Campaign*. What followed was a series of 'casual reports' purportedly dictated by Lawrence to Robinson at Akaba dating from 13th June 1916 to 10th May 1918. These end on the seventh page and the following ten pages cover *The Destruction of the Fourth [Turkish] Army*. A short introductory paragraph leads up to this section:

> This was the last of these casual reports given by Lawrence, but as the succeeding three months were devoted to intensive training interspersed by attacks necessary to our campaign for diverting the attention of the Turks from the Palestine Front, I do not think much interest will have been missed. The next report concerns an epic in the fighting annals of the world – and I give it exactly as dictated by Lawrence, tense, to the point and giving no hint of the hazards of the adventure, a fierce hand to hand fighting , hiding absolutely the fact that the campaign owed its success to his entire lack of fear, the unbounded belief of the Bedouin in 'El Orance', and in his own determination to realise his goal – mentioned so briefly in a little conversation when he first met Feisal at the commencement of the Revolt. 'It is far from Damascus', said Lawrence . . .

'It is far from Damascus' comes straight from *Seven Pillars of Wisdom,* which was not published generally until 1935. The second 'casual report' entry, purportedly dictated by Lawrence, concerned the attack on Wejh in 1917:

Jan. 25, 1917
Wemyss directed an attack on El Wejh in person. The naval guns outranged the Turks and I went into the heart of the port with my Arabs and drove the enemy out after terrific hand-to-hand fighting.

I have now got the Herb (between Medina and Mecca), the J'Heina (between Yanbo and Medina) and the Billee (Wejh) together after heart to heart talks with the sheikhs,

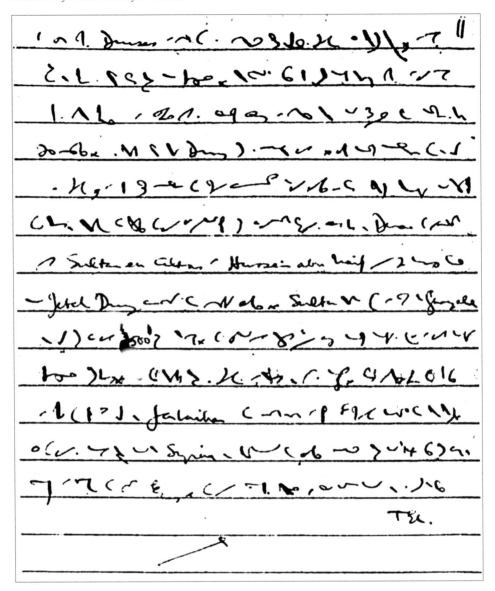

Copy of the final page of Edward Robinson's bogus shorthand notes he suggested were dictated by Lawrence that concerned the destruction of the Turkish 4th Army. (Imperial War Museum)

and think I shall soon able to move north to Akaba and Maan, where I hope I shall pick up with Beni Atiyeh. I want Akaba as a base, and to divert attention shall send flying columns north for feints against Amman.

Some time later A.W. Lawrence made a series of comments on Robinson's notes. One in particular referred to this attack: 'Authenticity [of Robinson's original typescript] would remain doubtful till another copy should turn up, but it can be said at once that certain portions are entirely false – e.g. Lawrence did not arrive at Wejh until after its capture.'

In fact the attack on Wejh took place on 23rd January, carried out after a bombardment by R.N. Admiral Wemyss's ships, by a force of 600 Arab regulars under a British officer, Vickery. Feisal and Lawrence, with over 8,000 Bedouin, did not arrive until the 25th, by which time the town had fallen. It was A.W.'s contention that the 'typescript style obviously isn't TEL' and the authenticity was 'doubtful throughout'. He had never seen Lawrence's report and thought Robinson's content may have come from a manuscript he stole from the War Archives or was perhaps translated from Arabic manuscripts originally owned by Arnold himself. Some time later a copy of the typescript was found by the police amongst Robinson's papers. To say the style 'isn't TEL' is certainly an understatement. The final section in the report is a comment on the part played by the Druses, who had not originally sided with the Allies. They were 'ignoble' soldiers:

> They hung around behind our horse, never entering the fight, and waited until Damascus was taken. They then paraded before the Sherif and began to loot the inhabitants. After the Arabs checked them at this and drove them out of the town to Jalainen they came to me and said that their real feelings were pro-British. As they were the only people in all Syria to volunteer for service against Egypt in 1914 this was hard to credit and I gave them little satisfaction. They are greedy braggarts, who soon knock under a show of force.

This last sentence in particular is totally out of character, as is the earlier, gauche description of 'heart to heart talks with the sheikhs'. These are only two of many obviously bogus quotes. A.W. Lawrence appears to have lent Robinson a number of original documents to assist with the first *Lawrence* book. A.W. realised something was wrong when these surfaced some time later in America: '...some such 'original' seems to have been sold by him in the U.S.A. . . . . The sale in New York 1937 did include some Arabic [documents].'

In 1937 the American Art Association Anderson Galleries published a catalogue of *First Edition Autographs, Americana, Stamps and Miniatures*. The sale included 'Manuscripts, maps, photographs and memorabilia by or relating to Colonel T.E. Lawrence'. On of the artifacts was 'Item 245: Lawrence, Colonel, T.E. Typewritten carbon copy, signed, of Lawrence's diary. 35pp. (Syria 1910)'. Arnold Lawrence's described this as a 'Typescript made after death of TEL with forged signature'. 'Item 249: [-] Manuscript expense account, written on one side of five leaves, 4vo. Written freehand in purple ink' purports to be a provision and general account presented to Lawrence shortly after Damascus had been taken. A.W's comment was 'I don't know whether this is genuine. R. may have added it'. Of all the entries in Item 249, page 5 only was a credit entry:

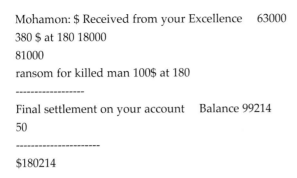

Mohamon: $ Received from your Excellence   63000
380 $ at 180 18000
81000
ransom for killed man 100$ at 180

Final settlement on your account   Balance 99214
50

$180214

Lawrence is referred to as 'His Excellence' on the front cover. A.W. said the ransom entry was forged. Item 25 was 'Lawrence, Colonel, T.E. Pen and ink sketches. PLAN signed 'T.E. Lawrence'. A.W.'s comment was: 'Copy by AWL of Marshall's plan with forged signature'. The Anderson Galleries remained ignorant of Robinson's duplicity. The catalogue's description was reassuring:

> The important comments accompanying much of this material were made by Edward Robinson Parliamentary Editor of Reuter's London news agency, who accompanied Lawrence upon many of his exploits in the East. Robinson has recently completed his second book on Lawrence which we believe is scheduled to appear this spring. The latter's brother, A.W. Lawrence, has written the preface to this work and considers it an authentic record of Lawrence's military career. We are informed that A.W. Lawrence does not intend to authorize any military record of his brother's career other than that written by Robinson.

It was all a well-worked hoax carried out by a man with few scruples. But the British saw through it. On receiving the Sale Catalogue from New York Arnold Lawrence realised some of the material had been stolen from him and other items forged. Included among the papers Lawrence lent Robinson had been a copy of the Arab Bureau Bulletin. Robinson later used this to concoct parts of his second biography, inserting his own false passages. Robinson also forged pencil notes, purporting to be in T.E.'s handwriting, about himself in Arnold's copy of the Bulletin, which had previously belonged to T.E. A.W. had never seen these notes before and realised they were forged. He contacted the Police Criminal Investigation Department and Robinson was arrested on a charge of criminal larceny. A charge of forgery would have been added to this if relevant evidence had arrived from New York in time for Robinson's trial. But this came too late.

On 16th July 1937 Robinson was sentenced to three months hard labour for selling manuscripts and other material lent to him by Arnold Lawrence. Robinson's defence admitted a previous term of imprisonment – reported to have been three years for around 70 charges of misappropriating funds by forgery. A.W received, that same day, a letter from Mrs. Katherine Arnold of Albany County, New York. She was the purchaser of Item 245 (Lawrence's diary) at the auction:

My Dear Mr. Lawrence,

Someone has sent me a clipping about the trial of Edward Robinson and I see that I am the possessor of stolen property. Before the sale I spoke to some of the officials at the Galleries about the various inaccuracies in Mr. Robinson's descriptions. The diary was so obviously not the diary of your brother's first trip to Syria that I thought it odd that Mr. Robinson should describe it as he did. Besides I had read his book about your brother and (in spite of your foreword) didn't think much about it.

She was later contacted by the New York Police acting for London and agreed to return the item to A.W. Robinson refused to give up. He must have realised from his previous success that big returns were to be made from a proper biography. On 11th January, 1938, by which time he had completed his sentence, he wrote to Lawrence's agent Raymond Savage. He still insisted that he served with T.E. in Arabia and that many of his staff would remember him.

Dear Mr. Savage,

You leave me a little breathless. The note I left at your office gave the signatory as Major W.F. Stirling. He should no doubt remember that I used Abu el Lissan, or rather 'T.E.' did, as Headquarters for reporting, and it was there I did quite a lot of report work, coming in by camel or car. (S.C. Rolls would probably remember driving Lawrence, Nasr and me several times).

I have at home – I am looking at it this morning and posting a duplicate later – a short recommendation which I asked Colonel Joyce to give me in 1919 when C.O.'s were asked to supply men with characters for use in civilian life. In addition, there is Captain R.G. Goslett, who should I think remember me at Rabegh, and certainly at Akaba. I would also remind you that I saw Colonel Joyce last year, to talk over certain parts of the manuscript with him. I saw Captain Goslett and Colonel Newcombe at the memorial service to 'T.E.' at St. Paul's and they both recognised me.

Of course I have a photograph of myself at Akaba – I hope you remember my showing you it – and I could go on ad lib. Unfortunately the law, like you, required proof that I served abroad, and I think my brother-in-law has the actual discharge certificate. Is the above sufficient? I fear the most you could get from an R.A.S.C. H.Q. is date of drafting from M.E.F. to E.E.F. and then the actual discharge date. But I see so much waste of time, and if I continue writing this letter a note of bitterness might creep in which would be unjustified in writing to you. I am 'phoning this morning.

Yours sincerely,
E.H.T. Robinson

P.S. I've found Joyce's note. Here's a copy. Can I help further?
The 'T.R. Robinson' in Lawrence's own book refers to me. There was only <u>one</u> Robinson.

Enquiries about the validity of Robinson's claims had been made some time before this. On 15th December 1937 W.H. Brookes, an old soldier from Ebbw Vale wrote to A.W. 'In answer to your query. There was positively no Britisher other than T.E., Yells and myself when we wrecked the train near Mudowwara in September 1917. I have never heard of Robinson – he may have come later in the campaign.'

M.A. Frost, a veteran from Reading, wrote in January 1938: 'Is the Robinson [in] question the chap that was in the office at Damascus? I knew him fairly well. His initials I am not sure of. This man was a sub-editor of a Nottinghamshire paper. Sure was most likely the man. He was married in Damascus. I was at the wedding.'

Lawrence's driver when he entered Damascus in 1918, S.C. Rolls himself, replied in February 1938, Writing from the Rolls Motor Company in Northamptonshire:

> In view of the Robinson complication, I have written a very discreet letter to A. Barnes, a very genuine little fellow, whose name appears on the nominal roll in *Seven Pillars*. He, of course, knew Driver Robinson to whom I refer as W.R., the camp watch repairer in *Steel Chariots*,[8] also he met Corporal Robinson of the Arab Bureau when we reached Damascus after the armistice. I have asked him to send the correct initial (if he remembers it), of the only Robinson I knew who took an actual part in the campaign.

A.W. Lawrence was only able to find one official confirmation of Robinson's presence in Arabia.

> An entry in Goslett's accounts of May 18 shows a Ration allowance of $1.40 issued by Goslett at Akaba to Corporal E.H.T. Robinson. Presumably to pay for his keep on a ship. No other record exists of his presence in Arabia but NB that his transcript of a report by TE dates within a week before the issue.

By all accounts Robinson was in a very bad metal state by the time he reached Damascus. In fact, the effect the war had on him seems to draw very strong parallels with Lawrence himself. Over a year later, in September 1939, David Forsyth wrote to Arnold Lawrence from Portland:

> Mr. J. Lotsky came to see me here yesterday. He is able to confirm that he met Mr. Robinson in Cairo in the early days of the war, that he knows he was at Akabah at some later date and that he ran across him again early in 1919.
>
> . . . He recalled beyond any doubt that in Damascus Mr. Robinson was in an exceptionally nervous state.

Many could not remember Robinson at all. Jock Mackay, who formerly served in the Hedjaz Armoured Car Battery, for one:

Now, as to E.H.T Robinson , I am perfectly certain that at no time was any such person in the armoured car batteries, and I can assure you that there is no possibility of him being there without you or I having some recollection of him. It is rather strange that since Lawrence died there have come to light, even in Edinburgh, certain persons who can write long screeds on him, and even give lectures on him, who I have never heard of in the old days at all.

Robinson was more than just a literary hoaxer and fraud. In 1939 the Cambridge University Press's *British Journal of Medical Psychology* published an article entitled 'The Case of a Middle-aged Embezzler' by the psychologist David Forsyth on one of his patients who had served in the Middle East war. The patient was, of course, Edward Robinson. He had been to see the psychologist for treatment as he was, he made out, suffering from amnesia as a result of his experiences in the war. Not only had Robinson written a book about Lawrence, he also appeared to have become him in his subconscious fantasies. He suggested, during the consultation, that he had been suffering a loss of memory for nearly twenty years. This was unique in its longevity from Forsyth's point of view. He decided radical treatment was needed and, after Robinson and his wife consented, attempted hypnotism.

> As soon as the first hypnosis had been induced, I began to uncover the most amazing account of war experiences that I have ever listened to. To find their like we would have to go back to the medieval adventures of Sir John Mandeville, or the exploits of our Elizabethan buccaneers.

Robinson appears to have spun him a yarn that the psychologist fell for, hook, line and sinker. It seems this was an amalgamation both of his own and T.E.'s experiences in the war. The patient said he had been sent out to Cairo in 1915 and, due to his intelligence and ability with Arabic, been attached to the Sherifian forces with Lawrence. Shortly after a shell exploded in front of him and killed all his Bedouin comrades. He lost his memory. It did not come back, he said, until he returned to England six months later. Under apparently successful hypnosis he began to recall what occurred in the missing months. His Arab companions he ended up living with insisted he was mad and tied him to a tent pole. After that Robinson's fantasies exploded:

> He decided that he ought to resume the same guerrilla warfare against the Turks, which he had been assisting in under Lawrence a few weeks ago. His military qualities must have been rather exceptional, because these Arabs readily accepted him as their leader . . . He recalled with evident horror how his party seemed to be forever killing. They blew up the railway line more than once. At other times they looted camels and sheep, and some Turkish women. In this way his fame as a leader spread, more and more Arabs joined him . . . and eventually he found himself at the head of a body of 300 or 400 of them.

Forsyth appeared to have been completely bamboozled by Robinson who, by that time, 1939, would have known the Lawrence story backwards. He had become an unrepentant serial hoaxer, who enjoyed carrying out the subterfuge, in this case, purely for its own sake.

> That these happenings in the twentieth century may make us rub our eyes. They recall Sir Walter Raleigh's exploits on the Spanish Main. The Elizabethan was an Englishman who was supported by followers, while the patient was alone in the interior of Arabia among a crowd of Bedouins.

One wonders how any intelligent, professional man could have been so easily duped. Forsyth was impressed by his subject's youth: 'The patient was barely out of his teens, and with no more knowledge of life and the world than he got in a provincial town.' What made Robinson so persuasive? Perhaps he actually believed what he said was true. The final part of Forsyth's account goes a long way to explaining his mental state and motivations:

> …when he was demobilized the patient was a mass of nerves. This was the impression that he gave his relatives. Within that wreckage, however, he still preserved enough of his personality to react powerfully to the treatment meted out to him by the Ministry of Pensions. He felt intensely resentful that the war should have smashed him up so completely that he was incapable of any work, and yet the request to the Government for assistance had been turned down. As he saw it the Medical Board had as good as told him he was both a liar and an imposter, simply because no War Office record existed that he had ever been a casualty. He brooded over the thought of the injustice that had been done to him, and was more and more determined to revenge himself, especially on the Government. In this way two different personalities began to develop in him, one law-abiding, the other criminal, and the conflict between them has continued down to the present time.[9]

Despite his unstable mental state Robinson was able to produce another biography and, in the spring of 1946 it was published as *Lawrence the Rebel* by the small publishing firm Lincolns-Prager. This ran to 228 pages in octavo, with each section, or chapter, commencing with an obscure Arab quotation, such as 'A camel does not sell his hump, and water in a jug does not turn to sour milk.' This one heads the chapter where Lawrence refuses his decorations from King George V, which makes some kind of connection, but many of the sayings do not appear to support any logical interpretation: 'Singing without remuneration is like a dead body which lacks perfume', or 'A barber learns to shave on the orphan's face'; 'If a camel gets his nose in the tent his body will soon follow.' The unintentional humour, along with many of the Lawrence quotes not ringing true, exposes the book as fraudulent. Like Jonathan Cape in 1938, Lincolns-Prager published the book in good faith, unaware of Robinson's record. The first edition rapidly sold out and the copies could not be recalled. None of A.W Lawrence's copyright matter was included, otherwise the text was almost identical with proof copies of *Lawrence the Patriot Rebel*. David Garnett when asked to review the book for the *New Statesman and Nation*, refused to do so unless the paper was prepared to indemnify him against possible legal consequences and unless A.W. Lawrence was ready to support his denunciation of Robinson as 'an impudent forger and a convicted thief'. Garnett did not want to be involved in a libel action as, even if he won, Robinson would be unable to pay. He quoted one glaring error he had come across in a letter of 26th May 1946 to A.W.L.:

> I have not read it yet but opening it at random I find he records himself as writing out a report for T.E. of an interview with Feisal who is made to say that Ibn Saud will inevitably conquer the whole of Arabia. Robinson puts a footnote: 'Amazing prescience in 1917'.
>
> If this were true it would alter one's view of Feisal's state of mind on going forward to Damascus and of T.E.'s hope to establish Feisal. And we may find it quoted in the history books unless the book is denounced and withdrawn.[10]

A.W.L. realised that 'A precise statement of the grounds for Robinson's first conviction would greatly strengthen a denunciation of the book as historically unreliable.' Robinson offered his own explanation for this conviction in his sessions with Forsyth:

> His first sentence was for embezzling money by forging cheques. The body employing him at the time was a national organization which had been specially established for the purpose of assisting ex-servicemen, and it had substantial funds at its disposal. He himself was an ex-serviceman, badly damaged in the war, but denied any help. He felt so very sore about this, that unconsciously he decided to take his revenge against the Government by helping himself to some of the money which had been for precisely those in his unhappy state. It galled him all the more at his work to see remittances being sent out readily to others, and nothing coming his way.[11]

Despite suffering a history of disappointments and instability Robinson had a dogged persistence. In August 1967 Gordon Grimley of Robert Maxwell publications asked Liddell Hart if he would inspect a 360 page manuscript 'by a civil servant who was close to Lawrence and through whose hands practically all the documents covering the campaign from Wejh to Damascus passed.' That September Grimley contacted Liddell Hart once more to say that Arnold Lawrence had 'cast such a light on the T.E. Lawrence manuscript and author that I am now returning the manuscript with a simple rejection slip. It would appear that the entire origin of the book is wholly questionable'. It was Robinson again. Whether the manuscript was simply a rehash of the 1946 text or not is impossible to determine.

The fact that Robinson was able to carry out his hoax successfully, find a publisher, dupe an experienced psychiatrist, and mislead A.W. Lawrence, the

---

Directors
VANDELEUR ROBINSON.
MARGARET HARPER-NELSON.
EUGEN PRAGER (Czechoslovakian Form. Aust. & Hung.)

LINCOLNS-PRAGER (PUBLISHERS) LIMITED

83 CLAREWOOD COURT, SEYMOUR PLACE, LONDON, W.1.

Phone:
PADdington
5985.

1st July 1946.

WITHOUT PREJUDICE

Prof. A. W. Lawrence
31 Madingley Rd.
Cambridge

Dear Prof. Lawrence,

    With reference to your call here the other day my directors have now considered the situation you put before us in regard to the author of LAWRENCE THE REBEL. Naturally we are impartial in this matter. However, we wonder whether it would meet your wishes if we cancelled our contract with the author and thus avoid any publicity.

    I shall be pleased to have your kind reply in due course and remain,

        Yours sincerely
    Lincolns Prager (Publishers) Ltd.

(Miss) J. Kuhn   Secretary.

Letter dated 1st July 1946 from Lincolns-Prager to A.W. Lawrence suggesting they cancel the contract with Edward Robinson. (Bodleian Library)

Anderson Galleries, numerous buyers of his auctioned merchandise and any of those who purchased his book must point to how far he had successfully deceived himself, as well as those who fell victim to him. Even a court judgement, imprisonment and hard labour failed to deter him. And he made one final attempt to repeat his success over 20 years later. *Lawrence the Rebel* remains the most eccentric of Lawrence biographies and is still in circulation.

Notes

1 *Meinertzhagen's Diary Ruse.* J.N. Lockman. Cornerstone Publications Ltd. Grand Rapids, USA. 1995.

2 Simpson told the author in 2006 that the Bilbo story was fabricated. Bilbo was an underworld racketeer.

3 Letter from A.W. Lawrence to H. Montgomery-Hyde, June 18th 1977.

4 *Meinertzhagen's Diary Ruse.* J.N. Lockman. Cornerstone Publications Ltd. Grand Rapids, USA. 1995.

5 T.E. Lawrence papers MS eng. c 6753, Bodleian Library, Oxford.

6 From *Lawrence the Patriot Rebel,* proof copy. E.H.T. Robinson. Jonathan Cape. 1938

7 This was probably Doctor Marshall. See Chapter Eighteen on John Bruce, p.288.

8 Rolls' account of the Hejaz campaign, *Steel Chariots in the Desert.*

9 'The Case of a Middle-aged Embezzler', *British Journal of Medical Psychology.* Cambridge University Press. 1939.

10 Letter from D. Garnett to A.W. Lawrence, 26th May 1946. T.E. Lawrence Archive, Bodleian Library.

11 'The Case of a Middle-aged Embezzler', *British Journal of Medical Psychology.* Cambridge University Press. 1939.

CHAPTER TWENTY

Postscript

The tiny village of Moreton was originally part of the Frampton estate. Lawrence's funeral service was held in the church of St. Nicholas, which was accidentally bombed in 1940 by German raiders probably trying to find the nearby airfield at Warmwell. It was rebuilt after the war. Lawrence's grave is in a plot of land separate from the church and originally owned by Henry Featherstonehaugh-Frampton, who donated the land in 1935. One walks down the church path, turns left at the gate and follows the road around to the left for about 100 yards. Down here on the right is a roofed gateway to the cemetery in which Lawrence and Pat and Joyce Knowles lie. There is a wooden bench by Lawrence's grave. One can sit in complete solitude and wonder at the countless thousands who must have passed this way.

I arrived at the cemetery when it was just beginning to grow dark and not a soul for miles. Wandering up the path I could feel the hairs on the back of my neck begin to rise. I sat next to the bones of T.E. Lawrence, one of the most revered of British folk heroes and in the darkening solitude I must confess I told T.E. what a remarkable man he was. The bushes rustled nearby and I decided I didn't have the courage to stay there overnight.

A number of friends of T.E. lie in the same cemetery. Immediately behind him is the grave of Sergeant Pilot Dick Knowles, Pat's brother, who was killed at the beginning of the Battle of Britain. A few dozen paces down the path is that of Tom W. Beaumont of the Machine Gun Corps in Arabia, who died in 1991. Also there lies the memorial to Henry Rupert Featherstonehaugh-Frampton, T.E.'s cousin, and his wife, who died in 1941. As well as that of Pat and Joyce Knowles, there is the grave of Pioneer Sergeant Arthur Knowles, Pat's father, but I could not find the plot. I said goodnight respectfully and walked away.

Basil Liddell Hart, in a moment when he overreached himself, once compared Lawrence's talents in warfare to those of Napoleon. He saw him, like the Duke of Wellington and Ulysses S. Grant, as one of the 'great captains' of history. In the First World War Lawrence defeated an enemy far superior in numbers and firepower to his own force, relying solely on stealth, speed, silence, and superior intellect, adapting his tactics to the desert terrain and all it offered him. He also understood and exploited the character of the enemy. One soldier of a later war who has been compared to him in skill and success is Orde Wingate. Wingate won a reputation for his exploits behind the lines in Ethiopia and later in Burma, but although a distant cousin of T.E.'s he was disapproving of some of the tactics he used as well as the cult that grew up around him. Like Lawrence, Wingate possessed a tremendous, almost messianic drive. He died on operations before his potential could be fulfilled.

One man who bears similarities to Lawrence in some respects – surprisingly perhaps – and who was from the same generation, but who came of age in a later war, was Bernard Law Montgomery. 'Monty' was born in 1887, the year before Lawrence. Like Lawrence he came from a large Victorian family with a dominant mother and a strong religious background. Like Lawrence, he honed himself for the future burden of military leadership. Although he became a dedicated professional, he was no intellectual or student of war: he confessed, for example, he had never understood Clausewitz. Contrast this with Lawrence quoting Clausewitz to an Arab ally before his only set-piece battle. The comparison makes more sense when one remembers that that both men suffered climactic events in their lives that changed their direction completely: Lawrence at Deraa and Paris, which led him to shun fame, command and the limelight, Montgomery at the First Battle of Ypres, 1914. He lay wounded and covered by the body of a dead comrade in No Man's Land for over three hours whilst the enemy continued firing. This surely left him with a sense of destiny – some would say of his own self-importance – and perhaps motivated his constant effort to ensure overwhelming firepower and numbers in battle.

Colin Wilson

In the summer of 1956 a controversial book was published by an unknown young man that went to the top of the best seller lists. The first four printings were sold out within three weeks. It was the summer of the 'angry young man', John Osborne's *Look Back in Anger* was playing in London to great acclaim. The book was *The Outsider* by Colin Wilson, a 25-year-old living in a sleeping bag on Hampstead Heath. Wilson's book popularized existentialism. It considered Classic 'outsiders' (a term taken from Camus's work *L'Etranger*) including Sartre, Kierkegaard, Herman Hesse, van Gogh, Nietzsche, Dostoyevsky, and T.E Lawrence.

> Once a man has seen it, the world can never afterwards be quite the same straight-forward place . . . The Outsider is a man who cannot live in the comfortable, insulated world of the bourgeois . . . He sees too deep and too much.

Lawrence shares a chapter in the book with Van Gogh and Nijinsky. Wilson saw Lawrence, unlike Hemingway, Sartre and Hesse, as a man more concerned with living than writing. The second period of Lawrence's life is regarded as most depressing:

> It is like considering some great machine that is made useless by a small break in the circuit.

T.E.'s self-doubts are seen as damaging:

> That he lacked the healthy conceit of a man of genius is one of the root causes of his tragedy of waste.
>
> The war had given him new insights; he returned from it a wiser and in no way happier man.
>
> His power of self analysis is profound. He cannot see himself and his mind as a whole, but he can construct the picture in fragments, and in The Seven Pillars, none of the fragments is missing.

One of the key quotes in Wilson's book is from Eric Kennington's contribution to *T.E. Lawrence by his Friends*. It concerns the comments of an old schoolmaster on *Seven Pillars*:

> The schoolmaster's comment was 'Reading this book has made me suffer. The writer is infinitely the greatest man I have ever known, but he is terribly wrong. He is not himself. He has found an 'I' that is not a true 'I', so I tremble to think what may happen. He is never alive in what he does. There is no exchange. He is only a pipe through which life flows. He seems to have been a very good pipe, but to live truly one must be more than that.' His comment not only penetrates to the roots of Lawrence; it is an accurate characterization of the Outsider. 'He is never alive in what he does'. . . It suggests that the Outsider's business is to find a course of action in which he is most himself, that is, in which he achieves the most self-expression.[1]

That is Wilson's primary definition of a true Outsider, a man who is 'never alive in what he does'.

If T.E. had lived?

What if Lawrence had left Bovington Camp five minutes earlier or five minutes later? Arriving at his cottage, he would have had time to prepare for the lunch with Pat Knowles and Joyce Dorey. That afternoon he would have been surprised when his friend Lord Carlow arrived. The following afternoon, Tuesday 14th, he would have welcomed Henry Williamson in his silver Alvis. Over lunch they may have discussed Yeates' manuscript. Williamson never asked Lawrence if he would meet Hitler. But if he had, Lawrence might have been amused at such foolishness, greeting it with the same mockery as the suggestion that he become dictator of England. But perhaps he might have reconsidered after Williamson left. Churchill, the 'voice in the wilderness', was fighting against the appeasement policies of Chamberlain and Halifax. If you accept Lawrence realised any Anglo-Nazi alliance was impractical, you must concede that any advice he gave to Churchill would have been to press for a more aggressive anti-Nazi line. The threatening political situation demanded a strong Home Defence force, and we have seen that Lawrence was deeply engaged in this, if only intellectually, at his death.

If a Middle East front had developed, advisory work would have been demanded of Lawrence. Like his brother, A.W., he would have been involved in Middle East Intelligence duties. Accelerated development of covert operations with the Long Range Desert Group and the Special Air Service might have resulted from his involvement. Orde Wingate and David Stirling owed their inspiration to him. Wavell's initial success could have been pushed further with Lawrence's help and the Nazis prevented from entering North Africa. The Arab Legion could have been more effectively employed. On a smaller scale, an optimum development of Air Sea Rescue operations would have been achieved. If Lawrence had survived his accident the course of the War might have been altered.

But this was not to be. In view of the recklessness of his driving an accident was inevitable. Even if he had survived the May 1935 crash he could have been killed later, probably before September 1939.

In 1987 Mr. Joseph Clark, a local, was staying in the small bungalow at Polstead Road. He was a Server at All Souls College. One night he was lying in his bed in the small living room when he felt a heavy pressure on his feet, then on his ankles, then his legs, his knees, on his thighs, and then his whole upper body. Although it was dark he saw Lawrence, who had a sad expression on his face. When questioned a number of times, asked if he had imagined it, Clark said he was positive he had seen Lawrence. Some time after that another local, a woman, had the same experience while sleeping in the same room. No similar experience has been recorded since.

Notes

1 Wilson, 2005: 'TEL was such an overtense left-brainer, so unrelaxed (except on rare occasions when his senses awoke before his intellect) that he was simply 'not himself' most of the time – the old existentialist dilemma. . . . The occult is nothing to do with it.'

Effigy in St Martin's Church, Wareham, by Eric Kennington, at one time destined for Salisbury Cathedral. The inscription on Lawrence's grave itself was chosen by his mother, the motto of Oxford High School, and means 'God is my light'. He might not have approved.

Bibliography

BOOKS

Aldington, Richard, *Lawrence of Arabia: A Biographical Enquiry,* Collins, London. 1955.

Arnold, Mathew, *On Translating Homer,* John Murray, 1905.

Artennieth, Dr. G., *Homeric Dictionary.* MacMillan Press Ltd. 1877/1979.

Baker, Anne I., *From Biplane to Spitfire: the Life of Sir Geoffrey Salmond,* Leo Cooper / Pen and Sword Books, 2003.

Barker, Ralph, *The Schneider Trophy Races,* Airlife Publishing Ltd. 1981

Beardow, Keith, *Sailors in the R.A.F,.* Patrick Stephens Ltd. 1993

Broughton, Harry, *Lawrence of Arabia – the Simple Facts,* H. Broughton, Wareham, Dorset, 1961.

Brown, Malcolm (ed.), *The Letters of T.E. Lawrence,* J.M. Dent, London, 1988.

Brown, Malcolm and Cave, Julia, *A Touch of Genius – The Life of T.E. Lawrence,* J.M. Dent, London. 1988.

Butcher and Lang (trans.), *The* Odyssey *of Homer,* MacMillan and Co., 1928.

Dixon, Alec M., *Tinned Soldier,* Jonathan Cape, 1934.

Doughty, C.M., *Travels in Arabia Deserta,* Jonathan Cape, 1933.

Eden, Anthony (the Rt. Hon. Earl of Avon), *The Eden Memoirs. Volume 3: Facing the Dictators,* Cassell, 1962

Garnett, David (ed.), *The Selected Letters of T.E. Lawrence,* Jonathan Cape, London, 1937.

Gilbert, Martin, *Churchill: The Wilderness Years,* Macmillan, London, 1981.

Green, W.G., *The Similes of Homer's* Iliad, Longman and Co. 1887.

Graves, Robert, *Lawrence and the Arabs,* Jonathan Cape, 1924.

Graves, Robert and Liddell Hart, Basil, *T.E. Lawrence to his Biographers,* Cassell, London, 1938.

Hunt, E.V.G. (ed.), *The Life and Times of Joyce Knowles,* Dorset, 1994.

Hunt, E.V.G. (ed.), with Pat and Joyce Knowles, *An Handful with Quietness,* Dorset, 1990.

Hyde, H. Montgomery, *Solitary in the Ranks,* Constable and Company. 1977.

James, Derek N., *Schneider Trophy Aircraft 1913–1932,* Putnam, 1981.

James, Lawrence, *The Golden Warrior,* Weidenfeld and Nicolson, London, 1990.

John, Augustus, *Chiaroscuro,* Jonathan Cape, 1952.

Jones, P.V. (trans.), *The* Odyssey *of Homer,* Bristol Classical Press, 1988.

Knight, Ronald, *Colonel T.E. Lawrence Visits Mr. and Mrs. Thomas Hardy*, Bat and Ball Press, Dorset, 1985.

Knightley, Philip, *A Hack's Progress*, Jonathan Cape, 1997.

Knightley, Philip and Simpson, Colin, *The Secret Lives of Lawrence of Arabia,* Thomas Nelson and Sons Ltd, 1969.

Knowles, Richard and Clabburn, P. (ed.), *Cats and Landladies Husbands: T.E. Lawrence in Bridlington*, Fleece Press, Yorkshire, 1995.

Lawrence, A.W, *T.E. Lawrence by His Friends*, Jonathan Cape, 1937.

Lawrence, T.E., *Seven Pillars of Wisdom*. Jonathan Cape, 1937.

Lawrence, T.E., (352087 A/C Ross, J.H.), *The Mint (unexpurgated version)*, Military Book Society, 1973.

Lawrence, T.E., (352087 A/C Ross, J.H.). *The Mint (expurgated version)*. Jonathan Cape,. 1955.

Lawrence, T.E., (as Shaw, T.E. (trans.)), *The* Odyssey *of Homer,* O.U.P., London 1935.

Legg, Rodney, *Lawrence in Dorset*, Dorset Publishing Company, Wincanton, 1988. Reprinted in a revised format as *Lawrence of Dorset*, 2005.

Liddell Hart, Basil, *T.E. Lawrence in Arabia and After,* (Revised Edition), Jonathan Cape, London, 1943.

Lockman, J.N., *Meinertzhagen's Diary Ruse*, Cornerstone Publications, Grand Rapids, U.S.A., 1995.

Mack, Dr. John E., Mack, *A Prince of Our Disorder,* Little, Brown and Co., U.S.A., 1973.

MacGillivray, J. Alexander, *Minotaur: the Life of Sir Arthur Evans,* Jonathan Cape, 2000.

Marriott, Paul and Argent, Yvonne, *A Leaf in the Wind: The Last Days of T.E. Lawrence,* Alpha Press, 1996.

McAlmon, Robert and Boyle, Kay, *Being Geniuses Together*, Paris, 1938.

Meinertzhagen, Richard, *Middle East Diary*, Cresset Press, London, 1959.

Norman, Dr. Andrew, *T.E. Lawrence - Unveiling the Enigma*, Halsgrove, Tiverton, Devon, 2003.

Pilsborough, Geoffrey, *The History of the Royal Air Force Marine Craft 1918–1986,* Canimpex Publishing, 1986.

Rance, Adrian, *Fast Boats and Flying Boats*, Ensign Publications, Southampton, 1989.

Rieu, E.V.(trans.) *The* Odyssey *of Homer* 1746/1991.

Robinson, Edward H.T., *Lawrence: the Story of His Life,* O.U.P., 1935.

Robinson, Edward H.T., *Lawrence the Patriot Rebel* (proof copy), Jonathan Cape, 1938.

Robinson, Edward H.T., *Lawrence the Rebel*, Lincolns-Prager, London. 1946.

Russo/ Fernandez/ Haverback, *A Commentary on Homer's Odyssey Vol. 3*. Clarendon Press, Oxford. 1992.

Smith, Alan, *The Schneider Trophy: High Speed Seaplanes 1913–1931,* Waterfront Publications, 1995.

Smith, Clare Sydney, *The Golden Reign*. Cassell and Co. Ltd., 1949.

Smith, J.C. and Hogan, Brian, *Criminal Law: Cases and Materials*, Butterworths, London, 1990.

Stuart, Desmond, *T.E. Lawrence*, Hamish Hamilton, London, 1977.

Sutherland, Jon and Cornell, Diane, *The R.A.F. Air Sea Rescue Service 1918–1986,* Pen and Sword Aviation Books, 2005.

Symonds, E.H., *Trial by Land and Sea,* Alderman, UK, 1980(?).

Thalman, W.G., *The Swineherd and the Bow,* Cornell U.P., 1998.

Thomas, Bertram, *Arabia Felix,* Jonathan Cape, 1932.

Tinsley, E.B., *One Rissole on My Plate,* Merlin Books, UK, 1984.

Tweedsmuir, Susan, *John Buchan by His Wife and Friends,* Hodder and Stoughton, 1947.

Wilson, Colin, *The Outsider,* Victor Gollancz, London, 1956.

Wilson, Derek, *The Astors,* Weidenfeld and Nicholson, 1993.

Wilson, J.M., *Lawrence of Arabia: the Authorized Biography,* Heinemann, 1989.

Williamson, Henry, *The Genius of Friendship,* Henry Williamson Society, London, 1937.

Winterbotham, F.W., *The Nazi Connection,* Panther, London, 1979.

Wood, Michael, *In Search of the Trojan War,* Guild Publishing/BBC, 1985.

Yardley, Michael, *Backing into the Limelight: A Biography of T.E. Lawrence,* Harrap, London, 1985.

Yeates, V.M., *Winged Victory,* Cape, London, 1934.

MAGAZINES & PERIODICALS

Caplan, Jerrold R., *The Lives of Lawrence and Odysseus.* T.E. Lawrence Society Journal Vol. V, No. 2 Spring 1996.

Bazzochi, Dr. E., *Technical Aspects of the Schneider Trophy and world speed record for seaplanes.* Aeronautical Journal, February 1972.

Banks, Air Commodore F.R., *Memories of the Last Schneider Trophy Contests.* Journal of the Royal Aeronautical Society, January 1966 (pp. 179-180).

De La Bere, Professor R, M.A., F.R.Hist.S., *Aircraftman Shaw in Lincolnshire (a Last Conversation),* The Lincolnshire Magazine, Vol. 2, No. 7, Sept. to Oct. 1935.

Eyles, Charles, article on Corporal Catchpole, T.E. Lawrence Society Newsletter No. 73, Spring 2005.

Forsyth, David, 'The Case of the Middle Aged Embezzler', *British Journal of Medical Psychology,* Cambridge University Press, 1939.

Graham, Colin, 'The Crash That Killed Lawrence of Arabia', *Dorset the County* Magazine, Summer 1968

Liddell Hart, Basil, 'Speed Boat Targets for R.A.F. Bombers', *Daily Telegraph,* 14th December 1933.

Findlay, C., 'The Amazing AC2', *The Listener,* 05/06/58.

McGowan, Malcolm, article, 'First Word' in *Wessex* magazine, Dorset, December, 1985.

Mitchell, R.J., 'Schneider Trophy Machine Design, 1927', *Journal of the Royal Aeronautical Society,* September 1928 Postlethwaite, Norman, 'Homer's *Odyssey* and Lawrence's', *T.E. Lawrence Society Journal* Vol. V No.1, Winter 1996.

Press, various: *Daily Mail,* 18/5/35.

   Daily Sketch, 4/5/35.

   Daily Telegraph, 22/5/35.

Dorset Daily Echo and Weymouth Dispatch, 21/5/35, 6/5/36.

Exeter Express and Echo, 21/5/36.

Rance, Derek, 'T.E. Shaw and the British Power Boat Company', *T.E. Lawrence Society Journal* Vol. II No. 1, Summer 1992.

Russell, Arthur, articles in *T.E. Lives* magazine, Dorset, 2000.

Sheppard, 'Motor Boats for the RAF', *The Times*, 30th March 1932.

'Voyage of an RAF Motor Boat', *The Times*, 16th April 1932.

Simpson, Colin, 'Death of a Hero', *Unsolved* magazine, Orbis Publications London, 1984.

Wasley, Gerald, *Plymouth Evening Herald* articles.

Wilson, Jeremy, *T.E. Lawrence and the Translation of the* Odyssey *1928–1931*, T.E. Lawrence Society Journal Vol. III No. 2 Spring 1994.

Yardley, 'Clouds Hill and the Lawrence Legend', *Dorset the County* Magazine, Issue 96, 1986.

ARCHIVES

Air Historical Branch:
(R.A.F.), Ministry of Defence, R.A.F. Bentley Priory, Stanmore, Middlesex.
Air Ministry , List of Staff and Distribution of Duties: 10/1918, 5/1926 & 10/1934.
Manning, Air Commodore F.J.: interview 20/11/1975.
Sims, Wing Commander R.G. Interview 2/3/1955, Eastgate, Hornsea, Yorks.

Bodleian Library, Modern Papers Room, Oxford:
MS Eng c.6738, MS Eng c.6742, MS Eng c. 6758, MS Eng c. 6753, MS Eng. d.3349.
Letters to T.E. Lawrence: selection from A.E. Chambers and E.S. Palmer.
Letters from T.E. Lawrence to Henry Field, Bertram Thomas, A.E.E. Weblin, Edward Spurr, Ralph Isham.
Ralph Isham: Account of the Translation of the *Odyssey*.

R.A.C. Tank Museum Bovington, Dorset, Archive Library:
Box Files Nos. 1 & 2: various newspaper and periodical clippings. Account of Colonel Nigel W. Duncan of his meeting with T.E. Lawrence in the Middle East and at Bovington c.1923, written 1982.

Dorset County Museum, Dorchester:
Copy of letter, T.E. Lawrence to Florence Hardy, 02/12/23.

Dorset County Record Office, Dorchester:
Various newspaper articles from 1935.

Imperial War Museum:
Documents relating to Dr. Leigh and the *Sunday Times* research, Box ref. Misc 196(2904) *Recollections of Life in the Tank Corps and T.E. Lawrence,* A.H.R. Reiffer M.M. (April 1970).
Imperial War Museum 23(-41)/3

Documents containing the correspondence of Captain H.W. Lettman-Johnson (Box Ref. 92/32/1)

Letters from T.E. Lawrence to:

  T.W. Beaumont 10/06/1931, 26/06/1934.

  John Campbell, 10/06/1931.

  C.P. Robertson 30/01/1929, 22/11/1929.

  Rev. D. Siddons, 26/04/1932.

Recollections of R. Hales, February 1971.

Autobiography of Group Captain R.J. Bone.

National Archives, Kew, London:

Air Ministry: Air Historical Branch: Papers (Series 1) AIR 1/2692, AIR 1/2693, AIR1/2694, AIR 1/2695, AIR 1/2696, AIR 1/2697, AIR 1/2701, AIR 1/2702, AIR 1/2703. Treasury: Social Services Division (SS and 2SS series) Files T 227/4280.

Patents Office, Monmouth:

Patent applications of Edward Spurr 1937/1938.

Royal Air Force Museum, Hendon:

Air Commodore Sydney Smith archive.

T.E. Lawrence archive.

R.J. Mitchell photo archive.

Southampton Maritime Museum External Collections:

Scott-Paine archive.

CORRESPONDENCE

Baker, Anne I. Letters to the author, 2005, 2006.

Bennett Richard M. Correspondence., November 2004.

Cripps, Tony. Correspondence, 2004.

Hammersley, Roland and Hughes, Mrs Joan. Correspondence. Bovington, February 1986.

Payne, S.S., H.M. Coroner for Bournemouth and Poole and Eastern Dorset. Correspondence. December 2004.

Runyard, Godfrey C. Correspondence. May to July 2005.

Saga magazine. Replies to author's advertisement, March 2005.

Sources and Abbreviations

Part 1

Primary Sources

Gordon, Frank, Interview. Bovington. 25/05/85.

Bodleian Library, Oxford, T.E. Lawrence papers; MS Eng c. 6738, MS Eng c. 6758, MS Eng. c. 6753, MS Eng. d. 3349. Letters to T.E. Lawrence.

Imperial War Museum, London, Documents relating to Dr. Leigh and the *Sunday Times* research. Box ref. Misc 196(2904). *Recollections of Life in the Tank Corps and T.E. Lawrence.* A.H.R. Reiffer M.M. (April 1970). Imperial War Museum 23(=41)/3.

R.A.C. Bovington Tank Museum Library. T.E. Lawrence archive. Box files 1 and 2. Various letters and personal accounts.

Runyard, Godfrey C. Correspondence, May to July 2005.

Russell, Arthur. Interview. Coventry. 07/12/85.

Saga Magazine. Replies to author's letter, March 2005.

Wareham Reference Library Wareham, Dorset. Various copies of *T.E. Lives* and newspaper cuttings.

Secondary Sources

Aldington, R. *Lawrence of Arabia – A Biographical Enquiry.* Collins, London. 1955.

Brown, M and Cave J. *A Touch of Genius – The Life of T.E. Lawrence.* J.M. Dent, London. 1988.

DG: Garnett, E., Ed. *The Selected Letters of T.E. Lawrence,* Cape, London, 1937.

MB: Brown, M., Ed. *The Letters of T.E. Lawrence,* J.M. Dent, London, 1988).

T.E. Lawrence to his Biographers Robert Graves and Basil Liddell Hart, Cassell, London, 1938.

T.E. Lawrence by his Friends ed. A.W. Lawrence, Cape, London 1937/1954.

Legg, R., *Lawrence in Dorset,* Dorset Publishing Company, Wincanton, 1988.

Hunt, B., *The Life and Times of Joyce Knowles,* E.V.G. Hunt, Dorset.

Liddell Hart, B., *T.E. Lawrence in Arabia and After* by Basil Liddell Hart, Cape, London, 1935.

Knowles, Pat and Joyce, and Hunt, B., *An Handful With Quietness,* E.V.G. Hunt, Dorset, 1992.

Robinson, E.H.T., *Lawrence the Rebel,.* Lincolns-Prager, London. 1946.

Stuart, D., *T.E. Lawrence,* Hamish Hamilton, London, 1977.

Tinlsey, A.B., *One Rissole on My Plate,* Merlin Books Ltd. 1984.

Williamson, H., *The Genius of Friendship,* Henry Williamson Society, London, 1937/1998.

Wilson, J.M., *Lawrence of Arabia – the Authorized Biography,* 1988.

Yardley, 'Clouds Hill and the Lawrence Legend'. *Dorset the County* magazine, Issue 96, 1986.

Part 2

Translation of the *Odyssey*

TELSJ-1: Caplan, Jerrold R. *The Lives of Lawrence and Odysseus.* T.E. Lawrence Society Journal Vol. V, No. 2 Spring 1996.

TELSJ-2: Wilson, Jeremy, *T.E. Lawrence and the Translation of the* Odyssey *1928–1931.* T.E. Lawrence Society Journal Vol. III No. 2 Spring 1994.

TELSJ-3: Postlethwaite, Norman. *Homer's* Odyssey *and Lawrence's* T.E. Lawrence society Journal Vol. V No. I Winter 1996.

Homer, *The* Odyssey. Shaw, T.E. (trans.) O.U.P., London, 1935.

Homer, *The* Odyssey. Rieu, E.V. (trans.), 1746.

Homer, *The* Odyssey. Butcher and Lang (trans.). MacMillan and Co., 1928.

Homer, *The* Odyssey. Jones, P.V. (trans.) Bristol Classical Press, 1988.

On Translating Homer. Arnold, Matthew, John Murray, 1905.

A Commentary on Homer's Odyssey *Vol. 3*. Russo/Fernandez/Haverback, Clarendon Press, Oxford. 1992

Green, W.G. *The Similes of Homer's* Iliad. Longman and Co. 1887

Thalman, W.G. *The Swineherd and the Bow.* Cornell U.P. 1998

Artennieth, Dr. G. *Homeric Dictionary.* MacMillan Press Ltd. 1877/1979

Page, Denys Tinsley, Antony Brian, *One Rissole on My Plate,* Merlin Books Ltd. 1984.

Wood, Michael. *In Search of the Trojan War*, Guild Publishing/BBC, 1985.

The Schneider Cup

Barker, Ralph, The *Schneider Trophy Races,* Airlife Publishing Ltd., 1981.

James, Derek N., *Schneider Trophy Aircraft 1913–1932.* Putnam, 1981.

RAF Museum, Hendon: Air Commodore Sydney Smith Archive; R.J. Mitchell Archive.

Solent Sky Museum, Southampton: Supermarine S5 aircraft.

Shipster, Pieter. 'Lawrence and the Schneider Cup.' T.E. Lawrence Society Lecture, March, 2006.

Smith, Alan. *The Schneider Trophy: High Speed Seaplanes 1913–1931,* Waterfront Publications, 1995.

Mitchell, R.J. 'Schneider Trophy Machine Design,1927.' *Journal of the Royal Aeronautical Society,* September 192 (pp. 744-762).

Bazzochi, Dr. E. 'Technical Aspects of the Schneider Trophy and world speed record for seaplanes.' *Aeronautical Journal,* February 1972.

Banks, Air Commodore F.R. 'Memories of the Last Schneider Trophy Contests.' *Journal of the Royal Aeronautical Society,* January 1966 (pp. 179-180).

Power Boats and Armoured Target Boats

Primary Sources

The Times: 30th March 1932 'Motor Boats for the RAF'. Sheppard; 16th April 1932. 'Voyage of an RAF Motor Boat'. Sheppard.

Daily Telegraph: 14th December 1933. 'Speed Boat Targets for R.A.F. Bombers', Liddel Hart.

Letters from T.E. Shaw to Henry Field, Bertram Thomas, A.E.E. Weblin, Edward Spurr, Ralph Isham.

Ralph Isham: Account of the Translation of the *Odyssey*.

RAF Museum Reading Room, Hendon: Air Commodore Sydney Smith Archive; T.E. Lawrence Archive; R.J. Mitchell photo archive. Communications with Deputy Curator.

Southampton Maritime Museum External Collection: Scott-Paine Archive.

Patents Office, Monmouth. Patent Applications of Edward Spurr 1937/1938

National Archives, Kew, London. Air Ministry: Air Historical Branch: Papers (series 1) AIR 1/2692, AIR 1/2693, AIR1/2694, AIR 1/2695, AIR 1/2696, AIR 1?2697, AIR 1/2701, AIR 1/2702, AIR 1/2703. Treasury: Social Services Division (SS and 2SS series) Files T 227/4280.

Beaufort-Greenwood, W.E.G. Lawrence of Arabia and the Marine Craft Connection. Interview. 1935. T.E. Lawrence Studies.

Air Historical Branch (RAF) Ministry of Defence, RAF Bentley Priory, Stanmore, Middlesex.

Manning, Air Commodore F.J. Interview 20/11/1975.

Sims, Wing Commander R.G. Interview 2/3/1955, White Cottage, Eastgate, Hornsea, Yorks.

Air Ministry, Lists of Staff and Distribution of Duties: 10/1918, 5/1926, & 10/1934.

Secondary Sources

Rance, Adrian. *Fast Boats and Flying Boats*, Ensign Publications, Southampton, 1989

T.E. Lawrence Society Journal Vol. II No. I Summer 1992: 'T.E. Shaw and the British Power Boat Company.'

Beardow, Keith. *Sailors in the R.A.F.* Patrick Stephens Ltd. 1993.

Sutherland, J. and Cornell, D. *The R.A.F. Air* Sea *Rescue Service 1918 – 1986.*

Gilbert, Martin. *Churchill: The Wilderness Years*, Macmillan, London, 1981.

Knowles, R. (ed.). *Cats and Landladies Husbands.*

Walsley, Gerald. *Plymouth Evening Herald*, articles; telephone conversations with the author, December 2006.

The Mint (expurgated version). 352087 A/C Ross. Jonathan Cape. 1955

The Mint (unexpurgated version). 352087 A/C/ Ross. Military Book Society. 1973

Pilsborough. *The History of the Royal Air Force Marine Craft 1918 – 1966: The 200 Class Seaplane Tender.*

Baker, Anne I. *From Biplane to Spitfire: the Life of Sir Geoffrey Salmond.* Leo Cooper/Pen and Sword Books, 200; Letters to the author, 2005, 2006.

General Sources and their Abbreviations

BLH & RG: Liddel Hart and Graves, T.E. *Lawrence to His Biographers*. Faber and Faber, London. 1961.

DG: D. Garnett (ed.) *Letters of T.E. Lawrence*. Jonathan Cape. 1938.

MB: M. Brown (ed.) *Letters of T.E. Lawrence*. J.M. Dent. London. 1988.

LTEL: A.W. Lawrence (ed.) *T.E. Lawrence by His Friends*. Jonathan Cape. London. 1937.

Friends: A.W. Lawrence (ed.) *T.E. Lawrence by His Friends*. Jonathan Cape. 1937.

Wilson: Wilson, Jeremy, *Lawrence of Arabia; the Authorised Biography*. London, Heinemann, 1989.

Golden Reign: Sydney Smith, Clare *The Golden Reign*. Cassell and Co. Ltd. 1949.

Mack: Mack, J.E., *A Prince of Our Disorder*.

Yardley: Yardley, M. *T.E. Lawrence*. Stein and Day, New York. 1985.

Hyde: Montgomery Hyde, H., *Solitary in the Ranks*. Constable and Company. 1977.

Marriott: Marriott, P. *A Leaf in the Wind – The Last Days of T.E. Lawrence*. Alpha Press, 1996.

K&S: Knightley, P. and Simpson, C., *The Secret Lives of Lawrence of Arabia*. Thomas Nelson and Sons Ltd. 1969

Aldington: Aldington, R., *Lawrence of Arabia – a Biographical Enquiry*. Collins, London. 1955.

Part 3

Primary Sources

Bennett, Richard M. Correspondence. November 2004.

Birnie, Nick. Telephone Conversation. Kings Langley, Herts. May 1985.

Bodleian Library, Oxford, T.E. Lawrence collection

Cripps, Tony. Telephone conversation and correspondence. 1985, 2004

Dorset Daily Echo and *Weymouth Dispatch* (15th to 21st May 1935). Various reports.

Gordon, Frank. Interview. Bovington. 25th May 1985.

Hammersley, Roland and Hughes, Mrs. Joan. Correspondence. Bovington. February 1986.

Imperial War Museum, London Correspondence of Captain H.W. Lettman-Johnson. (Box Ref. 92/32/1).

Knowles, Joyce. Conversation. Clouds Hill, Dorset. May 1985.

Legg, Rodney. Telephone conversations. August and November 2004.

Montague, Margaret. Conversation. Wimborne, Dorset. November 1985.

Payne, S.S. (H.M. Coroner for Bournemouth and Poole and East Dorset). Correspondence. December 2004.

Runyard, Godfrey C. Correspondence. May to July 2005.

Russell, Arthur. Interview. Coventry. 7th December 1985.

Secondary Sources

Broughton: *Lawrence of Arabia – the Simple Facts*, Harry Broughton (one time Mayor of Wareham, Dorset), Wareham, 1961.

Biographers: *T.E. Lawrence to his Biographers*. Robert Graves and Basil Liddell Hart (Cassell, London, 1938).

Brown and Cave. *A Touch of Genius – The Life of T.E. Lawrence* (J.M. Dent, London. 1988).

Graham: *The Crash That Killed Lawrence of Arabia.* Article by Colin Graham in *Dorset* magazine (Dorset, Summer 1968).

James: *The Golden Warrior*, Lawrence James (Weidenfeld and Nicolson, London, 1990).

Knight: *Colonel T.E. Lawrence Visits Mr. and Mrs. Thomas Hardy*, Ronald Knight (Bat and Ball Press, Dorset, 1985).

Knightley and Simpson: *The Secret Lives of Lawrence of Arabia*, Philip Knightley and Colin Simpson (Panther, London, 1971).

DG: *The Letters of T.E. Lawrence* ed. David Garnett, Cape, London , 1937.

MB: *The Letters of T.E. Lawrence* ed. Malcolm Brown, J.M. Dent, London, 1988.

Quietness: *An Handful With Quietness* by Pat and Joyce Knowles and Bob Hunt, E.V.G. Hunt, Dorset, 1992.

Friends: *T.E. Lawrence by his Friends,* ed. A.W. Lawrence, Cape, London 1937.

Seven Pillars: *The Seven Pillars of Wisdom* by T.E. Lawrence, Cape, London, 1937.

Legg: *Lawrence in Dorset*, Rodney Legg, Dorset Publishing Company, Wincanton, 1988. Reprinted as *Lawrence of Dorset*, 2005.

Liddell Hart: *T.E. Lawrence in Arabia and After*, Basil Liddell Hart, Cape, London, 1935.

Mack: *A Prince of Our Disorder*, John E. Mack, Weidenfeld and Nicolson, London, 1976.

Marriott: *A Leaf in the Wind – The Last Days of T.E. Lawrence*, Paul Marriott and Yvonne Argent, The Alpha Press, Brighton, 1996.

McGowan: 'First Word' in *Wessex* magazine, Dorset, December, 1985.

Norman: T.E. *Lawrence – Unveiling the Enigma*, Andrew Norman, Halsgrove, Tiverton, Devon, 2003.

Simpson: 'Death of a Hero', Colin Simpson. *Unsolved* magazine, Orbis Publications London, 1984.

Stuart: *T.E. Lawrence* by Desmond Stuart, Hamish Hamilton, London, 1977.

Williamson: *The Genius of Friendship*, Henry Williamson, Henry Williamson Society, London, 1937/1998.

Wilson C: *The Outsider*, Colin Wilson, Victor Gollancz, London, 1956.

Wilson J; *Lawrence of Arabia – The Authorised Biography of T.E. Lawrence*, Jeremy Wilson, Heinemann, London, 1988.

Winterbotham: *The Nazi Connection*, F.W. Winterbotham, Panther, London, 1979.

Yardley: *Backing into the Limelight – A Biography of T.E. Lawrence*, Michael Yardley, Harrap, London, 1985.

Yeates: *Winged Victory*, V.M. Yeates, Cape, London, 1934.

Smith and Hogan: *Criminal Law: Cases and Materials*, J.C. Smith and Brian Hogan, Butterworths, London, 1990.

APPENDICES

APPENDIX ONE

Clouds Hill

In Medieval times a French monk by the name of Claude had lived on the hill. The correct pronunciation of his name was 'Clowood' and so the hill became 'Clowood's Hill'. Lawrence paid for the rebuilding of his cottage at Clouds Hill initially by selling his dagger from Arabia, and later from the proceeds of his translation of the *Odyssey*. He began renting it in 1923 and finally bought it in 1929. He was helped in this work by Sergeant Knowles and Arthur Russell. Knowles did the roof, the window frames and sash bars on his own. He also made the larger dormer window, which Russell and Lawrence copied. If one examines these closely one can see where a purlin has been cut to install the window in the upstairs bunk room. The second upstairs bunk room was sheathed in sheet cork and had a port hole as a window, and the food room was lined with aluminium foil. The ceiling height on the stairs is so low that Lawrence fitted two leather pads to prevent his friends suffering concussion. This shouldn't have worried Lawrence, who was only 5'5½". Payne remembered seeing him looking up at his tall cleaning lady, Laura Day, to talk to her.

The 'Kraal'

For a number of years after Joyce Knowles died Mr and Mrs Mike Chapman took over the trusteeship of the cottage. They lived in the old Knowles' cottage opposite, 'the Kraal' until, in 1992, Frank decided it had had its day and would have to be knocked down. However, Lawrence enthusiasts will be pleased to learn that he used as many of the materials from the original building to rebuild it as possible. Thus the present roof tiles are from the original structure. He also confined himself faithfully to the outline of the old building, so that the new two-storey house has the same plan form as the original. The present two-storey ridge is at the same height as that of the original single storey bungalow.

The Fire Pool

The old fire pool, built by a local contractor for Lawrence in the 1930s, is still visible in the Chapman's garden. The original superstructure has long since disappeared but one can clearly see the old tank and the remains of Lawrence's study and rest area. Ken Payne used to go swimming in this. He remembered the water was from a local spring, temperature 52 degrees. If you dived in you would hit your head on the bottom. Arthur Russell remembered Lawrence used to lie on the bed at one end of the pool and read. To get to the study at the other end one had to swim across. Arthur never used the pool but remembered that the Jeddah doors were brought back from Egypt by a destroyer captain.

A Vulcan Ram Pump, installed by Lawrence, was used to pump water uphill to the swimming pool/static water tank which had a capacity of 7,000 gallons. At the end of 1934 Lawrence had discussed with Pat Knowles the practicalities of setting up a printing press in a room over the swimming pool, but the project did not proceed.

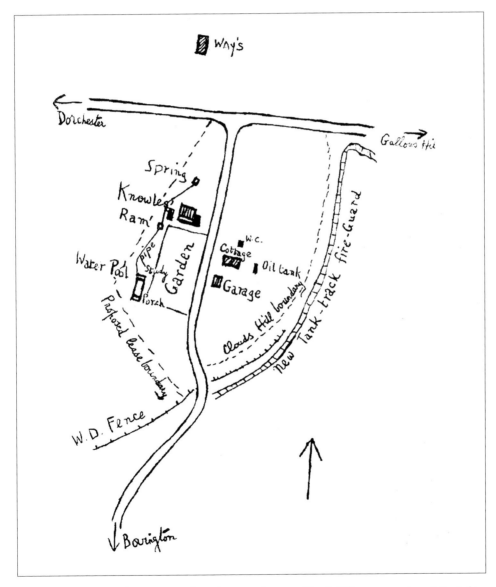

Lawrence's diagram of the location of the Vulcan Ram Pump at Clouds Hill accompanying a letter to his mother in 1934. It shows the location of the three bends in the road near Clouds Hill and the boundary of the Frampton Estate. (Via Legg)

In the new millennium the National Trust decided the cottage needed some restoration work. They employed their buildings expert, James Grazeby, to carry this out. Most of the work concerned the downstairs bathroom and the upstairs bunk room. In the course of restoring the bathroom, workers moved the bath and found a small lump of cork clinging to the wall. This was the remains of the original cork insulation. Grazeby commented:

> The cork is not of the modern square type, which is made of compressed cork shavings. It was covered in proper cork veneer, complete slices taken from entire trees and imported from Portugal. We managed to track down a firm there who could do the same thing for us and the effect is almost like having leather or marble on the walls.[1]

In 1933 Lawrence had lined the upstairs bunk room with aluminium foil for both thermal insulation and to prevent water seepage. The material was in those days a recent invention Lawrence came across it while working on the fast patrol boats, using it as a fuel proofer in the engine room.[2]

The Trust workers concluded Lawrence had carefully co-ordinated the look of the cottage. The restoration cost £5,000. Some find Clouds Hill a lonely, oppressive place with a peculiar atmosphere. But it remains the nation's most significant memorial to a strange, great man.

Notes

1 *Dorset Daily Echo* 17th August 2000; *The Times*, 15th August, 2000.
2 Ibid.

APPENDIX TWO

Arthur Russell's Recollections of Lawrence and Arabia

A.R: Arthur Russell.
A.S: the interviewer, the author.
Edited interview conducted at Arthur Russell's home in Coventry, December 1985.

A.R. He could think in five languages and speak in another seven. Marvellous, marvellous mind.

A.S. What were the languages he knew?

A.R.. I know French. I think German, Arabic – I don't know what the others were. I didn't speak them so I didn't use them. He did translate a book from the French while I was with him. I think it was called *The Tree*, but I think it's changed its name. But he translated it from the French and I was reading it, you know while he was doing it. He'd give it to me – 'here you are, read that.' I had to read all these things, give him my opinion.

A.S. When you were at Arishmael Cove you said he'd tell you more about the lashings on his back.

A.R. Oh, he told me all about that, how it happened and how he escaped. No, I don't think that . . . no it isn't in his book The *Seven Pillars of Wisdom* how he told it me, but when he escaped he said – I think this bit's in the book – the chap who gave him the key to the medicine room. He said he didn't know whether it was to get something to kill himself off, or to escape, but he said, 'He gave me the key and I got out of the window.' And then when he caught up with his Arabs – this isn't in the book, it's what he told me – he said the hardest job in the world he had was to mount that camel and not show them that he was hurt. 'Course he'd taped himself up here and his back was raw, but he didn't want to know. But they went back and cleared up.

A.S. Can you remember anything specifically he told you about his time in Arabia at all?

A.R. He used to tell me all of it. He used to tell me what he was going to write in the next chapter, how he used to set, do the dynamiting of the sleepers, for doing what he called 'the tulips' – blowing up their lines.

A.S. You must have been one of the first people to hear the true story of what his . . .

A.R. No. He had written The *Seven Pillars of Wisdom* but it was stolen on Reading Station.[1] . . . I think he wrote it three times actually. 'Cause it was a big book and it was a lot of writing but he was a fast writer, a fast reader as well – he taught me how to read fast. He also taught me how to go without sleep. When he was in Arabia he daren't sleep – had to keep awake.

A.S. How did he do that?

A.R. Oh, it's hard to describe it during later time. I wouldn't advise it to anyone. He wished he could sleep, 'cause it was such a habit he didn't sleep. He was conscious of everything that went on.

A.S. Did he tell you of the time he had to shoot one of the Arabs?

A.R. Oh yes, he told me about that. Of course, nobody else would do it – they had different factions. His biggest job with the Arabs, they would not work together. They had to work separately. So he wouldn't them all up and go in and fight a little battle. He had to get some way, some another. Now this was, I forget where they were travelling – it wasn't to Akaba was it, it was somewhere they were going up north, I know that. And this chap had done something wrong and he'd got to be shot and killed.

A.S. In the *Seven Pillars* he shot him three times didn't he?

A.R. Yes, well, just to make sure.

A.S. I don't know whether you saw the film? They made out that he'd enjoyed it.

A.R. He didn't. He didn't enjoy it. But he did it because it had got to be done and he couldn't get them to do it. And he said, 'All right, I'll do it', and then they could get on. He was waiting to go on. He had a hard time out there. A very hard life. There was nothing easy anywhere out there.

A.S. I recently read a report that he was in charge of his own bodyguard but really he was more of an adviser than a leader of the Arabs. Would you say that?

A.R. He had his own bodyguard for one reason. When they went out on a quick raid they had to have people on whom they could rely. There was one thing that's – I don't think this is in the book – but he told me, with his bodyguard everyone had to do the same as he could do – that was, mount a camel when it was standing. They daren't have them kneel because by the time they'd all have been shot. You know . . . get behind a sand dune . . . blow up a train (he only had about 60 feet of wire to his explosives). Now once . . . when the train went by and it didn't go off . . . but I think somebody had seen him and the train reversed and he blew it up when . . . the train got over it. But part of the train landed on his foot – 'cause all around him it was so close; he had also got five bullet grazes on him. He had to run – he'd got an armoured car that time – he had to run with a broken toe to get away from the Turks. I often say to people: in the First World War there's Kitchener; there's Allenby; and there's Lawrence – God's gift to the nation. If he hadn't have fought the Turks there, down in the Gulf and up to Akaba the Turks would have encroached upon Suez – we wouldn't have had any oil. We could have lost the War. But he stopped them. And I always say he was God's gift to the country. He stopped the Turks from stopping our oil.

A.S. Did he ever talk about what happened in Damascus?

A.R. Now he was supposed to get to Damascus after Allenby. But he got there first, a bit deliberately. He wanted to get the Arabs installed there and Allenby came in afterwards. This was to give the Arabs a little concession, which he knew he wouldn't get otherwise. So he got them there first. That was deliberate.

A.S. Were the Arabs actually sympathetic to these ideas?

A.R. Oh, yes. They thought the world of him. 'El Aurens' they called him. They called him 'El Aurens' because they couldn't say 'Lawrence'. They have to say 'El' instead of 'L'.

A.S. Why did they regard him so highly?

A.R. Well, because he was leading them. He was winning battles. Now when he blew up a train it burst the whole train, created them stuff they wanted. That was the hard part for him, 'cause he had to wait whilst they stole all the stuff from the train. Including the women.

A.S. I don't know whether you know, there was a recent British Army expedition went out there . . .[2]

A.R. Now they travelled his route. I did read a bit in the modern excerpt from this. They did a long journey and they said he must have made a mistake. They could not do it in the time he said.

A.S. He said nine hours, and they did it in three days.

A.R. Yes, well. There's one thing they missed out on. They just had ordinary camels. They didn't even know the languages. They had to work with an interpreter. They were not living the same as he was! Lying on the ground and riding. They were looking after themselves. Now if you want to read the *Seven Pillars of Wisdom* right through it says that he always used racing camels, not ordinary ones. They were the best of any available: the second or third best animal in Arabia.[3] Now he was on high speed travel, not low.

A.S. Did he ever talk about the American Lowell Thomas at all?

A.R. Oh yes, he told me a few things about him – the times he met him. I don't remember all the detail obviously. He did tell me about him.

A.S. He was the man responsible for promoting Lawrence after the war.

A.R. Yes. He told me all these things before he rewrote. I suppose, really, while he was telling me, he was refreshing his mind. Then he'd sit down and write it and I'd have to read it. Now the original book was going to be a hundred pounds and one hundred copies. They found out, by the way, that it had to be printed privately. It had to be a private edition 'cause of him being liable of [libellous concerning] some certain people. Well Magnus [Manning] Pike had already been bankrupt once so he didn't care, his 'don't worry' it was. He was summonsed good. As it was a private edition nobody could say anything.[4] He used to do digging in Egypt and round there. I think he'd done some in France, I'm not sure. But it was in Egypt when he started this. But I think he was a little bit involved with subversive work, spying as they call it. I think he was passing information back. But, it's like me; there are a lot of things that I can't talk about because they're on the Secret List. All those things are on the Secret List. He couldn't tell me about them.

A.S. So he didn't actually tell anything?

A.R. No! You can't talk about those things. He could only hint: 'I was there doing something' – that was all.

Notes

1 He left the original manuscript in an attaché case (lent to him by Alan Dawnay that morning) in the waiting room whilst changing trains.

2 This was an expedition to Arabia in 1984 by four men of the Royal Green Jackets retracing Lawrence's journeys. It was led by Captain Charles Blackmore. He wrote *In the Footsteps of Lawrence of Arabia* (1986).

3 The diminutive Lawrence was particularly suited to riding a camel at speed. Camels, apparently, have very long memories. If a man wounds or in some way injures a camel it can remember the perpetrator for up to 20 years and has a peculiar way of exacting revenge. It will chase after the man, then knock him over and sit on him. There is a large bone protruding from the base of the camel's neck. It may use this to crush the man to death.

4 *The Secret Lives of Lawrence of Arabia*: 'Whilst busy with his duties, Lawrence was still preparing the subscribers edition of *Seven Pillars* for publication. The printer, Manning Pike, had premises in London at 44, Westbourne Terrace North, W2, which he leased from George H. Noble at £1 a week. Lawrence would ride his motorcycle from Cranwell to check on progress and sometimes stay overnight, sleeping on a makeshift bed on the hot water pipes in the basement.'

APPENDIX THREE

Edward Spurr: a co-Designer?

Whilst he was working for Scott-Paine at Hythe, some time between December 1933 and November 1934, Lawrence met a young marine engineer named Edward Spurr who had some interesting ideas that corresponded in many ways to his own conclusions. These concerned how a boat performed at high speed. Although Lawrence had died before these ideas bore any fruit, Spurr continued working on the project for a number of years after T.E.'s death.

Spurr was a boat designer who was working at Southampton. What he and Lawrence appear to have become interested in was a phenomenon now quite well known in marine circles, but which in those times was revolutionary: the *Ground Effect*. This is a phenomenon used by large sea birds flying long distances to rest their wings. Any aircraft or airborne boat that flies close to the land or water surface creates a 'cushion of air' underneath it when pressurized air reacts against its under-surface. By 1935 the principle had long been known. In 1927 Charles Lindbergh used it to conserve fuel during his transatlantic flight and two years later Germany's Dornier Do-X, a 12 engined flying-boat, crossed the Atlantic using it.

Lawrence's interest in this appears to have remained concealed in the archives for years. It was only when an article appeared in the aviation press in the late sixties that heads began to turn. In February 1966 *Flight International* magazine published an article written by the editor H.F. King, entitled *Another Lawrence*. This claimed that Lawrence had been involved 'heart and soul' in the development of what would now be known as an 'air cushion craft'. King stated the boat was mentioned in at least one newspaper and one periodical of the day. In these the hull was described as 'like a short aeroplane wing' and 'a freak of aeroplane design'. Subsequent investigations by King revealed that a prototype was constructed by the engineering company R. Malcolm Ltd. of Slough, who had some experience of aircraft construction and Spurr was friendly with one of the executives there. The boat was named *Empire Day* by Baron Strabolgi[1], on 24th May, 1938, Empire Day, five years almost to the day after Lawrence died. King's article stated that Spurr and Lawrence worked together on 'new theories of aircraft design'. He gave no explanation how he came by this information.

Spurr had continued researches which had led to the building of *Empire Day*. It emerged also that Lawrence and Spurr had made nearly 70 miniature models; that these had been subject to 'innumerable tests'[5]; and that Lawrence was 'heart and soul in the work'.[2]

This does have some basis of truth and relates directly back to the work Scott-Paine did on fast boats and an occasion when he met Lawrence and Arthur Russell in his factory.

In September 1933 Scott-Paine took part in the US' Harmsworth Trophy in his purpose-designed boat *Miss Britain III*. The race was one of the most important powerboat races in America and was held in Detroit. *Miss Britain III* was a revolutionary design that, as well as using the 'hard chine principle', had a timber and metal reinforced frame that was clad in a skin of *Alclad*, an alloy comprising aluminium-based copper alloy, clad on each side with pure aluminium. The metal skin was fastened to the frames with thousands of duralumin screws with countersunk heads, rather like the fighters of World War Two. The design was incredibly light and incredibly dangerous: if it had flipped the pilot would have little chance of survival. Scott-Paine lost the Harmsworth Trophy Race to the American Garfield 'Gar' Wood. Wood's *Miss America X* packed 7,600 hp in comparison with *Miss Britain III*'s 1,400 – but the superior power-to-weight ratio of the tiny British boat and Scott-Paine's more or less reckless racing meant things were closer than they should have been. Scott-Paine returned to England and, on 24th September, had the engine of *Miss Britain III* removed after it caught fire during a race at Poole. Lawrence was then based at the British Power Boat Company yards at Hythe. Arthur Russell:

> I did visit him when I got back [from India] but the main visit, one I do remember vividly, was when he was at Hamble[3] with Scott-Paine. That was memorable. Scott-Paine had just come back from America, where he lost the race to Gar Wood. And he was showing us a film on his yacht to show how Gar Wood had manoeuvred him over the sandbank to make him do extra miles to get to the finishing point. He lost the race. We walked into the factory and his boat had just been unloaded. There was not an engine in it – that had come separately. And Lawrence said to him: 'There's no engine. If you want I'll try and get one. They are good engines.'
>
> Scott-Paine said, 'No, I'm happy with the one I've got, but I'm going to design another hull.'
>
> He [Lawrence] said, 'Oh, what are you going to do with this one?' It was only about 12 foot high.
>
> Scott-Paine said, 'Nothing, why, have you got designs on it?'
>
> He [Lawrence] said, 'Well yes as a matter of fact I could use it.' He had designs on this and he was asked what it was. He said, 'Well I would load a bomb with a torpedo on that and take it up and load it up onto a seaplane, instead of bringing the seaplanes on land to fit the bomb rack, bombs etc.'
>
> Scott-Paine said, 'Oh yes, it would do that wouldn't it?'
>
> He [Lawrence] said, 'Also I think I could launch a torpedo from that being low to the water.'
>
> . . . Also other people don't know it, but he was one of the forerunners [inventors] of the hovercraft[4]. I've seen pictures of him with the hovercraft.[5]

The boat they had been inspecting was the revolutionary *Miss Britain III*. Confirmation that Lawrence was impressed by the design comes from another source. On 2nd June 1934 he spent the evening with Liddel Hart and his family at Otterbourne. Whilst discussing the future of naval warfare Lawrence mentioned that in the future: 'a fleet would loose off 300–400 (quantity counts) of wireless-controlled speed-boats like *Miss Britain III* . . . carrying one torpedo and almost flush with [the] water – 1 foot showing in front being splinter-proof.

Only [a] direct hit could stop one, and no-one could hit such a target at 60 mph except by a fluke.'[6]

Lawrence had been working with flying boats, seaplanes and fast marine craft for nearly four and a half years by the time he met Spurr. From his work with the air and ground crews of the large Blackburn Iris and Supermarine Southamptons he must have heard of the ground effect phenomenon. His ideas appear to have stemmed directly from the work he did on the RAF 200. Here the flat bottom of the boat's hull was designed to plane across the water, reducing surface resistance to a minimum. Its development was a direct consequence of Scott-Paine's fast boat work.

On 18th June 1931 Lawrence wrote to Beauforte-Greenwood referring to surf board 'splash target' towing work he had done in Plymouth Sound:

> If we can go on playing with it, and get the wire right, I shall try some fast towing behind my own boat, and see if the board does 'take off' at speed. We could ballast it forward, or alter the pennant, if so, to make it fit up to 30 mph.[7]

His 'own boat' was the *Biscuit* speed-boat he had been given by Colin Cooper. 'Take off' in this instance, seems to suggest the surf board actually leaving the water surface, rather than

Scott-Paine's *Miss Britain III* at Poole after the Harmsworth Trophy Races of 1933, with a burnt-out engine. Lawrence and Russell saw her shortly after this at Southampton with the engine removed. Note the streamlining and *Alclad* cladding. It was possibly this boat that partly inspired Spurr's design.

accelerating away. One of the peculiarities of a 'wing in ground effect' is the tendency of the hull front to 'pitch up' as it rides an air cushion. This 'pitching up' was years later to have a critical effect on the design of ground effect craft. The Soviet Union did much research and experimentation into 'ground effect' flight in the 1950s and '60s. One of the problems they found was a change in the point where the pilot's trimming action (i.e. control of the angle of attack) acts. As the boat accelerated into ground effect the lift/weight balance changed and the point at which trim acted on the craft moved rearwards. Thus the nose tended to pitch upwards, i.e. there was an inherent instability. This would explain Lawrence's 1931 suggestion of adding forward ballast. The pennant was used to aid recognition from the air and may have created a lot of drag and he probably suggested reducing the size of it.

H.F. King in his article quoted another of Lawrence's letters to Beauforte-Greenwood, that of 14th July 1931 from Mount Batten. This concerned the towing of a 'splash target' in Plymouth Sound behind, at first, an RAF 35-foot launch, and later the *Biscuit*. The problem had been that the board hadn't been travelling fast enough, reaching sometimes 35 mph, but generally only 25. The *Biscuit*, on its own, could travel considerably faster than this. Halfway through his letter Lawrence told B-G:

> So I hooked it up onto the Biscayne baby and ran it [the surf board] off its keel! The rough days . . . were great fun, the sea being much too bad for a Southampton [flying boat] upon our last occasion. Once I got it [the surf board] up to 35 mph: but 20–25 is really its fastest decent speed. For a fast target you would have to re-design, with flared bows and a flattened after-moulding, I think, to plane: with scoop-tubes like air intakes thrust through the floor amidships. You could make it weigh only half of this target's weight, I think.[8]

King assumed this indicated 'that Lawrence had some knowledge or instinct concerning air lubrication'. However this appears to be a simple interpretation. The 'flared bows and flattened after moulding' were exactly what Scott-Paine had used on the RAF 200: this enabled it to plane across the water. But the penultimate sentence reveals a different system. If anything, the principle Lawrence advocated here was more akin to that of the 'ram wing': lift on take-off and landing is augmented by blowing a funnel of air under the aircraft's aerofoil surface and trapping it there for support. He suggested making air holes in the board and fitting some 'coin-scoop' air intakes on the surf board's top surface to enable slipstream-driven air to flow into the scoops and down underneath the board. Thus it rides on a cushion of air, reducing its weight.

Lawrence appears to have inadvertently solved one of the problems of ground-effect travel that baffled scientists for years. This was how to reduce the craft's 'drag' or resistance against the air and water surface. Water is eighty times denser than air. Consequently a very high 'drag' factor has to be overcome before a craft can leave the surface. Fifty years later a German engineer named Hanno Fischer used Lawrence's solution: he powered his boat with an airscrew set on a pylon. The pylon contained an open/close door that could funnel 7% of the slipstream down below the craft where the air was contained by two catamarans on each side of the hull with skirts fore and aft. Thus a static air cushion was built up beneath the hull.[9] This was exactly the principle Lawrence suggested in 1931.

View of bows of *Empire Day*, showing the nose logo dedication to Lawrence: 'To L of A – a compte'. (Via Pilsborough)

The only evidence that remains of Lawrence's correspondence with Spurr in 1935 is a lengthy letter written from the Ozone Hotel, Bridlington on 31st January. Scrawled across the top of this in A.W. Lawrence's minute handwriting are the words 'To be treated with great discretion':

Dear Spurr,

I lost your letter – or rather, I sent it to my cottage and so had no note of your address. Nor had Green whom I saw in Bridlington a month ago! A bright pair. Your letter interested me: I feel that engines – petrol engines – are at very nearly their best: that hulls are only in their beginnings, and propellors hardly even that. There is plenty of room for research indeed!

Our 37½ foot boats are about as far as planing displacement hulls have yet gone: that is, they are a pretty compromise between speed, cost and seaworthiness. Twenty years hence, I hope something very different will rule.

I'm here till Feb. 28, but tread by the leg. I have no motor-bike here, and no time to use it, if I had. The ten R.A.F. boats (five cruisers and five armoureds) are in a garage in the town, under refit, with myself to watch points for the Air Ministry.

You'll be glad to hear that your big gear box did admirably as linked to the Gardner light-fast Diesel. We ran if for 50 hours off Hythe without an adjustment. It is the softest and quickest clutch I've ever felt.

After February the R.A.F. discharge me, and thenceforward I've got to look after myself: not immediately for I have at least six months, but as soon as it is convenient. I have not an idea in my head: various jobs have been offered, but none of them attractive. Possibly I shall fall back in my cottage and see how much – or rather how little – I really need.

I hope your plans are satisfactory to yourself. Research is a sport, rather than a living: but you may be fortunate in getting something jog-trotting at Bradford to keep you in comfort while you do thinking.

Green was not too wise: he tried to persuade White's of Cowes to build an almost facsimile Power boat: they committed themselves some of the way, till the question of proprietary designs came up and then there was an almighty row behind the scenes. I'm out of it now but I fancy Scotty [Scott-Paine] strengthened his position, on the whole.

You are well away!

Yours,

T.E. Shaw[10]

We can infer from this that Spurr was interested in research, particularly engine development, had gearbox design experience and was looking for a reliable living. He might have been involved in some way with the design of the Power-Hyland system. It also suggests he may have been a mechanical, rather than marine engineer. The project they discussed never found tangible form during Lawrence's lifetime. However, on November 18th, 1936 Spurr registered a patent with the Patents Office entitled *Improvements in and relating to the Hulls of Motor-Boats*. Three months later, on February 17, 1937 he registered a second patent entitled *Improvements in and relating to the Construction of High Speed Motor Boats,* a development of the earlier one. In these applications lay the genesis of the craft Spurr claimed he and Lawrence had worked on.

Spurr's second application described specific features about his craft:

a) The main body of the hull was wedge shaped in plan tapering gradually towards the rear. This was of a cambered aerofoil shape in longitudinal section that extended the length of the boat. The idea was that, as the boat gained speed, the hull would act as a wing, lifting the boat out of the water.

b) Along the top centre of the hull was a 'cigar tube' shaped superstructure that contained the streamlined glazed cockpit, the front part of which was of a rounded shape that merged into the bows.

c) On the underside of the hull were two flat inclined planing surfaces, it being intended that these would 'plane or glide over the water . . . disposed one behind the other', and 'both inclined to the surface of the water'. The first of these stretched the entire width of the hull and was two-thirds the width of the rear surface. The rear surface acted as a 'tail skid' being 'nominally for trim purposes' and was one fifth the width of the front but longer by one fifth. The idea was

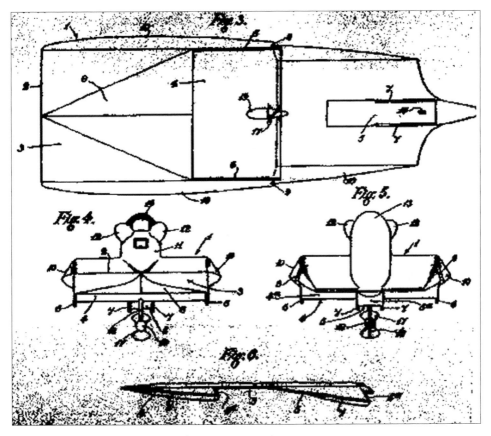

General Arrangement Drawing of Edward Spurr's *Empire Day*: plan of hull underside, front and rear elevations and side elevation of the planing surfaces below the hull. From *Improvements in and relating to the Construction of High Speed Motor Boats*. E. Spurr. Patents Office application, 17/02/1937. (Patents Office)

that as the boat's speed increased, the inclined surfaces would glide over the surface causing the nose and hull to be lifted clear of the water reducing drag to a minimum.

d) There were flanges or 'inwash fins' on each side of the planing surfaces to prevent side splash, cut a clear wake behind both the planes and 'confine the water beneath [them] . . ., giving a greater lifting force per unit area'.

e) In order to travel in choppy water the forward part of the hull before the front planing surface was a 'V-shaped' cut-water extending back to the front hydroplane. At the rear edge of the front plane was a step aligned transversely across the boat to break the suction effect.

f) As the front portion of the hull was wider than the rear, each side was stepped back above the underside step to reduce the width, providing less resistance by both rear sides of the boat to water. The sides of the boat were also shaped to prevent the craft 'digging' under the water when manoeuvring by being V-shaped in vertical cross section – the upper half overhanging the water. The top half of each side was inclined in towards the hull, the lower half was a convex curve down towards the inwash fins.

g) The engine was installed over the front planing surface. Since the greater the distance the engine, and consequently the centre of gravity, was from the rudder, the greater the turning

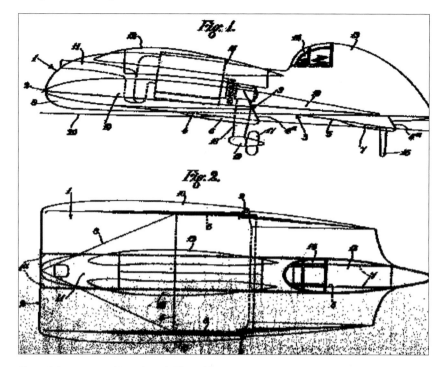

General Arrangement Drawing of Edward Spurr's Empire Day: side elevation and plan of hull top. From *Improvements in and relating to the Construction of High Speed Motor Boats*. E. Spurr. Patents Office application, 17/02/1937. (Patents Office)

moment of the boat would be. The rudder's effectiveness would increase, and the rudder's overall size reduce. With a slender rudder of high aspect ratio resistance to forward movement would also be reduced.[11]

Although highly futuristic in appearance, close examination reveals the patent application for *Empire Day* was naïve in its lack of technical detail. No powerplant was specified. If the accompanying photographs of are of an actual prototype, rather than a mock up, working drawings, materials specifications and construction details would have to have been prepared before it could be built. But the patent application gave only a very basic explanation of the design.

King stated that the craft had been under construction since November 1937, which would mean it took around five months to build (*Miss Britain III* took only nine weeks), and he described specifically that it was painted blue-and-white and that the first prototype had a 1.5 litre four-cylinder supercharged engine developing 150 hp at 6,000 rpm. It was 16 feet long, with a beam of six feet and weighed 850lb. The design was so tight the steering wheel had to be removed before the driver could get in.

A number of details point to Lawrence's involvement. One was the nose of the finished prototype of 1938 which carried the logo *To L of A a compte* (To Lawrence of Arabia on Account). Another was that Spurr used a cladding material on *Empire Day* exactly the same as that on

Miss Britain III. Since *Empire Day* used *Alclad* aluminium alloy for most of her construction, with a bottom of steel, and in view of the fact that Lawrence had had a particularly close inspection of *Miss Britain III* only months before he met Spurr, it is more than likely Lawrence mentioned this 'revolutionary' system to Spurr, if Spurr did not see it himself.

In his book on the RAF 200 seaplane tender, G.D. Pilborough concluded that *Empire Day* had anticipated by many years the effect of aerodynamic lift: 'The basic principle: in which hull design plays a big part is well known some fifty years later for use in racing water-born craft and in 'surface effect vehicles' requires speed to raise the craft up in the water, thereby reducing drag and displacement.'[12] Spurr stated in his patent application how on occasions the hull on *Empire Day* would ride 'completely clear of the water'. Eventually, when the boat attained an optimum speed, it was hoped that the ground effect would take over. Spurr was adamant in his patent that the boat was 'aerodynamically balanced' and 'perfectly stable'. At this point we must question whether Spurr was a genius or as Professor A.W. Lawrence believed, and Beauforte-Greenwood thought, a 'fatuous crank' or an imposter. T.E. thought similarly, his letter to Spurr notwithstanding.

In view of the fact that a boat moving into 'ground effect' is inherently unstable why would Spurr have stated the design was otherwise? There may be one reason for this.

In the 1960s Hanno Fischer hit on the solution to the inherent instability problem of a 'wing in ground effect'.[13] Experimenting with the delta wing shape developed by the Germans in World War Two,[14] he reversed the wing so that the leading edge was straight and the apex pointed to the rear, a configuration he found stable in ground effect flight. He controlled lateral movement by mounting the rudder and elevator control above the craft and out of the effect.[15] Spurr's craft was similarly 'wedge-shaped' tapering towards the rear and he may have accidentally lent stability to the craft without knowing why.

However *Empire Day* had few other redeeming features. The short wingspan suggested that it had very poor lateral stability when airborne and was hard to turn at speed. Also, in the ground effect the idea is that the drag coefficient is reduced to a minimum: with *Empire Day* however, the drive bracket, propeller and rudder remained well below the surface.

> When a load is moved via water, the various resistances increase as the velocity times itself, and the energy needed to affect an increase in speed rises as the energy cubed, or energy multiplied by itself three times (the exact power is 3.0) . . . a huge number.[16]

Thus, although the boat's velocity increased, and the craft rose free from the water surface, the parasitic drag of three elements submerged by one and a half feet below the surface required three times the normal energy to accelerate. Spurr appears to have ignored this:

> The only parasitic drag is caused by the central fuselage or [cigar tube] superstructure and the drive bracket and rudder. Otherwise every part of the design is serving a useful purpose.
>
> The deeply submerged drive bracket and propeller, and the deep, blade-like rudder allow the boat to be fully controlled when on occasions the hull rides completely clear of the water. In this case the hull becomes, momentarily, airborne, but loses nothing of its propeller thrust. It momentarily gains speed due to the total reduction of water resistance on the hull itself to zero,

yet retains full directional control as the drive bracket and rudder are still partly submerged and have a distance of approximately 40% of the hull length between them. The hull, therefore is, is fully guided by a two point contact with the water. At any speed over 100 miles per hour the water pressure on these submerged vertical surfaces is considerable and a very small area in contact with the water will be sufficient to keep the boat straight on its course.[17]

This is naïve: any of the advantages in speed the boat's design gave it would have been neutralised by the submerged elements.

The trial of *Empire Day* was not a success. Gerald Wasley recalled that he had heard there were trials of the boat on a lake in the Midlands, but they were not successful. There were probably a number of reasons for this. Not only because of the boat's huge total 'drag' but also because Spurr did not really understand the physics of ground effect. *Empire Day's* wings stretched the entire length of the hull, and were stubby. To ride on an air cushion the boat's height above the surface must be less than the width (or chord) of the wing:

> *Ground effect* is a function of the width of the wing; to take advantage of the ground effect, any vehicle must fly above the ground at an altitude less than the distance between the leading edge and the trailing edge of the wing.[18]

Her deep chord wing meant she would have had to reach a large height above the surface before entering ground effect.

The stubby wings may also not have done her any favours: one noticeable effect of air cushion flight is an increase in speed. This is not just because of a reduction in wetted area: in normal flight a large vortex of swirling air is carried backwards off each wing tip caused by the air attempting to leak around the wing tip from the wing bottom to the top. These vortices create huge additional 'drag' and limit the forward speed. In ground effect flight these are contained by the presence of the ground: the reduction in drag can be as much as 60%, resulting in great increases in speed and fuel saving.[19] But *Empire Day's* narrow wingspan would have substantially reduced this advantage.

J.M. Wilson concluded that, although Lawrence certainly knew Spurr, it was impossible that they met on many occasions and that there could never have been a close working partnership. He was dismissive of the *Flight International* article finding no evidence to support the statements it made, which he regarded as extraordinary.[20] Paul Marriott's conclusion was that although it was possible that the two did meet to experiment on a programme, with Lawrence's hectic time schedule Spurr appears to have wildly exaggerated his involvement. There was no time in 1934 to make so many models and conduct corresponding tests.[21]

King's article was controversial enough to warrant A.W. Lawrence to correspond with author Stanley Weintraub on the matter. Weintraub had written to him in July with a copy of the magazine. Professor Lawrence stated

> It was certainly interesting but I feel that the writer took Spurr's possibly eupeptic claims too readily at their face-value and may not have tested the practical validity of his ideas sufficiently; I have no knowledge of his qualifications however and may be wronging him.[22]

Photograph of Edward Spurr's *Alclad* alloy clad air cushion vehicle *Empire Day*, possibly taken in the manufacturing shed of Malcolm Engineering at Slough, London c.1938. It bears a superficial resemblance to Sir Malcolm Campbell's later *Bluebird II*, a much larger vessel that used hydrofoils. The bulbous canopy and streamlining can be seen. (*Flight International*)

Front underside view of Spurr's *Empire Day* c.1938. Probably taken before the first trial, this may have been a mock up. The stubby aerofoil shaped hull-wings, V cut-water and front planing surface can be seen. It appears to be resting on a stand. (*Flight International*)

A.W. said Spurr had written to him in 1937, probably around the time he made the applications to the Patents Office. He told A.W. that 'TEL had helped in his invention of a new type of boat, of which he had now completed a small model; he enclosed a photograph of it, a queer bulbous thing which I might have mistaken for a tin opener.'[23] A.W. contacted Beauforte-Greenwood, who was still head of the RAF's Marine Craft Section. Beauforte-Greenwood told him that Spurr had 'tried to tack himself on to them (the British Power Boat Co.–RAF combination)'. They had to push him away. The fact that T.E. did not mention Spurr to Beauforte-Greenwood confirmed this.

It is difficult to say how far Lawrence's work helped Spurr. Lawrence was interested in the ground effect phenomenon and Spurr tried to take his 'planing displacement hull' a step further, but appears to have lacked the genius or knowledge necessary to be successful. If Lawrence had survived his ability to see to the root of a problem might have corrected Spurr's work. But this did not happen. A.W. gave a fair summing up:

> It is conceivable that S[purr] could have been so far in advance of his time that the ablest designers saw no good in his ideas but should have done; if so, I am convinced that TE eventually shared in that misjudgement, which clearly was formed after opportunity for investigation.[24]

The fact that Spurr was able to build a prototype at all is testimony to his vision. He rebuilt and re-engined *Empire Day* with a Napier Sea-Lion engine in 1939. She was renamed *Empire Day II* and with an altered hull, was patented and advertised to attack the World Water Speed Record. She never did. Pilsborough suggested that she was influential in the design

	NAME	DATE	LENGTH	WIDTH	ENGINE	SPEED	LOCATION	DRIVER	DESIGNER
1	*Miss America VII*	1931	not known	not known	2 no. Packard aircraft engines	93	Indian Creek	Gar Wood	Napoleon 'Nap' Lisee
2	*Miss America X*	1932	36	not known	4 no. Packard aircraft engines (super-charged)	125	St. Clair River	Gar Wood	'Nap' Lisee
3	*Miss England III*	1932	not known	not known	2 no. R.R. aircraft engines	120	Loch Lomond	Sir Henry Seagrave/ Kaye Don	H. Scott-Paine
4	*Miss Britain III*	1933	25	not known	1 no. Power-Napier	120	Southampton Water	H. Scott-Paine	H. Scott Paine/ T. Quelch
5	*Bluebird K3*	1937	23	not known	1 no. R.R.	130	Lake Maggiore	Sir Malcolm Campbell	F. W. Cooper
6	*Bluebird K4*	1939	27	11	1 no. R.R. 'R'	142	Coniston Water	Sir Malcolm Campbell	Peter du Cane
7	*Empire Day*	1938	16	6	Napier Lion (for version II)		Slough		Edward Spurr

of Sir Malcolm Campbell's *Bluebird II*, but although there were superficial similarities the principles behind the design of the two boats were totally different – *Bluebird II* was a hydroplane, whilst *Empire Day*, as we have seen, relied on ground effect.

Notes

1 10th Baron Strabolgi, author of numerous books and Assistant Chief of Naval Staff in Gibraltar during the Second World War.

2 *Another Lawrence*, H.F. King. *Flight International*, London, February 1966.

3 Russell probably meant Hythe: Hamble was just across Southampton Water from Hythe.

4 This does not make a lot of sense: Spurr's 'hovercraft' or air cushion vehicle was not built until 1938. Russell may have been referring to Spurr, whom he saw with the 'hovercraft'.

5 Arthur Russell. Interview with author, December 1985.

6 B-LH

7 T.E. Shaw to W.E.G. Beauforte-Greenwood, Mount Batten, 18/06/1931.

8 T.E. Shaw to W.E.G Beauforte-Greenwood, Mount Batten, 14/07/1931.

9 Discussed in *Ekranoplan : the Caspian Sea Monster*, Equinox, Channel 4 1998.

10 T.E. Lawrence to Edward Spurr. Ozone Hotel, Bridlington 31/01/1935. Bodleian Library Special Collections.

11 Interpreted from *Improvements in and relating to the Construction of High Speed Motor Boats*. E. Spurr. Patents Office application, 17/02/1937.

12 *The History of the Royal Air Force Marine Craft 1918–1966: The 200 Class Seaplane Tender*, G.D. Pilsborough.

13 WIG

14 The 'Delta Wing' was developed by Dr. Alexander Lippisch in World War Two.

15 Discussed in *Ekranoplan : the Caspian Sea Monster*, Equinox, Channel 4 1998.

16 *History of the Hovercraft*, S. Herring/C. Fitzgerald, Neoteric Hovercraft, Inc.

17 *Improvements in and relating to the Construction of High Speed Motor Boats*. E. Spurr. Patents Office application 17/02/1937.

18 *History of the Hovercraft*, S. Herring/C. Fitzgerald, Neoteric Hovercraft, Inc.

19 As Footnotes 9, 15. Data presented by Pete Thomasson, Senior Lecturer in Flight Dynamics, Cranfield University.

20 Wilson

21 Marriott

22 A.W. Lawrence to S. Weintraub, 07/1966

23 Ibid

24 Ibid

APPENDIX FOUR

The Brough SS100 Superior 'George VII' after the crash

Following the accident, 'George VII' was picked up at the crash site by Godfrey C. Runyard and his brother Frank and taken back to Bovington. Here it was stored in the Red Garage for a few weeks.[1] The Runyard brothers were responsible for all the repairs on Lawrence's Broughs.

A photograph of George VII after the crash, taken in the goods shed at Wool Railway Station before being shipped to the Brough works at Nottingham for a complete rebuild, shows the damage to the right hand side of the machine.

The right handlebar was bent backwards, the kick start lever was bent back, the right hand footrest was missing, the gear change knob had been forced into the side of the petrol tank, and the headlamp rim was missing. To remove this one had to press and turn the fitting bayonet fashion. The leather fronted rear tool bag was bent and its right hand end flattened. The nose of the front mudguard was grazed on its right side by its contact with the road surface.

GW2275 was repaired by the Brough Company and sold as an ex-works bike to the firm Harper and King of Cambridge on 30 August 1935. It was later sold privately and remained undiscovered for nearly 30 years. In 1962 it was re-discovered by Leslie Perrin of Portsmouth. He found a Brough SS100 Reg. GW2275 rusting in a back garden in Hampshire.[2] He paid one pound for it and was almost immediately offered two hundred pounds by an interested party but did not sell. His son commented in 2006:

> My father [owned] the Brough Superior from about 1962 to 1976. The bike had suffered little damage from when Lawrence died on it, as he was thrown from the bike and hit a tree. Over the years he owned it, [my father] made many missing parts for the Brough. He is still interested in vintage motorbikes and owns several.[3]

Tony Cripps, Brough expert, commented on Lawrence's choice of mount: 'I doubt if anyone really knows why he chose a B.S. It is known that he owned a small c.c. motorcycle before Broughs . . . (probably a Triumph) . . . so his interest in motorcycles was there. . . The small oval gate is three speed, which 'GW' had. The four speed gate [model] is longer.'[4]

John Weekly, the present owner and a founder member of the T.E. Lawrence Society, purchased the Brough in 1977. Buying it was the realization of a lifetime's ambition, but

348

owning the bike has left him besieged by the curious and the avaricious. He worries about the bike being stolen and is reluctant to discuss the sale. British institutions seem unwilling to buy this remarkable piece of British history, despite the fact that this country is long overdue a Lawrence museum. 'I always wanted to own the bike that Lawrence was killed on. It sounds macabre, but that was my dream. In the ten years after I bought it, I spent every night reading about Lawrence. I also amassed a collection of documents, photographs and paintings associated with it.' But he is no longer able to cope with the demands and was recently looking for a British buyer 'I am nearly 60 . . . I tried moving the bike the other day and it was a massive struggle – it is seven-and-a-half-foot long and very heavy.'

Weekly floated the idea of a sale once but the press became flooded with stories of it being auctioned for two million pounds: 'The whole episode ended up as a shambles. I never agreed for it to go to auction, but suddenly people were calling me a money grabber. Ten years ago, when I loaned it to the National Portrait Gallery as the centrepiece of a Lawrence exhibition, around 100,000 people saw it. It should be the centrepiece of a Lawrence museum. This country does not have one, but we should. . . .People are always on at me about it – it's as if the bike and me are public property. I am always being tracked down by people making offers for the bike – mostly they come from overseas.'

GW2275 was until recently on display at the National Motor Museum Beaulieu. Lawrence paid £120 for it in 1932. It was brought to Beaulieu by the museum's motorcycle expert Frank Levy: 'It would have been a hard bike to ride, eight feet long with no brakes to speak of, no proper clutch. It was made for a man who loved motorbikes.'[5]

The Brough Superior came in both a three gear and a four gear form. The GW2275 on display in the Montague Motor Museum, Beaulieu is a three gear model. The museum commented that at least three machines claim to be Lawrence's final machine but Mr. Weekly's is the most likely one.

LAWRENCE'S BROUGH SUPERIORS

	BIKE NAME	REG. NO.	DATE	TYPE	COMMENTS
1	George I	?	1922	SS80	Side valve
2	George II	?	1923	SS80	Side car
3	George III	RK899	1924	SS80	
4	George IV	RK???	1925		Or XX7646
5	George V	RK4907	1925	SS100	
6	George VI	UL656	1929	SS100	
7	George VII	GW2275	1934	SS100	No sidecar
8	George VIII	BTO 308	1935	SS100	Not delivered

Notes

1 It was placed at the rear of the petrol pump from which he had his final refill. One account has it that the Brough was taken to Wool Police Station, where it was locked up to prevent it being seen by the public.

2 Perrin's son, Andrew, told the author in 2006 that a workmate sold the bike to Perrin in 1962. He kept it until 1976 making many of the missing parts himself. The brakes were almost non-existent, it had a side car fitted when bought, and it had previously collided with the back of a bus, which had had warped it slightly.

3 Andrew Perrin, communication with author, 24/04/2006.

4 Letter to the author. October 2004.

5 *Dorset Daily Echo*, June 20th, 2003.

APPENDIX FIVE

The *Middle East Diary* Hoax

In 1959 Richard Meinertzhagen published the *Middle East Diary*. This, he stated, was not a 'serious historical document'[1] on Zionism, but was intended to be a contribution to the subject, being based on diaries, correspondence and official documents covering a 40-year period from 1917 to 1956. It represented Colonel Meinertzhagen's own personal connection with the return of the Jewish people to their homeland after 2000 years. Thus it is not an original source but was 'reconstructed' in the mid-1950s from the documents mentioned. Meinertzhagen had no qualms about the criticisms he levelled in the book: 'I have criticized many persons who are dead; some may object that this is unfair; but never in history has death conferred on men immunity from criticism, and I make no apology for including in this book my opinion of those who cannot reply.'[2] One of the objects of this criticism was Lawrence, most of the discussion of whom occurs in one of the earlier chapters in the book. Some time after the *Diary* was published certain historians realised that some of the contents of the book were unsupportable. Meinertzhagen had himself admitted there were 'inconsistencies and repetitions'[3] in the book. As mentioned earlier there had been a number of exotic reports about Meinertzhagen's life: despite his supporter's regarding him as a 'great spook', he was known to have killed men with his bare hands.

In 1995 J.N. Lockman's book *Meinertzhagen's Diary Ruse (False Entries on T.E. Lawrence)* was published. It was written with the encouragement of two Lawrence experts, Malcolm Brown and Stephen Tabachurick. Lockman stated at one point:

> Upon first reading Meinertzhagen's Lawrence entries in the summer of 1992, and as a novice in Lawrence research, I sensed already that something was very wrong.
>
> . . . Months of research proved necessary to move from a state of strong suspicion to one of overwhelming certainty on numerous passages in all the entries.[4]

Lockman examined various entries in the *Middle East Diary* commenting on the reason for the falsehood of each one. Regarding the quote by Rodney Legg on the Director Designate theory he interprets 'C.O.' as 'Colonial Office' (where Meinertzhagen and Lawrence worked in 1922) whereas Legg, Lockman says, interprets it as 'Cabinet Office'. Since thirteen years had elapsed between Lawrence's resignation from the Colonial Office and 1935, something is wrong.

In the 19th June 1935 entry Meinertzhagen praised Lawrence in virtually unqualified terms. He stated he attended a memorial tribute to T.E. that day at the Grosvenor Hotel. The tribute took place the day before. Meinertzhagen even went so far as to comment on Lawrence's mother at the luncheon, gallantly stating she was 'charming'; on June 19th 1935 Mrs Lawrence and her son Bob were in the middle of the Indian Ocean, still en route to England, following missionary work in China. Lockman also comments: 'Meinertzhagen is only the tip of the iceberg among the dubious sources on Lawrence. For in the 1920s, while Lowell Thomas was beaming the Lawrence legend throughout the world, a second, much darker legend was inevitably forming . . . There is an ascending scale of irresponsibility among those who have quoted Meinertzhagen's diary entries. Some authors can only be lightly faulted. Deciding factors include the date of writing (pre- and post-Mack), the diary passages chosen for quotation, the length of the quotes, and the mother tongue.'

The most serious misuse of Meinertzhagen as a source is, he says, Lawrence James: 'His 1990 work *The Golden Warrior* quotes many dubious sources with hardly a word of caution. The work also contains a phenomenal number of factual errors (dates, names, places), sometimes several per page.'

In James's book, in the course of the author presenting a case for Lawrence being homosexual, there is the story of T.E. attended a flagellation party in Chelsea in the 1920s organised by Jack Bilbo. Lockman states the only connection between Lawrence and Bilbo (a.k.a. Hugo Buroch) is found in Bilbo's 1932 German spy story *Chicago – Shanghai*, in which Lawrence is featured as infiltrating the Chinese underworld. Lawrence tried to suppress this book, and, according to the Knightley and Simpson papers in the Imperial War Museum, the two men never met.[5] Michael Yardley's 1985 biography also questioned the reliability of Meinertzhagen's account, but quoted freely from him.

Desmond Stewart made a similar allegation to James in his 1977 book about a certain 'Bluebeard' (who bears a strong similarity in name, date, and location to Bilbo). Lockman thought that this, 'while more difficult to prove conclusively, seems extremely doubtful in any event'. There is so much gold in the Lawrence legend that some writers will employ almost any controversial source to create something marketable.

Notes

1 *Middle East Diary*. R. Meinertzhagen, Cresset Press, 1959.

2 Ibid.

3 Ibid.

4 *Meinertzhagen's Diary Ruse*, J.N. Lockman. Cornerstone Publications Ltd. Grand Rapids, USA. 1995.

5 Colin Simpson, who discovered the Bilbo story, commented in August 2006 that Bilbo was a racketeer and made the story up.

APPENDIX SIX

Henry Williamson's Letters to Lawrence: *Winged Victory*

1) Letter One: Shallowford, Filleigh, Barnstaple. 26.5.34

Dear Shaw,

Thanks for your two ripping letters, one welcoming me home, and the other about *Winged Victory*. As always, you not only hit the nail on the head, but have a collection of spikes, French nails, nobs drawn, forged, case hardened snigs, and all the technical rest of the driven and metallic points. I suggested the cutting of the economic talk, as being easily post-war in its confidence and explicitness: also the main character is too being daubed with recognizable primary colours . . .

It was started by him sending me a manuscript which had such a good flying chapter that I suggested this book; gave the theme, and outlined roughly how to do it; and forgetting this, was delighted as month by month the chapters came to me typed so tightly that all comments were difficult to put on paper. But it was a labour of delight. Only a teeny bit of the book is due to me. It is all his except the cut in the last chapter, to make the numbness after Williamson's death more effective. Thank you very much for reading it; and I'm so glad I didn't make an error in supposing you would like it. I knew you would, of course; there's some of you in the book, from you to me; and me to Yeates. Life's a compost . . .

2) Letter Two: 10.12.34

Dear Shaw,

. . . I am about to make a play out of WINGED VICTORY, tense drama, all natural too. (Yeates won't last much longer I fear. 1300 copies here, 559 in the U.S.) He's in a sanatorium at Hastings; I'm going to see him soon . . .

3) Postcard:

13 Feb '36 [actually '35]

Many thanks for your, as usual, refreshing letter. Yeates left me a 50,000 fragment FAMILY LIFE which I am hoping Faber will publish between an introduction and an Epilogue by me, thus making its form; for the contents Family Life are his life, and tied with such a lovely light touch, extraordinarily clear character, a minute by minute build up of daily life, so very amusing and instantly read.

APPENDIX SEVEN

E.S. Palmer's and A.E. Chambers' Letters to Lawrence 1933–34

34, Franklin Avenue,
Cheshunt
25.10.33

I wish I were R.T.C. and you R.T.C. and the date 1924. However . . .

You surprised one this time if ever you did and now I won't surprise you.

I am working jolly hard nowadays but not with a partner for a weekly wage, and a German from Silesia who loves Bach, Beethoven and work. I think I said this before to E.M.F.

I was in partnership for a year or [so] but things went wrong. I expected too much, as usual, both of us lacked experience, so we parted company. I am now a fully fledged typical Cheshunt gardener to outward appearance but not inwardly dam[n] it. I lead a sort of give and take life with Mrs. Palmer. I do the giving and she the taking.

Of course, and here it comes, I wrote to E.M.F. with an object

(1) to try and get in touch with you, (I did not know your address, and E.M.F.'s I did)

(2) The 'John'.[1] I have got to get rid of it. It has been a bane of contention between Mrs. Palmer and myself for some time now, she is jealous of it. She says I think more of the painting than I do of her. True I suppose, so the John has to go.

I cannot afford to give it away, and as you were responsible for it can you [give] any other suggestions? What about Clouds Hill?

I still hope to see it again and yet I am rather frightened at the thought. I have put so much behind me that seeing Clouds Hill again, would re-open old thoughts, and dreams, and things that I think had better remain buried.

I am glad you seem happier and doubly glad Clouds Hill has not altered much. The bath is great, gramophone greater, Beethoven greatest. A bed does not really matter. Glad Kirby is still at Bovington. Who is/are the storeman/men I wonder.

I am glad too that Mrs. Knowles is still near, and young Billy. I don't suppose I would know him now, and Dick, R.A.F. still? And dear old H.H.B. Surprised that he is married. How badly I treated you all.

How is Russell Ingham Willis, Jeffrey etc. Do you hear from them? I will try to make Clouds Hill but not yet.

E.S. (Palmer)

NOT Posh

26.11.33

I leave it to you, but wouldn't it be better to send 'the head'?

Somehow I don't trust sending it by rail. If however you have arranged with Mrs. Knowles I will send by rail and pray the Gods it arrives safely. I shall send (when you answer the letter) about Thursday I hope so it will arrive at Wool near or at the weekend.

'The sooner its over the sooner to sleep'.

I have been digging up, out, dahlias by the thousand sort to sort, class to class, very tedious, but as my employer says 'it has got to be done', a favourite expression of his. On Friday morning (24th) we pulled and bundled 5,000 wallflowers, our record, and the wind blew them from the North. Brrr. Beethoven's 7th came over nicely yesterday (Sat.) What do you think of 'Pacific 231' by Honneger? I like it.

Write soon and let me know the verdict, rail or post.

An endearing little beast?[2]

Not - - - (G.B.S.)

Good Night

Pip. Pip.

An accident,

just been on the wireless set.

Padd. Do.

7.10.34

Normal One!

Thanks. You are a good lad to write. I have one correspondent so that return service is swift. The books go by mail I'd finished them and just put off the sending away. The list is! Prawletts Poems, Ezra Pound XXX Cater, 'he lives to tell this tale' Cachalain Marthenene, (an old soldier) and Dudley and Silray. I've nowt else. If you want me to do a little scrounging round the stalls and bookshops for any ungettable ones . . .

I've camped out every weekend since April, and marvellous is the world regarding the weather. I'm due for leave Some when in Nov., so that's all right so far as I'm concerned , but I don't want to butt in if you've any posh blokes happening in. You sound happy and that's good although you say nothing of yourself or the fire and no mention of the bathing pool. Who wants hot water?

I've a new enthusiasm – galloping horse – which is, I believe, not interesting to you! But it's good. 500 feet up Amersham – wake in the morning with a tremendous view and to the 2nd part of a Russian bath. God's good these days ain't he?

Southampton smells of speedboats and you happily occupied. Posho! I hope its Nov. – Dorset for me.

Yours,

Jock Chambers

355

Paddington Do.
Sat., the 11th

Mak oh Chief,

It's 120! And I shall be too on arrival! I've mislaid or lost your letter probably coming from camp: there wasn't anything in it to point you out as you. I'd be glad if <u>you</u> would let Mrs. Knowles know of my happening. This is heifer Dust day; didn't think postmen were so military. I camp out tonight and hope it snows for the morn's awakening! Wind on the heath, brother! Roll on Wednesday, and thank you much for allowing me to write meself.

Jock Chambers
Sorter (of sorts)

Farm Raod³ [sic]
8.10.34

My dear T.E.,

It's been a bit of a sod however I'm back at light duty, able even to write this. Went to camp two weeks ago. Couldn't erect tent. Nearly got drowned, unable to cut bread – really was useless and got quite melancholy, not even able to ride my bike!!

Now? It's healing and in two month should be right again. I tripped whilst carrying a bottle of milk and fell on it. Commandeered a car, and inside two hours had been gassed, sewn up and sent home! In Nov. or Oct. late I get leave when I will gladly come down to Clouds Hill. You are a good spud to offer. Many people have been awfully kind to me lately. Hope it soon wears off except in your case!

I believe I wrote you that the Sassoon book was safe. I get it from my chum tomorrow and then must return the issue to you. Am just finishing 'Some Precious Stories'. You probably know it, and it's good to my mind. How the devil you kept quite happy with a broken wrist I can't think.⁴ You are inured to troubles of the sort, or probably!

It's good to be alive though, ain't it? Poor Pat – this woman business⁵. Had I has [his] capabilities and your cottage to muck about with, you would never have a chance to live in it. If the winter is wet that will mean [good] help to the new growth and a chance that the scars left by heath fires will be covered again.

In a month I possess my body in patience.

Yours again cheerfully,
Jock Chambers

Padd. DO.
8.4.35?

My dear Swede Basher!

The Wednesday foll[o]wing Easter Monday will see in residence. Don't have a fire, unless the pool is not swimmable. The Sphere had a picture of the cottage taken from the viewpoint chosen by me for Aussie when he took a snap. I chased him round and was pleased to find that his one was

<u>not</u> it. It's good that you like being down there. I do myself so much so that I hate the thought of it being yours. No, I'm glad, as no-one else would allow my using it as you do: I find that tree-climbing is still within my scope. Weekend in camp at Westerham. Posho, in spite of the rain.

Books of yours will be sent away during the week. All good. 'How the old woman got home' and how! The Claudius[6] goes slightly dopy. The last Axel I read right through immejutly.[7] I find that the sun and Spring keep me out. It's good to wake among the firs and pines of High Westerham. This morning, it was all mine, the sun shone, the fire went merrily, and I thought of poor Flecker[8] spoke so longingly of his pines in 'Binmania'. They did gossip last night. Scandalously! You seem happy now. The world will forget you soon and you'll simply be known as the 'queer bloke what lives up to Clouds Hill'. I have written a lot. Tea up. I must away to mail bag opening.

Yours

Jock Chambers

Notes

1 A portrait of Lawrence by Augustus John given to Palmer.

2 Appears to refer to the poem 'Diversions' quoted in RG-B. See also letter 235 to G.B.S. in Garnett: 'There is not a humbler little beast'.

3 Chambers' spelling was consistently poor.

4 Some time earlier Lawrence had broken his right wrist whilst starting a stranger's car up.

5 Refers to Pat Knowles and his relationship with Joyce Dorey.

6 *I, Claudius* by Robert Graves.

7 Some of Chambers' erratic spelling was due to his poor typing. At other times he simply couldn't spell, or was joking.

8 James Elroy Flecker, essayist and poet; Lawrence met him in Syria before WWI.

APPENDIX EIGHT

A Visit to Polstead Road, Oxford

Michael Asher in his book *Lawrence – the Uncrowned King of Arabia* described 2, Polstead Road as 'a slightly seedy building with overflowing rubbish bins and rusty Morris Minors parked in a concrete yard' but he did not attempt to enter it. My mistaken preconception of Lawrence's dwelling place during his formative years was of a stone Victorian house that fronted right onto the street. The four-storey house where Lawrence dwelt from 1896 to 1921 had a reasonable front garden originally, now concreted over. At the time of writing it is occupied by Terence Phillips. Phillips is a Welshman who was formerly a college lecturer. I was fully expecting to have the door slammed in my face or have no reply at all. Phillips turned out to be an extremely friendly, receptive and intelligent man who was quite willing to show me around the house and the adjacent bungalow.

The Polstead Road area of Oxford was developed in the 1880s into a residential area to provide accommodation for Oxford dons who had recently been allowed to marry. The Lawrence family owned the house from 1896 until the end of the Second World War. In 1945 Mrs Lawrence went to live in a larger house at Boar's Hill.

Asked about the continual enquiries he must get, Terence Phillips said he was not averse to them, but obviously it would be easier if people made an appointment. Every year there were hundreds of visitors from all over the world. He said the house was much the same as it had been when the Lawrences lived there. Above the old wooden posted porch a blue plaque is attached to the front brickwork, some 20 feet above ground level. This was erected by his mother, Mrs Phillips, with assistance from the authorities at All Souls and Jesus Colleges.

He led me into the back garden down towards the rear of the property to Lawrence's bungalow. For a long time there was a myth that 'Ned' had built it himself. In fact it was constructed by a local building firm. I was struck by how large it was. It appeared to be in reasonably good state of repair. He let me into the front room and we sat down. This, he said, was where Lawrence had written *The Wilderness of Zin* in 1910. Apparently the building has changed very little since Lawrence's time, although a modern kitchen had upgraded T.E.'s spartan requirements. In 1908 an application was made to Oxford City Council for permission to build. The present construction differs markedly from that originally proposed in having a third large sitting room on the opposite side of the dwelling to the room Lawrence originally used. The windows were exactly as they had been in Lawrence's time. Walking out of the first reading/writing area where T.E. used to curl up in front of the fire, we proceeded to a small rectangular room where T.E. slept. The timbering was in good shape. Turning left we went into the second study area. Again there were pine doors and shelving that Mr Phillips said were original, although they appeared to be brand new.

The building was larger than Clouds and in considerably better condition. In 1987 a small circular stained glass panel had been inserted into one of the front windows of the first reading room bearing an image of Lawrence in Arabian headgear, based on one of the John portraits. The unveiling of this had attracted a large number of local dignitaries from All Souls, Jesus and other Colleges.

We returned to the main house. The front door onto the porch still contains the stained glass panelling of fairy tale images from the Lawrences' time. Then he took me to the thing I had been most hoping to see. This was the cupboard door in the front living room where Mrs Lawrence had pencilled the heights of her sons as they grew up. And there it was, painted dark green timber in one corner of the room. Despite the shabby finish after opening the door one could still easily discern on its inner face the pencil and ink markings showing the boys' relative heights as they grew older. There were about 30 marks all over the painted timber – horizontal pencil and ink lines, with the boys' names after them, crossed out year on year. I saw Frank, Will, Bob, Ned and Arnie. The highest mark was Will's in 1908, who seemed to have attained over six feet. I measured Ned's final one. In 1906, when he was 18, T.E. Lawrence was about 5 feet 5 inches high. And that's as far as he got.

Since it is a large house it requires a lot to upkeep and Mr Phillips is struggling to find financial assistance. He has made some effort to keep it in a good state of repair. He has considered giving it to the National Trust but prefers to retain ownership. He has lived on the premises for nearly 40 years.

Other locations with Lawrence connections:

Wareham, Dorset
T.E. Lawrence exhibition, Wareham Museum, East Street, Wareham
Anglebury House and Restaurant, North Street, Wareham
St. Martin's Church, North Street, Wareham
Black Bear Hotel (where E.M. Forster stayed in 1924)
Bovington
T.E. Lawrence exhibition, R.A.C. Museum
Moreton, Dorset
St. Nicholas Church, Moreton
Moreton Tearooms (T.E. Lawrence display)
Clouds Hill, Dorset
Crash site and Lawrence's cottage
Hythe, Southampton
Myrtle Cottage, North Street, Hythe

Scott-Paine Drive
Dorchester
Max Gate, Thomas Hardy's house
Plymouth
3, Eliot Terrace, the Hoe
Mount Batten promontory
Picklecombe Point, Mount Edgecumbe
Thurlestone, near Kingsbridge
Bridlington
Ozone Hotel and memorial bird bath
Cambridgeshire
T.E. Lawrence Memorial Room, RAF Cranwell
North Wales
Lawrence's Café (birthplace), Tremadog

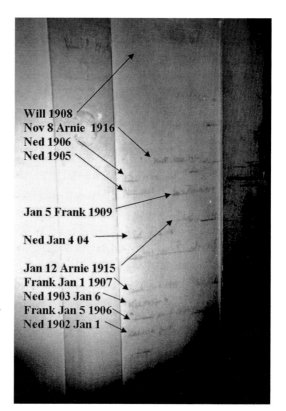

Will 1908
Nov 8 Arnie 1916
Ned 1906
Ned 1905

Jan 5 Frank 1909

Ned Jan 4 04

Jan 12 Arnie 1915
Frank Jan 1 1907
Ned 1903 Jan 6
Frank Jan 5 1906
Ned 1902 Jan 1

Upper half of the cupboard door at Polstead road in the ground floor front living room. It records the heights of the five Lawrence boys as they grew. There are about 30 marks, mainly between 1900 and 1910. Will is the highest at just over six feet in 1910. 'Ned' had numerous entries, but Bob and Frank only a few. At around January the first of each year Mrs Lawrence marked the new height of the boy with his name in pencil or ink, and crossed the old one out. (Author)

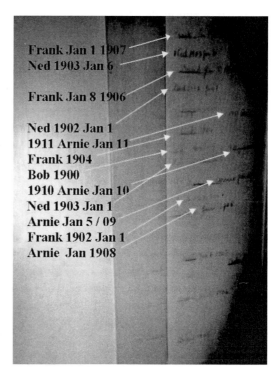

Frank Jan 1 1907
Ned 1903 Jan 6

Frank Jan 8 1906

Ned 1902 Jan 1
1911 Arnie Jan 11
Frank 1904
Bob 1900
1910 Arnie Jan 10
Ned 1903 Jan 1
Arnie Jan 5 / 09
Frank 1902 Jan 1
Arnie Jan 1908

Lower half of the cupboard door. Arnie is the smallest one to be measured, at just over one foot above floor level. (Author)

Index

Page references to illustrations are in *italic*.
Dates of the lives of prinicipal characters are given in parentheses.